Networking with Microsoft TCP/IP

Drew Heywood

New Riders Publishing, Indianapolis, Indiana

Networking with Microsoft TCP/IP

By Drew Heywood

Published by:
New Riders Publishing
201 West 103rd Street
Indianapolis, IN 46290 USA

Printed in the United States of America 1 2 3 4 5 6 7 8 9 0

CIP data available upon request

Warning and Disclaimer

This book is designed to provide information about Microsoft TCP/IP. Every effort has been made to make this book as complete and as accurate as possible, but no warranty or fitness is implied.

The information is provided on an "as is" basis. The author(s) and New Riders Publishing shall have neither liability nor responsibility to any person or entity with respect to any loss or damages arising from the information contained in this book or from the use of the disks or programs that may accompany it.

Publisher	*Don Fowley*
Publishing Manager	*Emmett Dulaney*
Marketing Manager	*Ray Robinson*
Managing Editors	*Tad Ringo*
	Carla Hall

Acquisitions Editor
Mary Foote

Production Editor
Phil Worthington

Copy Editor
Laura Frey

Technical Editor
John Flynn Matthew

Associate Marketing Manager
Tamara Apple

Acquisitions Coordinators
Tracy Turgeson
Stacia Mellinger

Publisher's Assistant
Karen Opal

Cover Designer
Nathan Clement

Book Design
Sandra Schroeder

Manufacturing Coordinator
Paul Gilchrist

Production Manager
Kelly Dobbs

Production Team Supervisor
Laurie Casey

Graphic Image Specialists
Sonja Hart, Clint Lahnen,
Laura Robbins, Craig Small,
Todd Wente

Production Team
Angela Calvert, Kim Cofer,
David Garratt, Tricia Flodder,
Beth Rago, Gina Rexrode,
Erich Richter, Scott Tullis,
Christine Tyner

Indexer
Ginny Bess

Production Analysts
Jason Hand
Bobbi Satterfield

About the Author

Drew Heywood is Vice President of InfoWorks, Inc., a company that specializes in technical communication and computer consulting. Drew is a busy author who has authored or co-authored seven books in the last three years. His most recent book is the popular *Inside Windows NT Server* from New Riders. Drew is also the author of NRP's *Inside NetWare 3.12* and has contributed to several volumes in NRP's NetWare Study Guide series of CNE certification books.

Trademark Acknowledgments

All terms mentioned in this book that are known to be trademarks or service marks have been appropriately capitalized. New Riders Publishing cannot attest to the accuracy of this information. Use of a term in this book should not be regarded as affecting the validity of any trademark or service mark.

Dedication

For Woody:

Your father is proud to dedicate this book to you, with all his love and hope.

Acknowledgments

Thank you to everyone who helped with this book.

Contents at a Glance

Table of Contents

Introduction

S ooner or later, almost all LAN administrators come face to face with TCP/IP. In today's world, as IS managers seek to base their systems on standards, and as everyone wants to connect to the Internet, TCP/IP has become practically unavoidable for anyone working with LANs. That doesn't make TCP/IP any less imposing, however. If you are among the many LAN administrators who find they need to get up to speed on TCP/IP, this book is for you.

TCP/IP is an extremely rich set of network protocols, probably the richest. After all, no other protocols have the Internet with its millions of users, many bent on making the Internet do more, which often means adding to TCP/IP. As a result, the family of TCP/IP can become a professional preoccupation, and has for many in the networking community. The vastness of TCP/IP forces any author addressing the subject to select a subset of the field, a subset that will meet the needs of the book's readers.

In selecting material for this book, I have tried to meet two goals: to tell you what you must know without overwhelming you, and to tell you everything you are ever likely to need to know. Although a lot of information is in this book, I have tried to organize it so that you can focus on the topics that are most relevant to your current needs. Later, as your experience grows and your responsibilities expand, you should find it profitable to return to this book to round out your knowledge. In short, this isn't a book you will read just once.

How Is This Book Organized?

Part I provides background information about the TCP/IP family of protocols. The information in these chapters applies to all implementations of TCP/IP. Although it may seem like the information goes overboard, you will find a use for nearly all of it in Part II, which examines in detail how TCP/IP is implemented on Microsoft networking products.

The first time you read Part I don't get caught up in the details. Try to get the gist of the information and remember what the main topics are and where they are discussed. Then you can return to these basic chapters when you need more theory to bolster your understanding of the more practical chapters in Part II. Don't try to understand every word you read. Just keep going back and each time your understanding will improve.

Part I takes the classic approach of discussing protocol stacks in layers. Both the OSI and the TCP/IP models are addressed, because both are in evidence in Microsoft networking products. Here is what happens in Part I:

Chapter 1, "Introduction to TCP/IP," is a general overview of TCP/IP. You will learn how TCP/IP protocols are developed, how standards are set, and how to obtain information.

Chapter 2, "TCP/IP Architecture," introduces the structures of the OSI Reference Model as well as the TCP/IP protocol stack architecture. You are introduced to the four layers of the TCP/IP architecture, which are the subjects of the next four chapters.

Chapters 3 through 6 discuss each layer of the TCP/IP protocol model in turn. You will learn how each layer functions and, more importantly, how the layers relate to each other.

With the theory of Part I behind you, you are ready to look at implementing specific features of Microsoft's TCP/IP implementation. Essentially, after a chapter of introduction, each TCP/IP subsystem gets its own chapter:

Chapter 7, "Introducing Microsoft TCP/IP," is just what the title implies. Here you will learn how Microsoft TCP/IP is organized and what the general features are.

Chapter 8: "Implementing TCP/IP on Windows NT Computers," describes the details of installing and configuring TCP/IP on Windows NT servers and clients.

Chapter 9, "Building Routed Networks," explores how Windows TCP/IP can be configured to handle traffic in routed internetworks.

Chapter 10, "Managing DHCP," shows you how to implement the Dynamic Host Configuration Protocol, one of the most time-saving administrative tools included with Microsoft TCP/IP.

Chapter 11, "Managing WINS," explains how to use the Windows Internet Naming Service to provide name resolution for Microsoft TCP/IP clients.

Chapter 12, "Managing DNS," shows how to set up a Domain Name Service name server on your network, enabling your hosts to participate in the DNS name service on the Internet.

Chapter 13, "Installing TCP/IP on Microsoft Clients," covers installation of TCP/IP on MS-DOS, Windows 3.x, and Windows 95 clients.

Chapter 14, "Managing Microsoft TCP/IP," explains how to configure Microsoft TCP/IP computers for SNMP monitoring and how to collect statistics using Performance Monitor.

Chapter 15, "Building an Internet Server," completes the picture by showing you how to connect to the Internet and build your own Internet Server.

Appendix A describes binary, decimal, and hexadecimal numbers, which you will encounter if you are working with TCP/IP.

Keep in Touch

No book is perfect. I am sure that I have missed topics readers want to know about, and I haven't seen a computer book yet that hasn't had an error or two. So I would like to hear from you, whether your words are blessings or curses. What questions have I left unanswered? What tips have I left unmentioned? How can I make the next edition of the book better? Please let me know.

You can send e-mail to me on CompuServe at 76415,140 or on the Internet at dheywood@iquest.net. Also, please feel free to send letters to me care of New Riders. Schedules and deadlines might prevent me from responding as promptly as you would like, but I will respond as quickly as possible.

Thank you for buying my book. Thank you for reading it. And thank you in advance for letting me know what you think.

New Riders Publishing

The staff of New Riders Publishing is committed to bringing you the very best in computer reference material. Each New Riders book is the result of months of work by authors and staff who research and refine the information contained within its covers.

As part of this commitment to you, the NRP reader, New Riders invites your input. Please let us know if you enjoy this book, if you have trouble with the information and examples presented, or if you have a suggestion for the next edition.

Please note, though: New Riders staff cannot serve as a technical resource for Microsoft TCP/IP or for questions about software- or hardware-related problems. Please refer to the documentation that accompanies Microsoft products.

If you have a question or comment about any New Riders book, there are several ways to contact New Riders Publishing. We will respond to as many readers as we can. Your name, address, or phone number will never become part of a mailing list or be used for any purpose other than to help us continue to bring you the best books possible. You can write us at the following address:

New Riders Publishing
Attn: Publishing Manager—Networking
201 W. 103rd Street
Indianapolis, IN 46290

If you prefer, you can fax New Riders Publishing at (317) 581-4670.

You can also send electronic mail to New Riders at the following Internet address:

`edulaney@newriders.mcp.com`

New Riders is an imprint of Macmillan Computer Publishing. To obtain a catalog or information, or to purchase any Macmillan Computer Publishing book, call (800) 428-5331.

Thank you for selecting *Networking with Microsoft TCP/IP*!

Part I

TCP/IP Concepts

Chapter 1 Snapshot

This chapter introduces several different aspects of TCP/IP, including its evolution as well as its standardization. The chapter covers the following topics:

- ◆ A brief history of TCP/IP

- ◆ The need for open computing standards

- ◆ Administration of the Internet

- ◆ The Internet standards process

- ◆ Obtaining RFCs and other Internet information

Introduction to TCP/IP

Until fairly recently, computer systems were islands that communicated with each other only with difficulty (with one significant exception). When you bought a computer, you bought a network communication system with it. IBM mainframes, for example, networked using the System Network Architecture. SNA is a robust network architecture, well-suited to the terminal-host environment of the mainframe computer, but IBM developed SNA to meet the needs of IBM computers, not the needs of the networking community as a whole. Consequently, few other vendors developed network equipment for SNA, preferring instead to develop their own network architectures to meet their visions of networking.

Dozens of network architectures populated the computers of the 1970s and 1980s. Equipment from the mainframe companies IBM, Digital, Sperry, Burroughs, Honeywell, and others frequently were islands, unable to communicate with one another because each company had designed a proprietary network architecture. When the computer vendors made most of their money by selling hardware, they tended to view a proprietary network architecture as a way to bind their customers to specific brands of computer and network equipment.

When LANs became more common in the late 1980s, they, too, tended to utilize proprietary protocols. To consider only a few examples, Novell promoted their IPX/SPX protocol suite, Apple had AppleTalk, and IBM and Microsoft focused on NetBEUI. Enabling computers on one brand of LAN to communicate with computers on a competing LAN architecture pr esented a daunting task. Getting a PC to talk to a mainframe required specialized technologies that would turn a smart PC into a dumb terminal that could be permitted within the mainframe's sphere of influence. Often, moving data from one computer environment to another meant dumping the files to a data tape or disk that could be loaded on the destination computer. Enabling different computer systems to transparently share files and data was practically unknown.

As the end of the 1980s approached, this isolation of computer systems was becoming unacceptable. Companies that once viewed LANs as noncritical began to realize that their LANs were now serving vital business needs. Moreover, LANs were being used to produce more than word processing documents and spreadsheets. LANs were becoming the repositories of critical company data that often needed to be shared with programs running on the mainframe.

Left to their own resources, computer manufacturers likely would still be fighting over the design of a common network architecture. Fortunately for the user community, however, a grass-roots movement has accomplished what commercial enterprise has not. Thanks to a serendipitous chain of events, an architecture for internetworking various types of computers has emerged.

That architecture was found on the Internet, the exception mentioned in the first sentence of this chapter. One group of users has been doing what everyone else wanted to do, and has been doing it for a long time. For more than 20 years, the Internet has provided a context for internetworking thousands of computers spread throughout the world. And TCP/IP is the language of the Internet.

This chapter introduces you to several aspects of TCP/IP. Because TCP/IP is best understood in its historical context, the first topic of discussion is the evolution of TCP/IP, starting with its early roots in the United States Department of Defense. That discussion introduces you to many of the networking problems that have stimulated the design and redesign of TCP/IP.

Next, this chapter examines the TCP/IP standardization process. Unlike vendor proprietary protocols, which tend to evolve in manufacturers' laboratories, TCP/IP standardization is open and public. As you become involved with TCP/IP, you should know about the standardization process so that you can monitor changes that might affect you. You might even decide to become involved in the standards-setting process.

A Brief History of TCP/IP

Perhaps no organization has more complex networking requirements than the United States Department of Defense (DoD). Simply enabling communication among the wide variety of computers found in the various services is not enough. DoD computers often need to communicate with contractors and organizations that do defense-related research, including most universities. Defense-related network components must be able to withstand considerable damage so that the nation's defenses remain operable during a disaster.

That the DoD initiated research into networking protocols, investigating the technology now known as *packet switching*, therefore, is not surprising. In fact, research on the protocols that eventually became the TCP/IP protocol suite began in 1969. Among the goals for this research were the following:

- ◆ **Common protocols.** The DoD required a common set of protocols that could be specified for all networks. Common protocols would greatly simplify the procurement process.

- ◆ **Interoperability.** If equipment from various vendors could interoperate, development efficiency could be improved and competition among vendors would be promoted.

- ◆ **Robust communication.** A particularly dependable network standard was required to meet the nation's defense needs. These protocols needed to provide reliable, high-performance networking with the relatively primitive wide-area network technologies then available.

- ◆ **Ease of reconfiguration.** Because the DoD would depend on the network, reconfiguring the network and adding and removing computers without disrupting communication needed to be possible.

In 1968, the DoD Advanced Research Project Agency (then called ARPA but since redubbed DARPA) initiated research into networks using the technology now called packet switching. The first experimental network connected four sites: the University of California at Los Angeles (UCLA), the University of California at Santa Barbara (UCSB), the University of Utah, and SRI International. Early tests were encouraging, and additional sites were connected to the network. The ARPAnet, as it came to be called, incorporated 20 hosts by 1972.

Originally intended to facilitate communication among the DoD, commercial research firms, and universities, the ARPAnet gradually became a medium for non-DoD communication as well. By the mid-1980s, the ARPAnet had become the backbone of an internetwork that connected large numbers of educational institutions and defense contractors, as well as the military network called MILnet. This extended network, which used the ARPAnet as its backbone, became known as the Internet.

 Note You will encounter the terms Internet and internet, and should be aware of an important distinction between them. An *internet* (short for *internetwork*) is any network comprised of multiple, interconnected networks. The *Internet* is the global internetwork that traces its lineage back to the ARPAnet.

In 1986, groundwork was laid for the commercialization of the ARPAnet. At that time, work to isolate military networks from the ARPAnet commenced. The ARPAnet backbone was dismantled, replaced by a network funded by the National Science Foundation. NSFnet now functions as the Internet backbone, managed by Advanced Network Services (ANS).

The evolutionary approach of the ARPAnet produced a community of users that became involved in debating and setting standards for the network. Most network protocols are developed under the control of the companies that develop them. Debate on the Internet protocols, however, has long taken place on a public forum. Consequently, these protocols are not "owned" by any particular company. Responsibility for setting Internet standards rests with an *Internet Activity Board*.

The TCP/IP protocols were developed in the early 1980s, and became the standard protocols for the ARPAnet in 1983. The protocols gained popularity in the user community when TCP/IP was incorporated into version 4.2 of the BSD (Berkeley Standard Distribution) UNIX. This version of UNIX is used widely in educational and research institutions, and was used as the foundation of several commercial UNIX implementations, including Sun's SunOS and Digital's Ultrix. Because BSD UNIX established a relationship between TCP/IP and the UNIX operating system, the vast majority of UNIX implementations now incorporate TCP/IP.

Evolution of the TCP/IP protocol suite continues in response to the evolution of the Internet. In recent years, access to the Internet has extended beyond the original community and is available to virtually anyone who has a computer. This dramatic growth has stressed the Internet and has pushed the design limitations of several protocols. On the Internet, nothing is permanent except change.

The Need for Open Computing Standards

As computing has escaped the MIS department and found a home on the desktop, the communication boundaries imposed by proprietary protocols have become less and less tolerable. The user community has come to demand more open standards: standards open to public debate, not controlled by a single commercial interest, and free to be used by all. Vendor-controlled, proprietary standards, however, present two disadvantages. Vendors who want to use the protocols must license them, often at considerable cost. Also, the controlling vendor can be unresponsive to requests from other vendors for changes in the protocols.

Given those requirements, the protocols used on the Internet are the only fully functioning protocols that can be regarded as truly open. Only TCP/IP is available freely and defined in an environment of public review.

> **Note**
>
> For several years, the International Organization for Standardization (ISO) attempted to define an open protocol suite called Open Systems Interconnection (OSI). As work on the OSI protocols progressed, it was widely assumed that they would supplant TCP/IP as the open protocol solution. The United States government announced that future computer purchases would conform to a government subset of the OSI protocols, called GOSIP, and the DoD indicated that GOSIP would replace TCP/IP on military networks.
>
> As often happens with international bodies, negotiations on the OSI protocol suite have bogged down. The OSI protocols have been slow to emerge and, in some instances, appear to be stalled. Interest in OSI has waned even as the fortunes of TCP/IP have prospered. Many industry analysts argued that OSI was not needed because a functional, open protocol suite already was available in TCP/IP. The DoD has backed off from its declaration that future procurements would require GOSIP. Although OSI might yet be resurrected, the immediate future of TCP/IP appears to be secure.

One consequence of this openness is that TCP/IP has evolved into an extremely rich suite of protocols and applications. The name by which the protocol suite is most commonly known is misleading because TCP and IP are only two of dozens of protocols that constitute the protocol suite. Some refer to the suite as the *Internet protocol suite* or the *DoD protocol suite*, to emphasize the distinction that TCP/IP is much more than just TCP and IP.

Here are but a few examples of protocols and services associated with TCP/IP:

◆ **Telnet.** A remote terminal emulation protocol that enables clients to log in to remote hosts on the network.

◆ **FTP.** A file transfer application that enables users to transfer files between hosts.

◆ **NFS (Network File System).** A more sophisticated remote file access service that enables clients to access files on remote hosts as though the files were stored locally.

◆ **SNMP (Simple Network Management Protocol).** Used to remotely manage network devices.

◆ **SMTP (Simple Mail Transfer Protocol).** Used to implement electronic mail systems.

◆ **DNS (Domain Name Service).** Puts a friendly face on the network by assigning meaningful names to computers.

Later chapters describe these applications in greater detail. Chapter 6 discusses Telnet, FTP, NFS, and SMTP. SNMP is one of several subjects addressed in Chapter 14, "Managing Microsoft TCP/IP." And Chapter 12, "Managing DNS," shows you how to set up a DNS server.

Another consequence of this openness is that TCP/IP has been implemented on virtually all hardware and operating system platforms. No other protocol suite is available on all of the following systems:

◆ Novell NetWare

◆ IBM mainframes

◆ Digital VMS systems

◆ Microsoft Windows NT Server

◆ UNIX workstations

◆ DOS personal computers

Administration of the Internet

The Internet Activities Board (IAB), established in 1983 and described as "an independent committee of researchers and professionals with a technical interest in the health and evolution of the Internet system," coordinates design, engineering, and management of the Internet. Figure 1.1 illustrates the organization of the IAB, along with its relationship to related groups. The IAB has two task forces: the Internet Engineering Task Force (IETF) and the Internet Research Task Force (IRTF).

Two organizations serve a liaison function with the IAB. The *Federal Networking Council* represents all agencies of the United States federal government involved with the Internet. The *Internet Society* is a public organization that takes its membership from the entire Internet community. Both organizations provide input on Internet policy and standards.

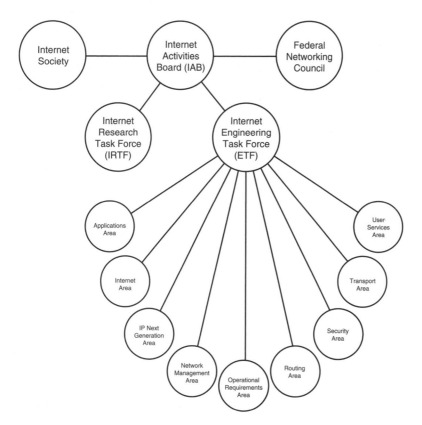

Figure 1.1

Organizations involved with the Internet.

The IETF is responsible for specifying the Internet protocols and architecture. By its own description,

> The IETF is not a traditional standards organization, although many specifications are produced that become standards. The IETF is made up of volunteers who meet three times a year to fulfill the IETF mission. There is no membership in the IETF. Anyone may register for and attend any meeting.

Could the Internet standardization process be any more open? RFC 1718, "The Tao of IETF," is an excellent introduction to the IETF.

 Note   The IAB makes most information public in the form of Request for Comments (RFC) memos. Nearly 2,000 RFCs have been published since 1969. Some RFCs describe Internet standards. Most are posted to promote discussion. A few are sheer whimsy. For a taste of the latter, check out RFC 968, "Twas the night before start-up," by Vint Cerf.

Work of the IETF is organized in areas that change over time. The directors for the technical areas comprise the *Internet Engineering Steering Group*, which is responsible for recommending protocol standards. The current IETF areas are as follows:

◆ Applications

◆ Internet

◆ IP: Next Generation Area

◆ Network Management

◆ Operational Requirements

◆ Routing

◆ Security

◆ Transport

◆ User Services

The IRTF is the research organization of the IAB. Membership of the IETF and the IRTF overlap considerably to promote technology transfer.

Figure 1.1 mentions two organizations that influence the IAB. The Federal Networking Council is the federal government's body for coordinating agencies that support the Internet.

The *Internet Society* is an open membership organization that involves educators, industry, users, and government in promoting use of the Internet. The Internet Society is involved in the Internet standards process. For membership information, contact the Internet Society using regular or electronic mail at either of the following addresses:

> Internet Society
> Suite 100
> 1895 Preston White Drive
> Reston, VA 22091
> U.S.A.
>
> E-mail: isoc@isoc.org
> (703)648-9888

The Internet Standards Process

As you review the documentation for the TCP/IP component of Windows NT, you will see a list of RFCs that the product supports. *Request for Comment (RFC)* documents are the means for developing and publishing standards for use on the Internet. Because the vast majority of TCP/IP systems connect to the Internet, a standard for the Internet is a standard for the TCP/IP protocol suite.

On its way to becoming a standard, a protocol passes through stages as a Proposed Standard, which the IESG may promote to a Draft Standard and finally to a full-fledged Standard. At each stage, the proposed standard is subject to review, debate, implementation, and testing. Proposed Standards, for example, are subject to at least six months of review before IESG may promote them to a Draft Standard. In general, promoting a standard requires two independent implementations of the protocol.[

A memo titled "Internet Official Protocol Standards" describes the standards for protocols to be used on the Internet. It also includes a thorough discussion of the standards process, which has been simplified considerably here. The memo is updated quarterly and is RFC 1800 as of this writing.

Note that not all RFCs are standards—many represent work in progress. Many RFCs, for example, have been posted to provide industry input to the process of updating the IP standard. All Internet standards are assigned a standard number.

Nor are all protocols in common use as Internet standards. A protocol developed outside the Internet review process occasionally achieves widespread acceptance in the TCP/IP community; for example, the Network File System (NFS) protocol developed by Sun Microsystems. NFS is a crucial TCP/IP protocol, in extremely wide use, but is not an Internet standard. A protocol cannot be described as a standard in an RFC unless the IAG engineering study group approves its status.

> **Note**
> After a document has been assigned an RFC number and published, it can never be revised using the same RFC number. Any published revisions are assigned a new RFC. If a new RFC obsoletes older RFCs, the obsolete RFCs are identified on the title page. Also, the old RFC is labeled as obsolete and classified as historical. Some Internet standards have been updated many times in this manner.
>
> You don't need to concern yourself, therefore, about having the latest version of an RFC; only one version of a given RFC ever exists. You do need to ensure that you have the current RFC for a given standard, however.

Internet protocols can be assigned several designations, depending on their state in the standards process:

◆ **Standard.** An official standard protocol for the Internet.

◆ **Draft Standard.** A protocol in the final stages of study prior to approval as a standard.

◆ **Proposed Standard.** A protocol under consideration for standardization in the future.

◆ **Experimental.** Protocols undergoing experimentation but not on the standards track.

◆ **Historic.** Protocols that have been superseded or are otherwise no longer under consideration for standardization.

You also see protocols identified as "informational." These are protocols that interest the Internet community but have not been through the IAG standards review process. RFC 1813 is an informational specification that describes the NFS Version 3 Protocol.

Internet standards have varying requirement levels:

◆ **Required.** Must be implemented by systems on the Internet.

◆ **Recommended.** Should be implemented.

◆ **Elective.** May be implemented.

◆ **Limited.** May be useful in some systems. Experimental, specialized, and historic protocols may receive this classification.

◆ **Not Recommended.** Historical, specialized, or experimental protocols not recommended for use on the Internet.

The matrix in figure 1.2 summarizes the various possible classifications that may be assigned to a protocol.

Internet-Drafts

At any time, IETF working groups are involved in a wide variety of projects that have matured to the point of producing RFCs. These projects are frequently documented in *Internet-Drafts*, which are available from the same sources as RFCs. Internet-Drafts are subject to modification at any time.

A useful document to obtain contains abstracts of the various Internet-Drafts. The file is `1id-abstracts.txt`.

	Required	Recommended	Elective	Limited Use	Not Recommended
Standard	●	●	●		
Draft Standard	●	●	●		
Proposed Standard		●	●		
Informational					
Experimental				●	
Historic					●

Figure 1.2

Classifications of Internet protocols.

Obtaining RFCs and Other Internet Information

Information about the Internet abounds and is most readily available through, guess what, the Internet. RFCs and other information are available through FTP, WAIS, electronic mail, and the World Wide Web (WWW).

A primary Internet resource is the InterNIC Directory and Database Services, which has two components:

- **Directory & Database Services, provided by AT&T.** This service is a source of information about the Internet, including RFCs. Another resource is WHOIS server providing a white pages directory of Internet users. A Gopher database provides access to numerous Internet documents.

- **Registration Services, provided by Network Solutions.** This service is used to register Internet addresses and domain names.

RFCs may be obtained in printed form, but the most expedient approach is to use one of the available techniques for using the Internet to obtain them. Recent information about obtaining RFCs is published in the "Internet Official Protocol Standards" document, discussed earlier in this chapter. However, several access options are not explained in the RFC.

RFCs may be obtained using FTP, WAIS, electronic mail, or the World Wide Web. To get up-to-date information about sources of RFCs, send electronic mail to rfc-info@ISI.EDU including the message `help: ways_to_get_rfcs`. The response message you receive includes a variety of options not included here.

The InterNIC Directory and Database Service is a primary depository that offers many options for information retrieval. Not all of the options discussed are available from all servers.

Unless you look for a specific RFC by number, you should retrieve a file named rfc-inde.txt, which lists all the RFCs. A typical entry is as follows:

```
1800 S  J. Postel, "INTERNET OFFICIAL PROTOCOL STANDARDS", 07/11/1995.
           (Pages=36) (Format=.txt) (Obsoletes RFC1780) (STD 1)
```

A letter that follows the RFC number indicates the status of the RFC:

S	Standard
DS	Draft Standard
PS	Proposed Standard
I	Informational
E	Experimental
H	Historic

Standards are assigned standard numbers. This RFC is Standard 1. A list of Internet standards is published in RFC 1800.

In many cases, some RFCs are obsolete or are rendered obsolete by other RFCs, as is clearly indicated in the index listing and on the title page of the document.

Anonymous FTP

FTP (File Transfer Protocol) provides a mechanism for transferring files between TCP/IP hosts. Chapter 6, "The Process/Application Layer," describes FTP. Anonymous FTP permits users to log in and access FTP files without having an account on the server. Enter "anonymous" as the login and your e-mail address as the password. In Chapter 6, FTP is used to perform an anonymous transfer of an RFC from the InterNIC server.

RFCs may be obtained via FTP from these servers:

DS.INTERNIC.NET (InterNIC Directory and Database Services)

NIS.NSF.NET

NISC.JVNC.NET

FTP.ISI.EDU

WUARCHIVE.WUSTL.EDU

SRC.DOC.IC.AC.UK

FTP.NCREN.NET

FTP.SESQUI.NET

NIS.GARR.IT

These hosts are primary depositories, updated when an RFC is first announced. Several secondary depositories also are available, although a few days might be required before they receive the most recent updates.

In most cases, such as the InterNIC server, RFCs are stored using the path **rfc/ rfc*nnnn*.txt**, where *nnnn* is the number of the RFC.

> **Note** RFCs can also be obtained in PostScript format by replacing "txt" with "ps" in the path.

WAIS

WAIS (Wide Area Information Servers) enables you to search a database for specific documents. Users can use their own WAIS clients or can Telnet to DS.INTERNIC.NET to access a WAIS client. Log in as **wais**, no password necessary. Help and a tutorial are available online. WAIS searches also may be conducted by using the WWW.

Gopher

The indexed document database can be searched using Gopher. To access the InterNIC Gopher server from a remote Gopher client, connect to `internic.net` using port 70. To access a Gopher client on the server, Telnet to DS.INTERNIC.NET and log in as **gopher**, no password required.

Archie

An Archie database is also maintained, and Archie searches can be performed using Telnet login or electronic mail. To access Archie, Telnet to DS.INTERNIC.NET and log in as **archie**, no password required, online help available.

To receive instructions on accessing Archie through e-mail, send a message to `archie@ds.internic.net`. Include the command **help** in the body of the message.

Finally, users who do not have FTP or Telnet access can obtain RFCs through electronic mail. To obtain an RFC from InterNIC, send a message to mailserv@ds.internic.net. Include the message **file** **/ftp/rfc/rfc*nnnn*.txt**, where *nnnn* is the number of the RFC.

World Wide Web

Certainly, the easiest way to access these resources is to use the World Wide Web. The URL for the InterNIC Directory and Database Services is as follows:

```
http://ds.internic.net/
```

The IETF also maintains a Web server, which can be accessed using the InterNIC server or reached directly using the following URL:

```
http://www.ietf.reston.va.us/
```

Summary

This chapter introduced you to several aspects of TCP/IP. The first topic of discussion was a brief history of TCP/IP, starting with its early roots in the United States Department of Defense. The TCP/IP protocols were developed in the early 1980s, and became the standard protocols for the ARPAnet in 1983. This discussion introduced you to many of the networking problems that have stimulated the design and redesign of TCP/IP.

Next, this chapter examined the TCP/IP standardization process. Unlike vendor proprietary protocols, which tend to evolve in manufacturer's laboratories, only TCP/IP is available freely and defined in an environment of public review.

Finally, this chapter looked at the administrating body of the Internet (The Internet Activities Board), and the Internet standards process. As you become involved with TCP/IP, you should know about the standardization process so that you can monitor changes that might affect you. You might even decide to become involved in the standards setting process.

Chapter 2 Snapshot

After discussing the OSI reference model, this chapter examines TCP/IP architecture. It covers the following topics:

◆ The communication process

◆ The OSI reference model

◆ Characteristics of layered protocols

◆ The Internet model

◆ Delivering data through internetworks

TCP/IP Architecture

The *architecture* of a computer system refers to overall system design. Microsoft designs its networking products using a fairly elaborate networking architecture that enables the products to support several popular networking protocols: NetBEUI, Novell's IPX/SPX, and TCP/IP. Chapter 7, "Introducing Microsoft TCP/IP," discusses the full scope of the Microsoft protocol architecture. The current chapter focuses on the characteristics of network protocol architectures in general and on the specific characteristics of the TCP/IP protocol architecture.

As Chapter 1 mentions, the name, *TCP/IP*, describes much more than the TCP and IP protocols. TCP/IP is a suite of protocols in which each protocol performs a subset of overall network communication tasks. Network implementors select among these protocols to achieve a desired network functionality. The TCP/IP protocol suite architecture defines the way the various TCP/IP protocols fit together.

Microsoft networks can involve multiple protocol suites, so establishing a model that clarifies the relations between the various protocols is essential. The conventional model for comparing protocol suites is the OSI reference model, which is the first topic this chapter covers. The discussion uses the OSI reference model to illustrate common characteristics all network protocol suites share. Chapter 7 also discusses the OSI reference model, using it to illustrate the way Microsoft products support multiple protocols concurrently.

After discussing the OSI reference model, this chapter examines TCP/IP architecture.

Understanding the Communication Process

The communication process is surprisingly complicated. We tend to take communication for granted because we are immersed in many forms of it every day of our lives. Even in the simplest of situations, however, communication can be quite involved. Data communication is a highly technical topic, one in which becoming bogged down in the details can be hard to avoid. Before things get too formal, looking at some examples of communication in which we humans engage should prove illuminating.

Dialogs

Humans and computers both exchange information in orderly conversations called *dialogs*. Consider the everyday event of meeting a friend on the street and holding a conversation, illustrated in figure 2.1. Even this simple situation has rules:

1. One person initiates communication by greeting the other person. They might need to negotiate some details, such as what language to use.

2. The other person acknowledges the greeting. This exchange initiates a conversation, which in data communication terminology is called a *session*.

3. The individuals undertake an orderly exchange of information. Generally, one person talks while another listens, then the parties exchange roles. A complex set of rules helps the speakers exchange roles without interfering with each others' utterances. Without these rules, orderly conversation breaks down and information exchange grinds to a halt. An example of failed communication is a shouting match when both parties are talking at once and receive little information.

4. Rules are observed for ending the conversation. Polite exchanges take place when both parties feel they have completed their messages. If the conversation breaks down mid-message, communication errors can occur. Data communication often requires a session termination procedure.

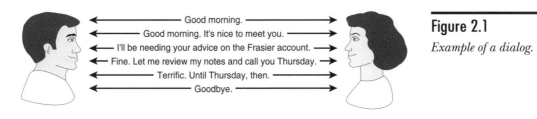

Figure 2.1

Example of a dialog.

Human communication is not always so formal. If you need to warn someone about a falling brick, you do not need to establish a conversation. A single, shouted warning might be the only communication that takes place. In such instances, however, the two parties must be in reasonable agreement about the rules of communication. A warning shout works if both parties speak the same language but might be useless if the warning is in Japanese and the potential victim speaks only German.

Computers establish communication in much the same way as humans. They exchange greetings and negotiate the rules under which communication takes place. The result is a *connection* between the devices that ensures an orderly dialog. After the need for the connection ceases, another orderly procedure closes it. In that way, neither device is left hanging with incomplete information.

Communication Protocols

Data communication is surprisingly similar to human conversation. People and computers both utilize formal communication for complex data exchanges, and informal processes for special purposes, such as warnings. Both follow *protocols*, rules that enable the subjects to exchange information in an orderly, error-free manner. Protocols are obeyed to establish and end communication, so that neither party is left hanging in an undesirable state. Just as the rude interruption of a conversation can offend a person, so too can the interruption of data communication without an orderly termination process confuse a computer.

The first characteristic to notice about the communication process, therefore, is that error-free communication can be achieved only by following communication protocols.

The inability of two entities to communicate directly complicates communication. Consider what happens when one person mails another person a letter:

1. Sender writes or types the letter on paper.

2. Sender inserts the paper in an envelope, and labels that envelope with his address and the intended receiver's address.

3. Sender places the envelope at a specific location, where the letter carrier picks it up and places it in a mail bag for transport.

4. The letter carrier takes the mail bag to the local post office branch, where yet another person or persons remove the letter from the bag, sort it, and place it in a mail bag destined for the city specified by the receiver's address.

5. Someone else transports the mail bag to the receiver's city.

6. After the mail bag arrives in the receiver's city, a person sorts the letters in the bag so that the letters can be given to the appropriate letter carriers for each region in the city.

7. The letter carrier transports the letter to the receiver's address.

8. Finally, the receiver removes the letter from its envelope to recover the original message from the sender.

This scenario illustrates several important characteristics of communication. The diagram of this scenario as shown in figure 2.2 closely resembles the architecture models that this chapter examines later.

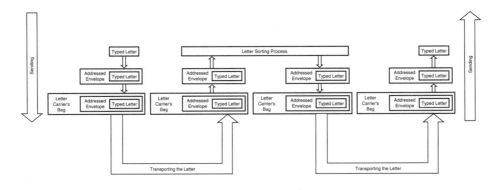

Figure 2.2   *A model for communicating by letter.*

One feature of the model shown in figure 2.2 is that communication takes place in layers, each of which has a specifically defined area of responsibility. When you want a letter delivered, you need only place it in an envelope and address the envelope. You need not be concerned with the other layers of the process. You don't need to worry about whether the letter is transported by truck or by plane—another layer is responsible for that decision.

This approach to designing a communication system is known as a *layered architecture*. Each layer has specific responsibilities and specific rules for carrying out those responsibilities, and knows nothing about the procedures the other layers follow. The layer carries out its tasks and delivers the message to the next layer in the process—and that is enough. Quite a few characteristics of layered architectures can be teased out of the preceding example:

◆ They break the communication process into manageable chunks. Designing a small part of a process is much easier than designing the entire process, and simplifies engineering.

◆ A change at one layer does not affect the other layers. The process of addressing an envelope does not change, whether the letter is being shipped by truck, train, or carrier pigeon. New delivery technologies can be introduced without affecting other layers. (This is the chief reason, in fact, for implementing protocols in layers.)

◆ When a layer receives a message from an upper layer, the lower layer frequently encloses the message in a distinct package. Letters are placed in mail bags when they are sent across the country, for example. In data communication terms, lower layer protocols frequently treat upper layer messages in a similar way, enclosing them in a "data envelope." The technical term for this process is *encapsulation*.

◆ The protocols at the various layers have the appearance of a stack, and a complete model of a data communication architecture is often called a *protocol stack*.

◆ Layers can be mixed and matched to achieve different requirements. By adding an overnight label to the envelope, the sender of a letter can have the letter routed through an overnight delivery service rather than standard first-class delivery.

◆ Layers follow specific procedures for communicating with adjacent layers. The interfaces between layers must be clearly defined.

◆ An *address mechanism* is the common element that allows letters to be routed through the various layers until it reaches its destination. Sometimes, layers add their own address information. The postal service often adds a bar code to letters, which enables letters to be routed more efficiently within the postal system. Postal addresses have two parts: a city and zip code that enable the postal service to deliver the message to the correct letter carrier, and a street address that enables the letter carrier to deliver the message to the correct recipient.

◆ Essentially, each layer at the sender's end communicates with the corresponding layer at the receiver's end. The process of putting the letter in a mail bag, for example, has a matching process of opening the mail bag in the destination city.

◆ Errors can occur at any of the layers. For critical messages, error-detecting mechanisms should be in place to either correct errors or notify the sender when they occur.

Each of these characteristics has its counterpart in data communication, and the time has come to examine some real data communication models. The first model this chapter considers is the OSI reference model, which is generic enough that it can serve to illustrate general characteristics of data communication models.

The OSI Reference Model

The International Organization for Standardization (ISO) developed the OSI reference model as a guide for defining a set of open protocols. Although interest in the OSI protocols has waned, the OSI reference model remains the most common standard for describing and comparing protocol suites.

Note If only TCP/IP were being discussed, bypassing the OSI model would be possible. Microsoft networks can be implemented with protocols other than TCP/IP, however, including NWLink (Microsoft's implementation of Novell's IPX/SPX) and NetBEUI. The architecture for integrating these protocols is best illustrated using the OSI model.

Figure 2.3 shows the seven-layer OSI reference model. Each layer provides a specific type of network service. This chapter describes each of these layers.

Figure 2.3

Layers of the OSI reference model.

| Application |
| Presentation |
| Session |
| Transport |
| Network |
| Data Link |
| Physical |

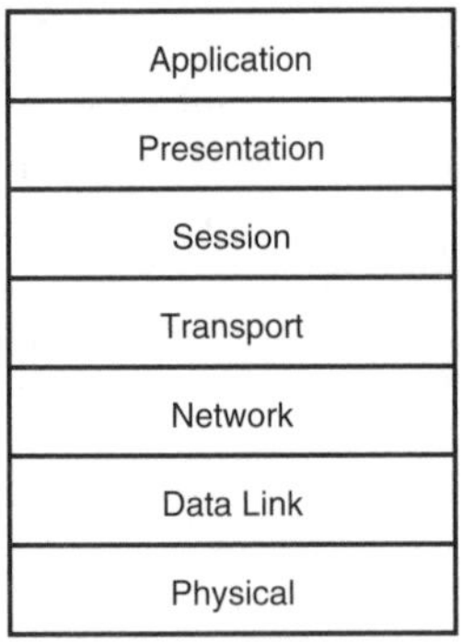

Figure 2.3 illustrates why groups of related protocols are frequently called *protocol stacks*. To an extent, network designers can build a protocol stack that meets their specific requirements by choosing an appropriate protocol for each layer. Layering makes changing the physical network easy, for example, from Ethernet to token ring without the need for changes at other layers.

The layers are numbered from the bottom of the protocol stack to the top. The following sections discuss each layer in turn, from the bottom up.

The Physical Layer

The physical layer communicates directly with the communication medium, and has two responsibilities: sending bits and receiving bits. A *binary digit*, or *bit*, is the basic unit of information in data communication. A bit can have only two values, 1 or 0, represented by different states on the communication medium. Other communication layers are responsible for collecting these bits into groups that represent message data.

Bits are represented by changes in signals on the network medium. Some wire media represent 1s and 0s with different voltages, some use distinct audio tones, and yet others use more sophisticated methods, such as *state transitions* (changes from high-to-low or from low-to-high voltages).

A wide variety of media are used for data communication, including electric cable, fiber optics, light waves, radio, and microwave. The medium used can vary—a different medium simply necessitates substituting a different set of physical layer protocols. Thus, the upper layers are completely independent from the particular process used to deliver bits through the network medium.

An important distinction is that the OSI physical layer does not, strictly speaking, describe the media themselves. The physical layer describes the bit patterns to be used, but does not define the medium; it describes how data are encoded into media signals and the characteristics of the media attachment interface. In actual practice, many physical layer standards cover characteristics of the OSI physical layer as well as characteristics of the medium.

The Data Link Layer

Devices that can communicate on a network frequently are called *nodes*. (Other names include *station* and *device*.) The data link layer is responsible for providing node-to-node communication on a single, local network. To provide this service, the data link layer must perform two functions. It must provide an address mechanism that enables messages to be delivered to the correct nodes. Also, it must translate messages from upper layers into bits that the physical layer can transmit.

When the data link layer receives a message to transmit, it formats the message into a *data frame.* (You also hear data frames referred to as *packets.*) Figure 2.4 illustrates the format of a typical frame. Chapter 3 presents actual frame formats in the context of Ethernet and token ring protocols. The sections of a frame are called *fields.* The fields in the given example are as follows:

◆ **Start Indicator.** A specific bit pattern indicates the start of a data frame.

◆ **Source Address.** The address of the sending node is also included so that replies to messages can be addressed properly.

◆ **Destination Address.** Each node is identified by an address. The data link layer of the sender adds the destination address to the frame. The data link layer of the receiver looks at the destination address to identify messages that it should receive.

◆ **Control.** In many cases, additional control information must be included. The specific information is determined by each protocol.

◆ **Data.** This field contains all data that were forwarded to the data link layer from upper protocol layers.

◆ **Error Control.** This field contains information that enables the receiving node to determine whether an error occurred during transmission. A common approach is *cyclic redundancy checksum (CRC),* which is a calculated value that summarizes all of the data in the frame. The sending node calculates a checksum and stores it in the frame. The receiver recalculates the checksum. If the receiver's calculated CRC matches the CRC value in the frame, it can safely be assumed that the frame was transmitted without error.

Figure 2.4

Start Indicator	Source Address	Destination Address	Control	Data	Error Control

Example of a data frame.

Frame delivery on a local network is extremely simple. A sending node simply transmits the frame. Each node on the network sees every frame, and examines the destination address. When the destination address of a frame matches the node's address, the data link layer at the node receives the frame and sends it up the protocol stack.

Data units at the data link layer are most commonly called *frames,* although the term *packet* is used with some protocols.

Network Layer

Only the smallest networks consist of a single, local network. The majority of networks must be subdivided, as shown in figure 2.5. A network that consists of several network segments is frequently called an *internetwork,* or an internet (not to be confused with *the* Internet).

These subdivisions may be planned to reduce traffic on network segments or to isolate remote networks connected by slower communication media. When networks are subdivided, it can no longer be assumed that messages will be delivered on the local network. A mechanism must be put in place to route messages from one network to another.

To deliver messages on an internetwork, each network must be uniquely identified by a *network address.* When it receives a message from upper layers, the network layer adds a header to the message that includes the source and destination network address. This combination of data plus the network layer is called a *packet.* The network address information is used to deliver a message to the correct network. After the message arrives on the correct network, the data link layer can use the node address to deliver the message to a specific node.

Forwarding packets to the correct network is called *routing,* and the devices that route packets are called *routers.* As you can see in figure 2.5, an internetwork has two types of nodes:

◆ *End nodes* provide user services. End nodes do use a network layer to add network address information to packets, but they do not perform routing. End nodes are sometimes called *end systems* (the OSI term) or *hosts* (the TCP/IP term).

◆ Routers incorporate special mechanisms that perform routing. Because routing is a complex task, routers usually are dedicated devices that do not provide services to end users. Routers sometimes are called *intermediate systems* (the OSI term) or *gateways* (the historic TCP/IP term).

The network layer operates independently of the physical medium, which is a concern of the physical layer. Since routers are network layer devices, they can be used to forward packets between physically different networks. A router can join an Ethernet to a token ring network, for example. Routers also are often used to connect a local area network, such as Ethernet, to a wide-area network, such as ATM.

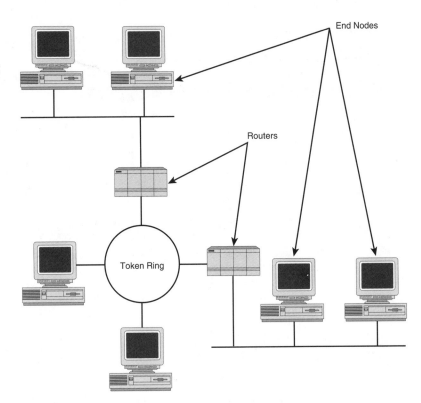

Figure 2.5

An internetwork consisting of several networks.

Transport Layer

All network technologies set a maximum size for frames that can be sent on the network. Ethernet, for example, limits the size of the data field to 1500 bytes. This limit is necessary for two reasons:

◆ Small frames improve network efficiency when many devices must share the network. If devices could transmit frames of unlimited size, they might monopolize the network for an excessive period of time. With small frames, devices take turns at shorter intervals, and devices are more likely to have ready access to the network.

◆ With small frames, less data must be retranslated to correct an error. If a message that consists of 100 KB encounters an error of a single byte, the entire 100 KB message must be retranslated. If the message is divided into 100 frames, each limited in size to 1 KB, a one byte error requires the retransmission merely of a single 1 KB frame.

One responsibility of the transport layer is to divide messages into fragments that fit within the size limitations established by the network. At the receiving end, the transport layer reassembles the fragments to recover the original message.

When messages are divided into multiple fragments, the possibility that segments might not be received in the order sent increases. Figure 2.6 illustrates how the network may route packets differently as routers attempt to send each packet by the most efficient available route. When the packets are received, the transport layer must reassemble the message fragments in the correct order. To enable packets to be reassembled in their original order, the transport layer includes a message sequence number in its header.

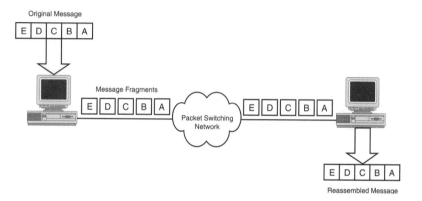

Figure 2.6

Fragmentation and reassembly of a message on a packet switching network.

Most computers are multitasking, running several programs at once. A user's workstation might, for example, be simultaneously running processes to transfer files to another computer, retrieve e-mail, and access a network database. The transport layer is responsible for delivering messages from a specific process on one computer to the corresponding process on the destination computer.

Under the OSI model, the transport layer assigns a *service access point (SAP) ID* to each packet. (The TCP/IP term for a service access point is *port*.) The SAP ID is an address that identifies the process that originated the message. The SAP ID enables the transport layer of the receiving node to route the message to the appropriate process.

Identifying messages from several processes so that the messages can be transmitted through the same network medium is called *multiplexing*. The procedure of recovering messages and directing them to the correct process is called *demultiplexing*. Figure 2.7 illustrates how message multiplexing and demultiplexing work. Multiplexing is a common occurrence on networks, which are designed to enable many dialogs to share the same network medium.

Figure 2.7

Message multiplexing and demultiplexing.

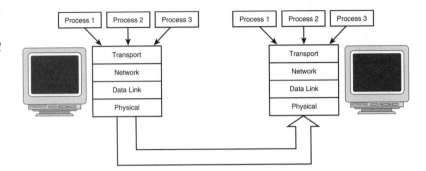

<table>
<tr><td>Note</td><td>Because multiple protocols may be supported for any given layer, multiplexing and demultiplexing can occur at many layers. Some examples of multiplexing are presented in the following list:</td></tr>
</table>

◆ Transport of different Ethernet frame types over the same medium (data link layer).

◆ Simultaneous support for NWLink and TCP/IP on Windows NT computers (data link layer).

◆ Messages for multiple transport protocols, such as TCP and UDP on TCP/IP systems (transport layer).

◆ Messages for multiple application protocols (such as TELNET, FTP, and SMTP) on a UNIX host (session and higher layers).

As subsequent chapters discuss layers of the TCP/IP protocol suite, the methods of multiplexing messages at each level are examined.

One more responsibility of the transport layer must be examined. Although the data link and network layers can be assigned responsibility for detecting errors in transmitting data, that responsibility generally is dedicated to the transport layer. Two general categories of error detection can be performed by the transport layer:

◆ **Reliable delivery.** Reliable delivery does not mean that errors cannot occur, only that errors are detected if they do occur. Recovery from a detected error can take the form of simply notifying upper layer processes that the error occurred. Often, however, the transport layer can request the retransmission of a packet for which an error was detected.

◆ **Unreliable delivery.** Unreliable delivery does not mean that errors are likely to occur, but rather, indicates that the transport layer does not check for errors. Because error checking takes time and reduces network performance, unreliable delivery often is preferred when a network is known to be highly reliable, which is the case with the majority of local area networks. Unreliable delivery generally is used when each packet contains a complete message, whereas reliable delivery is preferred when messages consist of large numbers of packets. Unreliable delivery is often called *datagram delivery*, and independent packets transmitted in this way frequently are called *datagrams*.

Assuming that reliable delivery is always preferable is a common mistake. Unreliable delivery actually is preferable in at least two cases: when the network is fairly reliable and performance must be optimized, and when entire messages are contained in individual packets and loss of a packet is not a critical problem.

The Session Layer

The session layer is responsible for dialog control between nodes. A *dialog* is a formal conversation in which two nodes agree to exchange data.

Communication can take place in three dialog modes, illustrated in figure 2.8:

◆ **Simplex.** One node transmits exclusively, while another exclusively receives.

◆ **Half-duplex.** Only one node may send at a given time, and nodes take turns transmitting.

◆ **Full-duplex.** Nodes may transmit and receive simultaneously. Full-duplex communication typically requires some form of *flow control* to ensure that neither device sends faster than the other device can receive.

Sessions enable nodes to communicate in an organized manner. Each session has three phases:

1. **Connection establishment.** The nodes establish contact. They negotiate the rules of communication, including the protocols to be used and communication parameters.

2. **Data transfer.** The nodes engage in a dialog to exchange data.

3. **Connection release.** When the nodes no longer need to communicate, they engage in an orderly release of the session.

Steps 1 and 3 represent extra overhead for the communication process. This extra overhead might be undesirable for brief communication. When devices are managed on a network, they send out periodic status reports that generally consist of single frame messages. If all such messages were sent as part of a formal session, the connection establishment and release phases would transfer far more data than the message itself.

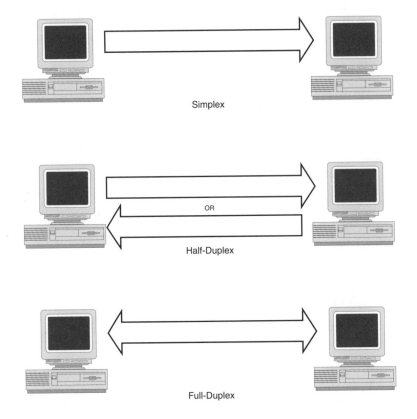

Figure 2.8

Communication dialog modes.

Simplex

OR

Half-Duplex

Full-Duplex

In such situations, communicating using a *connectionless* approach is common. The sending node simply transmits its data and assumes availability of the desired receiver.

A connection-oriented session approach is desirable for complex communication. Consider transmitting a large amount of data to another node. Without formal controls, a single error anytime during the transfer would require resending of the entire file. After establishing a session, the sending and receiving nodes can agree on a checkpoint procedure. If an error occurs, the sending node must retransmit only the data sent since the previous checkpoint. The process of managing a complex activity is called *activity management.*

The Presentation Layer

The presentation layer is responsible for presenting data to the application layer. In some cases, the presentation layer directly translates data from one format to another. IBM mainframe computers use a character encoding scheme called *EBCDIC*, whereas virtually all other computers use the ASCII encoding scheme. If data is being transmitted from an EBCDIC computer to an ASCII computer, for example, the presentation layer might be responsible for translating between the different character sets. Numeric data is also represented quite differently on different computer architectures and must be converted when transferred between different machine times.

A common technique used to improve data transfer is to convert all data to a standard format before transmitting the data. This standard format probably is not the native data format of any computer. All computers can be configured to retrieve standard format data, however, and convert it into their native data formats. The OSI protocol standards define Abstract Syntax Representation, Revision 1 (ASN.1) as a standard data syntax for use at the presentation layer. Although the TCP/IP protocol suite does not formally define a presentation layer, a protocol that serves a similar function is External Data Representation (XDR), which is used with the Network File System (NFS). Chapter 6, "The Process/Application Layer," discusses NFS.

Other functions that may correspond to the presentation layer are data encryption/decryption and compression/decompression.

The presentation layer is the least frequently implemented of the OSI layers. Few protocols have been formally defined for this layer. In the majority of cases, network applications perform the functions that might be associated with the presentation layer.

Application Layer

The application layer provides the services user applications needed to communicate through the network. Here are several examples of user application layer services:

◆ **Electronic mail transport.** A protocol for handling electronic mail can be used by a wide variety of applications. Application designers who use the e-mail protocols do not need to invent their own e-mail handlers. Also, applications that share a common e-mail interface can exchange messages through the e-mail message handler.

◆ **Remote file access.** Local applications can be given the capability to access files on remote nodes.

◆ **Remote job execution.** Local applications can be given the capability to start and control processes on other nodes.

◆ **Directories.** The network can offer a directory of network resources, including logical node names. This directory enables applications to access network sources by logical names rather than abstract numeric node IDs.

◆ **Network management.** Network management protocols can enable various applications to access network management information.

You frequently encounter the term *Application Program Interface (API)* used in conjunction with application layer services. An API is a set of rules that enables user-written applications to access the services of a software system. Developers of program products and protocols frequently provide APIs, which enable programmers to easily adapt their applications to use the services the products provide. A common UNIX API is Berkeley Sockets, which Microsoft has implemented as Windows Sockets.

Characteristics of Layered Protocols

The OSI reference model illustrates several characteristics of layered protocol stacks. When a device transmits data to the network, each protocol layer processes the data in turn. Figure 2.9 illustrates the steps involved for the sending and receiving devices.

Consider the network layer for the sending device. Data to be transmitted is received from the transport layer. The network layer is responsible for routing and must add its routing information to the data. The network layer information is added in the form of a header, which is appended to the beginning of the data.

Figure 2.9

Headers and the OSI protocol layers.

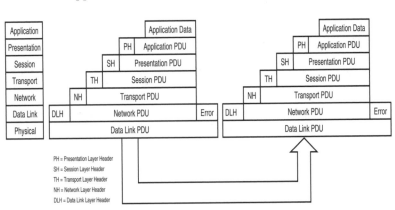

OSI terminology uses the term *protocol data unit (PDU)* to describe the combination of the control information for a layer with the data from the next higher layer. As figure 2.9 shows, each layer appends a header to the PDU that the next higher layer receives. The data field for each layer consists of the PDU for the next higher layer. (The data link layer also adds a trailer that consists of the error control data.) The physical layer does not encapsulate in this manner because the physical layer manages data in bit form.

When a layer adds its header to the data from a higher layer, the process resembles placing mail in an envelope. The envelope can be used to deliver the data to the correct location, where the envelope is opened and the data recovered. When a protocol uses headers or trailers to package the data from another protocol, the process is called *encapsulation*. We say that the network layer *encapsulates* the data from the transport layer.

As received data passes up the protocol stack, each layer strips its corresponding header from the data unit. The process of removing headers from data is called *decapsulation*. This mechanism enables each layer in the transmitting device to communicate with the corresponding layer in the receiver. Each layer in the transmitting device communicates with its *peer* layer in the receiving device, in a process called *peer-to-peer communication*.

The Internet Model

As discussed in Chapter 1, the protocol architecture for TCP/IP currently is defined by the IETF, which is responsible for establishing the protocols and architecture for the Internet. The model dates back to the ARPANET and often is called the *DoD model*. The DoD protocol architecture predates the OSI reference model, which was first described in 1979. As such, perfectly mapping the DoD model to the OSI reference model is impossible. Figure 2.10 illustrates the four-layer Internet model, mapping the Internet model layers as closely as possible to the OSI reference model. Each of the layers are discussed in a separate chapter (see Chapters 3 through 6), but a brief description is in order here.

OSI Reference Model	Internet Model
Application	Process/Application
Presentation	
Session	
Transport	Host-to-Host
Network	Internetwork
Data Link	Network Access
Physical	

Figure 2.10

Comparison of the Internet protocol model and the OSI reference model.

The *network access layer* is responsible for exchanging data between a host and the network and for delivering data between two devices on the same network. Node physical addresses are used to accomplish delivery on the local network. The DoD architecture was designed with the intent of using prevailing network standards, and

TCP/IP has been adapted to a wide variety of network types, including circuit-switching (for example, X.21), packet switching (such as X.25), Ethernet, the IEEE 802.x protocols, ATM, and frame relay. Data in the network access layer encode EtherType information that is used to demultiplex data associated with specific upper-layer protocol stacks.

The *internet layer* corresponds to the OSI network layer, and is responsible for routing messages through internetworks. Devices responsible for routing messages between networks are called *gateways* in TCP/IP terminology, although the term router is also used with increasing frequency. The TCP/IP protocol at this layer is the *internet protocol (IP)*. In addition to the physical node addresses utilized at the network access layer, the IP protocol implements a system of logical host addresses called IP addresses. The IP addresses are used by the internet and higher layers to identify devices and to perform internetwork routing. The *address resolution protocol (ARP)* enables IP to identify the physical address that matches a given IP address.

The *host-to-host layer* compares closely to the OSI transport layer and is responsible for end-to-end data integrity. Two protocols are employed at this layer: *transmission control protocol (TCP)* and *user datagram protocol (UDP)*. TCP provides reliable, full-duplex connections and reliable service by ensuring that data is present when transmission results in an error. Also, TCP enables hosts to maintain multiple, simultaneous connections. UDP provides unreliable (datagram) service that enhances network throughput when error correction is not required at the host-to-host layer.

The *process/application layer* spans the functionality of three layers of the OSI reference model: session, presentation, and application. Not surprisingly, therefore, a wide variety of protocols are included in this layer of the DoD model. Examples of protocols at this layer include the following:

◆ **File Transfer Protocol (FTP).** Performs basic file transfers between hosts.

◆ **Telnet.** Enables users to execute terminal sessions with remote hosts.

◆ **Simple Mail Transfer Protocol (SMTP).** Supports basic message delivery services.

◆ **Simple Network Management Protocol (SNMP).** A protocol that is used to collect management information from network devices.

◆ **Network File System (NFS).** A system developed by Sun Microsystems that enables computers to mount drives on remote hosts and operate them as if they were local drives.

Some of these applications encompass functions from several layers of the OSI reference model. NFS, for example, enables hosts to maintain a session (session layer), agree on a data representation (presentation layer), and operate a network file system (application layer).

Delivering Data Through Internetworks

When protocols are discussed in the following chapters, you encounter a variety of network concepts that are explained here. The way data are delivered through internetworks is involved—enough that it deserves more thorough discussion. It involves several topics:

◆ Methods for carrying multiple data streams on common media, a technique called *multiplexing*

◆ Methods for switching data through paths on the network

◆ Methods for determining the path to be used

Multiplexing

LANs generally operate in *baseband* mode, which means that a given cable is carrying a single data signal at any one time. The various devices on the LAN must take turns using the medium. This generally is a workable approach for LANs, because LAN media offer high performance at low cost.

Long-distance data communications media are expensive to install and maintain, and it would be inefficient if each media path could support only a single data stream. Imagine the expense if it was necessary to equip each telephone with its own communication satellite or transatlantic cable to enable it to connect to Europe. WANs, therefore, tend to use *broadband* media, which can support two or more data streams. Increasingly, as LANs are expected to carry more and different kinds of data, broadband media are being considered for LANs as well.

To enable many data streams to share a high-bandwidth medium, a technique called *multiplexing* is employed. Figure 2.11 illustrates one method of multiplexing digital signals. The signal-carrying capacity of the medium is divided into time slots, with a time slot assigned to each signal, a technique called *time-division multiplexing (TDM)*. Because the sending and receiving devices are synchronized to recognize the same time slots, the receiver can identify each data stream and re-create the original signals.

Figure 2.11

Time-division multiplexing.

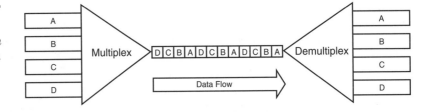

The sending device, which places data into the time slots, is called a multiplexer or mux. The receiving device is called a demultiplexer or demux.

TDM can be inefficient. If a data stream falls silent, its time slots are not used and the media bandwidth is underutilized. Figure 2.12 depicts a more advanced technique, called *statistical time-division multiplexing (stat-TDM)*. Time slots still are used, but some data streams are allocated more time slots than others. An idle channel is allocated no time slots at all. A device that performs statistical TDM often is called a *stat-MUX*.

Figure 2.12

Statistical time-division multiplexing.

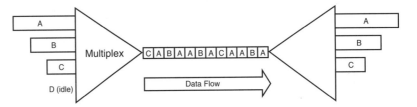

Switching Data

On an internetwork, data units must be switched through the various intermediate devices until they are delivered to their destinations. Two contrasting methods of switching data are commonly used: circuit switching and packet switching. Both are used in some form by protocols in common use. (A third, message switching, is useful in some situations, but not applicable to this book.)

Circuit Switching

Circuit switching is illustrated in figure 2.13. When two devices negotiate the start of a dialog, they establish a path, called a *circuit*, through the network, along with a dedicated bandwidth through the circuit. After establishing the circuit, all data for the dialog flow through that circuit. This approach quite resembles a telephone connection in which a voice circuit is established to enable the telephones at the end-points to communicate. The chief disadvantage of circuit switching is that when communication takes place at less than the assigned circuit capacity, bandwidth is wasted. Also, communicating devices cannot take advantage of other, less busy paths through the network unless the circuit is reconfigured.

Circuit switching does not necessarily mean that a continuous, physical pathway exists for the sole use of the circuit. The message stream may be multiplexed with other message streams in a broadband circuit. In fact, sharing of media is the more likely case with modern telecommunications. The appearance to the end devices, however, is that the network has configured a circuit dedicated to their use.

End devices benefit greatly from circuit switching. Since the path is preestablished, data travel through the network with little processing in transit. And, because multi-part messages travel sequentially through the same path, message segments arrive in order and
little effort is required to reconstruct the original message. For that reason, a form of circuit switching was used to design the new leading-edge technology ATM. The next chapter shows you how ATM uses a form of circuit switching without the inefficiencies just described.

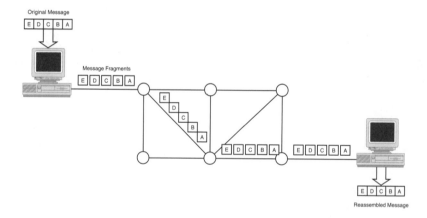

Figure 2.13

Circuit switching.

Packet Switching

Packet switching takes a different and generally more efficient approach to switching data through networks. In the late 1960s, packet switching was a new concept that the DoD sought to investigate in the early ARPA network research. As shown in figure 2.14, messages are broken into sections called *packets*, which are routed individually through the network. At the receiving device, the packets are reassembled to construct the complete message. Messages are divided into packets to ensure that large messages do not monopolize the network. Packets from several messages can be multiplexed through the same communication channel. Thus, packet switching enables devices to share the total network bandwidth efficiently.

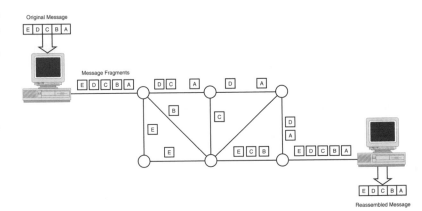

Figure 2.14

Packet switching.

Two variations of packet switching may be employed:

◆ *Datagram* services treat each packet as an independent message. The packets (also called *datagrams*) are routed through the network using the most efficient route currently available, enabling the switches to bypass busy segments and use underutilized segments. Datagrams frequently are employed on LANs and network layer protocols are responsible for routing the datagrams to the appropriate destination. Datagram service is called *unreliable*, not because it is inherently flawed but because it does not guarantee delivery of data. Recovery of errors is left to upper-layer protocols. Also, if several messages are required to construct a complete message, upper-layer protocols are responsible for reassembling the datagrams in order. Protocols that provide datagram service are called *connectionless* protocols.

◆ *Virtual circuits* establish a formal connection between two devices, giving the appearance of a dedicated circuit between the devices. When the connection is established, issues such as message sizes, buffer capacities, and network paths are considered and mutually agreeable communication parameters are selected. A virtual circuit defines a *connection*, a communication path through the network, and remains in effect as long as the devices remain in communication. This path functions as a logical connection between the devices. When communication is over, a formal procedure releases the virtual circuit. Because virtual circuit service guarantees delivery of data, it provides reliable delivery service. Upper-layer protocols need not be concerned with error detection and recovery. Protocols associated with virtual circuits are called *connection-oriented*.

For the TCP/IP protocol suite, datagram service is provided by the User Datagram Protocol (UDP). The vast majority of systems rely on the Transmission Control Protocol (TCP) to provide reliable delivery.

Bridges, Routers, and Switches

Data can be routed through an internetwork using the following three types of information:

◆ The physical address of the destination device, found at the data link layer. Devices that forward messages based on physical addresses generally are called *bridges.*

◆ The address of the destination network, found at the network layer. Devices that use network addresses to forward messages usually are called *routers,* although the original name, still commonly used in the TCP/IP world, is *gateway.*

◆ The circuit that has been established for a particular connection. Devices that route messages based on assigned circuits are called *switches.*

The following sections discuss each of these devices, respectively.

Bridges

Bridges build and maintain a database that lists known addresses of devices and how to reach those devices. When it receives a frame, the switch consults its database to determine which of its connections should be used to forward the frame. Figure 2.15 illustrates the process in terms of the OSI reference model. A bridge must implement only the physical and data link layers of the protocol stack.

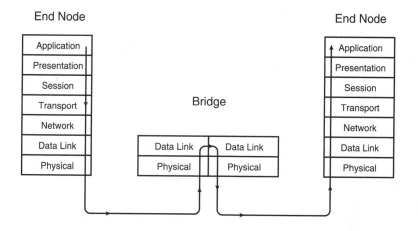

Figure 2.15

The protocol stack model for bridging.

Bridges are fairly simple devices. They receive frames from one connection and forward them to another connection known to be en route to the destination. When more than one route is possible, bridges ordinarily cannot determine which route is most efficient. In fact, when multiple routes are available, bridging can result in frames simply traveling in circles. Having multiple paths available on the network is desirable, however, so that a failure of one path does not stop the network. With Ethernet, a technique called the *spanning-tree algorithm* enables bridged networks to contain redundant paths.

Token ring uses a different approach to bridging. When a device needs to send to another device, it goes through a discovery process to determine a route to the destination. The routing information is stored in each frame transmitted and is used by bridges to forward the frames to the appropriate networks. Although this actually is a data link layer function, the technique token ring uses is called *source routing*.

Notice in figure 2.15 that the bridge must implement two protocol stacks, one for each connection. Theoretically, these stacks could belong to different protocols, enabling a bridge to connect different types of networks. However, Chapter 3 illustrates that each type of network, such as Ethernet and token ring, has its own protocols at the data link layer. Translating data from the data link layer of an Ethernet to the data link layer of a token ring is difficult (but not impossible). Bridges, which operate at the data link layer, therefore, generally can join only networks of the same type. You see bridges employed most often in networks that are all Ethernet or all token ring. A few bridges have been marketed that can bridge networks that have different data link layers.

Routing

A different method of path determination can be employed using data found at the network layer. At that layer, networks are identified by logical network identifiers. This information can be used to build a picture of the network. This picture can be used to improve the efficiency of the paths that are chosen. Devices that forward data units based on network addresses are called routers. Figure 2.16 illustrates a protocol stack model for routing.

Figure 2.16

A protocol stack model for routing.

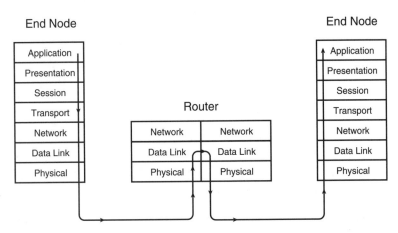

With TCP/IP, routing is a function of the internet layer, and is discussed more thoroughly in Chapter 4, "The Internet Layer." Discussion here is limited to briefly illustrating one technique. Figure 2.17 illustrates a network. By convention, the network on which the data unit originates counts as one hop. Each time a data unit crosses a router, the hop count increases by one. A wide variety of paths could be identified between A and E:

◆ A–B–C–E (5 hops)

◆ A–E (3 hops)

◆ A–D–E (4 hops)

By this method, A–E is the most efficient route. This assumes that all of the paths between the routers provide the same rate of service. A simple hop-count algorithm would be misleading if A–D and D–E were 1.5 Mbps lines while A–E was a 56 Kbps line. Apart from such extreme cases, however, hop-count routing is a definite improvement over no route planning at all.

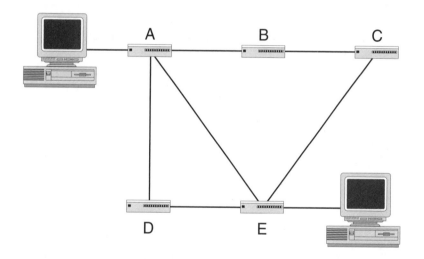

Figure 2.17

Hop-count routing.

Routing operates at the network layer. By the time data reach that layer, all evidence of the physical network has been shorn away. In figure 2.16, therefore, both protocol stacks in the router can share a common network layer protocol. The network layer does not know or care if the network is Ethernet or token ring. Therefore, each stack can support different data link and physical layers. Consequently, routers possess a capability—fairly rare in bridges—to forward traffic between dissimilar types of networks. Owing to that capability, routers often are used to connect LANs to WANs.

Building routers around the same protocol stacks as are used on the end nodes is possible. TCP/IP networks can use routers based on the same IP protocol employed at the workstation. However, it is not required that routers and end-nodes use the same routing protocol. Because network layer protocols need not communicate with upper-layer protocols, different protocols may be used in routers than are used in the end nodes. Commercial routers (such as Cisco and Wellfleet) employ proprietary network layer protocols to perform routing. These custom protocols are among the keys to the improved routing performance provided by the best routers.

Switching

Circuit-based networks operate with high efficiency because the path is established once, when the circuit is established. In figure 2.18, each switch maintains a table that records how data from different circuits should be switched. Switching is typically performed by lower-level protocols to enhance efficiency, and is associated most closely with the data
link layer.

Very seldom do real circuits resemble figure 2.18, with one cable dedicated to each communication circuit. More commonly, many circuits are multiplexed onto a single media channel, with the multiplexing hidden from the end nodes. Such circuits may then be referred to as *virtual circuits*, for they appear to the end nodes to be physical channels, whereas they actually share network bandwidth with many other virtual circuits.

Figure 2.18

Switching.

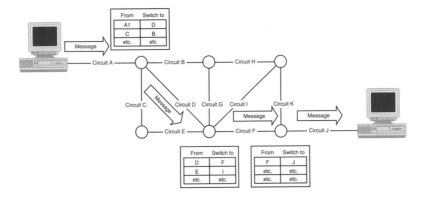

Note   When data are routed through internetworks using protocols higher than the network layer, the intermediate devices commonly are called *gateways*. This commonly confuses newcomers to TCP/IP, for historically the TCP/IP term for router has been *gateway*. You can expect to see the term router used increasingly in discussions of TCP/IP networks, but gateway remains in widespread use as a name for devices that perform routing with the IP protocol.

Summary

This chapter focused on the characteristics of network protocol architectures in general, and on the specific characteristics of the TCP/IP protocol architecture. It covered the communication process, including dialogs and communication protocols.

Next, this chapter began to describe the OSI Reference Model, explaining each of its layers in-depth. This was followed by a discussion of the characteristics of layered protocols like those found in the OSI model.

The Internet model was also described in terms of protocol. You learned that the protocol architecture for TCP/IP currently is defined by the IETF, which is responsible for establishing the protocols and architecture for the Internet. Protocols are discussed in the following chapters. A variety of network concepts that were discussed in this chapter will help you when you encounter these discussions.

Chapter 3 Snapshot

TCP/IP has come to adapt to virtually all kinds of network architectures. This chapter focuses on several protocol standards. It covers the following topics:

◆ Ethernet II

◆ IEEE LANs

◆ Digital Data Services

◆ X.25

◆ Frame Relay

◆ ATM

The Network Access Layer

The planners of TCP/IP intended the protocols to operate with existing physical network architectures. Over the years, the popularity of TCP/IP has inspired network designers to adapt TCP/IP to virtually all types of networks, too many to discuss in one chapter. This chapter focuses on the following protocol standards:

- Ethernet II

- IEEE 802.3 (IEEE Ethernet)

- IEEE 802.5 (IEEE token ring)

- X.25

- Frame Relay

- ATM

It is not the purpose of this chapter to exhaustively examine these standards. If you require more detailed information about the standards, please consult the following books from NRP:

- *Inside Windows NT Server*, for general discussions

◆ *Windows NT Server: The Professional Reference*, for greater detail

◆ *Network Optimization and Troubleshooting*, for thorough discussions of Ethernet and token ring

Ethernet II

Ethernet evolved from work by Robert Metcalf, David Boggs, and others at the Xerox Palo Alto Research Center (Xerox PARC). This early work laid the foundation for all networks that use the carrier sensing access control method. The early network was named Ethernet, after the mythical substance that allowed light to travel through space.

The first Ethernet standard, released in September 1980, was named DIX 1.0. The DIX acronym was derived from the names of the three companies that collaborated on the standard: Digital Equipment Corporation, Intel, and Xerox. A revised standard, released in November 1982, was called DIX 2.0, and is most commonly called Ethernet II.

Ethernet II became available at much the same time TCP/IP was being widely deployed. The two have become closely associated, and Ethernet II remains the dominant LAN for TCP/IP networks.

How Ethernet Works

Typically, local area networks permit a single node to transmit at a given time. This presents a problem, because all nodes at times need to transmit. *Access control methods* are systems that enable many nodes to have access to a shared network medium by granting access to the medium in an organized manner.

Ethernet uses an elegant access control method, called *carrier sensing*. When a node has data to transmit, it senses the medium, essentially listening to see if any other node is transmitting. If the medium is busy, the node waits a few microseconds and tries again. If the medium is quiet, the node begins to transmit. The full name for this approach is *carrier sensing multiple access (CSMA)*, permitting multiple nodes to access the medium through a carrier sensing method. CSMA often is called the "listen before talking" method.

A brief period of time must expire before a transmitted electrical signal reaches the furthest extents of the medium on which it is sent. Figure 3.1 shows how two nodes can sense a quiet network and begin to transmit at the same time. As the two signals flow through the medium, eventually they overlap in an event called a *collision*. Collisions always damage data, and having a mechanism for dealing with collisions when they occur is of paramount importance.

Ethernet nodes detect collisions by continuing to listen as they transmit. If a collision takes place, the nodes measure a signal voltage that is twice as high as expected. After detecting a collision, the nodes transmit a jamming signal that notifies all nodes on the network that
a collision has occurred and the current frame should be disregarded. Then the nodes wait a random amount of time before attempting to retransmit. Because each node delays for a different time, the likelihood of a new collision is reduced. This technique of managing collisions is called *collision detection (CD)*, making the complete abbreviation for the Ethernet access control method *CSMA/CD*.

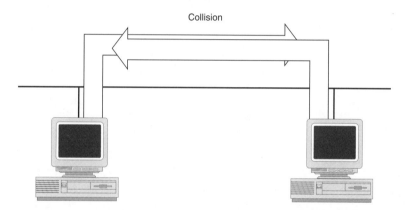

Collision

Figure 3.1

An Ethernet collision.

Note
Ethernet nodes detect collisions only when they are themselves transmitting. A potential collision detection problem is illustrated in figure 3.2. Nodes A and B have sent frames that have not yet reached each other. When the frames collide, neither node is transmitting and the collisions will not be detected. This situation arises because the frames were not long enough to reach other transmitting nodes during the time the frames were being sent.

The maximum diameter of an Ethernet is 2500 meters. Given the speed with which signals propagate (travel) through the medium, 576 bit-times are required to enable the first bits of a transmission to fully propagate through the network. As will be shown, Ethernet specifications require a 576-bit minimum frame size, ensuring that transmitting nodes will see all other transmissions that cause collisions.

Figure 3.2

How a collision may be undetected.

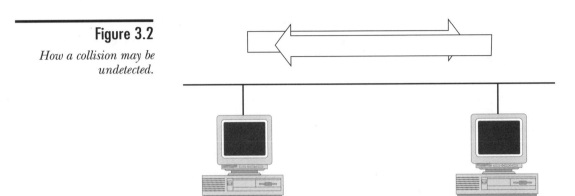

Collisions are part of the normal operation of an Ethernet. Because CSMA/CD is an exceptionally efficient access control method, normal collision activity does not seriously affect network performance. At some point, however, a heavily loaded network can experience high levels of collisions that seriously degrade network performance, possibly resulting in network gridlock. This disastrous condition seldom is seen on a properly designed Ethernet that has a reasonable number of nodes.

The CSMA/CD access method is elegant in its simplicity. Some networks, such as token ring, require elaborate mechanisms to maintain network access procedures. Ethernet requires few such mechanisms and consequently devotes a high proportion of network bandwidth to useful data transmission. The majority of networks are well-served by Ethernet. The simplicity of CSMA/CD has enabled the manufacture of extremely low-cost Ethernet hardware, and in most cases, Ethernet is the least expensive network media option. Engineers have been able to extend the scope of CSMA/CD, supporting its use on newer media options, such as unshielded twisted-pair (UTP).

Ethernet Media

Ethernet II is nearly 100 percent compatible with media specified by the IEEE 802.3 standard. Because the majority of developments in Ethernet media have been standardized by the IEEE, discussion of Ethernet media falls within the examination of the IEEE 802.3 standard. See the section "IEEE 802.3 Media" later in the chapter.

Ethernet II Frames

All protocol standards define a data structure used to transmit and receive data. Ethernet II data structures are called frames. The Ethernet II frame format is shown in figure 3.3. The *preamble* consists of a series of 8 bits in a specific pattern that notifies receiving nodes that a frame is beginning. The preamble begins with seven *octets* (8-bit groups, frequently referred to as *bytes*) of the pattern 10101010. The final octet of the preamble has the bit pattern 10101011. The purpose of the preamble is to signal the beginning of a frame, and the preamble is not formally part of the frame. Therefore, the octets in the preamble are not counted as part of the length of the frame.

Preamble (8 octets)	Destination Address (6 octets)	Source Address (6 octets)	Type (2 octets)	Data (46-1500 octets)	FCS (3 octets)

Figure 3.3

Structure of an Ethernet II frame.

The *destination* and *source addresses* each consist of 48 bits (6 octets). Each node on the network is assigned a unique 48-bit address. This information enables receiving nodes to identify frames that are addressed to them, and also enables the receiver of a message to reply to the sender. Ethernet addresses are discussed in the next section.

Note

Ethernet frame delivery is accomplished using a simple mechanism, illustrated in figure 3.4. The sending node includes the Ethernet address of the destination node in the destination address field of the frame. The frame is transmitted to the network medium, where each node on the network examines it. Each node decodes the destination address field of each frame. If the destination address in the frame matches the node's own Ethernet address, the frame is received. If the addresses do not match, the frame is discarded.

To make this delivery mechanism work, the sending node must be able to determine the Ethernet address of the intended recipient. Chapter 4, "The Internet Layer," includes a discussion of how this is accomplished for TCP/IP.

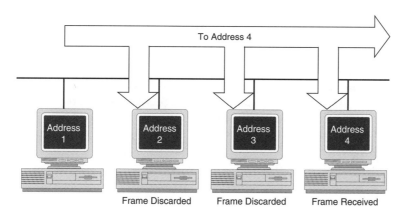

Figure 3.4

Delivery of an Ethernet frame.

The *type* field (also called the *EtherType*) is a 16-bit (two octet) field that designates the data type of the data field. The EtherType enables the network drivers to demultiplex the packets and direct data to the proper protocol stack. The type mechanism enables Ethernet networks to support multiple protocol stacks. Table 3.1 lists some common Ethernet type values, taken from RFC 1700. (All EtherType values are 5DDh (1501 decimal) or greater. Values of 5DCh or below are used to specify the data length for IEEE 802.3 frames.)

TABLE 3.1   EXAMPLES OF ETHERTYPE VALUES

EtherType (decimal)	EtherType (hex)	Type of Data
2048	0800	Internet IP (IPv4)
2053	0805	X.25 Level 3
2054	0806	ARP
24579	6003	DEC DECNET Phase IV Route
24580	6004	DEC LAT
24581	6005	DEC Diagnostic Protocol
32923	809B	AppleTalk
32981	80D5	IBM SNA Service on Ethernet
33079	8137-8138	Novell, Inc.

The *data* field contains the protocol data unit received from upper-layer protocols. Figure 3.2, drawn with TCP/IP in mind, shows that the data field is constructed of three components: the IP header, the TCP header, and the application data. The length of the data field can be from 46 to 1500 octets, inclusive. If the data field is less than 46 octets in length, upper-layer protocols must pad the data to the minimum length.

The *frame check sequence (FCS)* is a 32-bit code that enables the receiving node to determine if transmission errors have altered the frame. This code is derived through a *cyclic redundancy checksum (CRC)* calculation which processes all fields except the preamble and the frame check sequence. This CRC value is recalculated by the receiving node. If the CRC calculated by the receiver matches the value in the FCS, it is assumed that transmission errors did not occur.

The minimum length of an Ethernet frame is 6+6+2+46+4=64 octets, and the maximum length is 6+6+2+1500+4=1518 octets. Frames shorter than 64 octets are not permitted, and the data field must be padded to achieve the minimum length. The 64-octet size minimum, combined with the 8-octet preamble, results in a minimum 576-bit transmission length required to ensure proper operation of the collision detection mechanism.

Ethernet II Node Addresses

Ethernet II node addresses consist of 48 bits, organized in three fields, as shown in figure 3.3. The bits are numbered from bit 0 (the rightmost or low-order bit) to bit 47 (the leftmost or high-order bit). As these bits are discussed, they are examined both in binary and in hexadecimal notation. If you need a refresher on binary, decimal, and hexadecimal numbers, consult Appendix A.

The 48-bit Ethernet address is commonly organized in six octets, six groups of eight bits. To make it easier for humans to scan Ethernet addresses, the octet values are generally represented in hexadecimal notation. Each octet is represented by two hex digits. Pairs of digits are usually separated by periods, spaces, or hyphens. An example of an Ethernet address expressed in hexadecimal notation is 08–00–09–3A–20–1B.

Bit 47 (the high-order bit) is the Physical/Multicast bit. If this bit is 0, the address specifies the physical address of one device on the network. If the bit is 1, it specifies a multicast address that identifies a group of devices.

The remainder of the first three octets comprise a vendor code. Through a registration system formerly administered by Xerox and now by the IEEE, vendors are assigned unique vendor codes that are used to identify their adapters. This registration system ensures that each Ethernet device that is manufactured has a physical address that is unique in the entire world. Burned addresses are called *physical addresses*. They are also referred to as *globally administered addresses*, because all Ethernet addresses for the world are administered, formerly by Xerox, but now by the IEEE.

Table 3.2 lists a few of the vendor codes, which are documented in RFC 1700.

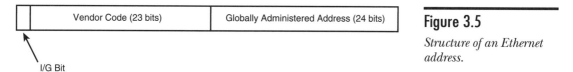

I/G Bit

Figure 3.5

Structure of an Ethernet address.

TABLE 3.2   EXAMPLE ETHERNET VENDOR CODES

Vendor ID	Vendor
0080C2	IEEE 802.1 Committee
00AA00	Intel
080008	BBN
080009	Hewlett-Packard
080014	Novell
080020	Sun
08002B	DEC
080056	Stanford University
08005A	IBM
080069	Silicon Graphics

The value of the remaining three octets is designated by the manufacturer of the Ethernet equipment. Because each manufacturer is assigned a unique vendor ID, and the manufacturers assign a different identification number to each equipment produced, the complete Ethernet ID for each Ethernet device is unique.

Note In some cases, network administrators may override the physical address with a *locally administered address* configured in the computer's network software.

Three general categories of Ethernet addresses can be identified, as follows:

◆ **Physical (globally administered) addresses.** Identified by a 0 value of the first bit (bit 47).

◆ **Multicast addresses.** Identified by a 1 value of the first bit (bit 47). The devices that will receive a message sent to a multicast address are defined by the network implementation. Some multicast addresses are specified in RFC 1700.

◆ **Broadcast address.** All bits are 1. Expressed in hexadecimal notation, the broadcast address is FF:FF:FF:FF:FF:FF. All nodes receive a message with the broadcast address in the destination address field.

IEEE LANs

The Institute of Electrical and Electronics Engineers (IEEE), the largest professional organization in the world, has been the major force in defining international standards for local area networks. The IEEE standards for LANs are defined by the 802 committee, so called because it first met in February, the second month of 1980.

The 802 committee has defined a wide variety of network standards. Not all are discussed in this book. This section focuses on examining the overall architecture of the 802 standards, along with the most widely implemented physical layer standards. International LAN standards have been established by the ISO, by adopting the IEEE 802 standards as the ISO 8802 standard.

Architecture of the IEEE 802 Standards

As a group, the IEEE 802 standards correspond to the OSI data link and physical layers. However, the architecture of the IEEE standards does not match the organization of the OSI layers. As you can see in figure 3.6, the IEEE architecture defines two sublayers that together correspond to the OSI data link layer:

◆ **Logical link control (LLC).** The *LLC* sublayer provides a network interface to upper-layer protocols and is concerned with transmitting data between two stations on the same network segment.

◆ **Medium access control (MAC).** The *MAC* sublayer provides the method by which devices access the shared network transmission medium.

Figure 3.6 illustrates how the 802 family of standards relates to the OSI reference model.

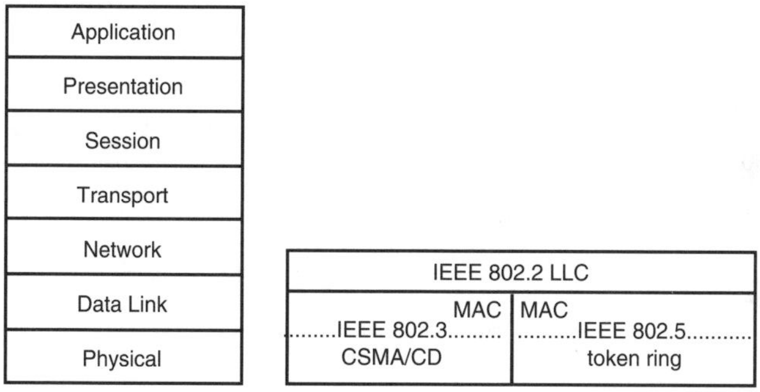

Figure 3.6

IEEE 802 standards related to the OSI reference model.

The work of the 802 committee is organized in subcommittees, designated as 802.x committees. Some committees directly define standards. Others serve an advisory function. The following 802.x standards are examined in this chapter:

◆ **802.2.** Defines the LLC sublayer protocol.

◆ **802.3.** Defines the MAC and physical layers for CSMA/CD (802.3 Ethernet) networks.

◆ **802.5.** Defines the MAC and physical layers for a token ring network based on IBM's Token-Ring technology.

The relationships of these standards are shown in figure 3.6. This figure illustrates an important design feature of the 802 standards: the 802.2 LLC protocol is used by all 802 LAN standards that define network physical layers. This approach to protocol layering simplifies the task of designing systems that can be easily adapted to different physical networks. A system can be converted from 802.3 Ethernet to 802.5 token ring with relative ease and without modification to upper protocol layers.

Another feature is that the 802.3 and 802.5 network standards span the functionality of the OSI physical layer, as well as the MAC sublayer for the data link layer.

802 LAN Physical Addresses

The 802 standards were designed to achieve as much uniformity as possible among the various LAN standards. The use of a common LLC layer for all LAN protocols has been discussed. Another area of uniformity is that all LAN protocols use the same address scheme.

Under the 802 model, physical device addresses are defined at the MAC protocol sublevel. Physical addresses, therefore, frequently are referred to as MAC addresses. MAC addresses can have 16-bit or 48-bit formats. All devices on the network must be configured to use the same address format. Since 48-bit addresses are used most commonly, only that format is examined in detail.

The format of a 48-bit MAC address was adopted from Ethernet and has been accepted for IEEE 802, ISO 8802, and other LAN standards. The 48-bit address format is shown in figure 3.7. This format is similar to the format discussed earlier for Ethernet II addresses.

Figure 3.7

Format of IEEE 802 MAC addresses.

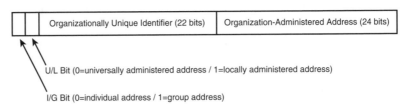

The first bit of the address (bit 47, the high-order bit) is the I/G bit. If the I/G bit value is 0, the address designates an individual address. If the I/G bit value is 1, the address designates a group address, which designates a multicast. An address of all 1s designates a broadcast. Apart from the different terminology, the I/G bit operates in the same manner as the Ethernet II Physical/Multicast bit.

Bit 46 is the U/L bit and indicates whether the address is universally or locally administered. When the U/L bit value is 0, the address follows a universal address format,
consisting of a 22-bit *organizationally unique identifier* and a 24-bit address assigned by the organization. When the U/L bit value is 1, the 46-bit address is locally administered, often by software running on the networked device.

Organizations that apply to the IEEE are assigned a 22-bit organizationally unique identifier, a function that was transferred from Xerox to the IEEE. When the organization combines its unique identifier with a 24-bit address assigned individually for each device made, a unique address is assigned to each piece of network equipment that is manufactured to conform with IEEE 802 LAN standards.

IEEE 802.2 Logical Link Control

LLC performs a variety of functions. Some of these functions are optional, and may be provided by upper-layer protocols.

Multiplexing and Demultiplexing

The LLC function most significant to this book is to multiplex and demultiplex data for multiple upper-layer protocols. Discussion of Ethernet II mentioned that the EtherType field is used to identify data that is associated with various upper-layer protocols. The mechanism used with IEEE 802 LANs differs significantly from that used with Ethernet II.

An interface between the LLC sublayer and upper-layer protocols is a *link service access point (LSAP)*. An LSAP is a logical address that identifies the upper-layer protocol from which the data originated or to which the data should be delivered. LSAPs serve a function similar to EtherType numbers with Ethernet II.

LLC Delivery Services

LLC was designed to provide a variety of delivery services, which determine the level of communication integrity established between devices. The three types of LLC delivery services provide various combinations of features.

Devices have a limited number of receive buffers, used to store frames that have been received but not processed. If the sending device continues to transmit while the destination receive buffers are full, frames not received are lost. *Flow control* ensures that frames are not sent at a rate faster than the receiving device can accept them. A variety of mechanisms can be used to provide flow control.

The simple *stop-and-wait* method requires the receiver to acknowledge received frames, signaling a readiness to accept more data. This simple mechanism is suitable to a connectionless, datagram service.

If the sender must wait for an acknowledgment of each frame, multiframe transmissions are handled inefficiently. The more sophisticated *sliding-window* technique enables the sender to transmit multiple frames without waiting for an acknowledgment. The receiver can acknowledge several frames at one time. A *window* determines the number of frames that can be outstanding at a given time, ensuring that the receiver's buffers do not overflow. The complexity of sliding-window flow control requires a connection-oriented LLC service.

Error detection is performed at the MAC layer, but error recovery, when performed at the data link layer, is a function of LLC. An *automatic repeat request (ARQ)* approach may be employed by the LLC, whereby a positive acknowledgment of each correctly received frame is sent. *Stop-and-wait ARQ* requires an acknowledgment for each frame and functions with acknowledged connectionless service; unacknowledged frames are retransmitted. *Go-back-N ARQ* enables the receiver to request retransmission of specific frames, and requires a connection-mode service.

LLC supports the following three types of delivery service:

◆ **Unacknowledged datagram service (Type 1 service).** This connectionless-mode service supports point-to-point, multipoint, and broadcast transmission. This service does not perform error detection and recovery or flow control.

◆ **Virtual circuit service (Type 2 service).** This connection-mode provides frame sequencing, flow control, and error detection and recovery.

◆ **Acknowledged datagram service (Type 3 service).** This mode implements point-to-point datagram service with message acknowledgments, and functions somewhere between Type 1 and Type 2 service.

To keep the lower-layer protocols trim and efficient, LLC is most commonly implemented with Type 1 service. Flow control and error recovery, if required, can be performed by a suitable transport protocol (such as TCP).

LLC Data Format

As with other protocol layers, the LLC layer constructs a *protocol data unit (PDU)* by appending LLC-specific fields to data received from upper layers. Figure 3.8 illustrates the format of the LLC PDU.

DSAP	SSAP	Control	Data

Figure 3.8

Format of the LLC protocol data unit.

The LLC PDU contains the following fields:

◆ **Destination Service Access Point (DSAP).** The LSAP address that identifies the required protocol stack on the destination computer.

◆ **Source Service Access Point (SSAP).** The LSAP address associated with the protocol stack that originated the data on the source computer.

◆ **Control.** Control information that varies with the function of the PDU.

◆ **Data.** Data received from upper-layer protocols in the form of the network layer PDU.

IEEE 802.3 Networks

Digital, Intel, and Xerox submitted their jointly developed Ethernet technology to the IEEE for standardization, resulting in the 802.3 standard for CSMA/CD LANs. The most significant changes required in adapting DIX Ethernet to the 802 architecture resulted from the decision to implement the 802.2 LLC layer as a common protocol for all 802.x LANs.

IEEE 802.3 networks utilize the same CSMA/CD access control mechanism that was developed for Ethernet II. The same media-signaling techniques are employed and 802.3 and Ethernet II network hardware are interchangeable. 802.3 and Ethernet II frames may be multiplexed on the same media. The primary difference between the 802.3 and the Ethernet II standards has to do with frame formats.

Note Xerox surrendered its trademark for Ethernet long ago, and no one any longer owns the term. Whether Ethernet should be used for Ethernet II or for IEEE 802.3 is a constant source of confusion. Unless Ethernet II disappears, however, the confusion seems likely to remain, so this book uses the term Ethernet fairly loosely when remarks apply to both network versions. When a distinction is necessary, the terms Ethernet II and IEEE 802.3 are used.

IEEE 802.3 Media

The 802.3 committee adopted cabling systems that were in use for Ethernet II, which were based on coaxial cable and data rates of 10 megabits per second. The committee has since developed a variety of newer media configurations. TCP/IP operates independently of the physical medium. Discussing the media options in detail, therefore, is unnecessary; however, a brief summary is appropriate. More detail can be found in NRP's books *Inside Windows NT Server* and *Windows NT Server: The Professional Reference.*

Each of the 802.3 cable standards has a three-part name, for example, 10BASE5. The first number indicates the data rate, with 10 indicating 10 megabit per second operation. BASE specifies baseband operation, and BROAD indicates a broadband network. The final designation suggests the cable type. 5, for example, indicates a configuration that can support cables up to 500 meters in length.

◆ **10BASE5.** This is the original Ethernet network configuration and employs a thick, 50-ohm coaxial cable. Cables can extend up to 500 meters without repeaters, and each cable section can support up to 100 station attachments. The cable for 10BASE5 is expensive and difficult to work with, and now is used less frequently than other cable options.

◆ **10BASE2.** This cable system was designed as a lower cost alternative to 10BASE5. It uses a thinner coaxial cable that supports segment lengths up to 185 meters (the 2 indicates a segment length of about 200 meters). 10BASE2 is economical and easier to install than 10BASE5, but does not adapt well to structured wiring systems, which are configured by running a cable from each device to a central hub. Structured wiring now is preferred in most cable installations of medium-to-large size.

◆ **10BASE-T.** The general trend in cabling is to use fewer coaxial and other shielded cables. Network designers have come to increasingly rely on *unshielded twisted-pair cable (UTP)*, which costs somewhat less than coaxial cable. The T in the standard name indicates use of twisted-pair cable. 10BASE-T uses a hub-based wiring system and adapts readily to a structured wiring approach.

◆ **10BROAD36.** A broadband cable system that enables multiple 10 Mbps channels to be carried by the same coaxial cable medium.

◆ **100BASE-TX.** A variety of 100 Mbps standards are being considered by various IEEE 802 committees. All utilize UTP cable, but differ in the grade of cable and number of wire pairs required. 100BASE-TX utilizes two pairs of high-grade UTP cable. Other 100 Mbps standards include 100 BASE-T4, which operates on four pairs of standard data grade UTP, and 100BASE-TF for optical fiber.

IEEE 802.3 Frames

Figure 3.9 illustrates the format of an IEEE 802.3 frame. The frame format is derived from Ethernet II and is similar to the format of an Ethernet II frame in most respects.

The 802.3 preamble consists of seven octets having the bit pattern 10101010. Following the preamble is a one octet *start frame delimiter* (SFD), with the bit pattern 10101011.

The *destination address* and *source address* have the same functions as the corresponding fields in an Ethernet II frame. Both 16 and 48-bit addresses are supported for IEEE 802.3. The format for 802 physical addresses is discussed in the prior section, "802 LAN Physical Addresses."

The *length* field consists of two octets that specify the number of octets in the LLC data field. This value must be in the range 46 through 1500, inclusive.

The *LLC data* field contains the protocol data unit received from the LLC sublayer, consisting of the LLC header and data. The size of this field is 46 to 1500 octets. If the data field falls short of the minimum 46 octets, octets with a value of 00000000 are appended to pad the field to the minimum length.

The *frame check sequence (FCS)* field stores a 32-bit checksum value that is used to detect transmission errors.

Assuming that 48-bit (6 octet) addresses are used, the minimum and maximum lengths of an 802.3 frame are the same as for Ethernet II frames: 64 and 1518 octets.

Preamble (7 octets)	Start Frame Delimiter (1 octet)	Destination Address (6 octets)	Source Address (6 octets)	Length (2 octets)	Data (46-1500 octets)	FCS (3 octets)

Figure 3.9

Format of a IEEE 802.3 frame.

Comparison of IEEE 802.3 and Ethernet II Frames

Network equipment manufactured to IEEE 802.3 specifications is compatible with Ethernet II frames and with much of the equipment manufactured to the Ethernet II standard. It also is in many cases compatible with older equipment designed to the DIX specification. Hardware designed to the DIX 1.0 specification, however, might not interoperate with hardware designed to the Ethernet II and IEEE 802.3 standards.

Note Older Ethernet equipment implements a feature called *signal quality error (SQE)* testing. The SQE circuitry sends a *heartbeat* signal that simulates a collision. The SQE signal interferes with operation of devices designed according to 802.3 specifications, particularly repeaters. Therefore, SQE operation should be disabled on Ethernet devices being connected to an 802.3 network.

Figure 3.10 compares the frame formats of 802.3 and Ethernet II frames. Notice that the 802.3 preamble and SFD combined have the same bit pattern as the Ethernet II preamble.

Figure 3.10

Comparison of IEEE 802.3 and Ethernet II frames.

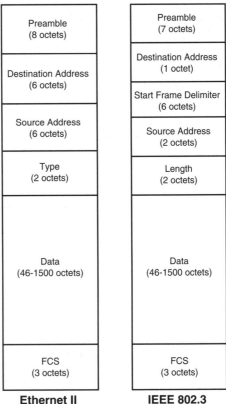

The organization identifiers used in Ethernet hardware addresses were originally administered by Xerox, but this responsibility has been handed over to the IEEE. A coherent catalog of identifiers has been maintained throughout the history of

Ethernet, permitting Ethernet II and IEEE 802.3 devices to coexist without risk of address conflict.

The IEEE 802 standards permit two-octet MAC addresses, but these are seldom used. More commonly, six-octet addresses are used, a format that is compatible with Ethernet II. As discussed, the body of Ethernet II addresses coexists seamlessly with 802.3 addresses assigned by the IEEE.

The most significant difference in frame formats is that the 802.3 format has a two-octet length field in place of the EtherType field found in Ethernet II frames. Distinguishing Ethernet II and 802.3 frames is possible by examining this field. EtherType values are restricted to decimal values of 1501 and greater. If the decimal value of this field is 1500 or less, therefore, the field identifies an 802.3 length field. With IEEE 802.3, type information must be supplied by the LSAP fields in the 802.2 LLC frame.

Implementing TCP/IP over IEEE 802.3

The original implementations of TCP/IP on Ethernet networks were based on Ethernet II and used the EtherType data field, which is not supported by the IEEE 802 standards. When TCP/IP is run over an IEEE physical layer, the EtherType information is encoded in the frame using the *Sub-Network Access Protocol (SNAP)*, which is an extension to the LLC header. SNAP is described in RFC-1042.

Figure 3.11 illustrates the format of the LLC and SNAP header data as they relate to an 802.2 frame. The presence of a SNAP header is indicated by DSAP and SSAP values of 170, a control value of 3 (unnumbered information) and an organization code of 0.

SNAP encapsulation increases the header overhead. On networks that specify maximum frame sizes, SNAP encapsulation necessarily reduces the number of octets available for upper-layer data. An IEEE 802.3 Ethernet frame has a maximum size of 1518 octets. Taking into an account 18 octets for the MAC header and trailer and 8 octets for the LLC and SNAP headers, an IEEE 802.3 frame with SNAP encapsulation can accommodate 1492 octets of data. This compares to 1500 octets of data available with Ethernet II.

SNAP is an extension to the 802.2 LLC sublayer and, therefore, is compatible with all IEEE 802.x LANs. The SNAP mechanism is frequently used to implement TCP/IP over IEEE 802.5 token ring physical layers. SNAP is general enough to be adapted to other networks as well.

Figure 3.11

Format of the SNAP header.

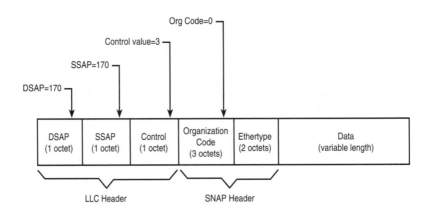

Note: maximum data size for
802.3 networks is 1492 octets.

IEEE 802.5 Networks

IBM developed the token ring network and submitted it to the IEEE for standardization, a task performed by the 802.5 subcommittee. IEEE 802.5 token ring is the second most commonly employed LAN physical layer, trailing significantly behind Ethernet. Several reasons can be cited for token ring's lower popularity:

◆ It was developed as an IBM technology. Although token ring technology is now offered by a great many vendors, many in the user community perceive it as proprietary.

◆ Ethernet is simple, reliable, and effective for the majority of networks, and at the same time, costs significantly less than token ring.

◆ TCP/IP has traditionally been wed to Ethernet II. Growing industry demand for TCP/IP has accompanied a recent surge in Ethernet popularity.

Nevertheless, token ring is an effective physical layer technology with features that make it preferable under some circumstances.

How Token Ring Works

Token ring was developed by IBM to circumvent a perceived shortcoming of the CSMA/CD access method. Each time a device needs to transmit, some probability exists that the network will be busy. And, even when the device successfully begins to transmit, some probability exists that another device will also transmit and cause a collision, forcing both devices to back off and try again. These probabilities increase as the network becomes busier, until a point is reached at which a device needing to transmit data becomes extremely unlikely to receive the opportunity to do so.

Because network access on a CSMA/CD network is uncertain, CSMA/CD is called a probabilistic access method.

The mere probability of access is unacceptable in certain critical situations such as industrial control. Suppose that an overheat sensor urgently needs to send a warning to the factory operators. If even a possibility exists that the sensor cannot access the network, the factory designers will not take the situation lightly.

Token access guarantees that every device on the network receives a periodic opportunity to transmit. The token access method chosen by IBM was implemented in a ring, as shown in figure 3.12.

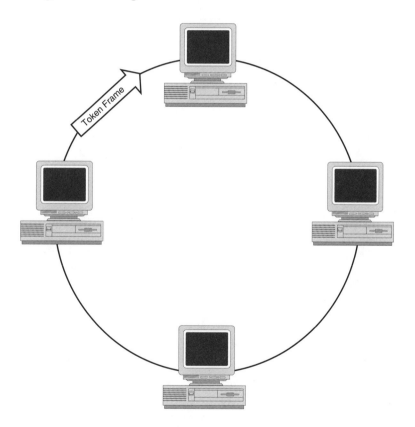

Figure 3.12

The token access method in a ring network.

The token consists of a special frame that circulates from device to device around the ring. Only the device that possesses the token is permitted to transmit. After transmitting, the device restarts the token, enabling other devices the opportunity to transmit.

IBM's initial 4 Mbps implementation of token ring permitted a single token to circulate on the network. Before releasing a token on the network that enabled other devices to transmit, a device that transmitted a frame waited for the frame to return after circulating the ring. A new feature, called *early token release*, introduced with the newer 16 Mbps token ring, enables a sending device to release a token immediately after it completes transmission of a frame. Thus a token can circulate at the same time as a data frame.

Although token access control appears simple, numerous problems lie beneath the surface.

◆ How does the network discover if the token frame is damaged or lost?

◆ How is a new token created?

◆ How does the network know when a device has malfunctioned and is no longer forwarding frames to the next device?

◆ How can the network recover from such a problem?

◆ How can the network identify a frame that is endlessly circulating the ring, destined for a node that does not exist?

◆ How can a frame be removed and a new token started?

The causes and solutions for these and other token ring errors are beyond the scope of this book. The point of introducing them is to illustrate that the control mechanisms token ring uses are significantly more complicated than those required for CSMA/CD. These control mechanisms take up network bandwidth, reducing the efficiency of token ring. For an excellent and thorough discussion of token ring, consult NRP's book *Network Optimization and Troubleshooting.*

To compensate for this added complexity, token ring offers significant benefits. Data throughput of a token ring can never reach zero, as is possible with an Ethernet experiencing excessive collisions. Although network performance slows as demand increases, every device on the network receives a periodic opportunity to transmit.

Token ring possesses a capability to set network access priorities, which is unavailable in Ethernet. High-priority devices can request preferred network access. This capability enables a critical device to gain greater access to the network.

Token ring was also designed to provide a higher level of diagnostic and management capability than is available with Ethernet. The mechanisms that compensate for token ring errors provide a capability for diagnosing other network problems, as well. Detecting devices causing network errors and forcing those devices to disconnect from the network, for example, is possible. Also, in the cabling system IBM designed, the network is serviced by two rings of cable. In the event of a cable break, using the extra media ring to reconfigure the network and keep it operating is possible.

Nevertheless, Ethernet—whether Ethernet II or IEEE 802.3—remains the most popular network physical layer. Ethernet works well in the majority of networks and costs considerably less than token ring. Equipment for token ring costs two-to-three times as much as corresponding Ethernet components.

Token Ring Media

IEEE 802.5 does not describe a cabling system for token ring, stopping with specifications for data rates, signaling, and the network interface. In most cases, manufacturers design their equipment around the IBM Cabling System, introduced in the early 1980s. The most popular cable type has been Type 1, a fairly heavy shielded twisted-pair cable, which has excellent electrical characteristics but is a bit bulky and expensive. Type 3 cable is a data-grade UTP cable. IBM provided early support a data rate of 4 Mbps over Type 1 and Type 3 cable. Although IBM engineers later sanctioned 16 Mbps operation with Type 1 cable, they were slow to change their early position that operation faster than 4 Mbps required Type 1 shielded cable.

Competing manufacturers were not so reticent, however, and introduced 16 Mbps token ring for UTP cable well in advance of IBM or of any IEEE standard. IBM finally yielded and offered a standard for 16 Mbps token ring over UTP cable. IBM has now announced a revised cable system that supports operation at up to 100 Mbps.

Although token ring networks operate logically as rings, they are cabled as physical stars so that each device is connected to a central hub through an individual cable. Figure 3.13 illustrates how the token ring is wired in a star configuration. Thus, token ring adapts naturally to a structured cabling plan.

A token ring can support up to 260 devices, but generally accommodates fewer than that number. Token ring networks are somewhat difficult to plan because the number of devices allowed on the ring varies with the size of the ring and the data rate.

IEEE 802.5 Frames

The token ring frame format is shown in figure 3.14. Three major sections can be identified, as follows:

◆ **Start-of-frame sequence (SFS).** This section signals to network devices that a frame is beginning.

◆ **Data section.** This section contains control information, upper-layer data, and the frame check sequence used for error checking.

◆ **End-of-frame sequence (EFS).** This section indicates the end of the frame and includes several control bits.

Figure 3.13

How token rings are wired in a star.

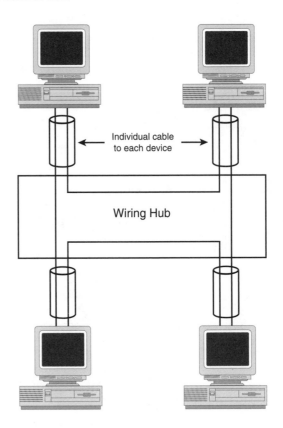

Figure 3.13

How token rings are wired in a star.

Figure 3.14

Format of a token ring frame.

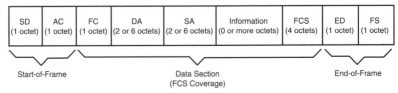

SD (1 octet)	AC (1 octet)	FC (1 octet)	DA (2 or 6 octets)	SA (2 or 6 octets)	Information (0 or more octets)	FCS (4 octets)	ED (1 octet)	FS (1 octet)

Start-of-Frame ⏝ Data Section (FCS Coverage) ⏝ End-of-Frame

SD = Starting Delimiter   SA = Source Address
AC = Access Control   FCS = Frame Check Sequence
FC = Frame Control   ED = Ending Delimiter
DA = Destination Address   FS = Frame Status

The *starting delimiter (SD)* field is a single octet that consists of electrical signals that cannot appear elsewhere in the frame. The SD violates the rules for encoding data in the frame and contains nondata signals.

The *access control (AC)* field includes priority and reservation bits used to set network priorities. It also includes a monitor bit, used for network management. A token bit indicates whether the frame is a token or a data frame.

The *frame control (FC)* field indicates whether the frame contains LLC data or is a MAC control frame. Several types of MAC control frame are used to control network functions.

The *destination address (DA)* specifies the station or stations to which the frame is directed. Multicasts and broadcasts are possible in addition to transmission to a single device. 16- and 48-bit addresses are supported.

The *source address (SA)* specifies the device that originated the frame. The DA and SA addresses must utilize the same format.

The *information* field contains LLC data or control information if it appears in a MAC control frame.

The *frame check sequence (FCS)* is a 32-bit cyclic redundancy check that is applied to the FC, DA, SA, and information fields.

The *ending delimiter (ED)*, like the starting delimiter, violates the network data format and signals the end of the frame. This field includes two control bits. The intermediate bit indicates whether this is an intermediate or the final frame in a transmission. The error bit is set by any device that detects an error, such as in the FCS.

The *frame status (FS)* field contains other control bits that indicate that a station has recognized its address and that a frame has been copied by a receiving device.

Note	As with IEEE 802.3 networks, token ring networks must encode EtherType information using the SNAP protocol.

Digital Data Services

When networks must span more than a few kilometers, new categories of technology come into play. Before considering WAN standards, it is useful to take a look at options that might be used by an organization that wants to build a private WAN. Not all options are examined.

Dedicated Leased Lines

Communication providers offer dedicated, leased lines at a variety of capacities. A dedicated line is a communication channel between two points that is leased by an organization for its exclusive use. The dedicated line almost certainly does not consist of a pair of wires that stretches continuously between the end-points, and a customer's signal can pass through any combination of copper and optical fiber cables as well as terrestrial and satellite microwaves. The appearance to the customer, however, is of a directly wired channel.

Dedicated lines may be analog or digital in nature. At one time, dedicated 56 Kbps analog lines were common way to interconnect mainframe computers. Increasingly, however, dedicated lines are digital, and 56 Kbps digital data service (DDS) lines are among the available options.

T1 is an example of a digital leased-line technology. T1 supports full-duplex communication between two points. Originally intended for digital voice communication, T1 adapts well to data communication, supporting data rates up to 1.544 Mbps in the United States. T1 circuits can utilize combinations of cables and microwave links.

A T1 line supports 24 multiplexed 64 Kbps channels. In some areas, *fractional T1* enables organizations to lease part of a T1 line in 64 Kbps increments, paying only for the bandwidth they require. Other standards include T2, T3, and T4 support data rates of 6.312, 44.736, and 274.176 Mbps.

An organization that wants to connect remote computers might choose to do so using a dedicated line, employing a configuration similar to that shown in figure 3.15. The interface to the leased line consists of the following components:

- ◆ A bridge or router to forward frames to the leased circuit.

- ◆ A channel service unit/digital service unit (CSU/DSU) to translate between LAN and DDS signal formats.

- ◆ A network interface provided by the communication service vendor.

Leased lines can be used to construct quite large networks. The Internet is a world-wide network that consists of thousands of hosts, most connected by leased lines. The participants in the Internet share the cost of operating the Internet by bearing the costs of one or more leased lines to connect to other host sites.

The downside of leased lines is that an organization bears the full cost of the capacity they have leased. Some allowance must be made for peak traffic periods, and a portion of the channel capacity being paid for may be idle a great deal of the time. Dedicated lines ensure an organization of a specified communication capacity, but come at a high cost.

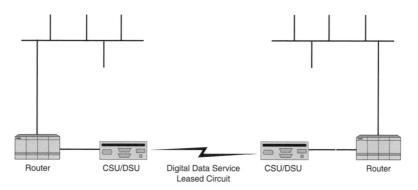

Figure 3.15

Connecting remote sites with a digital leased circuit.

Router   CSU/DSU   Digital Data Service   CSU/DSU   Router
                     Leased Circuit

Switched Digital Lines

Switched lines provide an alternative to dedicated lines. When remote hosts need to communicate, one dials the other to establish a temporary connection. Switched connections can be configured using conventional modems and voice-grade lines, enabling organizations that have very limited bandwidth needs to avoid the cost of a digital service. Switched digital services are available as well, and switched 56 Kbps CSU/DSUs are available.

A technology that promises to lower the cost of switched digital communication is the Integrated Services Digital Network (ISDN). A variety of ISDN services are possible, providing different amounts of bandwidth. A common basic rate service consists of two 64 Kbps digital channels. Although the potential bandwidth of this service is 128 Kbps, the 64 Kbps channels function separately. Equipment at the customer site must be capable of aggregating the separate 64 Kbps channels into a 128 Kbps logical channel. ISDN has the potential to make switched digital communication widely available at low cost. However, service providers have been slow to offer ISDN services. Only recently have the major providers committed to making ISDN available in their service areas. Smaller providers remain reluctant to jump on the bandwagon, however, and ISDN is less frequently an option away from larger metropolitan areas.

X.25

Dedicated leased circuits present a number of disadvantages. They are costly to operate and high setup costs are incurred when the circuit is configured or moved. And they are inflexible, so that moving a host site can be a big deal. Most often, buying data services the way you buy telephone services, by obtaining them from a network provider, makes more sense.

A network provider constructs a data network that covers a geographic area, with the capacity to support large amounts of customer traffic. Customers who need to connect hosts within that area connect into the existing network and pay for only a portion of the network bandwidth.

X.25 is one of the oldest WAN technologies and remains widely available. X.25 is a recommendation of the *International Telecommunications Union (ITU)*, formerly the *International Telegraph and Telephone Consultative Committee (CCITT)*. The ITU is an agency of the United Nations that establishes international communication standards.

X.25 is a packet-switching network. Devices communicate through the network by establishing virtual circuits. Much like dialing a telephone call, devices can set up switched virtual circuits to serve a short-term communication need. Permanent virtual circuits, which function much like dedicated circuits offered by telecommunication providers, also can be established.

As illustrated in figure 3.16, the X.25 standard uses three protocols, which correspond to the network, data link, and physical layers of the OSI model. Physical layer functionality is provided by X.21 for digital circuits and by X.21 *bis* for analog circuits. At the data link layer, full-duplex, synchronous communication is provided by the *Link Access Procedures-Balanced (LAPB)* protocol. Finally, the X.25 protocol provides for reliable service and flow control at the network layer.

Figure 3.16

The X.25 protocol stack.

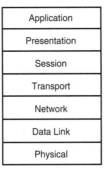

X.25 originated at a time when communication lines were slow and unreliable. The upper data rate for X.25 is 64 Kbps, adequate for character-based terminal-to-host communication and most mainframe host communications, but far too limited for today's more demanding real-time applications that demand LAN speeds.

Because X.25 was designed to provide reliable communication over unreliable lines, the X.25 protocol is responsible for both detecting errors and correcting them by requesting retransmission of damaged packets. Modern digital communication options are highly reliable, and the reliability features of X.25 simply add overhead and inefficiency to the communication process.

Figure 3.17 illustrates an X.25 network. The network itself consists of several X.25 switches that route frames through the network. The mechanics of the switching mechanism are hidden from the user, and WANs such as X.25 are frequently drawn as clouds to highlight the hidden nature of the switching process. Packets enter the network at one point and emerge at another, but the details do not concern the user.

Note	When remote computers communicate through a public network such as X.25, the public network operates independently of the protocols running on the end devices. If the end nodes are running TCP/IP, the IP datagrams are encapsulated in X.25 frames for transmission on the WAN. Decapsulation at the destination site recovers the original IP datagram.

Devices interface with the X.25 network through a *packet assembler-disassembler (PAD)*. The PAD can be located at the customer site, communicating with the X.25 network through a leased or dial-access line, or at a dial-in site with users accessing the network through dial-up modems.

Public X.25 networks are widely available and can be a cost-effective way to build a WAN to support moderate traffic. Private X.25 networks also can be constructed using leased circuits. For these reasons, X.25 is the WAN option Windows NT supports out of the box.

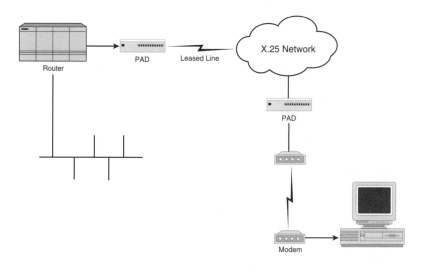

Figure 3.17

Example of an X.25 network.

Frame Relay

Frame relay is a packet switching, broadband, wide area network standard that is a streamlined update of X.25. The ITU (CCITT) is the body responsible for frame relay standardization. As shown in figure 3.18, the services provided by frame relay correspond to the data link and physical layers of the OSI reference model.

Figure 3.18

Relationship of frame relay to the OSI reference model.

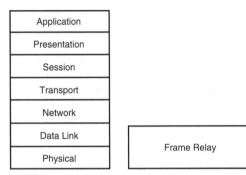

Frame relay was designed with the assumption that communication channels would be reliable. Therefore, frame relay is relieved of the responsibility to provide flow control and error correction. Frame relay performs error checking, discards frames with errors, and informs upper-layer protocols when errors occur. It is the responsibility of upper layers to recover from errors by requesting retransmission of frames. By moving error recovery to upper-layer protocols at end-nodes, processing at the switches is streamlined. X.25 networks must perform error detection and recovery at each switch.

Frame relay can operate over T1, T3, and other high-speed networks at speeds of 56 Kbps to 44.6 Mbps, sufficient to support most LAN-to-LAN communications. Frame relay network services may be obtained from a public data network, or private networks may be established.

Frame relay offers bandwidth-on-demand and better accommodates the bursty characteristics of LAN communication than does X.25. Terminal traffic, for which X.25 was designed, is limited in volume and fairly regular in nature. By contrast, LAN traffic demand tends to vary wildly between fairly quiet periods and very busy periods associated with high-traffic activities such as file transfers.

Subscribers to a public frame relay network service typically purchase a guaranteed amount of bandwidth called a *committed information rate (CIR)*. Some services permit customers to exceed the CIR temporarily on a pay-per-use basis. As a result, customers can purchase frame relay services that are closely tailored to their requirements without the risk that a temporary high demand will be unsupported.

Figure 3.19 illustrates a frame relay network. LANs are connected to frame relay through a *frame relay interface (FRI)*, generally incorporated into a router.

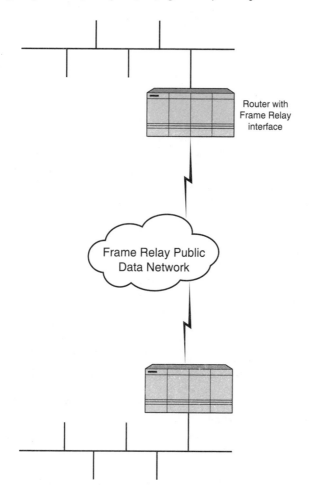

Router with
Frame Relay
interface

Frame Relay Public
Data Network

Figure 3.19

A frame relay network.

The data field of a frame relay frame is called the payload. The size of the payload field may be defined by the network implementation. Frame relay networks may thus be tuned to user requirements. TCP/IP protocol support utilizes SNAP encapsulation.

Frame relay is connection oriented, supporting switched virtual circuits and *permanent virtual circuits (PVC)*. A PVC establishes a fixed network path that enables devices to communicate efficiently. Up to 1,024 logical connections can be multiplexed through a PVC. Little processing is required as frames pass through the network. Consequently, frame relay operates at high speeds with little transmission delay.

ATM

The nature of network data is changing. Imaging is a commonplace technology, associated with large data files that often are many megabytes in size. Transfer of imaging data alone can stress a network, but even more demanding applications are evolving from state-of-the-art to everyday technologies. Networks must often cope with digitized video and audio, which not only demand high bandwidth but require data packets to arrive synchronized in real-time.

Both video and audio data may be represented in digital form, but the data requirements exceed those commonly encountered with computer data. A single, digitized full-motion video signal can require 6 Mbps or more of network bandwidth, but that is only one problem with networking video data. The picture and audio signals for a video signal constitute two separate data streams that must remain synchronized in real-time.

Asynchronous transfer mode (ATM) is an emerging technology that promises to solve these technical problems. ATM is flexible to an unprecedented degree and has been designed to integrate data, video, and voice support in a high-performance network.

A variety of organizations are involved in the ATM standards process. Much of ATM is derived from Broadband ISDN (B-ISDN), an extension of narrowband ISDN, a technology developed in 1988 by the CCITT. Standards from CCITT define the basic B-ISDN architecture but do not address many aspects of implementing ATM on LANs.

The ATM Forum is an industry consortium that formed to address problems of interfacing ATM to LANs. This group has developed the basic ATM-LAN architecture. The IETF is also addressing the problem of carrying LAN traffic over ATM. An Internet-draft document addressing these issues is Multiprotocol Interconnect over ATM Adaptation Layer 5.

Architecture of ATM LANs

ATM networks consist of two types of devices (see fig. 3.20): endstations and switches. The ATM Forum has designated two network interfaces. A *User-Network Interface (UNI)* connects an endstation to a switch. A *Network-Network Interface (NNI)* connects a switch to another switch.

LANs can interface with an ATM network through a router equipped with an ATM interface.

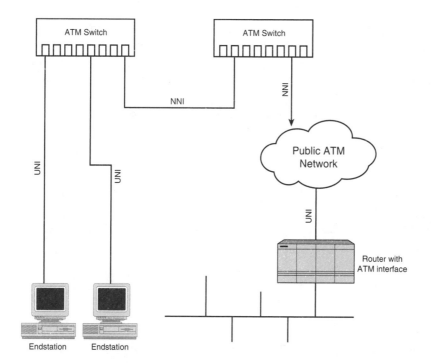

Figure 3.20

An ATM network.

Transfer Modes: STM, PTM, and ATM

Synchronous Transfer Mode (STM) uses time-division multiplexing, assigning time slots to data channels. Use of fixed time slots guarantees dedicated bandwidth and synchronous transmission of data. It is, for example, possible to ensure that voice and picture data remain synchronized for a video transmission. STM is best suited to voice and video data.

Packet Transfer Mode (PTM) uses packet switching to provide flexible services well suited to computer data. PTM adapts to packets of varying formats and sizes and provides flexible bandwidth.

Asynchronous Transfer Mode (ATM) provides a flexible transport method that is adaptable to voice, video, and computer data. Like X.25 and frame relay, ATM provides a mechanism for switching data units through networks. Unlike those packet switching protocols, which transmit data units of varying size, ATM operates with a fixed-size data unit called a *cell*. By standardizing on a data unit size, switch efficiency is greatly enhanced.

To satisfy the voice and video industries, ATM provides *cell synchronous* service, enabling ATM to provide guaranteed data rates and to synchronize data channels. ATM can *provide constant bit rate* service, compensating for any time irregularities encountered when transferring cells.

ATM cells are 53 bytes in length, incorporating a 5-byte header and a 48-byte payload, shown in figure 3.21. Clearly, a 5-byte header cannot accommodate two 48-bit addresses, as was the case with other protocols discussed in this chapter. The short header is possible because of the strategy used to define routes through ATM networks.

Figure 3.21

Format of an ATM cell.

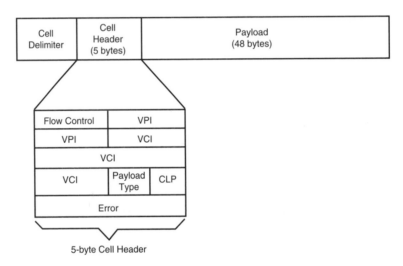

ATM is connection-oriented. Devices that communicate obtain a virtual circuit defining the route cells will follow through the network. Between any two ATM devices, a route is defined by two specifications. A specific *virtual channel (VC)* is assigned to the virtual circuit. A virtual channel functions on *a virtual path (VP)*. Virtual paths simply are collections of virtual channels.

Between ATM devices, one or more *virtual paths* exist. A T1 link between ATM switches might correspond to a virtual path. A path is virtual in the sense that a *physical path* is not dedicated to a given connection except during transference of a cell for that connection. At other times, the virtual path is available to service cells for other connections. Each virtual path can accommodate many *virtual channels*. An ATM virtual circuit is defined by a specific virtual channel on a specific virtual path.

The cell's virtual path between two given switches is represented by an 8-bit *virtual path identifier (VPI)* in the ATM cell header. A 16-bit *virtual channel identifier (VCI)* encodes the virtual channel information. Together, the VPI and VCI uniquely identify the virtual circuit associated with a given cell. With 24 bits to work with, ATM has the potential to support over 16 million virtual channels per switch, although most hardware supports fewer.

Each switch stores VPI and VCI information in a local connection database. For any given connection, it is likely that different VPI and VCI values will be selected between each pair of switches on the cell path. Switches consult their databases to determine the VPI and VCI to be used for the next step in forwarding a given cell. Figure 3.22 illustrates how VPIs and VCIs are used to route cells through a network.

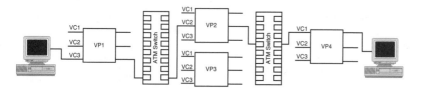

Figure 3.22

ATM switches and virtual circuits.

ATM Protocols

The CCITT has defined a three-level model for B-ISDN, shown in figure 3.21. This model corresponds to the lower three layers of the OSI model. To improve efficiency, all switching (the ATM equivalent of routing) is performed by protocols below the network layer.

The *ATM adaptation layer (AAL)* provides an interface to upper-layer protocols and performs message fragmentation and reassembly. IEEE 802.2 LLC encapsulation is employed when it is necessary to support multiple protocols over the same VC. The AAL provides a variety of services, including connection and connectionless, variable and constant bit rate.

The ATM layer defines cell formats and performs. Support is provided for *permanent virtual channels (PVC)* and *switched virtual channels (SVC)*.

The ATM physical layer defines how cells are transported on the network, and defines signaling for various media types. Data rates, however, are not specified. ATM can be adapted to virtually any data rate and medium.

ATM Media

ATM can operate over a wide variety of media, limited only by the physical transport. A common carrier is *Synchronous Optical Network (SONET)*, developed by BellCore. SONET data rates are specified by *optical carrier (OC)* levels ranging from OC-1 (52 Mbps) to OC-48 (2.5 Gbps). Current SONET implementations provide OC-9 service, 466 Mbps.

The ATM Forum has defined four types of interfaces:

◆ 45 Mbps DS3 WAN interface

◆ 155 Mbps OC-3 SONET

◆ 155 Mbps multimode optical fiber based on Fiber Channel

◆ 100 Mbps multimode optical fiber based on FDDI

Of these, two are likely to have an impact on LANs. The 100 Mbps option based on FDDI is designed to take advantage of newer FDDI developments, such as FDDI over copper (UTP and STP) cable. DS3 service supports copper and optical fiber media as a means of interfacing the LAN to telecommunications networks.

Other data rates seem likely. In an effort to lower cost, IBM has introduced a 25 Mbps ATM system intended to provide ATM service to the desktop.

One of the most intriguing characteristics of ATM is its capability to incorporate many data rates in an extended network. 25 Mbps ATM desktop connections could switch into a 100 Mbps ATM backbone which would in turn connect to a 455 Mbps public data network. Of available technologies, only ATM offers this level of flexibility to provide bandwidth as required for a specific environment.

An Emerging Technology

ATM has been voted the technology most likely to succeed by the majority of LAN pundits. At present, ATM costs hover around $1,000 per connection, a figure that naturally can be expected to decrease as the technology matures.

Nevertheless, ATM remains an emerging technology. A variety of LAN-related issues remain unresolved, and most standards are under development. At present, ATM is a technology for organizations that require its unique capabilities, and it is likely to coexist with current LAN and WAN technologies for quite some time.

Summary

This chapter discussed how TCP/IP has been adapted over the years to operate with various network architectures. The popularity of TCP/IP is too great to discuss every way these protocols have been adapted, so this chapter provided you with an overview of six protocol standards. You should have learned about the following:

◆ Ethernet II

◆ IEEE 802.3 (IEEE Ethernet)

◆ IEEE 802.5 (IEEE token ring)

◆ X.25

◆ Frame Relay

◆ ATM

Chapter 4 Snapshot

This chapter focuses on the internet layer. It covers the following topics:

- ◆ IP addressing

- ◆ Datagram fragmentation and reassembly

- ◆ IP routing

- ◆ Internet Control Message Protocol (ICMP)

C H A P T E R

4

The Internet Layer

T he internet layer is responsible for delivering data through an internetwork. The primary internet layer protocol is the *Internet Protocol, IP,* which bears the bulk of the responsibility for the layer. The current standard for IP is specified in RFC 791, as amended by RFCs 919, 922, and 950.

IP uses other protocols for special tasks. The Internet Control Messaging Protocol (ICMP) is used to deliver messages to the host-to-host layer. Also, routing protocols may be implemented to improve the IP's routing efficiency. This chapter discusses certain protocols, despite the fact that they do not function at the internet layer, because they are closely related to IP.

IP is a required Internet protocol that has the following primary functions:

◆ Addressing

◆ Datagram fragmentation and reassembly

◆ Delivery of datagrams on the internetwork

Of these, the function that most concerns network administrators is addressing. IP has a unique addressing scheme that takes some getting used to. Consequently, the bulk of discussion about IP will focus on IP addressing.

IP Addressing

The groundwork for TCP/IP was laid before LANs existed. No broadly accepted standards were in place for network protocol layering, and particularly no standards existed for assigning physical addresses to devices. The approach chosen for TCP/IP utilizes an address that the IP protocol uses, following a scheme that uniquely identifies each node on an internetwork. (Recall from Chapter 2 that identifying a node on an internetwork requires two pieces of information: the specific network to which the node is attached and the node's ID on that network.)

Upper-layer TCP/IP protocols do not directly use network hardware addresses. Instead, it was decided to use a system of logical addresses for identifying *hosts*. (The official name for an end station on a TCP/IP network is *host*.) The logical IDs, called IP addresses, provide several benefits. Routing is greatly simplified because network address information is encoded in the IP address. And logical addresses make TCP/IP resistant to changes in network hardware. If the network interface card is exchanged, its hardware address changes, or even if the network changes to a completely new technology, while the device remains on the same network, the IP address the upper-layer protocols use can remain the same.

You will appreciate this stability when you configure TCP/IP hosts, because a host configuration includes information about several other hosts, all expressed in the form of an IP address. Each host, for example, is configured with a default gateway. If the gateway address changed due to a hardware upgrade, every host on the network would require manual reconfiguration. The IP address scheme makes network configuration much simpler.

This capability is particularly important on the Internet, because users and applications frequently access other hosts on the network. If host addresses were to change frequently, disseminating those changes to the network community would be difficult. The availability of the Domain Name Service significantly reduces the severity of this problem, because it enables users to use names rather than numbers to identify hosts. At one time, however, host names and their related IP addresses were stored in manually maintained text files. A constant flux of new addresses would have made network administration impossible.

Note On TCP/IP networks, routers traditionally have been called gateways. That usage is gradually fading, and recent RFCs employ the term *router*, which is the term used in this chapter. Default routers continue to often be referred to as *default gateways*, however, a convention that this book observes as well.

IP Address Format

IP addresses are 32 bits in length and are divided into two fields:

◆ A *netid* field identifies the network to which the host is attached.

◆ A *hostid* field assigns each host on a given network a unique identifier.

In TCP/IP terminology, a network consists of a group of hosts that can communicate directly without the use of routers. All TCP/IP hosts that occupy the same network must be assigned the same netid. Hosts that have different netids must communicate through a router.

A TCP/IP *internetwork* is a network of networks, and can incorporate many networks, interconnected by routers. Each network on the internetwork must be assigned a unique netid.

Address Classes

When the IP address scheme was conceived, it was assumed that the following varieties of networks would exist:

◆ A few networks that had a very large number of hosts

◆ A moderate number of networks that had an intermediate number of hosts

◆ A large number of networks that would have a small number of hosts.

Consequently, it was decided to define classes of IP addresses tailored to each of these situations. This was achieved by assigning different numbers of bits to the netids for different classes.

Figure 4.1 illustrates the five classes of IP addresses. Notice that the bits in the addresses are organized into four octets.

◆ *Class A* addresses begin with a high-order bit of 0. The first octet of the IP address comprises the netid, and the remaining three octets are the hostid.

◆ *Class B* addresses begin with high-order bits of 10. The first two octets are the netid, and the remaining two octets are the hostid.

◆ *Class C* addresses begin with high-order bits of 110. The first three octets are allocated for the netid, and only one octet is available for the hostid.

◆ *Class D* addresses begin with the high-order bits 1110. Class D addresses are used to support multicasts.

◆ *Class E* addresses begin with the high-order bits 11110. These addresses are used for experimental purposes.

Figure 4.1

IP address classes.

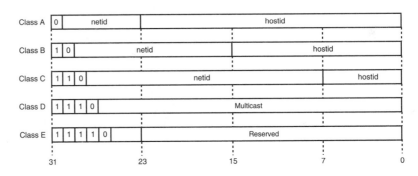

Class A | 0 | netid | hostid
Class B | 1 0 | netid | hostid
Class C | 1 1 0 | netid | hostid
Class D | 1 1 1 0 | Multicast
Class E | 1 1 1 1 0 | Reserved

31   23   15   7   0

Internet Address Registration

All networks that connect with the Internet must be configured with InterNIC-assigned IP addresses. The address registration service is managed by Network Solutions. Registration forms are available from several sources:

◆ Via FTP from DS.INTERNIC.NET

◆ From the World Wide Web, URL to http://ds.internic.net/

◆ By mail from the address cited below

Applications may be submitted by mail or e-mail to the following addresses:

Network Solutions
InterNIC Registration Services
505 Huntmar Park Drive
Herndon, VA 22070

HOSTMASTER@INTERNIC.NET

At this point, only class C addresses are available. All class A addresses were assigned long ago. The very few class B addresses are available only to industry heavy hitters. Unfortunately, available class C addresses are dwindling. The designers of IP, working before the PC revolution, expected that a few thousand addresses would be sufficient for any forseeable future. Work is proceeding on IP version 6, also called IP Next Generation (IPNG). A primary motivation for IPNG is to resolve the current address crunch.

> **Note** If you use a commercial Internet provider to connect to the Internet, your IP addresses must be obtained through the provider. Network providers are assigned blocks of addresses for that purpose.

Dotted-Decimal Notation

Humans cannot possibly reliably scan and remember 32-bit addresses, so the convention was developed of representing each octet as a decimal number ranging from 0 through 255. Consider this IP address:

```
11000001 00001010 00011110 00000010
```

Expressed in dotted-decimal form, the address would be: 193.10.30.2. By convention, when the hostid fields are 0, the address refers to the network. For example, 135.8.0.0 refers to the network with the netid 135.8.

> **Note** Although dotted-decimal representation is the rule, be sure to remember that IP addresses have a binary form. The majority of IP address configuration errors result because a network administrator fails to consider the binary address when setting up the network.

IP Address Restrictions

A few IP addresses have special uses, and cannot be used to identify networks or hosts.

◆ Netids and hostids of 0 (binary 00000000) are not permitted because ids of 0 means "this network." An IP address 155.123.0.0 identifies the network with the netid 155.123. An address of 0.0.0.35 identifies the host with hostid 35 on the local network.

◆ The netid 127 (binary 01111111) has a special use. It is a loopback address, used for testing host network configurations. Messages addressed to netid 127 are not sent to the network, but are simply reflected back.

◆ Hostids of 255 are restricted to use in broadcasts. A message sent to 255.255.255.255 is sent to every host on this network. A message sent to 183.20.255.255 is broadcast to every host on network 183.20.

◆ The last octet of an IP address cannot be 0 or 255.

Taking these restrictions into account, table 4.1 summarizes the available class A, B, and C addresses.

TABLE 4.1   AVAILABLE IP ADDRESSES

Class	From	To	Netids	Hostids
A	1	126	126	16,777,214
B	128	191	16,384	65,534
C	192	223	2,097,152	254

Addressing in a TCP/IP Internetwork

Figure 4.2 illustrates a TCP/IP internetwork that consists of three networks connected with routers. This internet incorporates networks with class A, B, and C addresses.

The following list describes a number of reasons for segmenting a network:

◆ **Different LAN technologies may be used in different places.** An organization might have token ring in manufacturing and Ethernet in engineering, for example. Routers can interconnect different network technologies.

◆ **LAN connection limits.** A given network cable can support a limited number of attached devices. If these limits are exceeded, additional networks can be connected with routers.

◆ **Congestion.** If a network is overwhelmed, performance quickly falls apart. Internetworks may be created to reduce traffic on individual network segments.

◆ **Wide area networking.** If the distance between two LANs exceeds the size limits of the cabling technology, they may be interconnected through a point-to-point link.

Subnet Addressing

If a network will never be connected to the Internet, network administrators may employ any of the available IP address classes. It is difficult to imagine any single organization that could run out of IP addresses on its own.

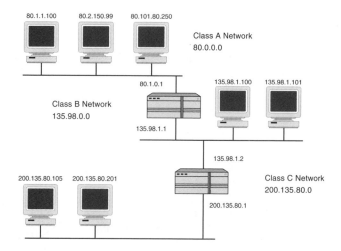

Figure 4.2

Example of a TCP/IP internetwork.

When a network is connected to the Internet, however, assigned addresses must be used. Unfortunately, the pool of available Internet addresses is dwindling, and even class C addresses are doled out reluctantly. As a result, many organizations find themselves with too few assigned IP addresses to assign a separate netid to each network.

To cope with this situation, a subnetting procedure was developed (RFC 950). Subnetting enables network administrators to distribute the hostids for a given netid to several subnetworks.

Figure 4.3 illustrates the formats of IP addresses with and without subnetting. The IP address always consists of 32 bits. *Subnetting* is a mechanism for using some bits in the hostid octets as a subnetid. Without subnetting, an IP address is interpreted in two fields:

netid + hostid

With subnetting, an IP address is interpreted in three fields:

netid + subnetid + hostid

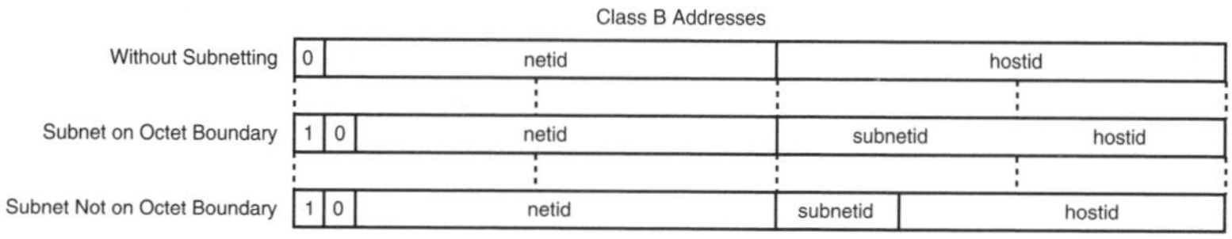

Figure 4.3

IP addresses with and without subnetting.

Subnet Masking

The subnetid is created by borrowing bits from the hostid field using a technique called *subnet masking*. Consider the following class B address:

```
10100001 01110101 10110111 10000111
```

The rightmost two octets of a class B address are the hostid. To encode a subnetid, some of the hostid bits can be reserved for the subnetid, by using a subnet mask. Figure 4.4 shows how a subnet mask could be used to reserve the first four bits of the hostid for the subnetid.

Figure 4.4

Subnet masking.

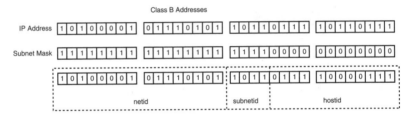

The subnet mask is a 32-bit number. A 1 in the subnet mask indicates that the corresponding bit in the IP address is part of the netid. A 0 in the subnet mask designates the bit as a part of the hostid.

Note

Subnet masks nearly always consist of adjacent, high-order bits. As a result, you need to remember only eight decimal numbers to be able to recognize the vast majority of subnet masks. The eight common subnet masks are as follows:

Binary	Decimal
00000000	0
10000000	128
11000000	192
11100000	224
11110000	240
11111000	248
11111100	252
11111110	254
11111111	255

The RFCs permit subnet masks with nonadjacent (noncontiguous) bits and even provide an example. It is difficult to imagine a case where a noncontiguous mask would provide an advantage.

The number of bits in the subnet mask is adjusted depending on the number of subnets required. With a class B address, the subnet mask 255.255.255.0 allocates the third octet for subnet addressing, yielding 254 possible subnetids.

Note   Like netids, subnetids cannot consist entirely of 0s or 1s. That is why, with a class B address, a subnet mask of 255.255.255.0 makes 254 subnetids available rather than 256.

Default Subnet Masks

When a network is configured to support subnet addressing, a subnet mask must be designated, even if no subnetting actually is in use. The default subnet masks are as follows:

◆ Class A: 255.0.0.0

◆ Class B: 255.255.0.0

◆ Class C: 255.255.255.0

The subnet mask must be configured with 1s for bits corresponding to the netid field of the address class. A subnet mask of 255.255.0.0 is invalid for a class C address, for example.

Example of Subnet Addressing

The advantages, disadvantages, and caveats of subnet addressing can be illustrated most clearly with an example based on a class C address. Figure 4.5 illustrates the example.

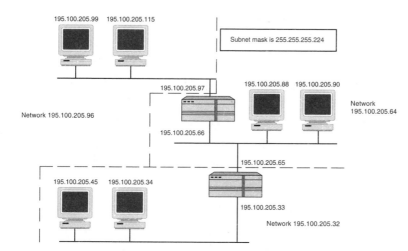

Figure 4.5

A class C network with subnetting.

The network will be based on the network address 195.100.205.0, which in binary is as follows:

```
11000011 01100100 11001101 00000000
```

The subnet mask used for the example is 255.255.255.224, which has the following binary equivalent:

```
11111111 11111111 11111111 11100000
```

Three bits of the hostid are set aside for subnetids. Because subnetids cannot be all 0s or all 1s, six subnetids are made available: 001, 010, 011, 100, 101, and 110. With 5 bits available, each subnet can support 30 hosts (hostids 00000 and 11111 are not available).

Consider the IP address 195.100.205.175. The binary form of the address is as follows:

```
11000011 01100100 11001101 10101111
```

Applying the subnet mask, the three bits allocated for the subnetid result in a subnetid of 10100000, which is 160 in decimal. The hostid is 01111, which is 15 decimal.

Table 4.2 summarizes the values that are valid for the fourth octet when using a subnet mask of 255.255.255.224. The table illustrates, among other things, that subnetting a class C address wastes many potential hostids. (Subnetting isn't nearly as costly with class A and B addresses.) If you have a budget of one class C address and you must segment your network, however, you don't have much choice. But NT offers the capability to help minimize the impact of subnetting, because NT can have one NIC represent several subnets. This helps overcome the problem of losing host IDs when subnetting with few subnets.

TABLE 4.2   CLASS C HOST ADDRESSES AVAILABLE WITH A SUBNET
MASK 255.255.255.224

Subnet (Binary)	Subnet (Decimal)	Fourth Octet Available Values (Binary)	Fourth Octet Available Values (Decimal)
001	32	00100001–00111110	33–62
010	64	01000001–01011110	65–94
011	96	01100001–01111110	97–126
100	128	10000001–10011110	129–158

Subnet (Binary)	Subnet (Decimal)	Fourth Octet Available Values (Binary)	Fourth Octet Available Values (Decimal)
101	160	10100001–10111110	161–190
110	192	11000001–11011110	193–222

Note It is essential to take the binary forms of addresses into account when planning subnets. Otherwise, selecting an invalid address becomes too easy. Another thing—if subnet masking is used on a subnet, all hosts must be configured with the same subnet mask.

Datagram Fragmentation and Reassembly

IP is responsible for delivering datagrams through the internetwork. An IP datagram can
be as large as 65,535. Many networks cannot support data units of that size, however. An Ethernet frame, for example, can support only 1500 bytes of upper-layer data.

So IP has the task of fragmenting large datagrams into datagrams that are compatible with the physical layer being used. The header for each fragment includes information that enables IP at the receiving host to identify the position of the fragment and to reassemble the original datagram.

IP Routing

IP is responsible for delivering datagrams on the internetwork. When IP datagrams must travel to a network other than the local one, IP performs routing for the network, ensuring that the datagram reaches the destination network.

Actual delivery to the destination host, however, is a function of the data link layer. Before examining how routing is performed, the process of delivering packets on a network must be understood.

Delivering Data on the Local Network

When two hosts communicate on the same local network, delivery of a datagram is a simple process. Actual delivery is performed by lower level protocols. On IEEE 802.x LANs frames are delivered under control of the medium access control (MAC) sublayer.

Recall from Chapter 2 that the MAC sublayer is responsible for node addressing. In fact, node hardware addresses are called MAC addresses in IEEE 802 terminology.

Figure 4.6 shows how simple delivering a frame on a local network can be. The source node simply builds a frame that includes the recipient's *destination address (DA)*. The sender's responsibility ends when the addressed frame is placed on the network. On LANs, each node examines each frame that is sent on the network, looking for frames with a destination address that matches its own MAC address. Frames that match are received. Frames that do not match are discarded (Ethernet) or forwarded to the next node (token ring). The only bit of information needed to send a frame to a node on the same network is the recipient's MAC address.

Figure 4.6

Delivering a frame on a local network.

Address Resolution Protocol

However, IP uses its own address scheme, consisting of logical IP addresses. To deliver a datagram on the local network, IP must provide the MAC layer with the physical address of the receiving host.

The *Address Resolution Protocol (ARP)* provides that information. IP calls ARP with the IP address of the destination host, and ARP returns the physical address for that node.

Figure 4.7 shows the method ARP uses to obtain address information. To identify a hardware address, the following steps take place:

1. ARP on host 140.1.1.3 sends an ARP request frame, which is broadcast to the local network. (On Ethernet, this is accomplished by sending the message to the address FF:FF:FF:FF:FF:FF.) The ARP request frame includes the sender's IP and MAC addresses, as well as the destination IP address.

2. All hosts on the network receive the ARP request frame and compare the destination IP address in the frame to their own addresses.

3. If a host finds that the addresses match, it creates an ARP response frame by placing its IP address in a field in the ARP request frame and returning the frame to the host that sent it.

4. When ARP on 140.1.1.3 receives the completed ARP response frame, the information is passed on to IP.

If ARP on each host were to broadcast an ARP request frame each time an address was needed, the traffic would overwhelm the network. To reduce the frequency of address requests, ARP maintains a cache table with recently received addresses. This cache table can be consulted in the future before broadcasting an ARP request. Information in the cache table has a limited life, and ARP reacquires an address after the cache table entry expires. (The system administrator determines the lifetime of a cache entry.)

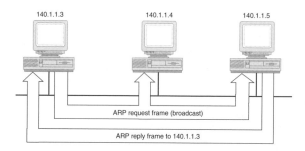

Figure 4.7

Operation of ARP.

Note A *Reverse Address Resolution Protocol (RARP)* compliments ARP, enabling a host to determine the IP address associated with a hardware address.

Local Delivery of IP Datagrams

To deliver a datagram, IP must determine whether it can be delivered on the local network or be routed to a remote network. Before examining routing, the local delivery process must be understood.

1. IP receives a frame from a higher-level protocol.

2. IP compares the destination netid of the frame to the netid of the local network (taking subnet masks into account if subnetting is employed). If the netids match, the frame can be sent directly to the hardware address of the destination host.

3. IP obtains the destination hardware address from ARP.

4. IP constructs a datagram that contains, among other things, the source and destination IP addresses.

5. IP passes the datagram to the network access layer protocol (for example, Ethernet II or IEEE 802.2 LLC) along with the source and destination hardware addresses.

6. The network access layer constructs a frame that incorporates the source and destination hardware addresses. The IP datagram is stored in the frame's data field. (See Chapter 3 for frame formats of various protocols.)

7. The destination host examines the frame, recognizes its hardware address, and receives the frame.

Delivering Data to Remote Networks

The previous section assumed that the datagram to be transmitted had source and destination addresses for hosts attached to the same network. On an internetwork, however, data must frequently be sent to *remote hosts*, hosts on other networks. On TCP/IP networks, delivery is performed through IP routing.

Simple IP Routing

When a datagram is to be routed to an adjacent network, as shown in figure 4.8, the procedure is fairly straightforward. Each host on the network is configured with the address of a default gateway, which specifies the host to which frames should be sent if they are directed to a host on a remote network.

An IP router (or gateway) essentially is a TCP/IP host equipped with two or more network connections. Such hosts are called *multihomed hosts*. A router can be a designated computer or a workstation host configured to perform routing.

In figure 4.8, host 128.1.0.3 must route a frame to host 128.2.0.2. The routing procedure illustrated in figure 4.8 is as follows:

1. Host 128.1.0.3 determines that the destination host is not on the local network by comparing the destination netid to its own netid. The frame must be routed.

2. To route the frame, host 128.1.0.3 performs an ARP request to determine the hardware address of its default gateway. IP then addresses the frame with the

destination hardware address of its default router. The destination IP address, however, is the address of the final destination 128.2.0.2. The address information used to address the frame is as follows:

- ◆ Source hardware address 1

- ◆ Source IP address 128.1.0.3

- ◆ Destination hardware address 4

- ◆ Destination IP address 128.2.0.2

3. IP on the router receives the frame from network 128.1.0.0. By examining the destination IP address, the router determines that it is not the final recipient of the datagram, which must be forwarded to network 128.2.0.0. Because the router is attached directly to the destination network, routing is a simple task.

4. IP on the router calls ARP to determine the hardware address for 128.2.0.2.

5. The router sends the packet on network 128.2.0.0 with the following address information:

- ◆ Source hardware address 5

- ◆ Source IP address 128.1.0.3

- ◆ Destination hardware address 6

- ◆ Destination IP address 128.2.0.2

The source IP address is that of the host that originated the datagram. The source hardware address corresponds to the router's network connection on network 128.2.0.0.

6. Host 128.2.0.2 recognizes its hardware address and receives the packet. Two things should be emphasized in this scenario:

- ◆ The source and destination IP addresses do not change as the datagram traverses the network

- ◆ Source and destination hardware address change each time the frame is sent.

Figure 4.8

Routing to an adjacent network.

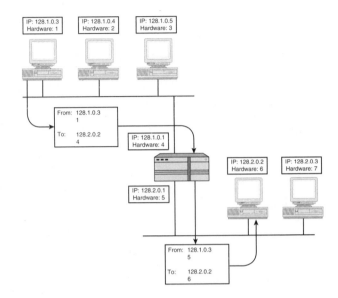

Complex IP Routing

The simple routing scenario just presented falls apart if the destination network is not directly attached to a router on the delivery path. Consider the example shown in figure 4.9. Router A is unaware of the existence of network 128.3.0.0 and has no information that enables it to forward the datagram.

For that reason, routing tables are maintained on IP routers. IP consults the routing tables to determine where to route a datagram for a particular destination network. On a complex internetwork, routing tables should offer all the available routes, along with an estimate of the efficiency for each route.

Routing tables can take the following two forms:

- ◆ **Static tables.** Maintained by the network administrator.

- ◆ **Dynamic tables.** Maintained automatically by a routing protocol.

Even though static routing tables are fairly archaic, they are the only routing supported by Windows NT as it ships. Taking a look at static tables before examining routing protocols, therefore, should prove worthwhile.

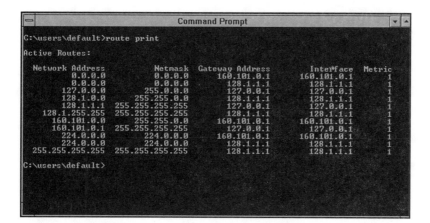

Figure 4.9

A Windows NT routing table.

Static Routing

Static routing tables are not automatically updated, but rather, must be manually maintained. On a dynamic network, router table maintenance can be tedious, but Windows NT administrators must face up to the task or buy commercial routers.

Figure 4.9 shows an example of a Windows NT routing table. Static routing tables are maintained by the **route** utility, which also was used to produce this listing.

The routing table lists known networks, along with the IP address that should be used to reach the networks. The entries in the table are as follows:

◆ **Network Address.** This column lists addresses of known networks. Notice that entries are included for the local network 0.0.0.0 and for broadcasts, 255.255.255.255.

◆ **Netmask.** This column lists the subnet mask in effect for each network.

◆ **Gateway Address.** This column lists the IP addresses that should receive datagrams destined for each network.

◆ **Metric.** This column is an estimate of the cost of the route in *hops*. A hop occurs each time a datagram crosses a router.

Clearly, maintaining such a table would be quite tedious. That is why the majority of networks rely on routers that employ a routing protocol to maintain routing tables.

Another problem with static routing is that it does not enable routers to automatically identify alternative routes. Figure 4.10 illustrates a situation involving three routers. If the link between A and 128.2.0.0 fails, router A cannot take advantage of the route A-C-B unless an entry for router C has been stored in A's router table.

Figure 4.10

A network path failure.

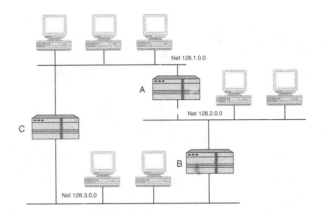

Routing Information Protocol

The Internet Routing Information Protocol (RIP; RFC 1058) is the protocol most commonly used to maintain routing tables on TCP/IP internets. If you have experience on Novell networks, you probably are familiar with the Novell RIP protocol, which is similar in function to Internet RIP (both were derived from the XNS protocol Xerox originated) but not interchangeable.

RIP is a distance vector routing protocol. As Chapter 2 explains, distance vector routing protocols represent routing information in terms of the cost of reaching destination networks. Cost is a fairly simple metric (measure) that represents the cost of using a route using a number from 1 through 15. In general, each network that a route must traverse is represented by a cost of 1. RIP is used to discover the costs of various routes to destination networks and store that information in a routing table, enabling IP to select the lowest-cost route.

A RIP routing table entry contains at least the following information:

♦ The IP address of the destination

♦ A metric that represents the sum of the costs to reach the destination

♦ The IP address of the next router on the path to the destination

♦ A flag indicating a recent change to the route

♦ Timers

In a router, RIP builds and maintains its routing table using a mechanism that is at its heart quite simple: each router periodically broadcasts its routing table, which other routers use to update their route information.

> **Note** In a routing table, the special address 0.0.0.0 describes a default route, which may be used if maintaining a complete network routing table is inconvenient.

Route Convergence

Figure 4.11 illustrates an internetwork with four routers. Assume that the entire internet has just come up and that all router tables have been newly initialized. The following steps describe how A initializes its routing table and how its information propagates through the internet.

1. After initialization, A knows only of the directly attached networks. A is 1 hop from NET1 and 1 hop from NET2 (1 is the minimum cost metric). A broadcasts a RIP response packet containing this information to its attached networks.

2. B receives A's broadcast. B is directly attached to NET2 at a cost of 1, and discards that information. B determines the cost to reach network 1 by adding its cost to reach A (1) to A's cost to reach NET1 (1). Consequently, B's cost to reach NET1 is 2.

3. B broadcasts a RIP response packet using its routing table, including its attached networks. A learns from this table that it has a route to NET3 at a cost of 2. C learns that it has routes to NET1 (cost 3) and to NET2 (cost 2).

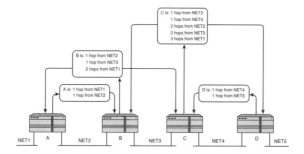

Figure 4.11

Route convergence on a simple internetwork.

Meanwhile, other routers have not been idle. D has broadcast its routing table as well, informing the other routers of routes to NET5. In this way, routers arrive on a complete picture of the network in terms of the costs to each destination and the routers through which a message should next be routed to reach a given destination. The process of bringing all routers up-to-date on the state of the network is called *convergence*.

Each router sends a route response packet to its neighbors on the network at 30-second intervals. The general rule is that a router updates its route tables after it discovers a route that has a lower cost. Routers eventually converge on the lowest-cost routes.

After a router is first initialized, it can solicit routing information from nearby routers by issuing an RIP request packet, which reduces the time required to converge the new router, and informs other routers of new routes the new router makes available.

Potential Convergence Problems with RIP

The RIP algorithm as described to this point has some potential for problems. Before examining techniques for alleviating the problems, the problems themselves must be examined.

Figure 4.12a illustrates an internetwork. Each of the networks shown is associated with a cost of 1, with one exception. The cost from C to D is 10, which might be the result of crossing many routers. Or it might result because the link is a low-speed link that should be used only in emergencies and the network administrator has manually assigned a high cost to it.

When the network is working properly, the routing information for the routers with respect to NET6 is as follows:

◆ A can reach NET6 through B at a cost of 3

◆ B can reach NET6 through D at a cost of 2

◆ C can reach NET6 through B at a cost of 3

◆ D can reach NET6 directly at a cost of 1

If NET4 fails between B and D, current routes are invalidated on A, B, and C. However, it takes some time for the routers to converge on a new route.

B rids itself of the old route fairly quickly by using a time out mechanism. If B fails to receive a route response packet from D after 180 seconds (three 30 second intervals), B times out the entries in its tables that route through D.

Timing out solves the immediate problem for B. But RIP routers have specific route knowledge only of the networks to which they are directly attached, causing problems in this instance because neither A nor C is aware that NET4 has failed and that B's route is invalid. A and C advertise that they have a route to NET6 with a cost of 3, but do not specify that the route requires the link between B and D. Therefore, C assumes it can use A's route and C assumes it can use C's route.

After B advertises that its route is gone, C looks for the least costly route available and discovers that A offers a route with a cost of 3. Similarly, A selects the route advertised by C, with a cost of 3. When A and C forward their routing tables, B sees routes to D through A or C with a cost of 4 and makes those entries in its routing table. Figure 4.12b shows the new routing status.

B's routing information causes A and C to update their costs to reach NET6, revising the costs to 5. This information, when received by B, prompts B to assign a cost of 6 to the routes through A and C. In this way, the cost metrics in the routing tables gradually ratchet up until the direct route from C to D, through NET5, becomes the low-cost route. Because RIP updates occur at 30 second intervals, considerable time might elapse before the network reconverges on the new route.

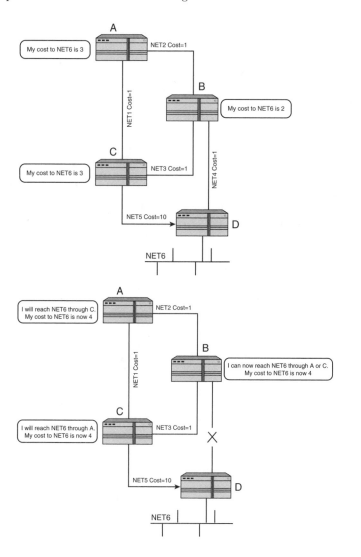

Figure 4.12

Convergence on a reconfigured network.

The Count to Infinity Problem

A more sinister scenario can take place if a network becomes inaccessible. In figure 4.13, if NET4 fails, D becomes unavailable. As before, vestiges of the route to D remain in A and C, and the process of ramping up the cost metrics begins. With D unavailable, a suitable route never becomes available, and the counting process can proceed indefinitely; hence, the *count to infinity problem.*

The technique for breaking this loop is to make "infinity" a suitably low number that is reached fairly rapidly. For RIP, the number chosen is 16. Any network that has a cost of 16 is considered unreachable. Any counting loop stops feeding itself when the metrics reach 16.

Convergence is simplified by making a simple change in B's behavior when a route times out. When B's table entry for D times out, B is aware that the route is invalid. Rather than simply discarding the table entries, B assigns a cost of 16 to its routes through D. When A and C do their next route updates, they arrive at costs of 17 to reach D through B. Consequently, all routers quickly become aware that D cannot be reached through B.

With distance-vector algorithms, the value used for "infinity" is a compromise between the capability to support a reasonably complex network and the need to promote speedy convergence. RIP's designers did not feel that diameters larger than 15 were appropriate for networks.

Figure 4.13

Counting to infinity.

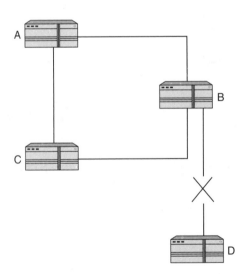

Split Horizon

Although setting infinity to 16 eventually stops hop counts from incrementing, eliminating the count to infinity problem altogether would be better. One technique for doing so is called split horizon. Examining the preceding scenarios reveals one source of problems: A relies on routes advertised by C, while C uses routes advertised by A. The self-referential nature of this relationship generates loops. *Split horizon* is a technique that helps routers be a bit more careful about the routing information they send.

If A advertises to C a route, C advertising that route back to A is never beneficial. Using the split horizon technique prevents a router from sending routes to a router from where it has learned the routes, which keeps two routers from getting into a self-referential loop.

A technique called *poison reverse* (see fig. 4.14) amplifies the safeguard provided by split horizon. If C can reach D through A, A's route cannot go back to C without forming a loop. Therefore, when C advertises its routes to A, C claims that D is unreachable by advertising a metric of 16 to reach D. A, thus, cannot attempt to route to D through C because the distance through C is infinite. Poison reverse informs attached routers that a route is invalid immediately, without the delay required for the route entries to time out. Poison reverse is useful on many complex internetworks and generally is safer than simple split horizon.

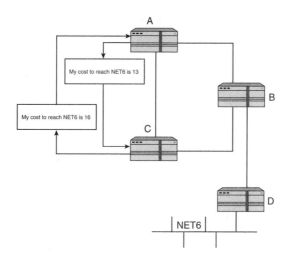

Figure 4.14

Poison reverse.

Limitations of RIP

RIP, as specified by RFC 1058, functions reliably and provides reasonably rapid route convergence. However, RIP has some undesirable traits.

The necessity for declaring some hop count to represent infinity places a size limitation on networks. RIP cannot provide routing on networks that have diameters of greater than 15 hops.

As shown earlier, some time might elapse before router tables converge after a network is reconfigured.

RIP requires routers to advertise their routing tables every 30 seconds. When many routers are present on a network, a significant amount of network bandwidth can be monopolized to send the many RIP response packets required.

For these reasons, the network community is gradually moving toward routing based on link-state algorithms. The protocol being developed for the Internet community is *open shortest path first (OSPF)*.

Open Shortest Path First

OSPF (RFC 1583) is a protocol on the Internet Standards track that is becoming increasingly popular for routing in autonomous systems. An *autonomous system (AS)* is a group of routers that share a common routing protocol. An entire TCP/IP internetwork does not have to use a common routing protocol.

OSPF is a link-state routing protocol, meaning that each router maintains a database that describes the topology of the local autonomous system. This topological database takes the form of a tree, with each router placed at the root of its own tree. Data to construct the database come from link-state advertisements sent by the routers in the AS.

To illustrate this process, consider the network illustrated in figure 4.15. As shown, link-state algorithms can use more flexible metrics than RIP. The network administrator can assign the cost of any given link, and the total cost for a path does not necessarily have a limit, which enables link-state routing to model AS that are indefinitely large. The upper limit for the metric used with OSPF is 65,535, which is sufficient to support networks of considerable scope.

Figure 4.15

Network illustrating the OSPF algorithm.

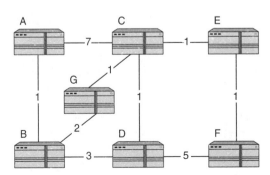

Each node places itself at the root of its tree. The tree constructed for router B in figure 4.15 is shown in figure 4.16. The link state database contains information about the most efficient route available to each destination. The tree shown in figure 4.16 contains the route B-G-C (cost 3) but has discarded the route B-A-C (cost 6).

Note When multiple routes of the same cost are available to a destination, OSPF routers can perform load balancing by distributing traffic across the available routes. RIP lacks this capability.

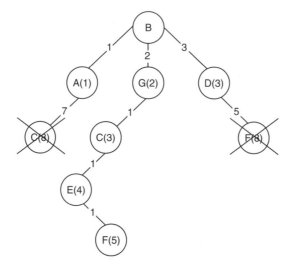

Figure 4.16

A router's link state database tree.

OSPF routers have the following two relationships:

◆ *Neighboring routers* connect to a common network.

◆ *Adjacencies* are relationships among selected neighboring routers used to share routing information. Not all neighboring routers become adjacent.

A router that starts up uses the OSPF Hello Protocol to acquire neighbors. On networks that support broadcasts, routers can dynamically discover neighbors; Hello packets are multicast to all routers on the local network. If a network does not support broadcast messaging, some level of configuration is required before the router can identify its neighbors.

Routers attempt to form adjacencies with newly acquired neighbors. Adjacent routers synchronize their topological databases. Adjacencies then are used to distribute routing protocol packets. A router advertises its state by transmitting a *link state update* packet to its adjacencies.

Link-state advertisements flood the routing area. Reliable delivery is used to ensure that each router in the area has identical information. Each router uses this information to calculate its own shortest-path tree.

OSPF operates directly above IP, unlike RIP, which utilizes UDP as a transport. When the fragmentation of OSPF protocol packets is necessary, the responsibility falls to IP.

OSPF uses several techniques to reduce the amount of messaging required to maintain the routing database:

◆ Although routers periodically transmit link-state advertisements, this is done at infrequent intervals. This contrasts sharply with RIP, which requires each router to send its entire routing table every 30 seconds.

◆ Apart from those infrequent updates, a router advertises its state only when it detects a change in the network.

◆ Link state update packets can contain routing information for multiple routers.

◆ Link state update packets are sent only to adjacencies. Adjacencies are responsible for forwarding the information until it has been flooded throughout the AS. Consequently, each OSPF packet travels a single IP hop.

This overview of OSPF has been necessarily brief. A full description in the RFC requires over 200 pages. The goal has been to illuminate the areas in which OSPF improves on RIP. In particular, OSPF eliminates incidents of self-referential routing information by enabling each router to build an unambiguous routing database. Also, maintenance of OSPF routing places more modest demands on network bandwidth than RIP, a capability of special importance on WAN links of limited bandwidth. Finally, OSPF need not impose an artificial size limit on the network, as with the 15-hop limit specified for RIP.

Exterior Gateway Protocols

RIP and OSPF are classified as *interior routing protocols*, protocols designed to support routing within an autonomous system. These are the routing protocols that LAN and private network administrators are most likely to encounter.

To route among autonomous systems, *external routing protocols* are employed. Figure 4.17 illustrates how an exterior routing protocol can be used to link autonomous systems running different interior routing protocols. This section briefly discusses two exterior router protocols that are mentioned in the RFCs.

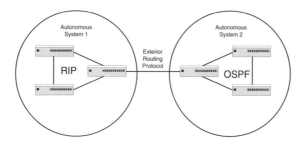

Figure 4.17

An exterior routing protocol linking two autonomous systems.

Exterior Gateway Protocol (EGP; RFC 827/904), introduced in 1982, performs exterior routing in a very rudimentary fashion. First EGP establishes other directly connect external routers as neighbors. Then EGP determines which networks are available through a given exterior router. Finally, EGP advertises route availability. Route information is limited to which destinations are available through which router. Therefore, no load balancing or route optimization are possible.

The more recent Border Gateway Protocol (BGP; RFC 1267) is an improved protocol that advertises full path information to BGP routers. This information enables BGP routers to select the best path between two autonomous systems.

IP Datagram Header Format

Figure 4.18 shows the format of the IP header. Operation of the IP protocol can be tailored with a variety of parameters which appear in the IP header, many of which can be managed in Windows NT TCP/IP.

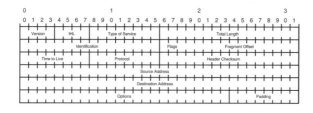

Figure 4.18

Format of the IP datagram header.

The IP header contains the following fields:

◆ **Version (4 bits).** Indicates the format of the internet header. The current version as described in RFC 791 is version 4.

◆ **Internet Header Length (IHL; 4 bits).** Describes the length of the header in 32-bit words. The minimum size for a correct header is 5 words.

◆ **Type of Service (8 bits).** Data in this field indicate the quality of service desired. The field is dissected in figure 4.19.

The effects of values in the precedence fields depend on the network technology employed, and values must be configured accordingly.

Not all options in this field are compatible. When special service is desired, a choice must be made among options of low delay, high reliability, and high throughput. Better performance in one area often degrades performance in another. Few cases call for setting all three flags.

Figure 4.19

Format of the Type of Service field.

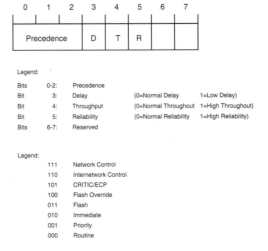

◆ **Total length (16 bits).** The length of the datagram in octets, including the IP header and data. This field enables datagrams to consist of up to 65,535 octets. The standard recommends that all hosts be prepared to receive datagrams of at least 576 octets in length.

◆ **Identification (16 bits).** An identification field used to aid reassembly of the fragments of a datagram.

◆ **Flags (3 bits).** This field contains three control flags.

   ◆ **Bit 0.** Reserved; must be 0

   ◆ **Bit 1 (DF).** 0=May fragment; 1=Do not fragment

   ◆ **Bit 2 (MF).** 0=Last fragment; 1=More fragments

If a datagram is fragmented, the MF bit is 1 in all fragments but the last.

◆ **Fragment Offset (13 bits).** For fragmented datagrams, indicates the position in the datagram of this fragment.

◆ **Time to Live (8 bits).** Indicates the maximum time the datagram may remain on the network. If this field has a value of 0, the datagram is discarded. The field is modified during IP header processing and generally is measured in seconds. Each IP module that handles the datagram, however, must decrement Time to Live by 1. This mechanism ensures that undeliverable datagrams eventually are removed.

◆ **Protocol (8 bits).** The upper layer protocol associated with the data portion of the datagram. Consult Assigned Numbers (currently RFC 1700) for values assigned for many protocols.

◆ **Header Checksum (16 bits).** A checksum for the header only. This value must be recalculated each time the header is modified.

◆ **Source Address (32 bits).** The IP address of the host that originated the datagram.

◆ **Destination Address (32 bits).** The IP address of the host that is the final destination of the datagram.

◆ **Options (0 to 11 32 bit words).** May contain 0 or more options. Options are described in RFC 791.

IP Version 6

Internet protocol version 4 has demonstrated remarkable durability. RFC 791 was published in 1981 and remains the standard specification for IP. New demands placed on the Internet, however, have stimulated the effort to define a new internet protocol.

The effort to develop IP version 6 (IPv6) is the responsibility of the IP Next Generation (IPNG) Working Group of the IETF. IPv6 is currently in the draft standards process, and numerous relevant Internet-Drafts have been published. At the time of this writing, the draft standard is available in the file **draft-ietf-ipngwg-ipv6-spec-02.txt** from sources
mentioned in Chapter 1.

Changes from IPv4 are concentrated in the following areas:

◆ Extending the IP address size from 32 to 128 bits. The new scheme will support more levels of addressing hierarchy, many more addressable nodes, and simpler auto-configuration of addresses.

◆ To simplify the header format, some fields have been dropped or made optional.

◆ Support for extensions and options will be improved.

◆ Greater support is provided for authentication, data integrity, and privacy. IPv4 is not a secure protocol, an obstruction to doing business on the Internet.

Internet Control Message Protocol (ICMP)

IP was not designed as a reliable protocol, and numerous potential problems can arise. ICMP (RFC 792) is a standard protocol that provides a messaging capability for IP. Although ICMP is described separately from IP, ICMP is an integral part of the internet protocol, and ICMP messages are carried as data in IP datagrams.

For a complete list of messages, consult RFC 792. A glance at some of the potential messages is sufficient for this discussion.

◆ **Destination Unreachable.** These messages provide information when a host, net, port, or protocol are unreachable.

◆ **Time Exceeded.** These messages notify the source if a datagram is undeliverable because its time to live expired.

◆ **Parameter Problem.** These messages report a parameter problem and the octet in which the error was detected.

◆ **Source Quench.** These messages may be sent by destination routers or hosts that are forced to discard datagrams due to limitations in available buffer space or if for any reason a datagram cannot be processed.

◆ **Redirect.** These messages are sent to a host when a router receives a datagram that could be routed more directly through another gateway. The message advises the host that was the source of the datagram of a more appropriate router to receive the datagram.

◆ **Echo Request** and **Echo Reply Messages.** These messages exchange data between hosts.

◆ **Timestamp Request** and **Timestamp Reply.** These messages exchange timestamp data between hosts.

◆ **Information Request** and **Information Reply.** These messages can be used to enable a host to discover the network to which it is attached.

ICMP Router Discovery Messages (RFC 1256) are an extension to ICMP that extend the capabilities of hosts to discover routes to gateways. *Router Advertisements* are multicast at periodic intervals, announcing IP addresses for its interfaces to networks. Hosts obtain route information by listening for these announcements. When a host starts up, it may send a *Router Solicitation* to request immediate advertisements. This technique provides information about available routers but cannot provide best-path information.

Summary

This chapter discussed IP, a required Internet protocol with the primary functions of addressing, datagram fragmentation and reassembly, and delivery of datagrams on the internetwork. This chapter focused primarily on IP's unique addressing scheme because it is this function that most concerns network administrators.

IP bears the bulk of the responsibility for delivering data through the internet layer. You learned that the current standard for IP is specified in RFC 791, as amended by RFCs 919, 922, and 950, but you also learned that IP uses other protocols for special tasks.

This chapter discussed these other protocols despite the fact that they do not function at the internet layer, because they are closely related to IP. The Internet Control Messaging Protocol (ICMP) is used to deliver messages to the host-to-host layer. Also, routing protocols may be implemented to improve the IP's routing efficiency.

Chapter 5 Snapshot

This chapter focuses on the host-to-host layer. It covers the following topics:

◆ Transmission Control Protocol

◆ User Datagram Protocol

The host-to-host Layer

T he host-to-host layer has the following two primary areas of responsibility:

◆ Providing upper-layer processes and applications with a convenient interface to the network.

◆ Delivering upper-layer messages between hosts.

Because upper-layer processes have different needs, two host-to-host protocols have been implemented.

Transmission Control Protocol (TCP) is a reliable protocol. It makes a concerted effort to deliver data to its destination, testing for errors, resending if required, and reporting errors to upper layers only if TCP cannot achieve a successful transmission. TCP was designed to meet a DoD requirement for robust network transmission in the days when wide-area networks were not very reliable, and remains well-suited to applications that require a reliable transport. The reliability of TCP is provided, however, at the cost of high network overhead. When high reliability is not required, a lower-overhead transport is preferable.

User Datagram Protocol (UDP) is an unreliable protocol that makes a best-effort attempt to deliver data. *Datagrams* are independent messages that are transmitted independently from other datagrams. UDP makes no attempt to discover lost datagrams, and upper-layer processes must take responsibility for detecting missing or damaged data and retransmitting data if required. UDP operates with less overhead than TCP and is used by a variety of prominent protocols.

The host-to-host layer is the middle layer in the TCP/IP protocol suite. Figure 5.1 displays protocols associated with the layers of the TCP/IP protocol stack, including some of the many process/application layer protocols. Data multiplexing for processes and applications uses ports, which identify data transmitted between two end-protocols on communicating hosts.

Figure 5.1

Protocols in the TCP/IP protocol stack.

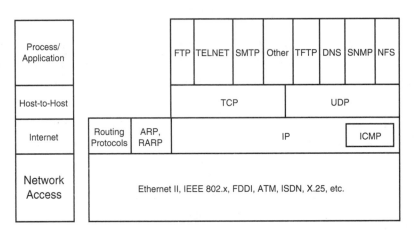

The remainder of this chapter examines more closely the features and operation of TCP and UDP.

Transmission Control Protocol

TCP (RFC 793) provides reliable communication between processes that run on interconnected hosts. This host-to-host communication functions independently of the network structure. TCP is not concerned with routing data through the internetwork; the network infrastructure is IP's responsibility. At the host-to-host layer, TCP on one host communicates directly with TCP on another host, regardless of whether the hosts are on the same network or remote from each other. In fact, TCP is not implemented on routers unless the router function is performed on a host that runs upper-layer processes. (Windows NT can perform routing on a computer being used as a workstation, for example.)

In fact, TCP is oblivious to the network. A wide variety of network technologies can be accommodated, including circuit switching and packet switching on local- and wide-area networks. TCP identifies hosts using IP addresses and does not concern itself with physical addresses.

Several characteristics and functions of TCP are discussed in the following sections, including:

◆ Maintenance of data streams with upper-layer processes and applications

◆ Provisions for reliable communication

◆ Connection maintenance

◆ TCP data communication

◆ Provisions for precedence and security

Following those discussions, the TCP header format is examined.

Data Stream Maintenance

From their perspectives, processes and applications in hosts communicate by transmitting streams of data. They are unconcerned with the underlying mechanisms that provide data fragmentation and flow control.

The interface between TCP and a local process is a *port*, which is a mechanism that enables the process to call TCP and in turn enables TCP to deliver data streams to the appropriate process.

Ports are identified by a port number. Implementors of TCP are permitted considerable freedom in assigning port numbers to processes, but specific port numbers have been assigned to a number of common processes by the Internet Assigned Numbers Authority (IANA). These port assignments, called *well-known ports*, are described in the Assigned Number RFC (currently RFC 1700). Well-known ports provide a convenient means for establishing connections between common processes. The Telnet-Server process, for example, is assigned a well-known port, easing the difficulty of initiating a Telnet session with a host.

To fully specify a connection, the host IP address is appended to the port number. This combination of IP address and port number is called a *socket*. Consequently, a given socket number is unique on the internetwork. A connection between two hosts is fully described by the sockets assigned to each end of the connection. The connection between two sockets provides a bidirectional (full duplex) communication path between the end processes. Figure 5.2 depicts process-to-process communication through a connection.

Figure 5.2

Process-to-process communication.

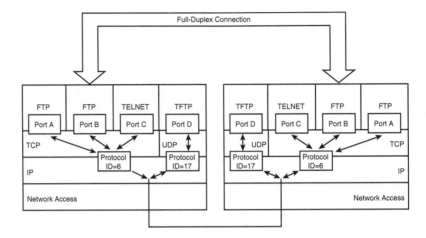

Sockets provide an *application-program interface (API)* between TCP and processes and applications. This API provides programmers with a clean interface between their applications and TCP.

 Note   The most common process API for UNIX is Berkeley (or BSD) Sockets, which was incorporated in Berkeley Standard Distribution UNIX. Microsoft Windows products utilize a Windows Sockets API, which is derived from Berkeley Sockets.

Managing Connections

From the perspective of the process, communication with the network involves sending and receiving continuous streams of data. The process is not responsible for fragmenting the data to fit lower-layer protocols. Figure 5.3 illustrates how data are processed as they travel down the protocol stack, through the network, and up the protocol stack of the receiver.

1. TCP receives a stream of data from the upper-layer process.

2. TCP may fragment the data stream into *segments* that meet the maximum datagram size of IP.

3. IP may fragment segments as it prepares datagrams that are sized to conform to restrictions of the network.

4. Network protocols transmit the datagram in the form of bits.

5. Network protocols at the receiving host reconstruct datagrams from the bits they receive.

6. IP receives datagrams from the network. Where necessary datagram fragments are reassembled to reconstruct the original segment.

7. TCP presents data in segments to upper-layer protocols in the form of data streams.

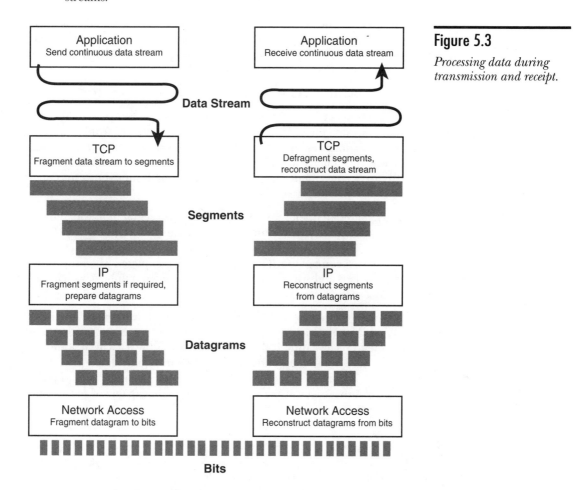

Figure 5.3

Processing data during transmission and receipt.

TCP has the responsibility of managing flow control between the hosts, which it does using *windowing*. The receiving host reports a window to the sending host, which specifies the number of octets that the receiving TCP is prepared to accept. The sending TCP does not transmit past the window unless it receives acknowledgments that verify the receipt of data.

Upper-layer processes request data transmissions by issuing SEND calls to TCP. Ordinarily, TCP queues data to be sent, but the process can specify an immediate send by setting a PUSH flag, which forces TCP to send queued data to its destination. A push also forces the receiver to flush its buffers and send outstanding data to upper-layer processes.

Processes can open, close, and obtain the status of a connection. Connections must be explicitly opened and closed. When TCP issues an *open* call, it specifies the local port and the remote socket. Upper-layer processes receive a name used to identify the connection. Connections may be active or passive:

◆ An *active open* is an attempt to open a connection with a remote TCP.

◆ A *passive open* sets up TCP to accept incoming connection requests, enabling the process that requested the passive open to accept connections from remote processes. Passive opens enable processes to make services available to outside requesters, which can make active open requests to form connections. Well-known ports are a convenient mechanism for enabling remote hosts to request connections with specific services.

When a process originates an open request, TCP prepares a segment in which the SYN (synchronize) control bit is set. Control bits are discussed in the section "TCP Header Format." The TCP receiving this segment matches the remote socket to a local socket to establish a connection. The connection is completed when the TCP modules exchange sockets and synchronize segment sequence numbers, which are described in the next section.

When a process requests closing of a connection, TCP sends a segment in which the FIN control bit is set. A connection must be closed from both ends. A TCP that sends a close may continue to receive until it receives a close from the TCP at the other end of the connection. This enables both ends of the connection to flush any untransmitted data. A TCP reliably receives all data sent before the connection was closed, and the process that receives the close should remain capable of receiving until it receives all data.

Providing Reliable Communication

TCP is a reliable protocol, and is responsible for delivering data streams to their destinations reliably and in order. To verify receipt of data, TCP uses *segment sequence numbers* and *acknowledgments.*

Every octet in a segment is assigned a sequence number, enabling every octet sent to be acknowledged. The TCP header specifies the segment sequence number for the first octet in the data field, and each segment also incorporates an acknowledgment number. When TCP sends a segment, it retains a copy of the segment in a queue, where it remains until an acknowledgment is received. Segments that are not acknowledged are retransmitted.

When TCP acknowledges receipt of an octet with segment sequence number *n*, it relieves the sending TCP of responsibility for all octets preceding the specified octet. The receiving TCP then becomes responsible for delivering the data in the segment to the appropriate upper-layer process. As has been shown, acknowledgments also are part of the windowing mechanism, determining the amount of transmitted data that can be outstanding at any given time.

Precedence and Security

The IP header provides a type of service field and a security option field, which TCP can use to implement precedence and security. TCP modules operating in a security environment must identify segments with required security information. TCP also enables upper-layer processes to specify required security.

 Note TCP is intended to be highly robust, and it is worth quoting this robustness principle from RFC 793: "Be conservative in what you do, be liberal in what you accept from others."

TCP Header Format

TCP formats a header for each segment transmitted to IP. When IP constructs an IP datagram, the TCP header follows the IP header in the datagram. Figure 5.4 shows the format of the TCP header.

TCP segments are organized into 16-bit words. If a segment contains an odd number of octets, it is padded with a final octet that consists of zeros.

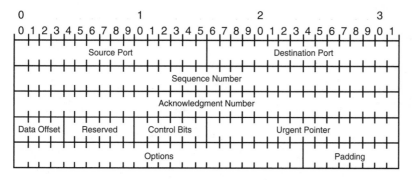

Figure 5.4

Format of the TCP header.

Fields in the TCP header are as follows:

◆ **Source port (16 bits).** Specifies the port on the sending TCP module.

◆ **Destination port (16 bits).** Specifies the port on the receiving TCP module.

◆ **Sequence number (32 bits).** Specifies the sequence position of the first data octet in the segment.

When the segment opens a connection (the SYN bit is set; see discussion on Control Bits later in this list), the sequence number is the initial sequence number (ISN) and the first octet in the data field is at sequence ISN+1.

◆ **Acknowledgment Number (32 bits).** Specifies the next sequence number that is expected by the sender of the segment. TCP indicates that this field is active by setting the ACK bit (see discussion on Control Bits), which is always set after a connection is established.

◆ **Data Offset (4 bits).** Specifies the number of 32-bit words in the TCP header. Options are padded with 0-value octets to complete a 32-bit word when necessary.

◆ **Reserved (6 bits).** Must be zero. Reserved for future use.

◆ **Control Bits (6 bits).** The six control bits are as follows:

   ◆ **URG.** When set (1), the Urgent Pointer field is significant. When cleared (0), the field is ignored.

   ◆ **ACK.** When set, the Acknowledgment Number field is significant.

   ◆ **PSH.** Initiates a push function.

   ◆ **RST.** Forces a reset of the connection.

   ◆ **SYN.** Synchronizes sequencing counters for the connection. This bit is set when a segment requests opening of a connection.

   ◆ **FIN.** No more data. Closes the connection.

◆ **Window (16 bits).** Specifies the number of octets, starting with the octet specified in the acknowledgment number field, which the sender of the segment can currently accept.

◆ **Checksum (16 bits).** An error control checksum that covers the header and data fields. It does not cover any padding required to have the segment consist of an even number of octets. The checksum also covers a 96-bit pseudoheader. The pseudoheader is discussed immediately following this list.

◆ **Urgent Pointer (16 bits).** Identifies the sequence number of the octet following urgent data. The urgent pointer is a positive offset from the sequence number of the segment.

◆ **Options (variable).** Options are available for a variety of functions, including: end of options list, no-operation, maximum segment size, and maximum segment size option data.

◆ **Padding (variable).** 0-value octets are appended to the header to ensure that the header ends on a 32-bit word boundary.

A 12-octet TCP *pseudoheader* (see fig. 5.5) includes source and destination addresses, the protocol, and the segment length. This information is forwarded with the segment to IP to protect TCP from misrouted segments. The value of the segment length field includes the TCP header and data, but does not include the length of the pseudoheader.

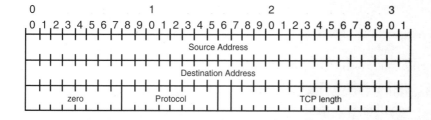

Figure 5.5

Format of the TCP pseudoheader.

User Datagram Protocol

TCP is a formal protocol that requires hosts to establish a connection that is maintained for the duration of a conversation, after which the connection is formally closed. The overhead required to maintain connections is justified when bulletproof reliability is required, but often proves to be misspent effort.

User Datagram Protocol (UDP; RFC 768) provides an alternative transport for processes that do not require reliable delivery. UDP is a datagram protocol that does not guarantee data delivery or duplicate protection. As a datagram protocol, UDP need not be concerned with receiving streams of data and developing segments suitable for IP. Consequently, UDP is an uncomplicated protocol that functions with far less overhead than TCP.

The following list describes some instances in which you might want to choose UDP as the transport protocol for a process:

◆ **Messages that require no acknowledgment.** Network overhead can be reduced by using UDP. Simple Network Management Protocol (SNMP) alerts fall into this category. On a large network, considerable SNMP alerts are generated as every SNMP device transmits status updates. Seldom, however, is loss of an SNMP message critical. Running SNMP over UDP, therefore, reduces network overhead.

◆ **Messages between hosts are sporadic.** SNMP again serves as a good example. SNMP messages are sent at irregular intervals. The overhead required to open and close a TCP connection for each message would delay messages and bog down performance.

◆ **Reliability is implemented at the process level.** Network File System (NFS) is an example of a process that performs its own reliability function and runs over UDP to enhance network performance.

Figure 5.6 illustrates the header format for UDP, which consists of two 32-bit words. The fields in the UDP header are as follows:

◆ **Source port (16 bits).** This field is optional and specifies the source port when enabling the receiver of the datagram to send a response is necessary. Otherwise, the source port value is 0.

◆ **Destination port (16 bits).** The port destination at the destination IP host.

◆ **Length (16 bits).** The length in octets of the datagram, including the header and data. The minimum value is 8 to allow for a header. Consequently, a UDP datagram is limited to a maximum length of 65,535 octets, making 65,527 octets available for data.

◆ **Checksum (16 bits).** A checksum value that covers data in the pseudoheader, the UDP header, and data.

Like TCP, UDP generates a pseudoheader that is passed with the UDP datagram to IP. The UDP pseudoheader guards against misrouted datagrams. Figure 5.7 depicts the UDP pseudoheader.

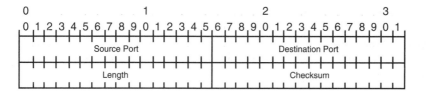

Figure 5.6

UDP header format.

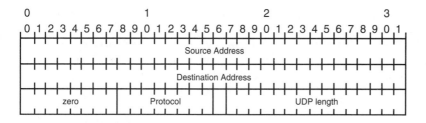

Figure 5.7

UDP pseudoheader format.

Summary

This chapter showed where the host-to-host layer has the following two primary areas of responsibility providing upper-layer processes and applications with a convenient interface to the network and delivering upper-layer messages between hosts. It also noted that because upper-layer processes have different needs, typically two host-to-host protocols have been implemented.

Transmission Control Protocol (TCP) is a reliable protocol. It makes a concerted effort to deliver data to its destination, testing for errors, resending if required, and reporting errors to upper layers only if TCP cannot achieve a successful transmission. TCP was designed to meet a DoD requirement for robust network transmission in the days when wide-area networks were not very reliable, and remains well-suited to applications that require a reliable transport.

User Datagram Protocol (UDP) is an unreliable protocol that makes a best-effort attempt to deliver data. *Datagrams* are independent messages that are transmitted independently from other datagrams. UDP makes no attempt to discover lost datagrams, and upper-layer processes must take responsibility for detecting missing or damaged data and retransmitting data if required. UDP operates with less overhead than TCP and is used by a variety of prominent protocols.

The host-to-host layer is the middle layer in the TCP/IP protocol suite. Figure 5.1 displays protocols associated with the layers of the TCP/IP protocol stack, including some of the many process/application layer protocols. Data multiplexing for processes and applications uses ports, which identify data transmitted between two end-protocols on communicating hosts.

Transmission Control Protocol TCP (RFC 793) provides reliable communication between processes that run on interconnected hosts. This host-to-host communication functions independently of the network structure. TCP is not concerned with routing data through the internetwork; the network infrastructure is IP's responsibility. At the host-to-host layer, TCP on one host communicates directly with TCP on another host, regardless of whether the hosts are on the same network or remote from each other. Several characteristics and functions of TCP were discussed in this chapter including maintenance of data streams with upper-layer processes and applications, provisions for reliable communication, connection maintenance, TCP data communication, and provisions for precedence and security.

Chapter 6 Snapshot

This chapter focuses on the process/application layer. It covers the following topics:

◆ Naming hosts on the Internet

◆ Mapping addresses to names

◆ TCP/IP applications

The Process/Application Layer

The process/application layer is why the other network layers exist. The lower protocol layers simply deliver messages. The process/application layer is where real work gets done. On it, you find programs that provide network services, such as mail servers, file transfer servers, remote terminal, and system management servers, as well as programs that interface with the end user, such as **ftp** and **telnet**.

Keep in mind that other layers may exist above the process/application layer, consisting of applications that use services that certain processes provide.

The *Simple Mail Transfer Protocol (SMTP)*, for example, is a protocol that users could operate directly to send and receive mail. More commonly, however, users interface with SMTP by way of an e-mail program, which generates messages in the SMTP protocol.

This section introduces several processes and applications commonly seen on TCP/IP networks. Before embarking on those discussions, however, examining the use of host names is necessary.

Naming Hosts on the Internet

Because users interface with the process/application layer, putting a friendly face on the network is desirable for this layer. Imagine using a network as vast as the Internet if you had to use IP addresses to address all messages and users. How many IP addresses could you remember?

Therefore, long ago the Internet community began to use *host names* as a convenient way to identify hosts. Most users agree that remembering ds.internic.net is much easier than 198.49.45.10.

To provide host names requires a system that can match host names to their IP addresses. Historically, two technologies have been employed on the Internet:

◆ Static naming using **hosts** files

◆ Domain Name System

Static Naming with HOSTS Files

In the early days, the ARPANET consisted of a few hundred hosts and was, by today's standards, relatively stable. Growth was measured in terms of a few hosts-per-year, not thousands of hosts per day. Host names were catalogued in a file named HOSTS.TXT, which was maintained on a host maintained by the Network Information Center, then maintained by Stanford Research Institute, dubbed the SRI-NIC. Every few days, the contents of HOSTS.TXT would be compiled into a table in a file named hosts.

The HOSTS.TXT and hosts files were maintained manually. ARPANET administrators would e-mail their changes to the NIC, where they would be recorded in HOSTS.TXT and complied to build a new hosts file, which would then be ftp'd to all hosts in the ARPANET to update the local copies.

The UNIX convention is to store a host table as a file named hosts in the directory / etc. Processes and applications consult /etc/hosts to obtain mappings between host names and IP addresses. Here is a sample of a hosts file:

```
#IP Address    Aliases
127.0.0.1      localhost loopback lb      #this host
200.235.80.1   x                          #x client host
200.235.80.5   sales1
200.235.80.6   sales2
```

Each entry in hosts consists of an IP address and one or more spaces, followed by one or more aliases that can be used to name the host. Characters following the # character are regarded as comments.

The hosts file remains an effective means of making host names available to users. It worked best in the days of timeshared host computers, when a single copy of hosts was sufficient for an entire site. By the early 1980s, however, the character of the ARPANET was changing. Increasingly, timeshare hosts were being supplemented or replaced by local area networks populated by single-user workstations. This produced several consequences: the number of host names was dramatically increasing, change was accelerating but it took longer for changes to make their way through the ARPANET, and local administrators were frustrated because their local names could not be locally administered. Moreover, the network traffic required to distribute the hosts file to all hosts via **ftp** was becoming a burden on the ARPANET.

 Note   Many administrators of moderate-sized LANs still rely on hosts files to provide naming on their networks. A naming service such as DNS can be time-consuming to maintain and generates some extra network traffic. If a LAN is fairly stable, hosts files may be the only naming support that is required.

Domain Name Service

Clearly, a better host naming mechanism was required for the ARPANET. After evaluating several proposals, the Domain Name System (DNS; currently standardized in RFC 1034/1035) was introduced as a standard in 1983. DNS indexes host names in a hierarchical database that can be managed in a distributed fashion. Before examining DNS in any detail, looking at the characteristics of hierarchies in general and of the DNS hierarchy in particular should prove useful.

Hierarchies

You are already familiar with a common form of hierarchical organization: the hierarchical directory structure used by virtually all operating systems, including UNIX, DOS, and Windows. Figure 6.1 illustrates a Windows NT directory hierarchy, more commonly called a *directory tree*. Even though real trees and family trees— perhaps the oldest hierarchical databases—frequently place their roots at the bottom, database trees are always upended (see fig. 6.1). The upside-down trees commonly used to depict computer data structures are called *inverted trees*.

Data in a tree are represented by the intersections, or end points, of the lines that describe the tree structure. These points are called *nodes*, of which there are the following three kinds:

◆ **Root.** Every tree has exactly one root node. On a file system, this is called the *root directory*, represented by a \ (DOS and Windows) or a / (UNIX).

◆ **Intermediate nodes.** An indefinite number of nodes can be made subordinate to the root node. Intermediate nodes may themselves have subordinate nodes. On file systems, intermediate nodes are called subdirectories and are assigned logical identifiers, such as WINNT35.

◆ **Leaf nodes.** A leaf node is the end of a branch in the tree.

Figure 6.1

Example of a file system directory tree.

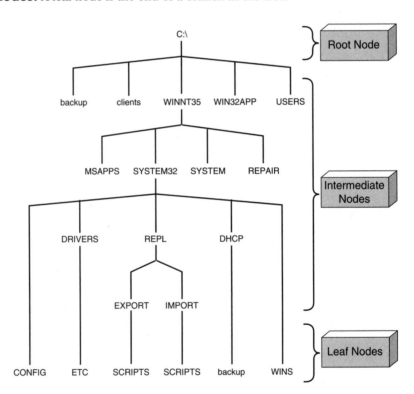

Nodes frequently are referred to as *parent* and *child* nodes. Leaf nodes are always children. Intermediate nodes are parents of their child (subordinate) nodes and children of their parent nodes. The root node is a parent to all first-level intermediate nodes. Nodes that are children of the same parent are known as *siblings*.

Any given node on the tree can be fully described by listing the nodes between itself and the root. Figure 6.1 shows an example identifying the node (in this case a subdirectory) \WINNT35\SYSTEM32\REPL\EXPORT. Names that list all nodes between a node and the root are called *fully qualified names.* Note that fully qualified names for file systems begin with the root and proceed down the tree to the node in question.

A fully qualified name can uniquely identify any node in the tree. The names \WINNT35\MSAPPS and \WINNT35\SYSTEM32 describe separate nodes (subdirectories) in the directory tree.

Figure 6.2 illustrates an important rule of hierarchies: siblings may not have identical node names. Thus, the \WINNT35 directory cannot have two subdirectories named MSAPPS. Having two nodes named MSAPPS is perfectly all right, however, if their fully qualified names differ. Naming directories \APPS\MSAPPS and \WINNT35\MSAPPS on the same file system, for example, is permissible.

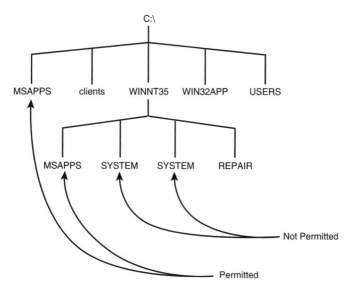

Figure 6.2

Each node in a hierarchy must have a unique fully qualified name.

The Domain Name Space

The DNS hierarchical database is called the *domain name space.* Each host in the domain name space has a unique fully qualified name. Figure 6.3 shows a simple DNS hierarchy that an organization might use. The root node of a DNS tree is called either "root" or the "root domain." The root domain often is designated with empty quotation marks (" ").

Each node in the tree has a name, which can contain up to 63 characters.

Figure 6.3

*DNS tree for an
organization.*

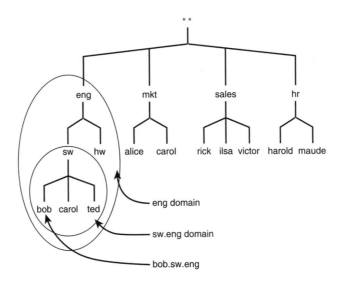

The fully qualified name for a DNS node is called the *fully qualified domain name
(FQDN)*. Unlike fully qualified path names in file systems, which start from the root,
the FQDN convention in DNS starts with the node being described and proceeds to
the root. Figure 6.3 illustrates bob.sw.eng as an example of a FQDN. The convention
with DNS names is to separate node names with a period (referred to as "dot"). The
root node may be represented by a trailing dot (as in bob.sw.eng.), but the trailing
dot ordinarily is omitted.

DNS trees can be viewed in terms of domains, which are simply subtrees of the entire
database. Figure 6.3 illustrates how subdomains can be defined within domains. The
eng domain has two subdomains: sw.eng and hw.eng. The name of a subdomain is
simply the FQDN of the topmost node in the domain. Subdomains always consist of
complete subtrees of the tree, a node and all of its child nodes. A subdomain cannot
be designated to include both eng and mkt, which are located at the same level of the
tree.

Subdomains are DNS management structures. Delegating management of any
subdomain to distribute management responsibility for the complete name space is
possible.

Figure 6.4 shows that DNS trees obey the same naming rules as directory trees:
siblings must have unique node names. Nodes that are children of different parents
may have the same node names.

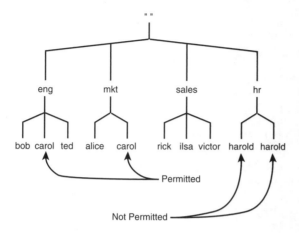

Figure 6.4

Naming rules for DNS nodes.

> **Note** Domain names can be assigned *aliases*, pointers from one domain name to another. The domain to which the alias points is called the *canonical domain name*.

Domain and subdomain are relative terms and are used somewhat interchangeably. Technically speaking, every domain except root literally is a subdomain. When discussion focuses on a particular node, however, that node generally is referred to as a domain. Use of the terms *domain* and *subdomain* is primarily a function of perspective. DNS domains typically are referred to in terms of levels:

◆ **First-level domain.** A child of root; the more commonly used name for a first-level domain is *top-level domain*.

◆ **Second-level domain.** A child of a first-level domain.

◆ **Third-level domain.** A child of a second-level domain, and so forth.

Notice that eng.widgets has two functions: it serves as a name of a host in the DNS hierarchy and points to a particular IP address. However, eng.widgets also is a structure in the DNS database that is used to organize its children in the database hierarchy.

> **Note** Note that the term *domains*, as used with regard to DNS, has no relationship to Windows NT Server domains. Windows NT Server domains provide a way to organize Windows NT computers into manageable groups that share a common security database. DNS domains are related only to the Internet naming service. A Windows NT computer quite certainly can participate in a Windows NT domain under one name and in a DNS domain with another name.

Domain Administration

DNS was designed to handle the Internet, which is too vast to be centrally administered as a single name space. Therefore, being able to delegate administration of subdomains was essential.

Name servers are programs that store data about the domain name space and provide that information in response to DNS queries. The complete name space can be organized into *zones*, which simply are subsets of the DNS tree. A given name server has authority for one or more zones. Figure 6.5 shows a sample tree as it might be organized into three zones. Notice that zones do not require regular boundaries. In the example, eng is maintained in a separate zone on its own name server. Notice that zones, unlike domains, need not be a simple slice of the DNS tree, but can incorporate different levels of different branches.

Administration for zones can be delegated to name servers as required. If administration for a domain is delegated to a name server, that name server becomes responsible for the domain's subdomains as well, unless administration for those subdomains is delegated away.

Figure 6.5

Zones and delegation of domain authority.

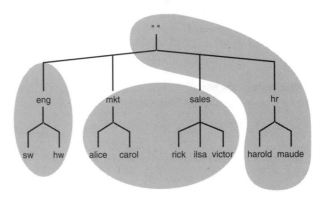

Each zone must be serviced by a *primary master name server*, which obtains the data for the zone from files on its host. Secondary master domain servers obtain zone data by performing *zone transfers* from the primary master name server for the zone. Secondary masters periodically update their databases from the primary to keep the various name servers for the zone synchronized.

DNS is very flexible in the way name servers and zones can be related. Recall that name servers may be authoritative for more than one zone. Beyond that, a name server can be a primary on some zone(s) and a secondary for other zone(s).

The provision for multiple name servers provides a level of redundancy that enables the network DNS to continue to function with secondaries even in the event of a failure of the primary master name server.

Resolving DNS Queries

When an application requires DNS data, it uses a *resolver* to query a DNS server. A resolver is the client side of the DNS client-server relationship. The resolver generates a DNS query and sends it to a name server, processes the response from the name server, and forwards the information to the program that requested the data.

Resolver queries are fulfilled by DNS servers (see fig. 6.6). The resolver in a host is configured with the IP address of at least one DNS server. When the resolver requires an IP address, it contacts a known DNS server, which is responsible for processing the request.

Resolution is a matter of querying other DNS servers starting with one that is authoritative for the root domain. The root name server provides the address of a first-level domain in the queried name. If required, the first-level domain supplies the address of a second-level domain server, and so on, until it reaches a domain server that can satisfy the query.

Note
The most popular implementation of DNS is *Berkeley Internet Name Domain (BIND)*, originally written for 4.3BSD UNIX and now at version 4.8.3. BIND has been ported to most versions of UNIX, and a Windows NT version is included with the *Windows NT Resource Kit*. BIND supports tree depths of 127 levels, sufficient to enable BIND to be used on the root name servers for the Internet.

BIND uses so-called *stub resolvers*. A stub resolver has no DNS search capability. It simply knows how to send a query to a DNS server. The name server performs the actual resolution of the query.

To diminish the effort required to resolve DNS queries, DNS servers cache the results of recent queries. Data in the cache can enable the server to satisfy a DNS query locally or to shorten the search by starting at a DNS server that is authoritative for a lower-level domain. In the event that cached information cannot be used to initiate a search, the process begins with the root domain. Entries in a DNS cache table are assigned a *time to live (TTL)*, which the domain administrator configures. Entries that exceed the TTL are discarded, and the next time a resolver places a request for that domain, the name server must retrieve the data from the network.

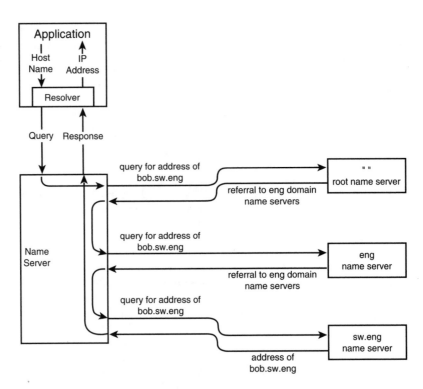

Figure 6.6

Resolution of a DNS query.

Resolvers are actually components of applications and processes running on a host. When compiling programs, developers include library routines for the name service to be supported. Thus, programs like **ftp** and **telnet** are compiled with the capability to construct DNS queries and to process the response. The DNS server, however, is responsible for searching the database.

Clearly, the capability of supporting secondary DNS servers in domains is crucial to providing a reliable name service. If no DNS server is available for the root domain, for example, all name resolution eventually fails as entries in the cache tables in lower-level DNS servers expire and require renewal.

Organization of the Internet Domain Name Space

All of the discussed DNS capabilities come into play on the Internet, certainly the largest name space on any network.

The critical nature of root name servers, along with the volume of DNS queries on the Internet, dictates the need for a large, broadly distributed base of root name servers. At this time, the Internet is supported by nine root name servers, including systems on NSFNET, MILNET, SPAN (NASA's network), and in Europe.

The root name servers are authoritative for the top-level domains in the Internet DNS database. On the Internet, no actual organization has a first-level domain name. *Top-level domains (TLDs)* organize the name space in terms of categories.

The only domains the Internet authorities administer are top-level domains. Administration of secondary and lower-level domains is delegated. Domain name registration is under the authority of the Internet Assigned Numbers Authority (IANA), and is administered by the *Internet Registry (IR)*. The central IR is INTERNIC.NET.

The Internet name space evolves too quickly to be centrally administered, and it has been shown how the DNS name space can be organized into subdomains and zones to enable administration to be flexible, efficient, and local. After establishing a new domain, a management authority for the domain is designated. In many cases, second- and lower-level domains are administered by the entities that requested establishment to them. Organizations such as universities, companies, and government agencies maintain name servers that support the DNS database for their portions of the DNS tree.

RFC 1591, "Domain Name System Structure and Delegation," describes the domain name structure for the Internet, as well as guidelines for administration of delegated domains. TLDs fall into the following three categories:

◆ Generic world wide domains

◆ Generic domains for only the United States

◆ Country domains

Figure 6.7 shows the overall organization of the Internet DNS name space.

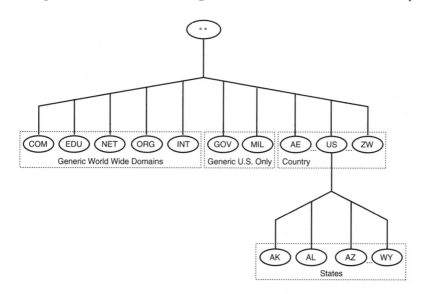

Figure 6.7

Organization of the DNS name space.

Generic World Wide Domains

If you have spent any time on the Internet, you have encountered these top-level domains, which organize the majority of Internet DNS names into five categories:

◆ **COM.** Identifies commercial entities. Because this domain comprehends virtually every company that has a presence on the Internet, the COM name space is getting quite large, and consideration is being given to organizing it in subdomains. Example of a commercial entity: microsoft.com.

◆ **EDU.** Originally embracing all educational institutions, this domain also is becoming quite extensive. Registration in this domain now is limited to four-year colleges and universities. Other schools and two-year colleges are registered under their respective country domains. Example of an educational entity: berkeley.edu.

◆ **NET.** Includes network providers and Internet administrative computers. Example of an Internet administrative computer: internic.net.

◆ **ORG.** Anything that does not fit in the other generic categories.

◆ **INT.** Organizations established by international treaties.

Registering second-level domains in these categories is the responsibility of the InterNIC (contact hostmaster@internic.net). InterNIC also is responsible for registering all new top-level domains.

Generic, United States Only Domains

Two top-level domains are reserved for the United States government:

◆ **GOV.** At one time, applied to any government office or agency, it has since been decided that new registrations will include only agencies of the U.S. federal government. State and local government entities are registered under country domains.

◆ **MIL.** The U.S. military.

Registration of second-level domains in GOV is the responsibility of the InterNIC (contact hostmaster@internic.net).

Second level domains under MIL are registered by the DDN registry at nic.ddn.mil.

Country Domains

Country TLDs are derived from ISO 3166. IANA recognizes the ISO as an international organization with mechanisms in place to identify bona fide countries.

The regional registry for Europe is the RIPE NCC (contact ncc@ripe.net). The registry for the Asia-Pacific region is APNIC (contact hostmaster@apnic.net). The InterNIC administers North America and other undelegated regions.

Table 6.1 lists the Internet top-level domains as of this writing. The information was obtained from the WHOIS server at rs.internic.net. Later in this chapter, the section "Obtaining Domain Information with WHOIS" explains how to conduct WHOIS searches.

TABLE 6.1   INTERNET TOP-LEVEL DOMAINS

Domain	
AE	United Arab Emirates
AG	Antigua and Barbuda
AI	Anguilla
AL	Albania (Republic of)
AM	Armenia (Republic of)
AN	Netherlands Antilles
AQ	Antarctica
AR	Argentina (Argentine Republic)
ARPA	Advanced Projects Research Agency Domain
AT	Austria (Republic of)
AU	Australia
AZ	Azerbaijan
BB	Barbados
BE	Belgium (Kingdom of)
BF	Burkina Faso
BG	Bulgaria top-level domain
BH	Bahrain (State of)
BM	Bermuda

continues

TABLE 6.1, CONTINUED

Domain	
BO	Bolivia (Republic of)
BR	Brazil (Federative Republic of)
BS	Bahamas (Commonwealth of the)
BW	Botswana (Republic of)
BY	Belarus
BZ	Belize
CA	Canada
CH	Switzerland (Swiss Confederation)
CI	Cote d'Ivoire (Republic of)
CK	Cook Islands
CL	Chile (Republic of)
CM	Cameroon
CN	China (People's Republic of)
CO	Colombia (Republic of)
COM	Commercial
CR	Costa Rica (Republic of)
CU	Cuba (Republic of)
CY	Cyprus (Republic of)
CZ	Czech Republic
DE	Germany (Federal Republic of)
DK	Denmark (Kingdom of)
DM	Dominica (Commonwealth of)
DO	Dominican Republic
DZ	Algeria (People's Democratic Republic of)
EC	Ecuador (Republic of)
EDU	Education
EE	Estonia (Republic of)
EG	Egypt (Arab Republic of)
ES	Spain (Kingdom of)

Domain	
FI	Finland (Republic of)
FJ	Fiji (Republic of)
FM	Micronesia (Federated States of)
FO	Faroe Islands
FR	France (French Republic)
GB	Great Britain (United Kingdom of)
GD	Grenada (Republic of)
GE	Georgia (Republic of)
GH	Ghana
GL	Greenland
GN	Guinea (Republic of)
GOV	Government
GR	Greece (Hellenic Republic)
GT	Guatemala (Republic of)
GU	Guam
GY	Guyana
HK	Hong Kong (Hisiangkang, Xianggang)
HN	Honduras (Republic of)
HR	Croatia / Hrvatska (Republic of)
HU	Hungary (Republic of)
ID	Indonesia
IE	Ireland
IL	Israel (State of)
IN	India (Republic of)
INT	International
IR	Iran (Islamic Republic of)
IS	Iceland (Republic of)
IT	Italy (Italian Republic)
JM	Jamaica

continues

TABLE 6.1, CONTINUED

Domain	
JO	Jordan (The Hashemite Kingdom of)
JP	Japan
KE	Kenya (Republic of)
KI	Kiribati
KN	Saint Kitts & Nevis
KR	Korea (Republic of)
KW	Kuwait (State of)
KY	Cayman Islands
KZ	Kazakhstan
LB	Lebanon (Lebanese Republic)
LC	Saint Lucia
LI	Liechtenstein (Principality of)
LK	Sri Lanka (Democratic Socialist Republic of)
LS	Lesotho (Kingdom of)
LT	Lithuania (Republic of)
LU	Luxembourg (Grand Duchy of)
LV	Latvia (Republic of)
MA	Morocco (Kingdom of)
MC	Monaco (Principality of)
MD	Moldova (Republic of)
MG	Madagascar
MIL	Military
MK	Macedonia (The former Yugoslav Republic of)
ML	Mali (Republic of)
MN	Mongolia
MO	Macau (Ao-me'n)
MT	Malta (Republic of)
MX	Mexico (United Mexican States)
MY	Malaysia top level domain

Domain	
MZ	Mozambique (People's Republic of)
NA	Namibia (Republic of)
NATO	NATO (North Atlantic Treaty Organization)
NC	New Caledonia (Nourvelle Caledonie)
NET	Network
NG	Nigeria
NI	Nicaragua (Republic of)
NL	Netherlands
NO	Norway (Kingdom of)
NP	Nepal
NZ	New Zealand
ORG	Organization
PA	Panama (Republic of)
PE	Peru (Republic of)
PG	Papua New Guinea
PH	Philippines (Republic of the)
PK	Pakistan (Islamic Republic of)
PL	Poland (Republic of)
PR	Puerto Rico
PT	Portugal (Portuguese Republic)
PY	Paraguay (Republic of)
RO	Romainia
RU	Russia (Russian Federation)
SA	Saudi Arabia (Kingdom of)
SB	Solomon Islands
SE	Sweden (Kingdom of)
SG	Singapore (Republic of)
SI	Slovenia
SK	Slovakia
SM	San Marino (Republic of)

continues

TABLE 6.1, CONTINUED

Domain	
SN	Senegal (Republic of)
SR	Suriname (Republic of)
SU	Soviet Union (Union of Soviet Socialist Republics)
SV	El Salvador
SZ	Swaziland (Kingdom of)
TH	Thailand (Kingdom of)
TN	Tunisia
TR	Turkey (Republic of)
TT	Trinidad & Tobago (Republic of)
TW	Taiwan
TZ	Tanzania (United Republic of)
UA	Ukraine
UG	Uganda (Republic of)
UK	United Kingdom of Great Britain
US	United States of America
UY	Uruguay (Eastern Republic of)
UZ	Uzbekistan
VA	Vatican City State
VC	Saint Vincent & the Grenadines
VE	Venezuela (Republic of)
VI	Virgin Islands (US)
VN	Vietnam (Socialist Republic of)
VU	Vanuatu
WS	Samoa
YU	Yugoslavia (Federal Republic of)
ZA	South Africa (Republic of)
ZM	Zambia (Republic of)
ZW	Zimbabwe (Republic of)

Subdomains in the US Domain

Within the US domain, second-level domains have been established for each state, using the standard postal abbreviations for the state domain names; for example, NY.US for New York.

RFC 1480 describes some conventions for establishing subdomains within the states (examples are taken from the RFC):

- ◆ **Locality codes.** Cities, counties, parishes, and townships. Example: Los-Angeles.CA.US or PORTLAND.OR.US.

- ◆ **CI.** City government agencies, used as a subdomain under a locality. Example: Fire-Dept.CI.Los-Angeles.CA.US.

- ◆ **CO.** County government agencies, used as a subdomain under a locality. Example: Fire-Dept.CO.San-Diego.CA.US.

- ◆ **K12.** For public school districts. Example: John-Muir.Middle.Santa-Monica.K12.CA.US.

- ◆ **CC.** All state-wide community colleges.

- ◆ **PVT.** Private schools, used as a subdomain of K12. Example: St-Michaels.PVT.K12.CA.US

- ◆ **TEC.** Technical and vocational schools.

- ◆ **LIB.** Libraries. Example: <*library-name*>.LIB.<*state*>.US.

- ◆ **STATE.** State government agencies. Example: State-Police.STATE.<*state*>.US.

- ◆ **GEN.** Things that don't fit comfortably in other categories.

Parallel to the state names, some special names have been designated under US:

- ◆ **FED.** Agencies of the federal government.

- ◆ **DNI.** Distributed national institutes, organizations with a presence in more than one state or region.

Figure 6.8 describes the structure of the US domain, including its use of state and lower-level codes.

Figure 6.8

Organization of the US domain.

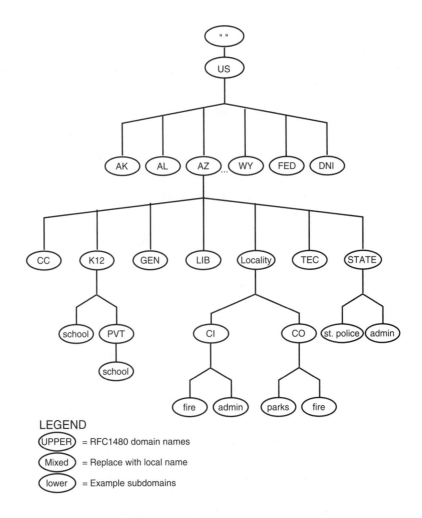

Administration of subdomains of US has been extensively delegated to local contacts. To obtain a list of contacts for the US subdomains via anonymous **ftp**, retrieve the file in-notes/us-domain-delegated.txt from venera.isi.edu. Other useful files are located on this host, and you should find browsing around worthwhile.

Another way to receive this list is to send an e-mail message to RFC-INFO@ISI.EDU. Put the following message in the body of the message:

```
Help: us_domain_delegated_domains
```

> **Note** The RFC-INFO service is yet another way to obtain Internet documents, including RFCs, FYIs, STDs, and IMRs. To obtain instructions, send e-mail to RFC-INFO@ISI.EDU with the text **Help** in the body of the message.

Subdomains in Non-Government Organizations

Below the second-level domain name assigned by InterNIC Registration, the organization that obtains the name is responsible for subdomain administration and has complete freedom to establish the subdomain structure. Any organization that wants to establish a subdomain must arrange for a name server to support the subdomain name space.

DNS services usually are supported on a DNS server operated by the domain's organization. Because a given DNS server can support several zones, however, establishing a new domain on an existing DNS server is possible, such as on one an Internet provider operates.

Earlier examples of an organization's name space (as in figure 6.3) indicated the topmost node as the root of the tree. When an organization joins the Internet, that can no longer be the case. An organization must apply for a domain name, to be a subdomain of one of the standard domains. If the organization in figure 6.3 is named Widgets, Inc., they might apply for the domain name widgets.com. In that case, their portion of the Internet name space would look like figure 6.9. It would be the responsibility of Widgets, Inc., to administer their portion of the name space, starting from the widgets domain.

In this manner, every host on the Internet may be assigned a unique FQDN. Bob's desktop workstation would now have the FQDN bob.sw.eng.widgets.com.

Obtaining Domain Information with WHOIS

WHOIS is a "white pages" directory of people and organizations on the Internet. One way to use WHOIS is for obtaining information about top-level domains, including the contacts.

WHOIS searches are based on keywords. Each top-level domain is keyword-indexed with the domain name concatenated to "-DOM". To search for the COM domain, for example, you would search for COM-DOM.

If your host is on the Internet and has WHOIS client software, you can query WHOIS directly. To find the contact person for the EDU top-level domain, enter the following WHOIS query:

```
whois -h rs.internic.net edu-dom
```

Figure 6.9

An organization in the Internet name space.

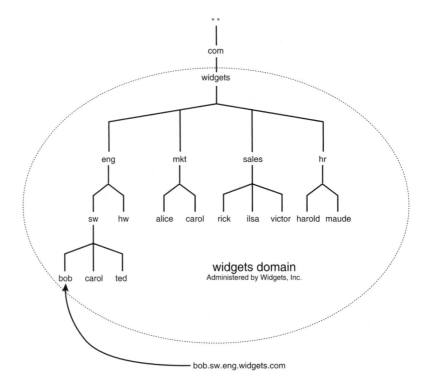

This command directs a WHOIS query using the keyword **edu-dom** to the host rs.internic.net.

On the World Wide Web, use the URL http://ds.internic.net to access the InterNIC WEB site. Enter the AT&T Directory and Databases Home Page, and select the InterNIC Directory Services ("White Pages"). From there, choose WHOIS Person/Organization to reach the WHOIS query form. Enter the keyword (such as NET-DOM) in the form. You can use this query page to obtain information from three WHOIS servers:

◆ InterNIC Directory and Databases Services (ds.internic.net) for domains other than MIL and non-point-of-contact information

◆ DISA NIC for the MIL domain

◆ InterNIC Registration Services (rs.internic.net) for point-of-contact information

An excellent way to access the InterNIC WHOIS database is to **telnet** to rs.internic.net. No login is required. Enter the command **whois** to start a WHOIS client. The following dialog shows the results of querying for EDU-DOM:

```
Whois: edu-dom
Education top-level domain (EDU-DOM)
   Network Solutions, Inc.
   505 Huntmar park Dr.
   Herndon, VA 22070

   Domain Name: EDU

   Administrative Contact, Technical Contact, Zone Contact:
      Network Solutions, Inc.  (HOSTMASTER)  HOSTMASTER@INTERNIC.NET
      (703) 742-4777 (FAX) (703) 742-4811

   Record last updated on 02-Sep-94.

   Domain servers in listed order:

   A.ROOT-SERVERS.NET        198.41.0.4
   H.ROOT-SERVERS.NET        128.63.2.53
   B.ROOT-SERVERS.NET        128.9.0.107
   C.ROOT-SERVERS.NET        192.33.4.12
   D.ROOT-SERVERS.NET        128.8.10.90
   E.ROOT-SERVERS.NET        192.203.230.10
   I.ROOT-SERVERS.NET        192.36.148.17
   F.ROOT-SERVERS.NET        39.13.229.241
   G.ROOT-SERVERS.NET        192.112.36.4

Would you like to see the known domains under this top-level domain? n
As can be seen, it is sometimes possible to drill down to lower level domains,
although the number of subdomains frequently exceeds reporting capacity.
```

This list contains the names and addresses of the nine name servers that service the Internet root domain. If you would like to know more about one of these hosts, you can query WHOIS as follows:

```
Whois: 128.63.2.53
Army Research Laboratory (BRL-AOS)
   Aberdeen Proving Ground, MD  21005-5066
```

```
Hostname: H.ROOT-SERVERS.NET
Address: 128.63.2.53
System: SUN running UNIX

Host Administrator:
    Fielding, James L.  (JLF)  jamesf@ARL.MIL
    (410)278-8929 (DSN) 298-8929 (410)278-6664 (FAX) (410)278-5077

domain server

Record last updated on 17-Aug-95.

Would you like to see the registered users of this host? n
Whois:
```

Mapping Addresses to Names

As described to this point, DNS is adept at resolving domain names to IP addresses. Sometimes, however, exactly the opposite is required. Given an IP address, it may be necessary to determine the domain name associated with the address. To support reverse mapping, a special domain is maintained on the Internet: the in-addr.arpa domain.

Figure 6.10 illustrates in-addr.arpa's structure. Nodes in the domain are named after IP addresses. The in-addr.arpa domain can have 256 subdomains, each corresponding to the first octet an IP address. Each subdomain of in-addr.arpa can in turn have 256 subdomains, corresponding to the possible values of the second octets of IP addresses. Similarly, the next subdomain down the hierarchy can have 256 subdomains corresponding to the third octets of IP addresses. Finally, the last subdomain contains records associated with the fourth octets of IP addresses.

The value of a fourth-octet resource record is the full domain names of the IP address that defines the resource record.

Figure 6.10 shows how a record could be stored in the IN-ADDR.ARPA hierarchy. The domain name mcp.com is associated with the IP address 198.70.148.1. To locate the domain name, DNS searches down the tree beginning with 198.in-addr.arpa. The search continues until reaching the resource record 1.148.70.198.in-addr.arpa. The value of that resource record is mcp.com.

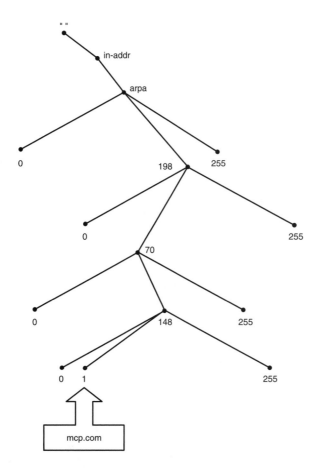

Figure 6.10

Resolving an address to a domain name in in-addr.arpa.

TCP/IP Applications

This section examines several common TCP/IP applications. Some, like **ftp** and **telnet**, are tools that end users frequently access. Others, although not often seen by users, are main-stays of TCP/IP networking. Specifically, this section examines the following applications:

◆ File Transfer Protocol (**ftp**)

◆ Trivial File Transfer Protocol (**tftp**)

◆ **Telnet**

◆ Simple Mail Transport Protocol (SMTP)

◆ Simple Network Management Protocol (SNMP)

◆ Network File System (NFS)

Incidentally, DNS name servers also function at the process/application level. Operation of DNS is described above, and will not be considered further.

File Transfer Protocol

ftp is both a protocol and a program that can be used to perform basic file operations on remote hosts and to transfer files between hosts. As a program, **ftp** can be operated by users to do file tasks manually. **ftp** also can be used as a protocol by applications that require its file services.

ftp is a secure, reliable application. To ensure reliability, **ftp** operates over TCP. Users who access a host through **ftp** undergo an authentication login which may be secured with usernames and passwords. These usernames and passwords can be tied into the host's security, enabling administrators to restrict access as required.

> **Note**   Although secure, FTP sends passwords as CLEARTEXT, which can pose problems.

Anatomy of ftp

As figure 6.11 shows, **ftp** includes client and server components. A host that makes its file system available to users must run an application that operates as an *ftp server*. Users who access the **ftp** server must run *ftp client* software on their computers.

When the **ftp** client opens a connection to an **ftp** server, a logical pipeline (a virtual circuit defined by two sockets) is established between the client and server hosts. This pipeline enables the **ftp** components to communicate. The end result is very much like mounting the remote file system for limited local file access. You cannot execute remote files as programs, but you can list directories, type file contents, manipulate local directories, and copy files between the hosts.

> **Note**   A word about capitalization is in order. UNIX commands, directories, and file names are case-sensitive, and the command `FTP` is not interchangeable with `ftp`. Therefore, authors of UNIX books conventionally typeset this and other commands entirely in lowercase.

Windows NT recognizes upper- and lowercase characters in file names, but is not case-sensitive when commands are entered from the keyboard. It does not matter whether you type **ftp**, **FTP**, or **fTp**.

Because this book primarily addresses Windows NT, Microsoft conventions have been followed in this book. The Microsoft convention is to typeset commands in lowercase, boldface type, unless case is significant (as when the example involves being logged into a UNIX host).

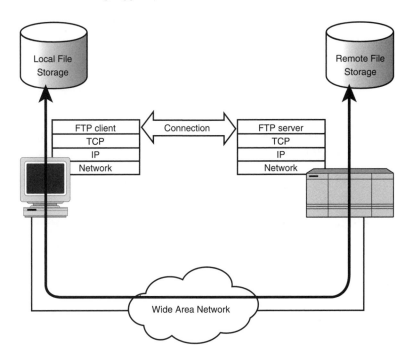

Figure 6.11

*Anatomy of an **ftp** session.*

Using ftp

Chances are high that you connect your Windows NT computers to the Internet in some way. When that happens, you leave the realm of Microsoft networking and need to use **ftp** to perform remote file operations.

Until fairly recently, **ftp** has been a text-only application, used from the command line. The new popularity of the Internet, combined with the wide availability of graphical user interfaces, has lead to the development of Windows-based applications that provide a point-and-click interface to **ftp**.

Windows NT, however, ships with command-line **ftp** only. Fortunately, that is all you need. Chapter 15, "Building an Internet Server," tells you everything you need to know to connect Windows NT computers to the Internet. After doing so, you can use **ftp** as it ships with Windows NT to access **ftp** sites that can supply you all of the tools you need to set up your Windows NT Internet environment, including the previously mentioned graphical interface to **ftp**.

Example of an ftp Session

This section presents an example of an **ftp** session. The example is designed to show you how to retrieve an RFC document from the InterNIC server DS.INTERNIC.NET.

Before beginning, you must establish an Internet connection, using either a dial-in service or a direct network connection.

Starting ftp

You can start an **ftp** session by simply opening a command prompt and typing the command **ftp** as in this dialog (text entered by the user is in bold):

```
C:\ftp
ftp>
```

The prompt changes from C:\ to ftp>. At this point, only **ftp** commands are accepted.

Getting Help

To obtain a list of **ftp** commands, use the **?** command:

```
ftp> ?
Commands may be abbreviated. Commands are:
!          delete     literal   prompt      send
?          debug      ls        put         status
append     dir        mdelete   pwd         trace
ascii      disconnect mdir      quit        type
bell       get        mget      quote       user
binary     glob       mkdir     recv        verbose
bye        hash       mls       remotehelp
cd         help       mput      rename
close      lcd        open      rmdir
ftp>
```

ftp betrays its UNIX origins in many ways. Many of the file and directory management commands originated in the UNIX environment. Some will be familiar to DOS and

Windows users (no points for guessing which OS originated the commands). Others, such as **pwd** (print working directory) and **ls** (list files) are unfamiliar to DOS users, but quite understandable after they are explained.

You can obtain brief help on any of these commands by typing **help** followed by the command for which you seek advice. The descriptions aren't very elaborate, but they can help, as in this example:

```
ftp> help ls
ls              nlist contents of remote directory
```

Opening a Session

After starting **ftp**, you can open a session with an **ftp** server by using the **open** command, as follows:

```
ftp> open ds.internic.net
Connected to ds.internic.net
220-             InterNIC Directory and Database Services
220-
220-Welcome to InterNIC Directory and Database Services provided by AT&T
220-These services are partially supported through a cooperative agreement
220-with the National Science Foundation.
220-
220-Your comments and suggestions for improvement are welcome, and can be
220-mailed to admin@ds.internic.net.
220-
220-AT&T MAKES NO WARRANTY OR GUARANTEE, OR PROMISE, EXPRESS OR IMPLIED,
220-CONCERNING THE CONTENT OR ACCURACY OF THE INTERNIC DIRECTORY ENTRIES
220-AND DATABASE FILES STORED AND MAINTAINED BY AT&T. AT&T EXPRESSLY
220-DISCLAIMS AND EXCLUDES ALL EXPRESS WARRANTIES AND IMPLIED WARRANTIES
220-OF MERCHANTABILITY AND FITNESS FOR A PARTICULAR PURPOSE.
220-
220-
220-            ****************************
220-
220-DS0 will be rebooted every Monday morning between 8:00AM and 8:30AM est.
220-
220-            Please use DS1 or DS2 during this period
220-
220-            ****************************
220-
220 ds FTP server (Version 5.3 Tue Nov 23 19:25:19 EST 1993) ready.
User (ds.internic.net:(none)):
```

You can start **ftp** and open a session with an **ftp** server by including the domain name for the server as a command-line parameter. The session with InterNIC could also have started using this command:

`C:\ ` **ftp ds.internic.net**

Logging in to Anonymous ftp

Like many **ftp** servers, ds.internic.net accepts anonymous logins. Any user may log in with limited access rights by using the username **anonymous** and entering a password. By convention, most systems request that users enter their e-mail addresses as their passwords. The login process is shown below:

```
User (ds.internic.net:(none)): anonymous
331 Guest login ok, send ident as password.
Password: (password does not echo)
230 Guest login ok, access restrictions apply.
ftp>
```

Changing Directories

You now are logged in to the root directory of ds.internic.net. At any given time, you will be working with two working directories: one on the **ftp** server and one on your local computer. You can change these directories if you need to determine where to copy files from and to.

Two commands are available for changing directories:

◆ cd. Changes your working directory on the **ftp** server

◆ lcd. Changes your current directory on your local computer

At any time, you can view your current directory on the **ftp** server by using the **pwd** (print working directory) command:

```
ftp> pwd
257 "/" is the current directory
```

When you complete a login to an **ftp** server, you enter the realm of that server's operating system. ds.internic.net is a Sun system running on SunOS UNIX—the majority of **ftp** servers run UNIX—and you must apply UNIX conventions to the names of files and directories.

Remember that case is significant in UNIX. You cannot retrieve the file rfc1800.txt with the command parameter RFC1800.TXT. Also, UNIX subdirectories are delimited with forward slashes (/) rather than the back slashes (\) with which DOS and Windows users are familiar.

Similarly, in UNIX, case matters in directory names. If a directory is named /pub/Libraries/Programs, you must be sure to match case when you enter the subdirectory names.

RFC files are stored in the /rfc directory. You can access files by specifying the file name with a directory path, or can change your working directory to /rfc. To change your working directory on the server, use the **cd** (change directory) command:

```
ftp> cd /rfc
250 CWD command successful
ftp> pwd
257 "/rfc" is the current directory
```

To change the current directory on your local computer, use the **lcd** command. To store files in \docs, enter the command:

```
ftp> lcd \docs
Local directory now c:\docs
```

Figure 6.12 illustrates a directory tree along with some examples of commands for moving around:

◆ To move up the directory tree (to the parent directory of the current one) enter the command **cd ..** or **cdup**. The symbol .. simply means "one directory up."

◆ To change to a subdirectory of the current directory, use a *relative* reference. If your working directory is /ietf, you can change to **/ietf/95jul** simply by typing **cd 95jul**. A directory specification that does not begin with a / is a relative reference that begins with the current directory.

◆ You can change to any directory on the system by using an absolute reference that begins with the root directory. The command **cd /ietf/95apr** changes you to the 95apr directory, no matter what your current directory is.

Figure 6.12

Navigating a UNIX directory tree.

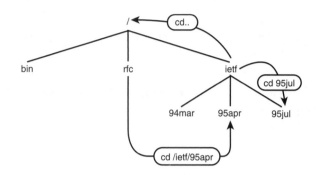

Listing Directory Contents

This directory contains nearly 2,000 files. You could see them all by typing the **ls** command, but you probably want to use wild cards to delimit the file list.

Directory contents may be shown as file names alone or as detailed file lists. The **ls** (list) command shows only file and directory names. You can use the familiar * and ? wild cards with **ls**. The following example was chosen to highlight several important documents that you should retrieve during your first session with InterNIC.

```
ftp> ls rfc-*.txt
200 PORT command successful.
150 Opening ASCII mode data connection for file list.
rfc-index.txt
rfc-instructions.txt
rfc-retrieval.txt
226 Transfer complete.
56 bytes received in 0.01 seconds (5.60 Kbytes/sec)
ftp>
```

Processing wild card characters is called *globbing*. When globbing is turned on, ? and * are treated as wild cards. If required, you can turn globbing off by using the **glob** command. Enter the command again to turn globbing on.

Note   Even though some of the commands resemble UNIX commands, you cannot freely use UNIX commands while in an **ftp** session. The commands are processed by **ftp**, not by a UNIX shell.

When you know you are working on a UNIX host, however, some command options are supported. The **ls** command accepts the following parameters (note the use of uppercase in some options):

-a   Lists all files, including hidden ones

-C   Produces a column listing (similar to the DOS /W switch)

-d   Lists directory names only

-F   Displays the file type (directory or executable)

-l   Produces a long listing

-R   Specifies a recursive (continuous) listing

To display more detail, use the dir command. The details you see depend on the OS running on the **ftp** server. This list originates on a UNIX computer and includes UNIX security information (called *permissions*) in the leftmost column. Because this server permits unsecured anonymous logins, you are unlikely to see any files that are not secured with read-only (r) permissions. (Consult NRP's *Inside UNIX Second Edition* if you are interested in more information about UNIX.) In the following example, a ? wild card was used as a single-character placeholder to display all files starting with the characters "rfc170".

```
ftp> dir rfc170?.txt
200 PORT command successful.
150 Opening ASCII mode data connection for /bin/ls.
-r--r--r--  1 welcome  ftpguest    458860 Oct 19  1994 rfc1700.txt
-r--r--r--  1 welcome  ftpguest     15460 Oct 20  1994 rfc1701.txt
-r--r--r--  1 welcome  ftpguest      7288 Oct 20  1994 rfc1702.txt
-r--r--r--  1 welcome  ftpguest     17985 Oct 21  1994 rfc1703.txt
-r--r--r--  1 welcome  ftpguest     42335 Nov  1  1994 rfc1704.txt
-r--r--r--  1 welcome  ftpguest     65222 Oct 25  1994 rfc1705.txt
-r--r--r--  1 welcome  ftpguest     19721 Oct 21  1994 rfc1706.txt
-r--r--r--  1 welcome  ftpguest     37568 Oct 28  1994 rfc1707.txt
-r--r--r--  1 welcome  ftpguest     26523 Oct 25  1994 rfc1708.txt
-r--r--r--  1 welcome  ftpguest     66659 Nov 22  1994 rfc1709.txt
226 Transfer complete.
670 bytes received in 0.54 seconds (1.24 Kbytes/sec)
ftp>
```

If the directory contains subdirectories, you see an entry similar to the following. The d at the beginning of the permissions indicates that the entry is a directory.

```
drwxr-xr-x  3 welcome  1          25600 Sep 20 04:07 rfc
```

Retrieving Files

To retrieve an RFC file, use the **get** command. Keep in mind as you do so that file names in UNIX are case-sensitive. The following example gets the file rfc1700.txt from the working directory on the **ftp** host and retrieves it to the working directory on the local computer:

```
ftp> get rfc1700.txt
200 PORT command successful.
150 Opening ASCII mode data connection for rfc1700.txt (458860 bytes).
226 Transfer complete.
471743 bytes received in 92.04 seconds (5.13 Kbytes/sec)
ftp>
```

You do not have permissions to copy files to DS.INTERNIC.NET. For hosts on which you have file write permissions, the **put** command works very similarly to **get**.

Note

As disclosed in the **ftp** dialog, the preceding example was of an ASCII transfer, which generally is preferable for text documents. UNIX and DOS/Windows have different conventions for indicating the ends of lines in text files. UNIX uses the linefeed character alone, while DOS/Windows uses a carriage return/linefeed combination. When **ftp** transfers in ASCII mode between different host environments, the proper character translations take place.

To turn off end-of-line character translation, enter the **cr** command. Enter **cr** again to restore translation. You use the **cr** command if the file's ultimate destination is a DOS or Windows computer.

If you transfer program or data files, you do not want any character translation or format changes to take place. Before getting the file, enter the command **binary** to instruct **ftp** not to convert file contents.

Enter the command **ASCII** to restore ASCII-mode file transfers.

ftp supports a variety of commands that determine how files transfer and display the information. If you want to know what settings currently are in effect, enter the **status** command, as in this example:

```
ftp> status
Connected to ds.internic.net.
Type: ascii; Verbose: On; Bell: Off; Prompting: On
Globbing: On; Debugging: Off; Hash mark printing: Off
ftp>
```

Ending an ftp Session

After you finish your operations on the **ftp** server, you need to close your connection by entering the **close** command:

```
ftp> close
221 Goodbye.
ftp>
```

You can then exit **ftp** by using the command **bye**. Typing **bye** while in session with an **ftp** host both closes the connection and exits **ftp**.

```
ftp> bye
C:\
```

ftp Command Reference

You probably will use **ftp** to obtain files to set up your Internet host or server, and probably will need to become familiar with command-mode **ftp**. You might find the command-mode approach preferable to a graphical one. A graphical **ftp** front-end must transfer entire directory contents to make the file names available for mouse actions. This is unnecessary in command mode, and you can connect to a familiar **ftp** server and retrieve files with a very few commands while a graphical front-end would still be transferring directory lists.

Table 6.2 includes an alphabetical listing of **ftp** commands supported on Windows NT with brief explanations of their functions. Many commands are toggles. Each time these commands are executed they reverse the status of the current function (on-to-off or off-to-on).

TABLE 6.2   FTP COMMANDS

Name	Function
append *local remote*	Appends the contents of the local file *local* to the end of the remote file *remote*.
ASCII	Specifies that file transfers should be performed in 7-bit ASCII text mode. End-of-line characters will be translated as appropriate for the destination host.
binary	Specifies that no translations should be performed when files are transferred between hosts. This mode should be used for data, program, and 8-bit ASCII text files.

continues

TABLE 6.2, CONTINUED

Name	Function
bye	Stops **ftp**. If a host connection is active, the connection is closed first.
case	Toggles conversion of upper- to lowercase characters when using the mget command.
cd *path*	Changes the working directory on the **ftp** server to the directory specified in *path*.
cdup	Changes the working directory on the **ftp** server to the parent of the current working directory.
close	Closes the host connection but leaves **ftp** running.
cr	Toggles the translation of carriage return characters when transferring text files
delete *file*	Deletes the file named *file* from the **ftp** server.
dir	Obtains a detailed directory of files in the working directory on the **ftp** server.
dir *path*	Obtains a detailed directory of files in the working directory specified by *path*.
get *remote local*	Retrieves the file *remote* from the **ftp** server and stores it with the name *local* on the local host. Omit *local* to retain the original file name.
glob	Toggles use of file name expansion.
help ?	Lists the names of available commands.
help *command*	Displays a brief message about *command.*
lcd *path*	Changes the working directory on the local computer.
ls	Lists files in the working directory on the **ftp** server. On a UNIX host accepts UNIX ls options.
mdelete *name*	Deletes all files on the **ftp** server that match *name*, which may include ? and * wild cards.
mget *name*	Retrieves files from the **ftp** server that match *name*, which may include ? and * wild cards.
mkdir *directory*	Creates a subdirectory named *directory* on the **ftp** server.

Name	Function
mput *name*	Copies to the **ftp** server all local files that match *name*, which may include ? and * wild cards.
open *hostname*	Open a connection to the specified hostname, which must be running **ftp** server software to accept the connection.
prompt	Switches prompting on or off during operations on multiple files (wild cards are used). You may find prompting irritating for routine operations such as mput and mget, but may prefer to have prompting active for deleting files with mdelete.
put *local remote*	Copies the local file *local* to the **ftp** host with the name *remote*.
pwd	Prints the working (current) directory on the **ftp** server.
rename *old new*	Renames a file on the **ftp** host from the name *old* to the name *new*.
rmdir *directory*	Removes a directory named *directory* from the **ftp** server.
runique	Toggles unique file mode when receiving files. To ensure that all received files have unique names an extension from .1 through .99 will be appended to each successive file name. One use is to ensure unique file names when copying many files with long names to a system that supports short file names such as the DOS 8.3 format.
status	Shows current session settings.
sunique	Toggles unique file mode when sending files. To ensure that all received files have unique names an extension from .1 through .99 will be appended to each successive file name.
user *username*	Initiates a login to the **ftp** host with the username specified. **ftp** prompts for a password.
verbose	Switches verbose mode on or off. Verbose mode provides information you might not care about, such as file transfer statistics.

Trivial File Transfer Protocol

ftp was designed to provide robust and secure file operations over unreliable networks and uses TCP as a transport protocol to provide reliable delivery. To operate over TCP virtual circuits, **ftp** requires hosts to establish a connection before file operations can commence. Part of **ftp** connection establishment incorporates logins for security.

When the network is reliable, as on a local area network, the overhead of **ftp** might not be desirable. Consequently, a simpler protocol was developed, Trivial File Transfer Protocol (*Tftp*; RFC 1350). **tftp** uses the unreliable UDP protocol as a transport, and does not require establishing a connection or logging on before file transfer requests are possible.

tftp's lack of security makes offering **tftp** services a bit risky for a computer on a public network, because it provides an entrée to the computer that could allow an outsider to gain unsecured access. Therefore, system administrators quite commonly disable **tftp** on publicly available computers. File access available to **tftp** must be carefully secured.

Note	**tftp** is not available in 3.51.

tftp is a small and efficient protocol easily embedded in a computer's boot ROM. Sun UNIX workstations, for example, use **tftp** to download a central operating system image when booting the system on a network.

telnet

Remote terminal access is a critical feature on many computers. One way to provide remote terminal access is through dial-in telecommunications. But when you have a network as widespread and functional as the Internet, does having to dial California to gain access to a computer at Berkeley make much sense? Why not communicate through the Internet? **telnet** is a program that makes possible remote terminal access through a network.

How telnet Works

Figure 6.13 illustrates the architecture of **telnet**, which like **ftp,** is based on client and server processes. A **telnet** server process on the remote host maintains a virtual terminal, an image running entirely in software of a terminal that can interact with the remote host. A user initiates a **telnet** session by running **telnet** client software and logging on to the **telnet** server. The **telnet** server receives keystrokes from the client and applies them to the virtual terminal, which in turn interacts with other processes on the host. The **telnet** server also receives screen display data directed to the virtual terminal and communicates the data to the **telnet** client. To the user, it appears that the terminal session is taking place on the local computer, whereas the remote host has the viewpoint that it is interacting with a local terminal.

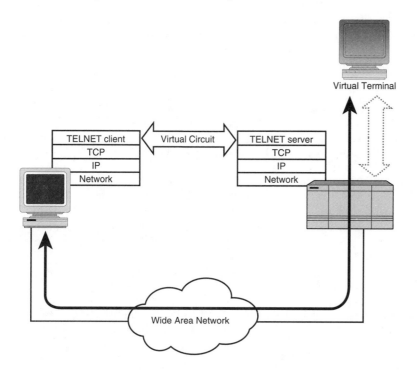

Figure 6.13

telnet operation.

There is nothing terribly fancy about **telnet**. **telnet** is based on emulation of one of several models of text-mode terminals, most commonly the Digital VT220, VT100/VT102, or the VT52. These terminals can perform sophisticated text-based operations, such as displaying menus that permit option selection using arrow keys. But they remain text-based.

Another limitation of **telnet** is that it does not enable the local computer to participate in processing. All processing takes place on the remote **telnet** server, and the local host functions as a "dumb" terminal. Therefore, **telnet** cannot be used as a foundation for sophisticated network operations, such as file sharing. In fact, **telnet** offers no mechanism for file transfer, which must take place under a separate **ftp** session.

Nevertheless, many good reasons promote familiarity with **telnet**. A great many services on the Internet still are available only through **telnet** operation. Even though alternatives exist for other services, **telnet** remains a functional way to access many things on the Internet, including:

◆ **archie.** archie is a database service that catalogs tens of thousands of files on a thousand or so anonymous **ftp** servers. **archie** was developed as a project by McGill University School of Computer Science in Montreal, Canada, and now is widely available as a resource. Several useful documents can be **ftp**'d from archie.ans.net. Look in the directory pub/archie/doc, and start by obtaining the file whatis.archie.

◆ **gopher.** Originally created to provide a database for documents in a distributed computing environment, **gopher** (developed at the University of Minnesota, home of the Golden Gophers) now provides access to a wide variety of files and network services. **ftp** a guide to gopher from boombox.micro.umn.edu and retrieve the file pub/gopher/00README.

◆ **Veronica.** gopher provides a database of files on a local computer. **Veronica** is to **gopher** what **archie** is to **ftp**, providing an index to the contents of the majority of gopher sites. **Veronica**, incidentally, stands for "very easy rodent-oriented net-wide index to computerized archives." You can **ftp** a good introduction to gopher and Veronica from **ftp**.cso.uiuc.edu. Retrieve the file doc/net/uiucnet/vol6no1.txt.

◆ **WAIS.** An Internet tool that enables users to search indexes of cataloged resources. An InterNIC WAIS server is available as a convenient way to find Internet-related documents. To access a WAIS client on the InterNIC server, **telnet** to DS.INTERNIC.NET, and log in with the username `wais`. An online tutorial is available.

You can access **archie**, **gopher**, **Veronica**, and **WAIS** by running local client software. If you do not have the appropriate client installed, however, you can access remote clients using **telnet**. The next section provides an example of using **telnet** to access a remote **archie** client.

Example of a telnet Session

If you need a file, but don't know which **ftp** servers provide it, or even precisely what the file name is, you need **archie**. In this example, telnet is used to locate sources for Netscape, the popular browser for the World Wide Web. Obtain this file as one step in getting Windows NT well-hooked-into the Internet.

The dialog begins by using **telnet** to access an **archie** server. Table 6.4 lists a wide variety of **archie** servers. The one used in this example is archie.rutgers.edu.

The **telnet** that ships with Windows NT, unlike **ftp**, is Windows-based. After starting Windows NT **telnet**, select the **<u>R</u>emote System** option in the **<u>C</u>onnect** menu to enter a host name and initiate a **telnet** connection. This box permits you to specify a terminal type (VT100 or ANSI). It also can be used to access different ports, but the **<u>P</u>ort** setting should be left as **telnet**. Choose **<u>C</u>onnect** to reach out and touch archie.rutgers.edu.

After establishing a connection, a login dialog appears. To access an **archie** client, log in using the username **archie**. Here is the login sequence:

```
login: archie
# Message of the day from the localhost Prospero server:


        Welcome to the Rutgers University Archie Server!
-------------------------------------------------------------------
7/31/95  -  The Rutgers Archie server has been moved to its new home;
            A Sun SPARCserver 20/71!  Please let us know if you
            encounter any problems.

-------------------------------------------------------------------


        Type "help" for information on how to use Archie.

# Bunyip Information Systems, Inc., 1993, 1994, 1995

# Terminal type set to 'vt100 24 80'.
# 'erase' character is '^?'.
# 'search' (type string) has the value 'sub'.
```

Note the terminal type shown. If it differs from the terminal you have configured for **telnet**, you might experience erratic operation. Correct the **telnet** terminal type setting if required.

archie informs you that `'search' has the value 'sub'`, which means that it will conduct a case-insensitive search, reporting any and all files and directories that contain a substring that matches your search parameter. As you can see, substring searches are a good way to find things when you don't know the exact name. First, here is an example of a search for programs containing the string "netscape":

```
archie> prog netscape
# Search type: sub.
# Your queue position: 1
# Estimated time for completion: 5 seconds.
working... =
```

```
Host karanet.edu.uni-klu.ac.at     (143.205.42.57)
Last updated 14:25 26 Aug 1995

    Location: /pub/systems/mac/netscape
        FILE    -rw-r--r-- 1562241 bytes  01:07 31 Mar 1995  netscape-1.1b2.hqx

Host graffiti.univ-lille1.fr    (134.206.1.36)
Last updated 15:37 15 Sep 1995

    Location: /pub/unix/infosys/www/netscape
        FILE    -rw-rw-r-- 982816 bytes  15:00 12 Jan 1995  netscape.i486-
unknown
-linux.B10N.tar.gz

Host ftp.cs.umn.edu    (128.101.227.20)
Last updated 02:11  9 Sep 1995

    Location: /packages/netscape/unix
        FILE    -r--r--r-- 982816 bytes  06:00 17 Dec 1994  netscape.i486-
unknown
-linux.B10N.tar.gz

Host umigw.miami.edu    (129.171.97.1)
Last updated 02:09 20 Sep 1995

    Location: /oscar/.. /appz
        DIRECTORY    drwxr-xr-x    512 bytes  20:21 10 Sep 1995  netscape

Host plaza.aarnet.edu.au    (139.130.23.2)
Last updated 15:23 15 Sep 1995

    Location: /pub/misc
        DIRECTORY    drwxr-xr-x    512 bytes  15:00 14 Oct 1994  netscape

archie> mail dheywood@iquest.net
archie>
```

This listing includes only a representative sample of the locations reported. The
majority of entries are directories, because the NetScape product distribution file
does not contain the text "netscape." However these results are sufficient to give you
some likely **ftp** servers that should have the file you want.

You probably want a record of the search results. You could use **telnet** logging to capture a record of your dialog with **archie**, but a better way is to e-mail yourself the results of the latest search. As in the preceding example, simply enter the command **mail** followed by your Internet mail ID.

If you know that the file for the 32-bit version of Netscape, the version most appropriate for Windows NT and Windows 95, begins with the characters "n32", you can conduct a different search:

```
archie> prog n32
# Search type: sub.
# Your queue position: 1
# Estimated time for completion: 5 seconds.
working... =

Host alfred.ccs.carleton.ca    (134.117.1.1)
Last updated 14:56 19 Sep 1995

    Location: /pub/civeng/viewers
       FILE    -r--r--r-- 1269110 bytes  15:00 16 Jun 1994  win32s.zip

Host ftp.bt.net    (194.72.6.51)
Last updated 14:55  9 Sep 1995

    Location: /pub/computing/information-systems/WWW/Netscapes/netscape1.2b3
       FILE    -r--r--r-- 1339223 bytes  15:30 18 Jul 1995  n3212b3.exe

Host venera.isi.edu    (128.9.0.32)
Last updated 02:51 19 Sep 1995

    Location: /pub/httpd/htdocs/sims/sheila
       FILE    -rw-r--r-- 1198241 bytes  21:49 22 Jun 1995  n32e11n.exe
```

Again, this listing includes only a representative sample of the files reported. Notice that the files win32s.zip and n3212b3.exe both meet the substring search criteria. After completing each search, you can e-mail the results.

After you finish using **archie**, enter the command **bye** to end the session:

```
archie> bye
# Bye.
```

You can learn more about **archie** from the documents on archie.ans.net. Table 6.4 lists some more **archie** servers.

TABLE 6.4   ARCHIE SERVERS

Host Name	Location
archie.au	Australia
archie.univie.ac.at	Austria
archie.mcgill.ca	Canada
archie.funet.fi	Finland
archie.univ-rennesl.fr	France
archie.th-darmstadt.de	Germany
archie.ac.il	Israel
archie.unipi.it	Italy
archie.wide.ad.jp	Japan
archie.hama.nm.kr	Korea
archie.uninett.no	Norway
archie.rediris.es	Spain
archie.luth.se	Sweden
archie.switch.ch	Switzerland
archie.ncu.edu.tw	Taiwan
archie.doc.ic.ac.uk	United Kingdom
archie.unl.edu	USA (Nevada)
archie.internic.net	USA (New Jersey)
archie.rutgers.edu	USA (New Jersey)
archie.ans.net	USA (New York)
archie.sura.net	USA (Maryland)

Simple Mail Transfer Protocol

Electronic mail probably is the single most important application on the Internet. The protocol that supports Internet e-mail is SMTP (RFC 821; RFC 822 defines the message format), which is the protocol used to transfer e-mail messages between different TCP/IP hosts. Although a knowledgeable user quite possbily can communicate directly using the SMTP protocol, doing so is not the standard way of working. Usually, several communication layers are involved.

Architecture of SMTP Mail

Figure 6.14 illustrates the architecture of an SMTP-based mail system. Hosts that support e-mail use a *mail transfer agent (MTU)* to manage the process. The most popular MTU in the UNIX community is **sendmail**. Broadly speaking, the MTU has two responsibilities:

◆ Sending messages to and receiving messages from other mail servers

◆ Providing an interface that enables user applications to access the mail system

The MTU is responsible for providing users with addressable mailboxes. When e-mail is addressed to frodo@bagend.org, bagend.org is the domain name that identifies the host running the MTU. The MTU is responsible for ensuring that messages to frodo arrive in the correct mailbox.

Note Microsoft does not offer a native SMTP-compliant MTU, although you can use an e-mail gateway to exchange e-mail between Microsoft Mail and the Internet.

Endusers interface with the MTU, using one of the many available *user agents (UAs)*. The UA puts a friendly face on the network e-mail, shielding the user from a fairly complicated process. UAs use a mail protocol to communicate with the MTA, such as Post Office Protocol - Version 3 (POP3; RFC 1460).

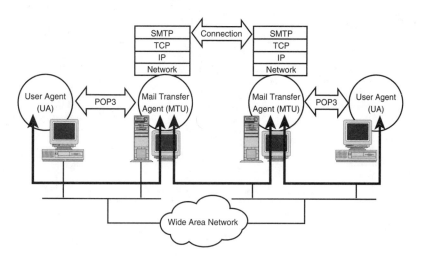

Figure 6.14

Architecture of SMTP-based messaging.

A common UA in the UNIX world is the text-based program named **mail**. In the Windows environment, a popular program is Eudora, available in both shareware and commercial versions for a variety of platforms. But e-mail is so ubiquitous on the Internet that large numbers of Internet applications, such as Web browsers and newsgroup viewers, now provide at least a rudimentary e-mail front end.

Delivering Electronic Mail

Electronic mail systems are not designed to provide real-time message interchange. For that, users can employ tools such as chat programs. Instead, e-mail systems are designed to route large volumes of messages in a reasonable (but not necessarily short) amount of time with as little network overhead as possible. If every mail message were rushed through the Internet via packet switching, the Internet would quickly be bogged down. So e-mail is implemented with the understanding that limited message transit time is permissible if it reduces network loading.

E-mail servers use a store-and-forward method for delivering messages. Figure 6.15 illustrates an example of an e-mail system in which B must forward messages between A and C. B would need to work very hard if it had to route IP datagrams in real time. However, B takes a more relaxed approach. When B receives a message from A, B receives the entire message, storing it on a local hard drive. If B has other priorities, such as receiving other incoming messages, B may wait until things quiet down before forwarding the message to C. B may even be configured to send to C only when several messages are queued or after a time interval has expired. It is more efficient for B to transfer several messages with one connection than to open a connection for every message. These techniques can slow transit time for a message to minutes or hours, but greatly increase overall efficiency.

Figure 6.15

Forwarding electronic mail messages.

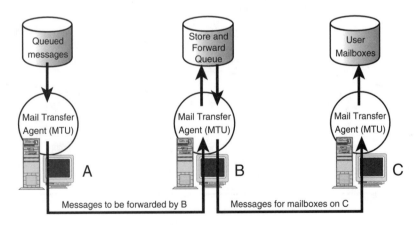

Characteristics of SMTP

SMTP is a fairly old protocol that predates widespread use of graphic terminals. Many of the data types being transported on modern messaging systems were undreamed of in 1982 when RFC 821 was published. Who could have imagined that we would be e-mailing pictures, voice messages, even video clips? In keeping with then-current technology, SMTP was designed to transfer messages consisting of 7-bit ASCII text.

When binary data must be sent through SMTP mail systems, the data must be encoded to a format compatible with 7-bit character transmission. The receiving site then decodes the message to retrieve the binary data. Many user agents now perform these translations automatically for attached binary files.

The most common encoding scheme in the UNIX community is **uuencode** (UNIX-UNIX encode), which has a companion program named **uudecode**. Programs are available to perform uuencodes and uudecodes on DOS, Windows, and Macintosh computers.

The Multipurpose Internet Mail Extensions (MIME; RFC 1521) is an Internet elective protocol that supports transfer of nontext messages via SMTP.

Note	SMTP was developed to handle nonsensitive messages in a fairly close-knit Internet community that operated with a high level of trust. Consequently, SMTP has weak security and does not encrypt messages. A knowledgeable person can readily extract messages from the raw protocol data that travels through the public network. Sensitive data, therefore, should be encrypted before transmission through SMTP mail.

Simple Network Management Protocol

A wide variety of activities can fairly be described as "network management." With regard to SNMP, network management means collecting, analyzing, and reporting data about the performance of network components. Data collected by SNMP include performance statistics and other routine reports, as well as alerts that report potential or existing network problems.

SNMP is one of a family of protocols that comprise the Internet network management strategy:

◆ SNMP is the protocol that enables network management stations to communicate with managed devices.

◆ MIB, the *management information base*, is the database that stores system management information.

◆ SMI, *structure and identification of management information,* describes how each object looks in the MIB.

Before looking at these protocols, you should understand how an SNMP-based network management system is organized.

Organization of SNMP Management

As figure 6.16 illustrates, SNMP is organized around two types of devices:

◆ *Network management stations* serve as central repositories for the collection and analysis of network management data.

◆ *Managed devices* run an *SNMP agent,* which is a background process that monitors the device and communicates with the network management station. Often, devices that cannot support an SNMP agent can be monitored by a *proxy* device that communicates with the network management station.

Information is obtained from managed devices in two ways: polling and interrupts. These methods support different network management goals.

Figure 6.16

Organization of an SNMP-managed network.

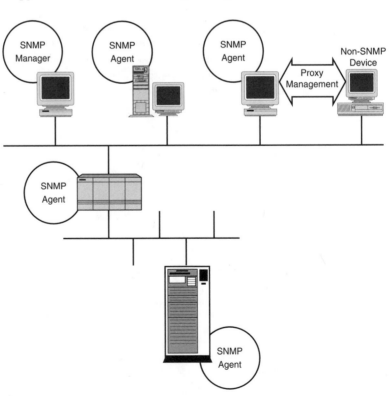

One goal of network management is to maintain a history of network performance that consists of "snapshots" of various characteristics of the network. These snapshots can be used to analyze trends, anticipate future demand, and isolate problems by comparing the current state of the network to prior conditions. The most efficient way to obtain snapshots is to have the management station *poll* managed devices, requesting that they provide the required information. Polling (see fig. 6.17) occurs only at defined intervals, rather than continually, to reduce network traffic. A snapshot of the performance characteristics of a healthy network is called a *baseline*.

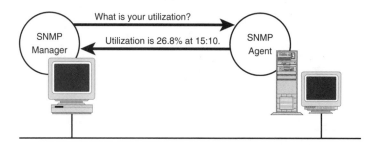

Figure 6.17

Polling an agent for information.

Another goal is to quickly notify managers of sudden changes in the network. When operational conditions for a device alter abruptly, waiting for the next poll from the management station is not timely. Managed devices can be configured to send *alerts* (also called *traps*) under predefined conditions. Network managers define thresholds for specific network performance characteristics. When a threshold is exceeded, the agent on a managed device immediately sends a trap to the management station (see fig. 6.18).

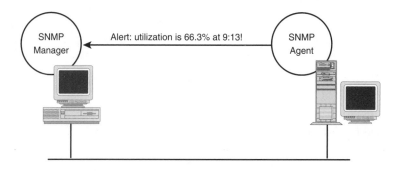

Figure 6.18

Network management agent sending a trap.

Essentially, a network management station and an agent can perform the following tasks:

◆ The network management station can poll agents for network information.

◆ The network management station can update, add, or remove entries in an agent's database. A router's router tables, for example, might be updated from the management console.

◆ The network management station can set thresholds for traps.

◆ The agent on a managed device can send traps to the network management station.

The Management Information Base

A MIB is a set of objects (types of network entities) that are included in the network management database. The MIB specification states the nature of the objects, whereas the SMI describes the appearances of the objects.

Three Internet MIB standards have been associated with SNMP.

◆ **MIB-I (RFC 1156).** This was the first MIB specification, initially published as RFC 1066 in 1988. MIB-I defined eight object groups.

◆ **MIB-II (RFC 1213).** This is the current recommended standard, defining ten object groups and 171 objects.

◆ **RMON-MIB (RFC 1513/1217).** The Remote Monitoring MIB is oriented around monitoring network media rather than network devices.

Additionally, a number of experimental and private (or *enterprises*) MIBs are available. Some enterprises MIBS are provided by vendors to support unique features of their products.

Experimental MIBs are undergoing trial as they are considered as possible extensions to the MIB standards. MIBs that are proven of value during experimentation may be considered for inclusion in the standard MIB-space.

SNMP

Although SNMP (RFC 1157) was designed for the Internet, SNMP is not dependent on the TCP/IP protocols, and can operate above a variety of lower-level protocols such as Novell's IPX/SPX. With TCP/IP, SNMP runs over the UDP datagram protocol to reduce network overhead.

SNMP requests are identified by a *community name*, a 32-character, case-sensitive identification which serves somewhat as a password. SNMP implementations may impose limitations on the characters that can appear in community names. Community names serve to identify SNMP messages but are transmitted as open text and, therefore, are not secure. The three types of community names are as follows:

◆ **Monitor Community.** This community name grants read access to MIBs, and must be included with each MIB query. The default monitor community name is "public."

◆ **Control Community.** This community name grants read and write access to MIBs.

◆ **Trap Community.** This community name must accompany trap messages. An SNMP console rejects trap messages that do not match its configured trap community name. The default trap community name is "public."

SNMP entities operate asynchronously. A device need not wait for responses before it can send another message. A response is generated for any message except a trap, but network management stations and managed devices communicate fairly informally.

The current SNMP standard, version 1, can perform four operations:

◆ **get.** Retrieves a single object from the MIB.

◆ **get-next.** Traverses tables in the MIB.

◆ **set.** Manipulates MIB objects.

◆ **trap.** Reports an alarm.

get, get-next, and set commands originate from the network management station. If a managed device receives the command, a response is generated which is essentially the command message with filled in blanks.

SNMP v1 has several shortcomings, most particularly in the area of security. SNMP names are sent as clear text, which can be observed by anyone who can observe raw network traffic. SNMP v2 (RFC 1441-1452) is a proposed standard that improves security by encrypting messages. SNMP v2 also improves efficiency, for example, by enabling a management console to retrieve an entire table in one request, rather than record-by-record with get-next.

Network Management Stations

Network management is of little value if the management data is not available for report, analysis, and action. Among the available network management console products are the following:

◆ Hewlett-Packard OpenView (DOS, Windows, and UNIX)

◆ Sun Microsystems SunNet Manager (UNIX)

◆ Novell Network Management System (NMS) (Windows)

◆ Synoptics Optivity (Windows)

◆ Cabletron Spectrum (Windows, UNIX)

Functions of the network management station include receiving and responding to traps, maintaining a trap history database, and getting object data from managed devices. More sophisticated—and costly—management consoles provide a graphic interface to the network and can construct a logical picture of the network structure. High-end management consoles generally are costly and require fairly powerful hardware.

The record-keeping capability of a management console is critical. It enables you to record baseline measurements of the network when it operates normally. These baseline measurements can be used to set thresholds for traps, which alert you to changes in network operation. They also provide a point of comparison that you can use to identify causes of network performance problems.

Network File System

Examination of the limitations of **ftp** and **telnet** shows that they leave much to be desired where network computing is concerned. **ftp** can be used to transfer files, and **telnet** can be used to run terminal sessions on a remote computer. But what if you want to run an application on your computer when some or all of the application files are stored on another computer? What if you want, for example, to open a spreadsheet program on your computer and update a spreadsheet on another computer? With **ftp**, you need to transfer the file to your computer for work and back to the original computer when changes were complete. To complicate the matter further, what if the spreadsheet program itself is located on the remote computer? Must you **ftp** all the application files as well? **ftp** just isn't up to the job.

Network File System (NFS) provides the TCP/IP equivalent of Microsoft products' file sharing capability. NFS was developed by Sun Microsystems and is widely licensed to other vendors who have implemented NFS on most platforms.

An NFS server can export a portion of its directory tree for use by NFS clients. Clients can mount the exported directories as if they are part of the clients' native file systems. DOS users, for example, access the exported directory as if it is a drive letter in the local DOS file structure. Figure 6.18 furnishes an example of exporting an NFS directory.

NFS is a sophisticated, reliable protocol that does not use TCP as a transport. For efficiency, NFS operates over UDP. NFS performs any required security, message fragmentation, and error recovery.

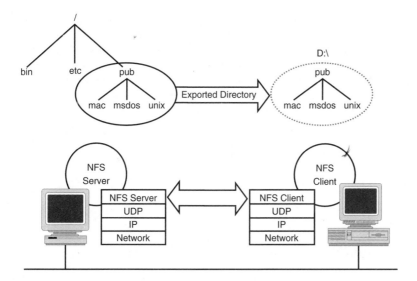

Figure 6.19

Exporting a directory with NFS.

Microsoft does not offer an NFS product for Windows NT, but NFS is available from third-party vendors. Sources of NFS for Windows NT include the following:

◆ Chameleon32NFS from NetManage (408) 973-7171

◆ Connect NFS for NT from Beame & Whiteside (919) 831-8989

Summary

This chapter introduced several processes and applications commonly seen on TCP/IP networks, specifically naming hosts on the Internet and TCP/IP applications. When naming hosts on the Internet users interface with the process/application layer. The naming process puts a friendly face on the network. Remembering the thousands of IP addresses necessary to nagivate the Internet is an insurmountable task. Hence, that is why long ago the Internet community began to use *host names* as a convenient way to identify hosts. As a result, an address such as ds.internic.net is used more frequently that its equivalent 198.49.45.10.

To provide host names requires the operator to program the system so that host names match their IP addresses. Historically, two technologies have been employed on the Internet to accomplish this, namely static naming using hosts files and Domain Name System (DNS).

This chapter also examined several common TCP/IP applications. Some, like ftp and telnet, are tools that end users frequently access. Others, although not often seen by users, are mainstays of TCP/IP networking. Specifically, this section examined applications such as File Transfer Protocol (ftp), Trivial File Transfer Protocol (tftp), telnet, Simple Mail Transport Protocol (SMTP), Simple Network Management Protocol (SNMP), and Network File System (NFS). All of these functions are important in recognizing the role TCP/IP plays as it transfers information through the process/application layer.

Part II

Implementing NetWare TCP/IP

Chapter 7 Snapshot

This chapter links TCP/IP to Microsoft networking products. It covers the following topics:

◆ Microsoft network protocols

◆ Dynamic Host Configuration Protocol (DHCP)

◆ Windows Internet Name Service (WINS)

◆ Windows NT routing

◆ SNMP

Introducing Microsoft TCP/IP

The preceding chapters provide a fairly thorough introduction to the technologies and protocols in the TCP/IP protocol suite. This chapter begins by putting TCP/IP to work with Microsoft networking products. Microsoft has long included TCP/IP in its network-ready operating systems, beginning with the LAN Manager server product, be-cause the native Microsoft network protocol NetBEUI cannot function on a routed network. TCP/IP was included to support networks that required routing, and to provide compatibility with other vendors' networks.

Discussion focuses on Windows NT, because NT serves as the backbone technology for any extensive Microsoft TCP/IP network. Yes, Windows 3.1 and Windows 95 can function in a TCP/IP network, but you need at least one Windows NT computer if you want to provide services, such as automatic IP address assignment, or a Windows naming service. Also, the most robust Microsoft networks are based on Windows NT Server, which provides central file and security services.

These chapters assume that you are reasonably comfortable with Windows, and particularly with Windows NT. You are shown all the steps for accomplishing a procedure, but not all the operations of Windows management. If you need more information about Windows NT Workstation or Server, please consult the author's book, *Inside Windows NT Server*, published by New Riders. New Riders also offers thorough books on Windows 3.1x and Windows 95: *Inside Windows 3.11* and *Inside Windows 95*.

Microsoft Network Protocols

Current Microsoft operating systems support three network transport protocols: NetBIOS Frame protocol (NBF), NWLink, and TCP/IP. (A fourth standard protocol not discussed in this book, DLC, supports network-attached printers.) These protocols are integrated using two technologies: the *Network Driver Interface Specification (NDIS)* and the *Transport Driver Interface (TDI)*. Before launching into the network protocols, the next section examines the overall architecture of Microsoft protocol stacks, including NDIS and TDI.

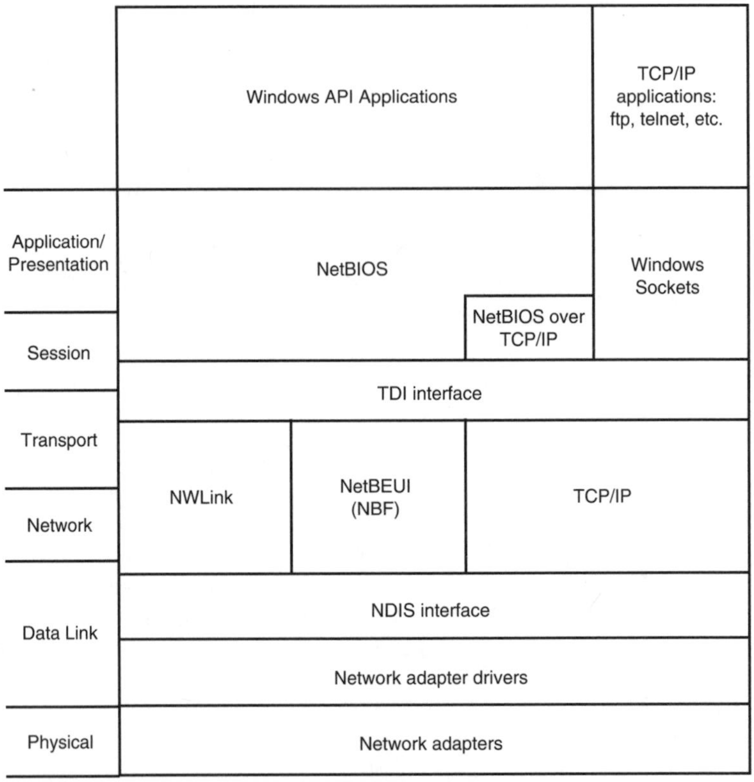

Figure 7.1

The Microsoft Network Protocol Architecture.

The Microsoft Network Protocol Architecture

As shown in figure 7.1, NDIS and TDI act as the unifying layers that enable Microsoft workstations to support multiple protocol stacks over a single network interface.

At the lowest levels of the protocol model are network interface adapters and the driver software that enables them to connect with upper layers. NDIS, developed jointly by Microsoft and 3Com, is a standard interface between MAC layer protocols and the network layer. At the MAC layer, NDIS provides a well-defined interface that enables vendors to write drivers for their network interface products. NDIS also provides a standard protocol layer that upper-layer protocols can use, enabling multiple NDIS-compliant network layer protocols to interface with any NDIS-compliant network adapter. Windows NT 3.5x supports drivers written to NDIS version 3.0.

NDIS enables a computer to support multiple network adapters, which might be of the same or mixed types. These adapters communicate with the same upper-layer protocol stacks, mediated by the NDIS interface. This arrangement could permit a computer to access the following environments through a single network adapter: a Windows 3.1 workgroup using NBF, a Novell NetWare 3.12 server using NWLink, and a UNIX host using TCP/IP.

The Transport Driver Interface defines a protocol interface between session layer protocols and the transport layer. Transport protocols, therefore, can be written to standard interfaces both above (TDI) and below (NDIS) in the protocol stack.

Above the TDI, Microsoft provides support for two application programming interfaces (APIs). NetBIOS is the historic API for Microsoft network products. The majority of network-ready programs written for the Microsoft environment are written to the NetBIOS interface.

On the other hand, the standard API for TCP/IP applications is Berkeley sockets, which Microsoft has implemented as Windows sockets. For environments that choose to implement TCP/IP without NetBEUI, and to support the nonroutable NetBIOS protocol over internetworks, Microsoft has provided a NetBIOS over TCP/IP feature (NBT) that enables NetBIOS applications to access the TCP/IP transport.

NetBIOS Frame Protocol

Starting with MS-Net in the mid-1980s, Microsoft's traditional networking protocol has been NetBEUI, an efficient protocol that functions well in local networks. Although still often called NetBEUI, the protocol was updated for Windows NT and is now more properly called the *NetBEUI Frame protocol (NBF)*. NBF is compatible with the earlier NetBEUI implementations found in LAN Manager and Windows 3.*x*.

NBF provides two service modes (reliable connectionless mode is unavailable):

◆ Unreliable connectionless communication (datagram)

◆ Reliable connection-oriented communication (virtual circuit)

Connection-oriented communication is used in many situations on peer-to-peer networks. When a station uses a shared directory, the NET USE command initiates a dialog that establishes a connection between the two computers.

NBF depends heavily on broadcast messages, however, to advertise network names. When a NetBIOS computer enters a network, it broadcasts a message announcing its name to ensure that no other computer on the network already has the same name. This essential NetBIOS mechanism fails in internetworks because broadcasts do not cross routers. Ordinarily, therefore, NBF is restricted to nonrouted networks.

NWLink

NWLink is a Microsoft implementation of the two protocols that are the standard transport on NetWare networks: IPX and SPX. Beginning with Windows NT 3.5, NWLink became the standard Microsoft transport protocol, replacing NetBEUI, now optional. Then, starting with version 3.51, NT's default network protocol became TCP/IP.

Internetwork Packet Exchange (IPX) is a datagram network layer protocol that serves as the primary workhorse on NetWare LANs. The majority of NetWare services operate over IPX. *Sequenced Packet Exchange (SPX)* is an optional transport-layer protocol that provides connection-oriented, reliable message delivery.

IPX is a routable protocol, and NWLink can be used to construct routed networks using Microsoft products. The network/hardware address mechanism differs significantly from the mechanism used for IP.

Usually, nodes on IPX networks utilize their burned-in hardware addresses as network addresses, ordinarily 48-bit addresses. For networks based on standards that maintain a centralized address registration process, such as the IEEE 802 names described in Chapter 3, "The Network Access Layer," this approach guarantees unique hardware addresses throughout any conceivable internetwork without the need for manually configuring host IDs.

Network logical addresses are maintained as part of the server configuration. Each server connection must be configured using a 32-bit network address shared by all computers using a given protocol on that cabling segment. Stations that insert themselves on a network segment undergo a "get nearest server" dialog that, among other things, determines the network address of the local cabling segment. As a result, the network address must be specified at relatively few points, limited to the servers that connect directly to the network. All other nodes can discover the network address locally or through routing protocols. Novell provides a network address registry service that enables organizations to obtain a unique IPX network number for use on a public data network. Figure 7.2 illustrates the IPX addressing scheme.

IPX uses sockets (similar to TCP/UDP ports) to direct messages to and from the correct upper-layer processes. In most cases, upper-layer functions are performed by the *NetWare Core Protocols (NCP)*, which provide network services at the session, presentation, and application layers. NCP is not part of NWLink, although Microsoft has implemented a NetWare client requester that implements the client side of NCP.

The IPX/SPX protocols offer high performance and—because node IDs need not be maintained manually—great ease of administration. Use of IPX/SPX, however, has been confined primarily to the NetWare environment. In part, this has resulted from the proprietary nature of the protocols. Novell maintains control of the protocols and IPX/SPX are not as accessible for public input or extension. Many network planners have developed a strong distaste for anything proprietary.

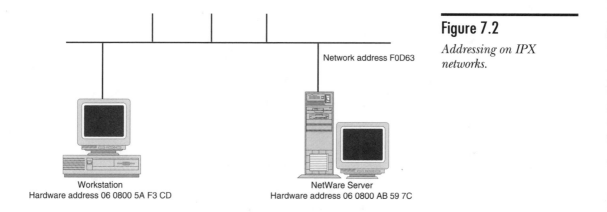

Network address F0D63

Workstation
Hardware address 06 0800 5A F3 CD

NetWare Server
Hardware address 06 0800 AB 59 7C

Figure 7.2

Addressing on IPX networks.

The primary reason, however, probably is the Internet, which functions quite well with TCP/IP. Although cracks have appeared, most notably the limitations on IPv4 address space, mechanisms are in place to enable TCP/IP to evolve on the Internet, and there has been no need to replace the Internet protocols. Now that the Internet is evolving into the fabled Information Superhighway, everyone needs TCP/IP connectivity and the Internet protocols seem to be here to stay.

Novell and AT&T are working to establish an Internet-like wide area network based on the IPX/SPX protocols. Success of this commercial venture might expand the influence of IPX/SPX, but is unlikely to put a dent in the TCP/IP marketplace.

TCP/IP

Microsoft has been including TCP/IP support in network products since LAN Manager. TCP/IP was Microsoft's choice as a routable protocol for use when the nonroutable NetBEUI was not functional. TCP/IP is available on Windows NT and on Windows 3.x and Windows 95 clients.

Table 7.1 summarizes the RFCs that Microsoft NT TCP/IP supports. Many are recognized from discussion in the foregoing chapters.

TABLE 7.1   RFCs SUPPORTED BY MICROSOFT NT TCP/IP

RFC	Title
768	User Datagram Protocol (UDP)
783	Trivial File Transfer Protocol revision 2 (TFTP)
791	Internet Protocol (IP)
792	Internet Control Message Protocol (ICMP)
793	Transmission Control Protocol (TCP)
826	Ethernet Address Resolution Protocol (ARP)
854	Telnet Protocol (TELNET)
862	Echo Protocol (ECHO)
863	Discard Protocol (DISCARD)
864	Character Generator Protocol (CHARGEN)
865	Quote of the Day Protocol (QUOTE)
867	Daytime Protocol (DAYTIME)
894	Transmission of IP Datagrams over Ethernet
919	Broadcasting Internet Datagrams
922	Broadcasting Internet Datagrams in the Presence of Subnets
959	File Transfer Protocol (FTP)
1001, 1002	NetBIOS Service on a TCP/UDP Transport: Concepts, Methods, and Specifications
1034, 1035	Domain Name System
1042	Transmission of IP Datagrams over IEEE 802 Networks (SNAP)
1055	Transmission of IP Datagrams over Serial Lines: SLIP
1112	Host Extensions for IP Multicasting

RFC	Title
1122	Requirements for Internet Host Communication Layers
1123	Requirements for Internet Host Application and Support
1134	Point-to-Point Protocol (PPP)
1144	Compressing TCP/IP Headers for Low-Speed Serial Links
1157	Simple Network Management Protocol (SNMP)
1179	Line Printer Daemon Protocol
1188	Transmission of IP Datagrams over FDDI
1191	Path MDU Discovery
1201	Transmitting IP Traffic over ARCNET Networks
1231	IEEE 802.5 Token Ring MIB
1332	PPP Internet Protocol Control Protocol (IPCP)
1334	PPP Authentication Protocols
1533	DHCP Options and BOOTP Vendor Extensions
1534	Interoperation between DHCP and BOOTP
1541	Dynamic Host Configuration Protocol (DHCP)
1542	Clarifications and Extensions for the Bootstrap Protocol (BOOTP)
1547	Requirements for an Internet Standard Point-to-Point Protocol (PPP)
1548	Point-to-Point Protocol (PPP)
1549	PPP in High-Level Data Link Control (HDLC) Framing
1552	PPP Internetwork Packet Exchange Control Protocol (IPXCP)
1553	Compressing IPX Headers over WAN Media
1570	PPP Link Control Protocol (LCP) Extensions
Draft	NetBIOS Frame Control Protocol (NBFCP)
Draft	PPP over ISDN
Draft	PPP over X.25
Draft	Compression Control Protocol

As implemented, Microsoft NT offers a solid implementation of the majority of core Internet protocols. Some notable omissions include the following:

◆ **Native support for SMTP.** Windows NT does not include an SMTP message transfer unit similar to the UNIX **sendmail** MTU.

◆ **Dynamic routing.** The only routing support included with Windows NT is based on static routing tables and the **route** utility.

◆ **Network File Service (NFS).** Although not an Internet standard, NFS is used extensively in the TCP/IP networking community. NFS is available as an option from third-party vendors.

The remainder of this chapter examines some Microsoft TCP/IP features in greater detail.

Dynamic Host Configuration Protocol (DHCP)

Chapter 4, "The Internet Layer," takes a close look at IP addressing. Clearly, maintaining IP addresses in a changing network can pose a significant challenge. Doing so is one problem DHCP can help correct.

Very few hosts require fixed IP addresses. Routers and DNA servers are examples of hosts to which you should assign fixed IP addresses, because those addresses frequently are entered into the configurations of hosts. But the garden variety host does not require a fixed IP address and can be assigned any valid IP address from the network address space.

DHCP renders unnecessary assigning fixed IP addresses to the majority of hosts. DHCP enables administrators to specify groups of IP addresses, called *scopes*. When a host is configured to obtain its IP address from DHCP, it is automatically assigned an address from a DHCP scope.

DHCP even permits a network to support more hosts than the number of available addresses. If users require only infrequent TCP/IP protocol support, they can lease an IP address when they need it. When the host no longer needs use of the address, the address is returned to the address pool.

DHCP also enables administrators to specify numerous parameters that tune the operation of IP, TCP, and other protocols. Because DHCP is managed centrally, administrators can manage many characteristics of the hosts for which they are responsible without having to physically visit the hosts.

Chapter 10, "Managing DHCP," includes an examination of the details of DHCP.

Windows Internet Name Service (WINS)

Chapter 6, "The Process/Application Layer," explores naming services in general and DNS in particular. Clearly, a naming service makes it considerably easier for users to access network services. In the Microsoft TCP/IP environment, the standard naming service is WINS.

Microsoft networks traditionally have used a naming system based on NetBIOS, and Microsoft TCP/IP networks can continue to use NetBIOS names, as long as routers are not involved. On the other hand, NetBIOS does not maintain a central database of names. Instead, a computer seeking to enter the network attempts to register it by broadcasting messages on the network. If no computer challenges the name, the computer establishes itself on the network and announces itself. This mechanism works on a local network, but fails on an internetwork because broadcast messages do not cross routers.

WINS provides a way to integrate NetBIOS with TCP/IP. Under WINS, NetBIOS computer configurations continue to specify names. No central management is required (or, if you prefer, available).

NetBIOS over TCP/IP provides a way to disseminate NetBIOS names throughout an internetwork. A WINS server must be supported on each network segment that requires NetBIOS name support. The WINS servers exchange information via directed host-to-host messages rather than broadcasts, enabling NetBIOS names to cross routers and be advertised on other network segments.

WINS is a Microsoft-only technology and cannot, unfortunately, work in conjunction with DNS. Therefore, a company cannot put itself on the Internet and use WINS to manage its local domain name space. To advertise host names on the Internet, a DNS name server still is required.

Therefore, WINS is only one of several name services supported. Others include the following:

◆ **LMHOSTS.** A static file-based naming convention that was used with LAN Manager. LMHOSTS files are still supported on WINS networks.

◆ **hosts.** A static file-based naming convention for TCP/IP networks.

◆ **DNS.** The dynamic naming service used on the Internet. A Windows NT implementation of the DNS program **bind** is included with the *Windows NT Resource Kit.*

WINS and LMHOSTS are discussed in Chapter 11, "Managing WINS." DNS receives further coverage in Chapter 12, "Managing DNS."

Windows NT Routing

In TCP/IP terminology, hosts equipped with two or more network adapters on different network segments are called *multihomed* hosts. Any multihomed Windows NT computer can provide IP routing.

Routing is configured using static tables, which you manage by using the **route** utility. This approach offers the benefits of being efficient, producing little or no network overhead traffic. Networks of substantial scope can be routed using static tables.

Chapter 9, "Building Routed Networks," includes a discussion of Windows NT routing.

SNMP

Windows NT supports SNMP, including MIB II, as well as MIBs for LAN Manager, DHCP, and WINS. Chapter 14, "Managing Microsoft TCP/IP," includes a discussion of SNMP.

Summary

Chapter 7 focused on understanding the various protocols and technologies that exist in the TCP/IP protocol sequence. Topics that were discussed include the Microsoft Network Protocols, which include the Microsoft network protocol architecture, the NETBIOS frame protocol, and NW Link.

The chapter also focused on several dynamic host configuration protocols, such as the Windows Internet Name Service and Windows NT Routing.

Chapter 8 Snapshot

This chapter examines the basics of installing and configuring TCP/IP on Windows NT computers, including some troubleshooting procedures. It covers the following topics:

- ◆ Planning the installation

- ◆ Installing networking on a computer for the first time

- ◆ Installing and reconfiguring the TCP/IP protocols on a networked computer

- ◆ Testing the TCP/IP configuration

Installing TCP/IP on Windows NT Computers

I f you have installed Windows NT, you already appreciate the general simplicity of the Windows NT installation process. That simplicity carries over to the procedures for installing TCP/IP. All procedures are performed from the graphic interface using the Network utility in the Control Panel.

This chapter examines the basics of installing and configuring TCP/IP on Windows NT computers, including some troubleshooting procedures. After this chapter covers the fundamentals, subsequent chapters examine more advanced topics, including implementing DHCP, WINS, internetworking, DNS, and SNMP.

Discussion assumes familiarity with Windows NT operations and does not delve into procedures that don't relate directly to TCP/IP.

Planning the Installation

Before you install TCP/IP, you must obtain information that defines the computer's TCP/IP configuration. The following list delineates the items you need to determine before you begin installing:

◆ If network adapter drivers must be installed or configured, you must determine for each card in the computer the manufacturer and model, as well as the card's settings, such as IRQ, DMA, and I/O memory address.

◆ Whether the machine obtains its IP address from its own configuration or from DHCP (discussed in Chapter 10). This chapter assumes manual addressing.

◆ With manual addressing, you must know the IP address to be assigned for each network adapter that supports TCP/IP.

◆ Addresses of any default IP gateways the computer uses. This chapter assumes a single network without routing.

◆ How the computer obtains NetBIOS host names. This chapter assumes NetBIOS names are automatically supported on local segments. NetBIOS names for routed segments can come from WINS or from LMHOSTS files, both of which are discussed in Chapter 11.

◆ Whether the computer obtains TCP/IP host names from DNS. See Chapter 12 for more information about running a domain name service. This chapter assumes DNS naming is not active.

◆ SNMP community names, traps, and IP addresses of SNMP management hosts (see Chapter 14).

On a basic, single segment network, the only essential information is the IP address and subnet mask to be assigned to the computer.

All the required files are included on the Windows NT Workstation and Windows NT Server distribution disks or CD-ROM. You need to have the appropriate disks on hand.

Installing Networking on a Computer for the First Time

If the system on which you work already operates on a network, you do not need to install network adapter drivers. Please proceed to the section "Installing and Reconfiguring the TCP/IP Protocols on a Networked Computer."

If this is a first-time installation, however, you need to install the adapter hardware and software. After you install the network adapter card, record its settings. Also, if you add the computer to a Windows NT Server domain, you need to create the appropriate computer and user accounts in the domain before login attempts can be successful. Consult *Inside Windows NT Server* for detailed information about setting up computer and user accounts.

TCP/IP installation and configuration is performed by using the Network utility, which is one of the tools in the Control Panel. This section walks you through the procedures for installing TCP/IP for the first time on a Windows NT computer.

1. Check the computer name on the computer. The computer name was specified during installation and is visible in the login dialog box. All Microsoft networks rely on NetBIOS names to identify computers, and each computer must be assigned a unique NetBIOS name. After network drivers and protocols are installed on the computer, Setup attempts to enter the network. If it discovers that another computer on the network is already using the NetBIOS name or the IP address you have specified, the new computer is not permitted on the network.

    You are presented with an opportunity to change the computer name in Step 12.

2. Open the Network utility by double-clicking on the Network icon in the Control Panel (see fig. 8.1).

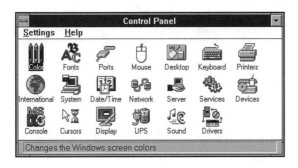

Figure 8.1

The Network icon in the Control Panel.

3. If networking has never been installed on the computer, you see a prompt like the one shown in figure 8.2. Select **Yes**. You are prompted for the location of the installation files. Specify the path to your CD-ROM or floppy installation disks. The network files are copied.

Figure 8.2

Installing networking for the first time.

4. The next dialog box (see fig. 8.3) enables you to specify that NT detect your network adapter card. Automatic detection is generally pretty reliable, and you normally should select **Continue**. The result in the demonstration computer appears in the **Network Adapter Card Detection** dialog box (see fig. 8.4).

Figure 8.3

Initiating automatic network adapter detection.

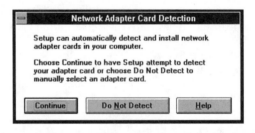

Figure 8.4

Results of detecting a network adapter.

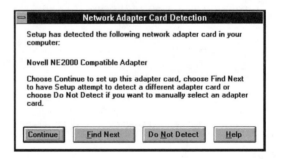

This box offers the option of detecting additional cards. If this computer has more than one network adapter, choose **Find Next**. After all cards are detected, choose **Continue**.

This function will find only one of many cards. To install multiple cards, they must be added when the network portion of the install is shown.

5. After the network adapter drivers are installed, you must specify the network card setup parameters in a dialog box similar to that shown in figure 8.5. Choose **Continue** when the settings are correct.

6. You might see a **Setup Message** box that contains the message The current netcard parameters are not verifiably correct and may result in usage problems or system failure. Use them anyway? Verify that the settings you entered match the settings for the card and that the settings do not conflict with other hardware. Then choose **OK** to continue.

7. Next, Setup presents the dialog box shown in figure 8.6. Check the protocols you intend to install. If you want your network to run TCP/IP alone, check only the **TCP/IP Transport** box. The **NWLink** and **NetBEUI** boxes are optional. After you select protocols, choose **Continue**.

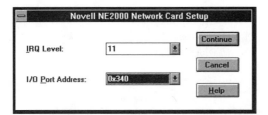

Figure 8.5

Entering network adapter settings.

Figure 8.6

Selecting network protocols.

8. The **Windows NT TCP/IP Installation Options** dialog box appears next (see fig. 8.7). If this example had been performed on a Windows NT Server computer, the box would show additional options for installing DHCP and WINS.

   Only the basic **Connectivity Utilities** are installed in this example. These utilities include a **telnet** client and some other TCP/IP utilities. Other options are demonstrated in other chapters. Choose **Continue** after checking the desired options. Several message boxes appear during installation and configuration of the software.

9. Next, the **Network Settings** dialog box appears (see fig. 8.8). You will become very familiar with this dialog box, for it is the focal point for installing and reconfiguring network adapters and protocols on Windows NT. If you scroll the **Installed Network Software** list, you see, among the entries, drivers for your network adapter and the TCP/IP protocol.

Figure 8.7

Selecting TCP/IP options.

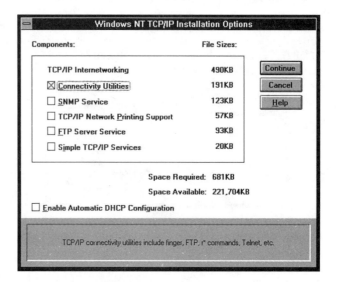

10. You may choose to manually add adapters or protocols in this screen, but for a basic installation, click on **OK** to continue. Next, the **TCP/IP Configuration** dialog box appears (see fig. 8.9).

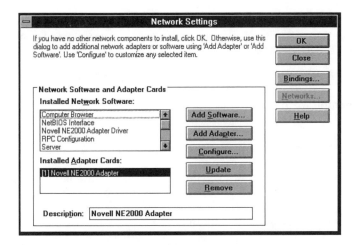

Figure 8.8

The Network Settings dialog box.

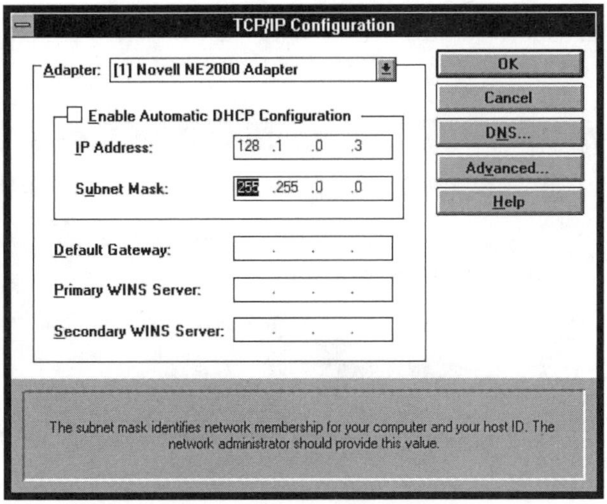

Figure 8.9

Configuring a host IP address.

11. Only two settings are required. Other optional settings (such as the default gateway and WINS server addresses) are examined in later chapters.

Fill in the **IP Address**, typing a decimal (period) if required to skip to the next field. The example is 128.1.0.3.

After you enter the IP address, the **Subnet Mask** fields are automatically filled in with the default mask for the corresponding address class. If subnet masking is employed, edit the **Subnet Mask** fields as required.

No other fields currently require attention. Choose **OK** to continue.

12. Setup now attempts to open a network connection and announce the computer on the network. This process can fail for several reasons, including the following:

    ◆ An incorrect driver or driver parameter for the network card. In this case, installation fails and you must reenter the network utility and reconfigure the adapter manually.

    ◆ The computer does not have a unique NetBIOS name.

    ◆ The computer does not have a unique IP address.

    If the NetBIOS name or IP address already in use fails, you are returned to the **Network Settings** box, which now resembles figure 8.10.

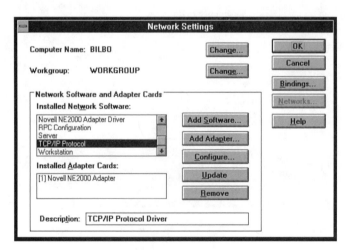

Figure 8.10

Changing network settings.

To change the computer name, click on the **Computer Name Change** button and enter the new name in the **Computer Name** dialog box that appears.

To change the IP address, select **TCP/IP Protocol** in the **Installed Network Software** scroll box. Then click on **Configure** to open a **TCP/IP Configuration** dialog box, in which you can change the IP address and other TCP/IP settings.

13. After the computer successfully enters the network, the **Domain/Workgroup Settings** dialog box appears (see fig. 8.11).

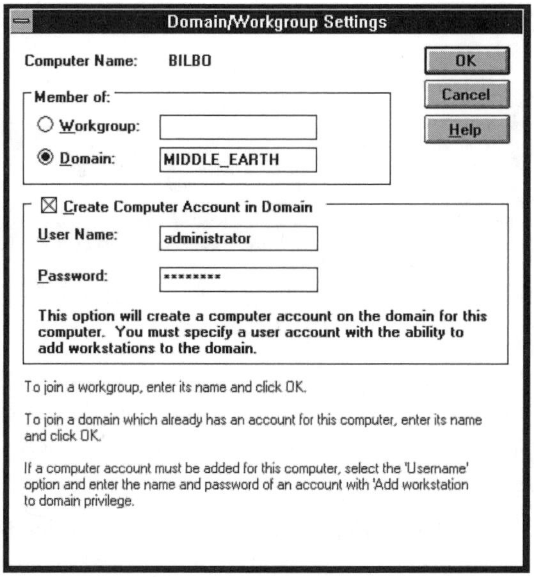

Figure 8.11

Changing domain/ workgroup settings.

If the computer participates in a peer-to-peer workgroup, click on the **Workgroup** button and enter the workgroup name.

If this computer participates in a Windows NT Server domain, click on the **Domain** button and enter the domain name. If a computer account for this computer has already been created in the domain, choose **OK**. If you must create a domain account, you can do so now by checking **Create Computer Account in Domain** and specifying a domain administrator account in the **User Name** and **Password** fields.

Choose **OK** after you specify the workgroup or domain settings. If you check **Domain**, Setup attempts to enter the domain and create a computer account if necessary. If Setup cannot locate the domain, you receive the message The domain controller for this domain cannot be located. You can enter a new domain name or configure the computer using the **Workgroup** option and add it to the domain in the future.

14. You are prompted to restart the computer, which activates the network connection.

Installing and Reconfiguring the TCP/IP Protocols on a Networked Computer

The same general procedure is used to add TCP/IP to an already-networked computer, to reconfigure TCP/IP, and to add TCP/IP options.

If the computer already functions on a network, you do not need to reinstall the network adapter drivers. You need only add TCP/IP to the network adapter configuration. This procedure is demonstrated on a computer running Windows NT Server, currently configured with the NetBEUI protocol.

1. Double-click on the Network icon in the Control Panel to open the **Network Settings** dialog box (see fig. 8.12). In the figure, the NetBEUI Protocol is listed in the **Installed Network Software** scroll box.

Figure 8.12

A computer on which NetBEUI is installed.

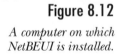

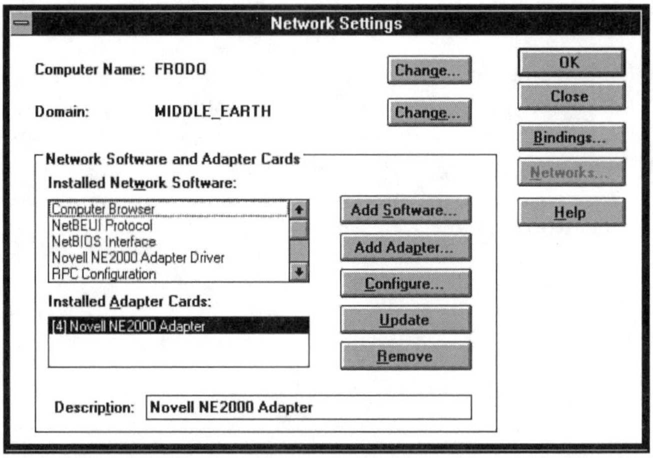

2. NetBEUI and NWLink are not required to run TCP/IP. If these protocols are installed but no longer supported on the network, you can remove them from the computer. To remove a protocol, select the protocol in the **Installed Network Software** list and click on **Remove**. You are asked to confirm your decision to remove the software.

3. To add TCP/IP, choose **Add Software** to open the **Add Network Software** dialog box (see fig. 8.13). Click on the arrow to pull down the **Network Software** list, and scroll the list until you can select **TCP/IP Protocol and related components**. Then choose **Continue**.

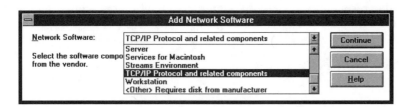

Figure 8.13

Selecting network software to add.

4. Next, the **Windows NT TCP/IP Installation Options** dialog box appears, as shown in figure 8.14. This computer runs Windows NT Server, and offers two options not seen in the earlier example using Windows NT Workstation: **DHCP Server Service** and **WINS Server Service**. The only option needed for a basic installation is **Connectivity Utilities**.

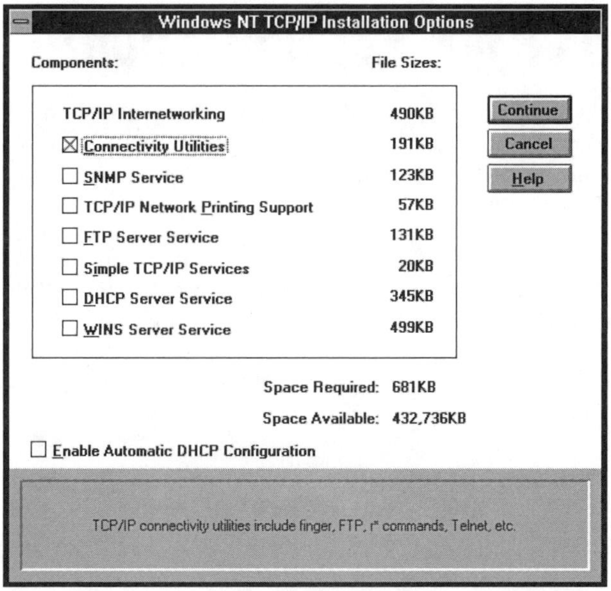

Figure 8.14

Selection TCP/IP options for Windows NT Server.

After you specify the desired options, choose **Continue** to return to the **Network Settings** dialog box, and **TCP/IP Protocol** has been added to the **Installed Network Software** box. Before you return, required files are copied from the installation disks, and you need to supply the appropriate disk and specify a drive path.

5. You still have not supplied any TCP/IP configuration parameters, such as the IP address. If you choose **OK** in the **Network Settings** dialog box, the **TCP/IP Configuration** dialog box appears (refer to figure 8.9), in which you must enter at least an IP address and a subnet mask.

   If you need to reconfigure any TCP/IP setting, start the Network utility. Then bring up the **TCP/IP Configuration** dialog box by selecting **TCP/IP Protocol** in the **Installed Network Software** box and then choosing **Configure**.

6. Choose **OK** in the **Network Settings** dialog box to exit the Network utility.

Note

Repeat the preceding steps when you need to install additional TCP/IP components. When you reach the **TCP/IP Options** dialog box, check the components you want to add and continue the installation. Only new software is added.

Return to the **TCP/IP Configuration** dialog box whenever you need to reconfigure TCP/IP settings.

Testing the TCP/IP Configuration

Installing the TCP/IP connectivity utilities adds several useful troubleshooting tools to the computer. Some, such as **arp**, **hostname**, and **finger**, are best discussed in Chapter 12, which examines DNS. Chapter 6, "The Process/Application Layer," sufficiently examines **ftp** and **telnet.**

Two of the utilities, **ping** and **ipconfig,** are useful for checking out the network connections of TCP/IP hosts. They are illustrated in the context of the simple network shown in figure 8.15, consisting of two hosts with IP addresses 128.1.0.1 and 128.1.0.2.

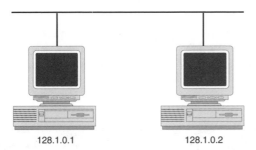

Figure 8.15

Example of a TCP/IP network.

128.1.0.1   128.1.0.2

Using ping

ping is used to verify connections between hosts by sending ICMP echo packets to the specified IP address. **ping** waits up to one second for each packet it sends and reports the numbers of packets sent and received. By default, **ping** sends four echo packets that consist of 32 bytes of data. (The Microsoft documentation indicates that **ping** defaults to 64-byte packets, but the example seems to indicate an actual size of 32 bytes.)

Figure 8.16 illustrates the results of successfully and unsuccessfully pinging a host. When a host does respond, **ping** displays the message Request timed out.

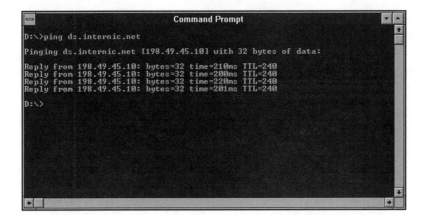

Figure 8.16

Pinging an existent and nonexistent IP address.

During Chapter 4's examination of IP addresses, you encountered a special address, called the *loopback address*, which refers to any valid address that has a netid of 127. The network adapter reflects back any packet sent to the loopback address without letting it enter the network. Pinging the loopback address tests the configuration of the local TCP/IP interface. Figure 8.17 shows an example of pinging the loopback address.

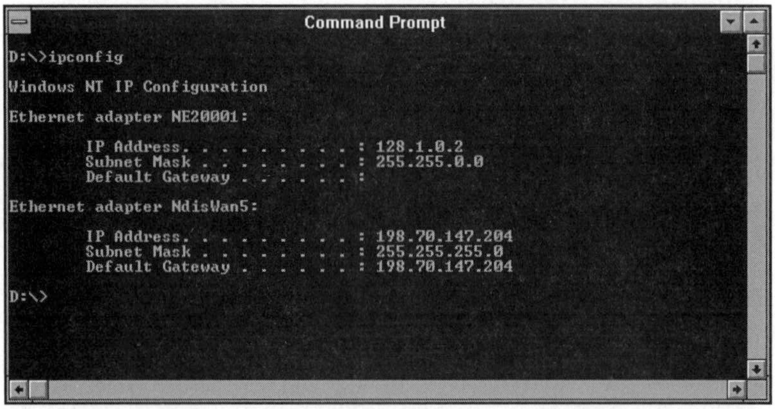

Figure 8.17

Pinging the loopback address.

```
                              Command Prompt
D:\>ipconfig

Windows NT IP Configuration

Ethernet adapter NE20001:

        IP Address. . . . . . . . . : 128.1.0.2
        Subnet Mask . . . . . . . . : 255.255.0.0
        Default Gateway . . . . . . :

Ethernet adapter NdisWan5:

        IP Address. . . . . . . . . : 198.70.147.204
        Subnet Mask . . . . . . . . : 255.255.255.0
        Default Gateway . . . . . . : 198.70.147.204

D:\>
```

When you add a TCP/IP computer to the network, using **ping** to test it is a good idea.

1. First, ping the loopback address.

2. Then, ping the host's own IP address.

3. Finally, ping other hosts on the network, particularly servers to which the host will connect.

ping can accept IP addresses or DNS host names. Figure 8.18 furnishes an example of pinging a host name. If you can ping a host by its IP address but not by its host name, a name resolution problem exists. **ping** does not recognize NetBIOS host names, however.

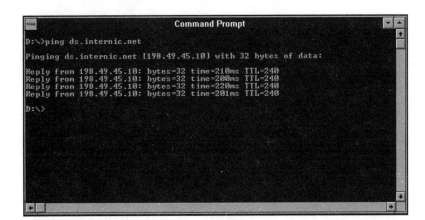

Figure 8.18

Pinging a host name.

Table 8.1 lists options that can be used with **ping**. The syntax of the **ping** command is as follows (where square brackets enclose optional parameters):

```
ping [-a][-f][-i ttl][-j host-list][-k host-list][-l length][-n count][-r count]
     [-s count] [-t][-v tos][-w timeout] hosts
```

TABLE 8.1   PING OPTIONS

Option	Function
hosts	Specifies one or more hosts to ping.
-a	Addresses should be resolved to hostnames.
-f	Sets the Do Not Fragment flag in the packet so that it will not be fragmented by routers on an internet.
-i ttl	Sets the Time to Live field to the value *ttl*.
-j host-list	Specifies a list of hosts through which the packet is to be routed. Hosts may be separated by routers. The maximum number of hosts is 9.
-k host-list	Specifies a list of hosts through which the packet is to be routed. Hosts *may not* be separated by routers. The maximum number of hosts is 9.

continues

TABLE 8.1, CONTINUED

Option	Function
-l *length*	The *length* parameter specifies the number of data bytes in the echo packets. Maximum is 8192.
-n *count*	The *count* parameter specifies the number of packets to be sent. Default is 4.
-r *count*	Records the route of the outgoing and returning packet in the Record Route field. The *count* parameter specifies a minimum of 1 and a maximum of 9 hosts.
-s *count*	Instructs **ping** to report time stamps for the number of hops specified by *count*.
-t	Pings the host until interrupted.
-v *tos*	Sets the value of the Type of Service field to *tos*.
-w *timeout*	Specifies a timeout interval in milliseconds.

Using ipconfig

The **ipconfig** command displays TCP/IP configuration settings for a host. This utility is particularly useful when the host obtains address information dynamically from DHCP or a host name from WINS. Consequently, Chapters 10 and 11 revisit **ipconfig**.

TABLE 8.2   IPCONFIG OPTIONS

Option	Function
/all	Specifies display of all data. Without this option, **ipconfig** displays only the IP address, subnet mask, and default gateway values for each network card.
renew [*adapter*]	On systems that run the DHCP Client service, this option renews DHCP configuration parameters. To specify a specific adapter, use the optional *adapter* parameter. For adapter, specify the name that appears when **ipconfig** is entered without parameters.
release [*adapter*]	On systems running the DHCP Client service, this option releases the DHCP configuration and disables TCP/IP on the host. To specify a specific adapter, use the optional *adapter* parameter. For adapter, specify the name that appears when **ipconfig** is entered without parameters.

> **Note** In place of **ipconfig** Windows 95 substitutes a GUI utility named WINIPCFG. To run WINIPCFG, open the **Start** menu, select the **Run** command, and enter `WINIPCFG` in the **Open** field of the **Run** dialog box.

Summary

This chapter primarily focused on installing TCP/IP on Windows NT computers. It covered planning an installation, as well as providing step-by-step guidelines for those new to installing a network. From that point, the chapter discussed installing and reconfiguring TCP/IP protocols on a networked computer. The chapter concluded with information on testing a TCP/IP configuration using ping and ipconfig commands.

Chapter 9 Snapshot

This chapter examines configuration of Windows NT routers in simple and complex internetworks. It covers the following topics:

◆ Rules of routing

◆ Routing with two networks

◆ Configuring a Windows NT router

◆ Adding default gateways to hosts

◆ Configuring default gateways on internets with three networks

◆ Routing with more than two networks

◆ Building static routing tables

◆ Routing with multiple default gateways

Building Routed Networks

C hapter 4, "The Internet Layer," pays considerable attention to routing, and by now, you should have a good grasp of basic routing concepts, including how IP delivers datagrams through an internetwork. You have yet to learn how Windows NT computers can be configured as routers, and how to configure a large, routed network. This chapter examines configuration of Windows NT routers in simple and complex internetworks.

Rules of Routing

Before you examine the procedures for configuring routers, take a moment to review some basic rules of routing.

When subnetting is not in effect, two hosts attached to the same network segment can communicate directly only if they have matching netids. In figure 9.1, hosts A and B can communicate directly. However, neither A nor B can communicate with C, because they have different netids (assuming a subnet mask of at least 255.255.255.0).

Figure 9.1

*Host communication
on a local network.*

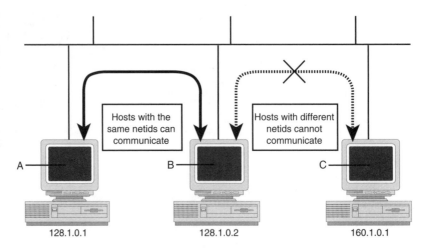

When subnetting is in effect, two hosts attached to the same network can segment only if both their netids and subnetids match. If either the netids or the subnetids differ, a router must be employed. In figure 9.2, hosts A and B can communicate directly. C has the same netid as A and B, but C has a different subnet ID. Therefore, C cannot communicate directly with A or B.

Figure 9.2

*Host communication
with subnetting.*

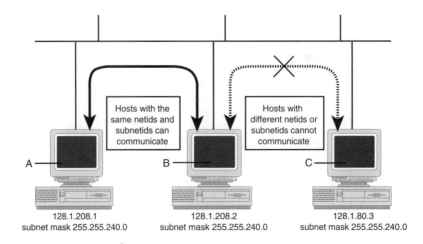

Finally, all hosts that occupy different networks must communicate through a router.

Note   As figures 9.1 and 9.2 illustrate, hosts on the same network segment do not have to share common network IDs. Even though these hosts share a common cable, an IP router is required to enable them to communicate.

Routing with Two Networks

Figure 9.3 illustrates a basic internet with two networks: 128.1.0.100 and 128.2.0.100. The common element that connects the two networks is Windows NT host A, which is equipped with a network adapter on each of the two networks. A host that connects to two or more networks is called a *multihomed* host. To turn a multihomed Windows NT computer into an IP router, the IP Routing feature must be turned on.

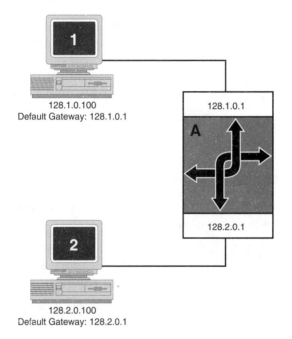

128.1.0.100
Default Gateway: 128.1.0.1

128.1.0.1

A

128.2.0.1

128.2.0.100
Default Gateway: 128.2.0.1

Figure 9.3

Routing between adjacent networks.

After routing is activated on a multihomed Windows NT computer, the computer forwards IP datagrams from one of its connected networks to another connected network. Here is an example of what happens:

1. Host A needs to send a datagram to host C, which is not on the local network. A does not know how to reach C, and therefore sends the frame to its default gateway, host B.

2. Host B receives the frame on adapter 128.1.0.1. The frame is identified by the physical address of B, but the destination IP address is 128.2.0.2. B knows that it is not the ultimate destination, and proceeds to forward the datagram.

3. Host B consults its routing table and determines that it has a route to network 128.2.0.100.

4. Host B resends the datagram from its adapter 128.2.0.1. The frame is addressed with the physical address and the IP address of host C.

5. Host C receives the frame and recovers the datagram.

Two things must be done to enable this simple routing system to work:

◆ A router (host B in the example) must be installed between the networks, configured with network adapters on each network, and have its routing function enabled.

◆ Other hosts must be configured with a default gateway.

Those tasks are performed in the following sections.

Configuring a Windows NT Router

An IP router is a multihomed host that has its routing function turned on. Two steps are involved in setting up a Windows NT Router:

1. Install a second network adapter and configure it for TCP/IP.

2. Activate routing.

After installing the network adapter hardware, add it to the Windows NT configuration, using the following steps:

1. Start the Network utility in the Control Panel.

2. In the **Network Settings** dialog box, choose **Add Adapter**.

3. In the **Add Network Adapter** dialog box, select an adapter from the list in the **Network Adapter Card** box. (Or select **<Other> Requires disk from manufacturer** to install a nonlisted card.) Choose **Continue** after specifying a card.

   If the new card is the same type as the one already installed, you are shown the message A network card of this type is already installed in the system. Do you want to continue?. Choose **OK**.

4. Specify the card settings in the **Network Card Setup** dialog box and choose **OK**. The **Network Settings** dialog box reappears, which now shows two adapters, as in figure 9.4. The new adapter will be identified as adapter [2].

5. Choose **OK** after you finish adding adapter drivers. After some software installation, the **TCP/IP Configuration** dialog box appears.

6. Each adapter must be configured. Select an adapter from the list in the **Adapter** box. Figure 9.5 shows the configuration of adapter [1]. First, a default gateway must be added to the configuration for adapter [1]. Usually, the default gateway is the address of a router interface that is on the same network as the adapter being configured. In the case of a computer that is also a gateway, the default gateway address probably will be the same as the IP address assigned to the adapter being configured.

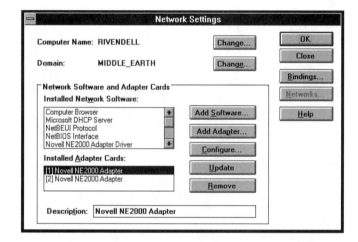

Figure 9.4

Network Settings after adding a second network adapter.

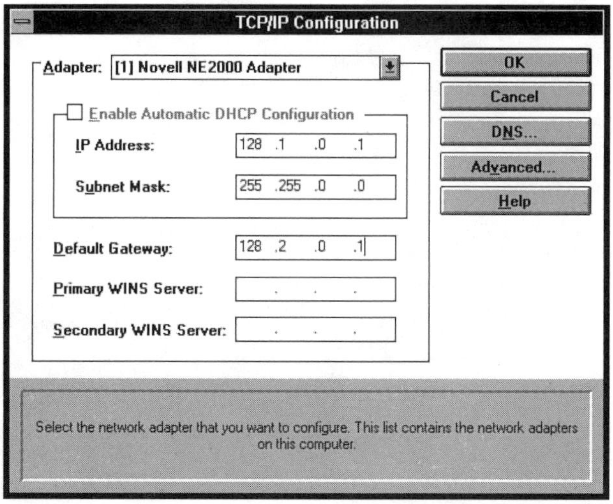

Figure 9.5

Configuration of adapter [1] on the example gateway.

7. In figure 9.6, adapter [2] has been selected and configured with the appropriate addresses.

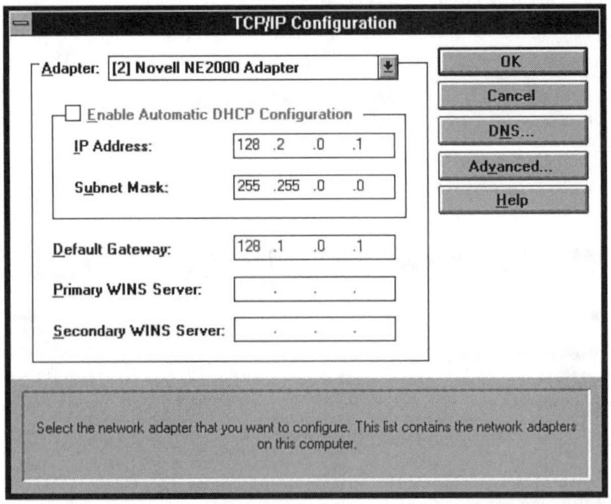

Figure 9.6

Configuration of adapter [2] on the example gateway.

8. The remaining required step is to activate IP routing. Select either network adapter. Then choose **Advanced** in the **TCP/IP Configuration** dialog box. Figure 9.7 shows the **Advanced Microsoft TCP/IP Configuration** dialog box.

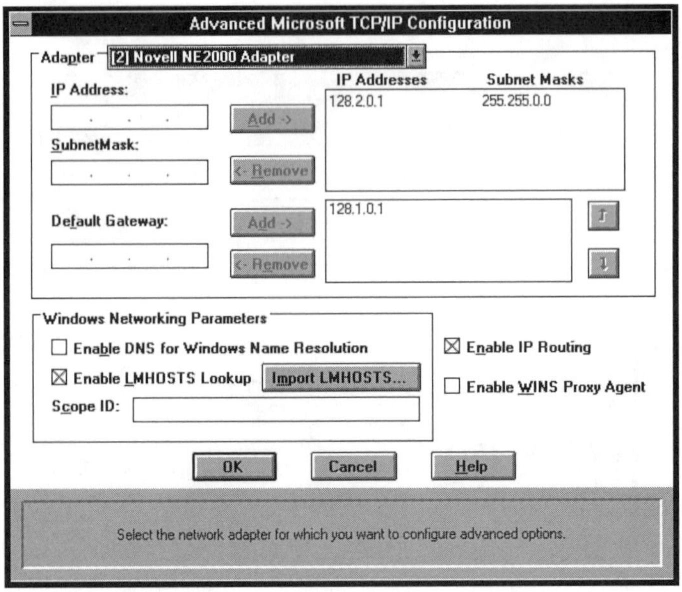

Figure 9.7

TCP/IP advanced configuration.

The advanced configuration option of interest here is **Enable IP Routing**. When this option is checked, as in figure 9.7, the computer routes IP datagrams among the installed adapters. Checking this option for one adapter activates routing for the entire computer.

Note	IP routing can be enabled only when at least two IP addresses have been configured on the computer. Usually, this means having two or more network adapters, but assigning multiple addresses to the same adapter also is possible.

9. After TCP/IP has been configured for all adapters and IP routing has been enabled, return to the **Network Settings** dialog box and choose **OK**. Restart the computer to activate the new features.

Adding Default Gateways to Hosts

The **TCP/IP Configuration** dialog box also serves to configure default gateway addresses on Windows NT hosts. A default gateway must be configured for any host that must communicate with hosts that do not reside on the same subnet.

To configure a default router for a Windows NT computer:

1. Start the Network utility in the Control Panel.

2. In the **Network Settings** dialog box, select **TCP/IP Protocol** from the **Installed Network Software** box. Then choose **Configure** to open the **TCP/IP Configuration** dialog box.

3. On a multihomed host, select the adapter to be configured in the **Adapter** box.

4. Enter the address of an IP router in the **Default Gateway** box.

5. Choose **OK**.

6. Exit the Network utility and restart the computer.

Configuring Default Gateways on Internets with Three Networks

Figure 9.8 illustrates an internet that consists of three networks connected by two gateways. On this network, all required routing can be performed using default gateways. Arrows on the figure illustrate the paths that are followed when datagrams are routed from host 1 to host 2 and from host 1 to host 3.

Consider the behavior of router A when it receives a datagram to be delivered from host 1 to host 2. Router A has direct knowledge of network 128.2.0.100 on which host 2 resides, and uses that knowledge to address the datagram to host 2 and route it to network 128.2.0.100.

Figure 9.8

Routing in an internet with three networks and two routers.

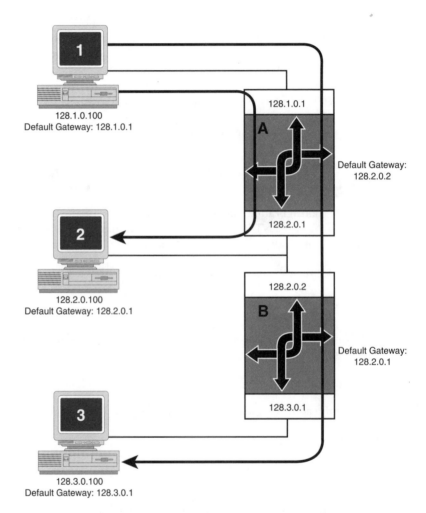

Now consider what happens when host 1 needs to send a datagram to host 3. Router A examines the destination IP address and determines that 128.3.0.100 does not reside on either of the subnets to which A is connected. Therefore, A uses its default gateway and routes the datagram to 128.2.0.2 on router B. Router B can deliver the datagram to network 128.3.0.0.

A mirror of this process occurs when 3 sends a datagram to 1. Host 3 sends the datagram to its default gateway, 128.3.0.1 on B. B sends the datagram to its default gateway, 128.2.0.1 on A, and A can deliver the datagram.

Finally, the case of routing datagrams from host 2 must be examined. When 2 sends a datagram to 1, 2 sends the datagram to its default gateway on A, and A can deliver the datagram.

The route to 3 is a bit more indirect (see fig. 9.9). 2 sends to its default gateway on A. A is not aware of the network 128.3.0.0 and sends the datagram to its default gateway on B, from which the datagram can be delivered. Therefore, routing from 2 to 3 requires an extra hop.

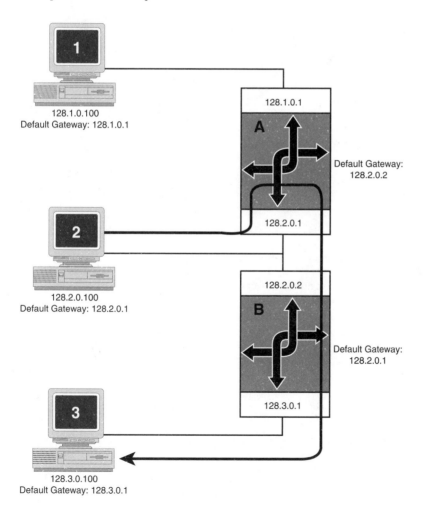

Figure 9.9

Routing from host 2 to host 3 on a three-network internet.

Routing with More Than Two Networks

Can default gateways be used to route datagrams to networks of any size? To see, examining a network, such as the one illustrated in figure 9.10, is necessary.

As figure 9.10 illustrates, routing datagrams to network 128.4.0.0 can be performed using default routers. If you trace the routes, you find that the following situations all are covered:

◆ 1 can route to 2, 3, and 4.

◆ 2 can route to 1, 3, and 4.

◆ 3 can route to 2 and 4

The sting in the tail of this diagram is apparent when 3 attempts to route a datagram to 1. Here is the sequence, which is illustrated in figure 9.11:

1. Host 3 sends the datagram to its default router, 128.3.0.1.

2. Router B has no direct knowledge of network 128.1.0.100. B, therefore, routes the datagram to B's default router, 128.3.0.2.

3. Router C has no direct knowledge of network 128.1.0.100. C, therefore, routes the datagram to C's default router, 128.3.0.1. The datagram has now arrived back at router B.

4. B routes the datagram to its default router, C.

5. C routes the datagram to its default router, B.

The datagram cannot be delivered to network 128.1.0.100 because it never reaches a router that is aware of the destination network. A loop has developed between B and C that could continue indefinitely, which is the reason for the `time to live` parameter in the IP header. Time to live is decremented by some amount each time it passes through a router. For any datagram not delivered, time to live eventually reaches 0 and the datagram is removed from the network.

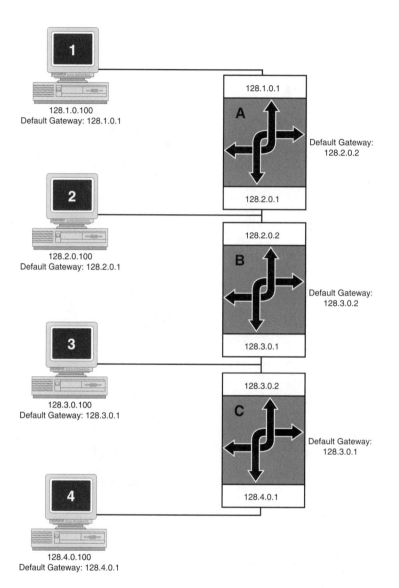

Figure 9.10

Routing on an internet with four networks.

Figure 9.11

A routing loop.

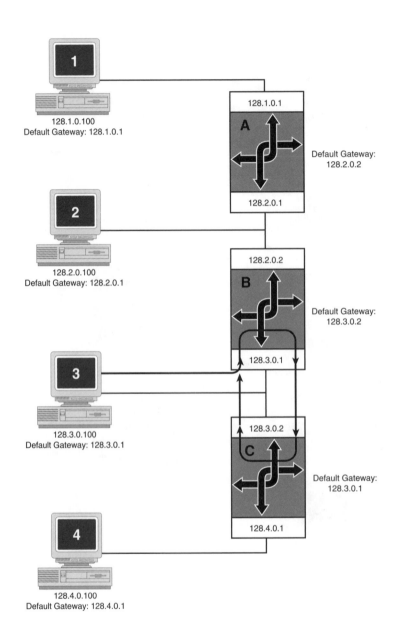

Building Static Routing Tables

The default router mechanism is extremely limited. Although hosts can be configured with default routers, backup default routers are used only when the primary default router is unavailable. In other words, any given host is limited to a single default route at any given time, which is why the network shown in figure 9.11 occasionally fails to deliver datagrams properly.

To solve problems such as the one shown in figure 9.11, you need to improve the knowledge that hosts and routers possess of possible routes to remote networks. You do so by adding entries to the computer's routing tables.

The problem in figure 9.11 is that router B is unaware of the existence of network 128.1.0.0. Adding a path to that network to B's routing table eliminates the problem.

Figure 9.12 shows the same network. This time, router B has been configured with a routing table that supplements the default gateway specifications. The routing table describes the next hop on the route to network 128.1.0.0 on the internet.

Returning to the problem of routing a datagram from host 3 to host 1, now the sequence of events is as follows:

1. Host 3 sends the datagram to its default router, 128.3.0.1.

2. Router B has an entry in its routing table for network 128.1.0.0. Any datagram directed to 128.1.0.0 will be routed to 128.2.0.1 on router A.

3. Router A is attached to the destination network and can deliver the frame.

Figure 9.12 illustrates the routes from hosts 3 and 4 to host 1, showing how the routing table entry in router B also enables host 4 to reach any network.

The tool used to maintain static routing tables is **route**, a command-line utility. Figure 9.13 shows a router table for router B in figure 9.12. The table includes information about default routers and routing to adjacent networks.

Figure 9.12

Routing with routing tables.

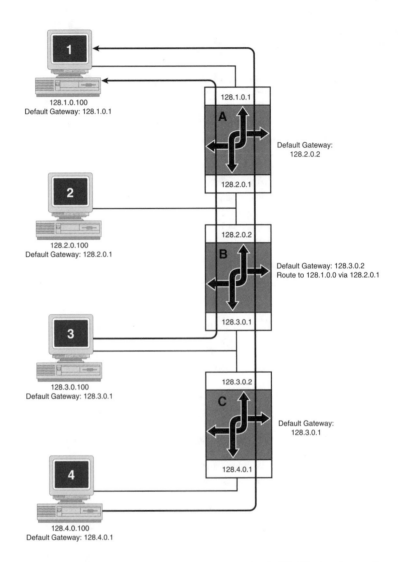

All of the entries shown in figure 9.13 were created using the **TCP/IP Configuration** utility. When installing TCP/IP, IP addresses were declared for each adapter in the host. It is worth examining the entries in the table:

◆ **0.0.0.0.** Specifies the default router, address 128.3.0.2.

◆ **127.0.0.0.** The loopback network. Any datagrams sent to 127.0.0.0 are routed to 127.0.0.1 and reflected back.

◆ **128.2.0.0.** A network address. Datagrams destined for that network are routed through adapter 128.2.0.2.

◆ **128.2.0.2.** The network adapter on the router. Notice that datagrams sent to that address are routed through the loopback address.

◆ **128.2.255.255.** A broadcast address for network 128.2.0.0. Broadcasts are routed to the network through adapter 128.2.0.2. Entries such as this should be added if broadcast messages are to be routed to remote networks.

◆ **128.3.0.0.** The other attached network. The routing table includes entries for 128.3.0.0 that are similar to the entries discussed for 128.2.0.0.

◆ **224.0.0.0.** A multicast address used internally by Windows NT.

◆ **255.255.255.255.** The local broadcast address. (Routers do not forward broadcasts to other networks.)

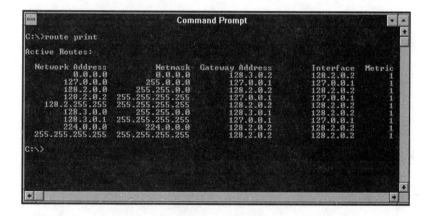

Figure 9.13

A routing table with adjacent routing entries only.

Figure 9.14 illustrates two routing attempts using **ping**, both performed on router B. In the first attempt, it proves possible to ping 128.2.0.1, which is not surprising because that host is attached to a network that is directly attached to B.

An attempt to ping 128.1.0.1 fails, however. B attempts to reach 128.1.0.1 via its default router, 128.3.0.2. This attempt does not succeed and times out.

To solve the problem, an entry must be added to the router table for B. This entry must specify that network 128.1.0.0 may be reached via router 128.2.0.1. Figure 9.15 was made on router B. First, an attempt to ping 128.1.0.1 fails. Then a **route** command is entered, after which the ping succeeds. Figure 9.16 shows the updated routing table for B. The third entry in the table reflects the **route** command that was entered.

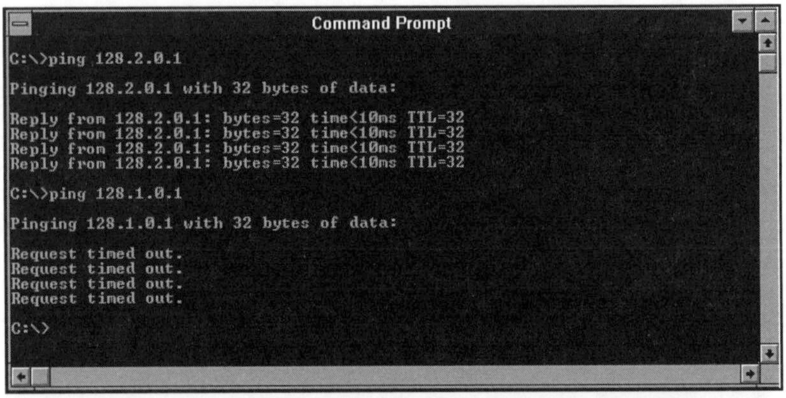

Figure 9.14

Pinging routed and nonrouted addresses.

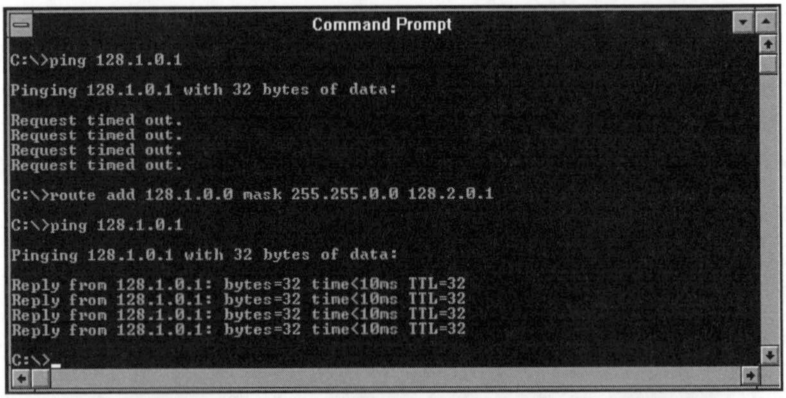

```
─                              Command Prompt                         ▼ ▲
                                                                        ↕
C:\>ping 128.2.0.1

Pinging 128.2.0.1 with 32 bytes of data:

Reply from 128.2.0.1: bytes=32 time<10ms TTL=32
Reply from 128.2.0.1: bytes=32 time<10ms TTL=32
Reply from 128.2.0.1: bytes=32 time<10ms TTL=32
Reply from 128.2.0.1: bytes=32 time<10ms TTL=32

C:\>ping 128.1.0.1

Pinging 128.1.0.1 with 32 bytes of data:

Request timed out.
Request timed out.
Request timed out.
Request timed out.

C:\>
                                                                        ↓
◀ ▐                                                                  ▶
```

Figure 9.15

Example of using the **route** *command.*

```
─                              Command Prompt                         ▼ ▲
                                                                        ↑
C:\>ping 128.1.0.1

Pinging 128.1.0.1 with 32 bytes of data:

Request timed out.
Request timed out.
Request timed out.
Request timed out.

C:\>route add 128.1.0.0 mask 255.255.0.0 128.2.0.1

C:\>ping 128.1.0.1

Pinging 128.1.0.1 with 32 bytes of data:

Reply from 128.1.0.1: bytes=32 time<10ms TTL=32
Reply from 128.1.0.1: bytes=32 time<10ms TTL=32
Reply from 128.1.0.1: bytes=32 time<10ms TTL=32
Reply from 128.1.0.1: bytes=32 time<10ms TTL=32

C:\>_
                                                                        ↓
◀ ▐                                                                  ▶
```

Figure 9.16

The routing table after execution of the example **route** *command.*

```
─                              Command Prompt                         ▼ ▲
                                                                        ↑
C:\>route print
Active Routes:
   Network Address          Netmask  Gateway Address     Interface  Metric
           0.0.0.0          0.0.0.0        128.3.0.2      128.2.0.2       1
         127.0.0.0        255.0.0.0        127.0.0.1      127.0.0.1       1
         128.1.0.0      255.255.0.0        128.2.0.1      128.2.0.2       1
         128.2.0.0      255.255.0.0        128.2.0.2      128.2.0.2       1
         128.2.0.2  255.255.255.255        127.0.0.1      127.0.0.1       1
     128.2.255.255  255.255.255.255        128.2.0.2      128.2.0.2       1
         128.3.0.0      255.255.0.0        128.3.0.1      128.2.0.2       1
         128.3.0.1  255.255.255.255        127.0.0.1      127.0.0.1       1
         224.0.0.0        224.0.0.0        128.2.0.2      128.2.0.2       1
   255.255.255.255  255.255.255.255        128.2.0.2      128.2.0.2       1

C:\>
                                                                        ↓
◀ ▐                                                                  ▶
```

The syntax for **route** is as follows:

```
route [-f][-p] [command] [destination] [mask netmask] [gateway]
```

route accepts four command options:

◆ **add** adds a route to a table.

◆ **delete** removes a route from a table.

◆ **change** modifies the routing for a table entry.

◆ **print** displays the router table.

destination is an optional parameter that specifies the network address that is the destination to be specified in the routing table entry. It must be supplied with the add, delete, and change options.

mask is an optional parameter. When mask appears, it specifies that the following IP address is an address mask. The default value for *netmask* is 255.255.255.255. Other values must be fully specified.

gateway is an optional parameter that specifies the IP address of the gateway that is to be used when routing datagrams to the destination.

-f is an optional parameter that specifies that the routing table is to be cleared of all entries. It can be included with routes to clear the table before the routes are entered.

-p is an optional parameter that is used with the **add** command to make an entry persistent. Persistent entries remain in effect after the router restarts. If this parameter is not specified, the table entry does not appear after the router restarts.

Note The -p option is available, beginning with Windows NT version 3.51. With earlier versions, the route commands must be reentered when the computer restarts.

The example command is

route add 128.1.0.0 mask 255.255.0.0 128.2.0.1

This command adds a table entry for network 128.1.0.0 with a network mask of 255.255.0.0. The router to be used to reach 128.1.0.0 is 128.2.0.1.

Static routing requires some thought, effort, and troubleshooting to ensure that all datagrams can be routed properly to all required destinations. It might appear, therefore, that network administrators would be better served by dedicated, commercial routers that maintain routing tables automatically.

Dynamic routing with a routing protocol, such as RIP or OSPF, is certainly preferable when networks are dynamic or incorporate large numbers of routers. Maintaining routing for a large, evolving organization using static routing would be difficult or impossible.

Dynamic routing also is often preferable when networks provide multiple paths to destinations. Dynamic routing can adapt to failed segments, selecting the most optimum path available on the changed network. This again argues for dynamic routing on large networks.

Static routing, however, might be just the thing for networks of moderate size or networks that change infrequently. Static routing is built into Windows NT and, therefore, is free. Dynamic routers are among the most expensive pieces of equipment you can have on a network. Also, static routing requires no network overhead. Dynamic routing protocols require routers to communicate to exchange routing data. With protocols such as RIP, routing messages can utilize a significant portion of available bandwidth. NT will include a version of RIP in NT version 3.56.

Routing with Multiple Default Gateways

Any TCP/IP computer can be configured with more than one default gateway. Unfortunately, only the first configured gateway will be used for routing. The additional gateways are used only if the primary gateway becomes unavailable. Consequently, multiple gateways cannot be used to take better advantage of network bandwidth. On the other hand, they do provide a greater degree of network fault tolerance.

Figure 9.17 shows an example of a network that can take advantage of multiple default gateways. Host 1 offers two possible routes to host 2:

◆ Via router A

◆ Via routers C and B

Assuming that routing through A is more efficient, the primary default gateway for host 1 should be 128.1.0.1. However, host 1 can have a second route to host 128.4.0.1, which enables 1 to reach 2 should router A fail.

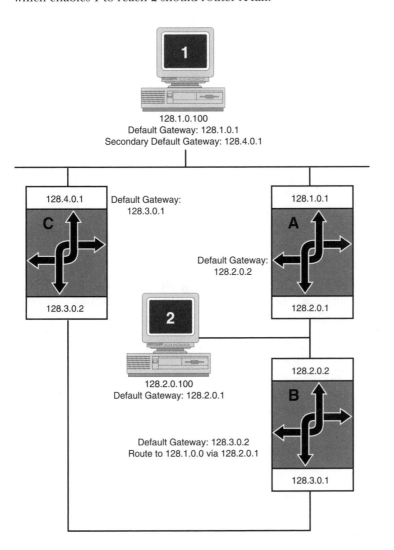

Figure 9.17

A network using multiple default gateways.

Additional default gateways are configured using Advanced TCP/IP Configuration. To add a default gateway:

1. Start the Network utility in the Control Panel.

2. In the **Network Settings** dialog box, select **TCP/IP Protocol** in the **Installed Network Software** box. Then choose **Configure** to open the **TCP/IP Configuration** dialog box.

3. On a multihomed host, select the adapter to be configured in the **Adapter** box.

4. If a default gateway has not been entered, add the gateway in the **Default Gateway** field of the **TCP/IP Configuration** dialog box.

5. Choose the **Advanced** button to enter advanced configuration for the selected adapter. Figure 9.18 illustrates the **Advanced Microsoft TCP/IP Configuration** dialog box for the selected adapter.

   The box to the right of **Default Gateway** contains two entries. 128.1.0.1 is the default gateway address specified in the **TCP/IP Configuration** dialog box. 128.4.0.1 was added with the following steps.

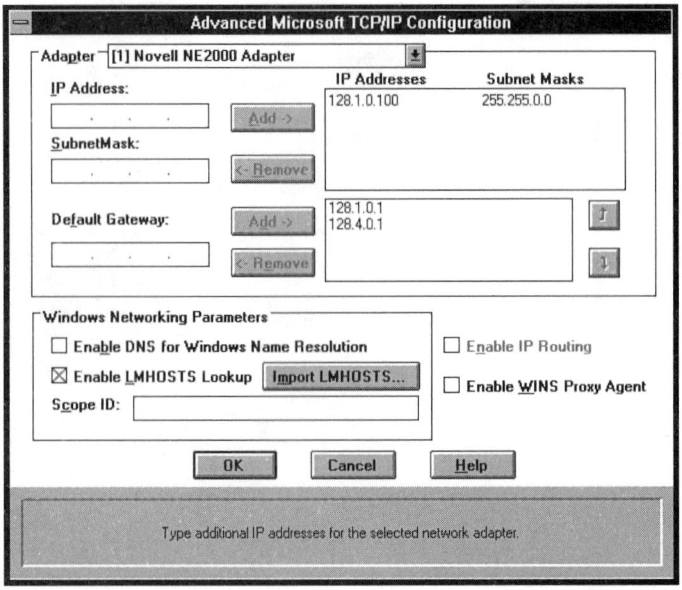

Figure 9.18

Adding a gateway in advanced TCP/IP configuration.

6. To add a default gateway, enter the address in the **De̲fault Gateway** address fields. Then choose **A̲dd** to move the entry to the default gateway list.

7. Choose **OK**, exit the Network utility, and restart the computer to activate the new address.

The **Advanced Microsoft TCP/IP Configuration** box is used for all TCP/IP configuration entries, except the basics. Chapter 11 describes how this box is used to configure hosts to use LMHOSTS files and to function as WINS proxy agents. Chapter 13 demonstrates how to configure a host to access a DNS server.

Summary

In this chapter, you learned how to configure Windows NT computers as routers for both simple and complex internetworks. The chapter began by introducing the basic rules of routing. You then learned how to connect two networks. The common element that connects the two networks is a Windows NT host, which is equipped with a network adapter on each of the two networks. A host that connects to two or more networks is called a *multihomed* host. The following section discussed how to configure Windows NT routers. The steps include installing a second network adapter and configuring it for TCP/IP, and then activating routing. A default gateway must be configured for any host that must communicate with hosts that do not reside on the same subnet.

The default router mechanism is extremely limited, however. Although hosts can be configured with default routers, backup default routers are used only when the primary default router is unavailable. In other words, any given host is limited to a single default router at any given time. To solve this problem, you need to improve the knowledge that hosts and routers possess of possible routes to remote networks. You do so by adding entries to the computer's routing tables. To gain a greater degree of network fault tolerance, you can configure multiple default gateways.

Chapter 10 Snapshot

This chapter provides an overview of DHCP. It covers the following topics:

- ◆ DHCP concepts and operation

- ◆ Installing DHCP servers

- ◆ Setting up DHCP scopes

- ◆ Enabling DHCP clients

- ◆ Viewing and managing active leases

- ◆ Establishing reservations

- ◆ Activating, deactivating, and deleting scopes

- ◆ Managing leases

- ◆ Managing multiple DHCP servers

- ◆ Managing the DHCP database

- ◆ DHCP configuration options

- ◆ Configuring DHCP in the Registry

C H A P T E R

10

Managing DHCP

The Dynamic Host Configuration Protocol (DHCP) can make TCP/IP network administration much more efficient by dynamically assigning IP addresses to hosts, practically eliminating the need to configure host addresses manually. A DHCP client host can even move to a new network without any need for manual reconfiguration.

DHCP also provides a mechanism for local management of the majority of TCP/IP clients on the internetwork. Parameters such as default routers can be configured centrally without visiting each host and making changes manually.

Microsoft DHCP client and server are implemented under RFCs 1533, 1534, 1541, and 1542.

This chapter provides an overview of DHCP, defines it, and explains how it works. Then it proceeds to examine DHCP, beginning with installation, then examining configuration and management issues.

DHCP Concepts and Operation

DHCP is based on *DHCP servers*, which assign IP addresses, and *DHCP clients*, to which addresses are assigned. Figure 10.1 illustrates a simple network that consists of a single DHCP server and a few clients. As shown, a single DHCP server can supply addresses for more than one network. To support DHCP on an internetwork, routers must be configured with BOOTP forwarding (see RFCs 1533, 1534, and 1542).

Figure 10.1

Example of a network running DHCP.

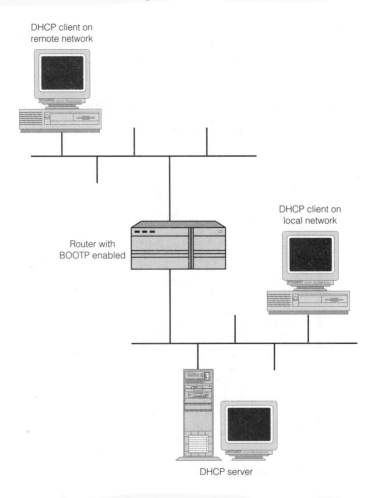

The DHCP server maintains pools of IP addresses, called *scopes*. When a DHCP client enters a network, it requests and is granted a *lease* to use an address from an appropriate scope.

, because DHCP clients are not ordinarily granted
ad, they receive a lease of limited duration. When
tiated. This approach ensures that unused
by other clients.

HCP server can support clients on several networks
to different networks are assigned IP addresses

takes place when a DHCP client obtains a lease from
cts the life cycle of a lease. The stages in the life cycle

nters a network enters an *initializing state* and broad-
the local network. This message may be relayed to other
DHCP servers in the internet. (Routers must be config-
rotocol, RFC 1542, to support DHCP.)

receives the discover message and can service the request
essage that consists of an IP address and associated
ion.

s a *selecting state* and examines the offer messages that it

t selects an offer, it enters a *requesting state* and sends a
ppropriate DHCP server, requesting the offered configura-

ants the configuration with an *acknowledgment message* that
dress and configuration along with a *lease* to use the configu-
time. The local network administrator establishes lease

eceives the acknowledgment and enters a *bound* state in which
n is applied to the local TCP/IP protocols. Client computers
ration for the duration of the lease and may be restarted
g a new lease.

pproaches expiration, the client attempts to renew its lease with

8. If the lease can...ot be renewed, the client reenters the binding process and is
assigned a lease to a new address. Nonrenewed addresses return to the available
address pool.

---

(513) 298-6540

Thank you for being our customer. Our only goal is to serve you well.

Truffles Cafe
Corporate Orders
Phone & FAX Ordering
Free Gift Wrap
Shipping Worldwide
Newspapers & Magazines
Gift Certificates
Newsletters
Special Orders
Children's Events
Author Signings & Special Events
Knowledgeable Booksellers

We are pleased to offer you...

If you like books, you'll love Books & Co., a lively, friendly place to browse and talk with people who know books. Our helpful booksellers offer great customer service, and we have the most comprehensive selection of books in our region, currently 125,000 titles.

Wide aisles and comfortable places to sit and make it easy for you to browse. Our performance area in the center of the store is the site of frequent author signings, children's programs, live music and other special events. We invite you to visit us often.

BOOKS&CO.

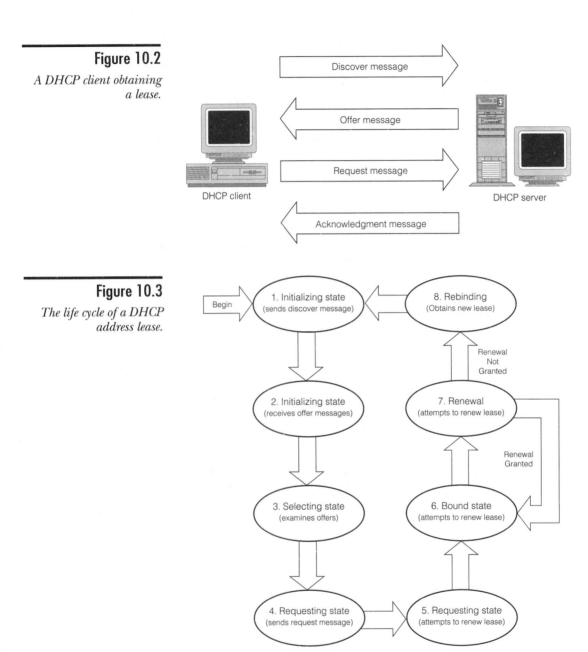

Figure 10.2

A DHCP client obtaining a lease.

Discover message

Offer message

Request message

DHCP client

Acknowledgment message

DHCP server

Figure 10.3

The life cycle of a DHCP address lease.

Begin

1. Initializing state
(sends discover message)

8. Rebinding
(Obtains new lease)

Renewal
Not
Granted

2. Initializing state
(receives offer messages)

7. Renewal
(attempts to renew lease)

Renewal
Granted

3. Selecting state
(examines offers)

6. Bound state
(attempts to renew lease)

4. Requesting state
(sends request message)

5. Requesting state
(attempts to renew lease)

This process is completely transparent to the client and requires little ongoing maintenance on the part of the network administrator.

DHCP can be configured to assign specific addresses to specific hosts, which enables administrators to use DHCP to set host protocol options while retaining fixed address assignments.

Several types of hosts must be assigned fixed, manual addresses so that other hosts can enter the addresses into their configurations, including, among others, the following examples:

◆ Routers (gateways)

◆ WINS servers

◆ DNS servers

Installing DHCP Servers

DHCP Server services may be installed on computers running Windows NT Server. To install DHCP services, follow these steps:

1. Open the Network utility in the Control Panel.

2. Choose **Add Software** in the **Network Settings** dialog box.

3. Select **TCP/IP Protocol and related components** in the **Network Settings** box of the **Add Network Software** dialog box, then choose **Continue**.

4. Check **DHCP Server Services** in the **Windows NT TCP/IP Installation Options** dialog box. Then choose **Continue**.

5. Supply disks and path information as required to install the software.

6. Choose **OK** to close the **Network Settings** dialog box and restart the computer.

Setting Up DHCP Scopes

Before DHCP clients can obtain IP addresses from a DHCP server, at least one scope must be created. A *scope* is a range of IP addresses along with a set of configuration options that apply to clients that receive IP addresses assigned from the scope. All scopes have the following properties:

◆ A scope name

◆ A subnet mask

◆ A lease duration

DHCP is administered using the DHCP Manager utility. An icon for DHCP Manager is created in the Network Administration program group when DHCP Server services are installed. DHCP Manager can also be started from a command prompt by entering the command **start dhcpadmn**.

Figure 10.4 shows the **DHCP Manager** dialog box. As yet, no scopes have been defined. Before defining a scope, determine the following:

◆ The starting IP address of the range to be assigned to the scope

◆ The ending IP address to be assigned

◆ The subnet mask to be in effect

◆ Any addresses in the range that are to not to be made available to clients obtaining addresses from the scope

◆ The duration of the lease (default value is three days)

Figure 10.4

DHCP Manager prior to creating scopes.

Drag to adjust split

DHCP server

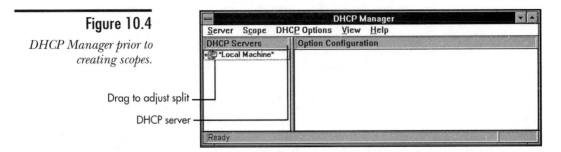

To create a scope, perform the following steps:

1. Start DHCP Manager. The display in figure 10.4 shows DHCP Manager before defining any scopes. If a DHCP Server service is running on this computer, it is identified as Local Machine.

2. Select a DHCP server in the **DHCP Servers** list. The example will create a scope on Local Machine. A scope is always created on a specific DHCP server.

3. In the **DHCP Manager** dialog box, choose **Create** in the **Scope** menu, which opens the **Create Scope** dialog box (see fig. 10.5). Data fields in the figure have been filled to reflect typical scope properties.

4. Enter the appropriate addresses in the **Start Address**, **End Address**, and **Subnet Mask** input boxes.

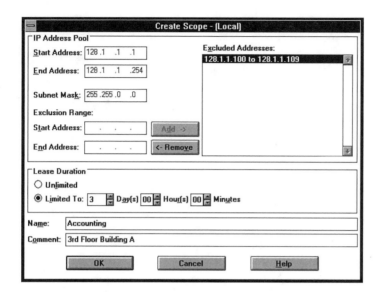

Figure 10.5

Creating a scope.

5. To exclude an address or range of addresses, under **Exclusion Range**, enter the appropriate addresses in the **Start Address** and **End Address** boxes. (An *end address* is not required when you exclude a single address.) Then choose **Add** to move the addresses to the **Excluded Addresses** list.

6. To remove an excluded address range, select the range in the **Excluded Address** list. Then choose **Remove**.

7. Choose **Unlimited** if leases for this scope are to be unlimited in duration. Choose **Limited To** and enter a period in days, hours, and minutes to set a lease duration for the scope. Limiting lease duration, even when plenty of addresses are available, is best so that unused leases are eventually released.

8. Optionally, enter a name and comment for the scope in the **Name** and **Comment** boxes. This information helps identify the scope in the DHCP Manager.

9. Choose **OK** to return to the DHCP Manager main dialog box. For a new scope, you receive the message shown in figure 10.6. To activate the scope, choose **Yes**.

10. As figure 10.7 reveals, the scope you have defined appears under the DHCP server
    for which the scope was defined. Because it was activated, the lightbulb icon is illuminated.

Note
To modify a scope, select the scope in the **DHCP Servers** box and choose **Properties** in the **Scope** menu, which opens a **Scope Properties** dialog box in which you can change scope properties. Choose **OK** after you make the necessary changes.

Figure 10.6

The scope activation message.

Figure 10.7

DHCP Manager after a scope has been defined.

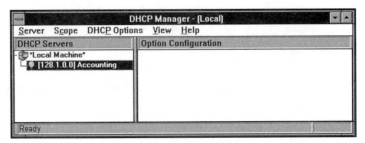

Stop

Notice in figure 10.5 that the address range is from 128.1.1.1 through 128.1.1.254, so that the scope range does not contain invalid hostid values. Remember that the last octet of a hostid may not be all 0s or all 1s (although those addresses are permitted on some systems). If the IP address 128.1.0.0 is assigned to a DHCP client, the client might have difficulty communicating.

Be sure that the scope address range does not include the IP addresses of any hosts for which addresses have been manually assigned. This includes all DHCP servers. Fixed IP addresses must be outside the scope address range or must be excluded from the scope. The next step explains how to exclude addresses from scopes. Figure 10.8 shows an error message that DHCP Manager displays when it determines that an address it has assigned conflicts with an address already in use.

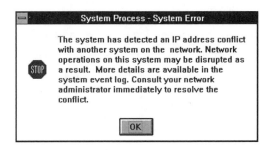

Figure 10.8

Message resulting from an address conflict.

Enabling DHCP Clients

After DHCP has been configured, DHCP clients can be activated. Microsoft operating systems that can be DHCP clients are as follows:

◆ All versions of Windows NT

◆ Windows 95

◆ Windows 3.11 with the 32-bit TCP/IP client

◆ MS-DOS workgroup connection 3.0, which is the DOS-client included with Windows NT.

Configuration of Windows 95 and 3.11 is covered in Chapter 13, "Installing TCP/IP on Microsoft Clients."

To enable a Windows NT computer as a DHCP client, perform the following steps:

1. Open the Network utility in the Control Panel.

2. In the **Installed Network Software** box, select **TCP/IP Protocol** and choose **Configure**.

3. In the **TCP/IP Configuration** dialog box, select the adapter to be configured from the list in the **Adapter** box.

4. Check **Enable Automatic DHCP Configuration**. Any IP address or submask that already has been entered is greyed out to identify it as inactive.

Note The option to **Enable Automatic DHCP Configuration** is not available if DHCP Server services or WINS Server services are installed on the computer. DHCP or WINS servers must be configured using fixed IP addresses.

5. Choose **OK** twice to exit Network Settings. Then restart the computer.

> **Note**
>
> When a DHCP client obtains an address lease from a DHCP server, you can determine the address assignment by entering the command `ipconfig /all` at a command prompt on the client.
>
> Windows 95 users can run the `winipcfg` command at a Run prompt. WINIPCFG is a GUI program that performs most of the same functions as ipconfig. The Advanced button will show all other DHCP configured information.

Viewing and Managing Active Leases

DHCP clients can obtain addresses after the following have been accomplished:

◆ DHCP Server services have been installed on at least one Windows NT Server computer.

◆ At least one scope has been defined that applies to the network on which the DHCP client resides, or a reservation has been established for the client.

◆ **Enable Automatic DHCP Configuration** has been selected in the client's TCP/IP Protocol configuration.

After those steps are accomplished, restarting a DHCP client causes it to obtain a lease for an IP address from a DHCP server. To view active leases, select a scope in the **DHCP Servers** box. Then choose **Active Leases** in the **Scope** menu. Figure 10.9 shows a scope with two active leases.

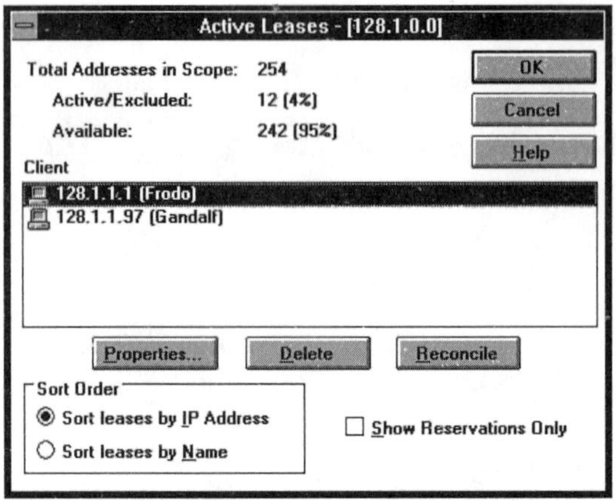

Figure 10.9

Active leases for a scope.

The following information is available in the **Active Leases** dialog box:

◆ The NetBIOS name of the computer that has obtained each lease.

◆ The total number of addresses in the scope.

◆ The number of addresses currently unavailable for leasing. This number is the total of numbers of active leases, excluded addresses, and reserved addresses.

No direct way exists for determining the number of active leases. To determine the number of active leases, record the total number of active/excluded addresses. Then check the **Show Reservations Only** box to determine the number of reserved addresses. Subtract the number of reservations from the total of active/excluded addresses to determine the number of nonreserved leases. Then subtract the number of excluded addresses, which must be determined from the scope properties.

◆ Whether leases should be sorted by IP Address or by Name.

◆ Whether leases should be displayed with reservations.

When a DHCP client restarts, what events take place depend on whether the client holds a lease to an IP address.

◆ If the DHCP client does not hold an address lease, it enters an initializing state in which it attempts to obtain an address lease.

◆ If the DHCP client holds a lease to an address, it sends a message to DHCP declaring its configuration. A DHCP server must confirm this information if the client is to continue using the lease. If the DHCP server sends a negative reply, the client must enter an initializing state and acquire a new lease.

Usually, a client is permitted to retain its IP address assignment and may use the same address indefinitely. Changes in scope properties can force the DHCP client to accept a new IP address lease when it restarts.

Note When a client starts TCP/IP with an address obtained from DHCP, it transmits an ARP request frame to determine whether the IP address is active on the network. If it is discovered that another host is using the IP address, TCP/IP is not started and the client reports an error message. Resolve the conflict before attempting to restart the client.

Viewing and Modifying Properties for an Active Lease

To view or modify the properties for a lease, select the lease in the **Active Leases** dialog box and choose **Properties** to display the **Client Properties** box (see fig. 10.10).

For leases assigned from a scope address pool, no fields in the **Client Properties** box may be modified.

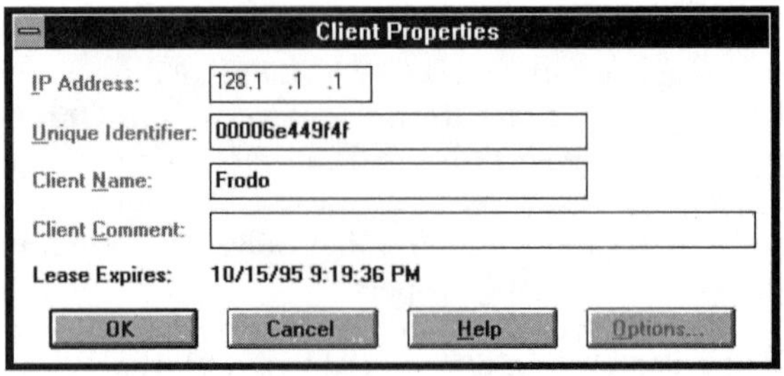

Figure 10.10

Properties for an active lease.

	Client Properties
IP Address:	128.1 .1 .1
Unique Identifier:	00006e449f4f
Client Name:	Frodo
Client Comment:	
Lease Expires:	10/15/95 9:19:36 PM

OK   Cancel   Help   Options...

If the lease has been assigned to a reserved address, three fields may be modified: **Unique Number**, **Client Name**, and **Client Comment**. The **IP Address** field may not be modified. To change the IP address reserved for the client, you must delete the current reservation and create a new one. You also must force the client to release its old address, which you do by executing the command `ipconfig /release` at a command prompt on the client computer. Windows 95 users can run the `winipcfg` command at a Run prompt and choose the **Release** button to accomplish the same result.

Deleting Active Leases

Deleting an active lease is not quite what it appears. Selecting a lease in the **Active Leases** dialog box and choosing **Delete** removes the lease from the display but leaves the client free to use the lease for the duration of the current session.

When an active lease is deleted, the result is identical to when the client's lease has expired. The client is not forced off the network but continues to use the IP address until the client is restarted. The next time it reconnects to the network, the client enters a *renewing* state. DHCP denies the client's request to renew the lease on its old address. This forces the DHCP client into a *rebinding* state, in which the client requests a new address lease from DHCP.

> **Note**
> Do not delete an active lease when a client is logged in using that lease. The client may continue to use the IP address until it logs out of the network. The IP address, on the other hand, is returned to the pool of available addresses and can be leased by other DHCP clients. As a result, two active clients might find themselves sharing the same IP address.
>
> To force a client to release its current lease and free up its IP address, enter the command `ipconfig /release` at the command prompt of the client. Windows 95 users should run the `winipcfg` program at a Run prompt and choose **Release**. Doing so forfeits the client's IP address and effectively disconnects it from the network. Restarting the client and logging back in to the network to obtain a new IP address is necessary.

Establishing Reservations

In some cases, it is important that a client always obtain the same IP address, but it remains advantageous to manage the IP address and its properties through DHCP. To support clients that require fixed addresses, *reservations* can be specified in DHCP Manager. A reservation consists of an IP address and associated properties, keyed to the physical (MAC) address of a specific computer. Only that computer can obtain a lease for the IP address.

> **Note**
> All computers can be configured to obtain their addresses from DHCP, except for computers running DHCP Server services or WINS Server services.
>
> Here are some examples of situations that may require reserved IP addresses:
>
> ◆ A constant address is required, such as the address of a default gateway or a DNS server.
>
> ◆ A domain controller obtains its address from an LMHOSTS file. (See Chapter 11, "Managing WINS.")
>
> ◆ A host does not obtain its address from DHCP and address conflicts must be prevented.

To define a reservation, the physical address of the client must be determined. After TCP/IP protocols are installed on a computer, either of the following procedures can be used to identify the physical address:

◆ Enable the computer as a DHCP client and have it obtain a lease to an address in any active scope. Then view the properties for the client as described in the section "Viewing and Managing Active Leases" earlier in this chapter. One of those properties is the host's physical address. You can copy this address to the Clipboard by selecting it and pressing Ctrl+C. This makes pasting the address into the reservation properties easy.

◆ At the client host, open an MS-DOS prompt and enter the command `ipconfig` `/all`, discussed in Chapter 9, "Building Routed Networks." One of the items in the listing produced reports the physical address of the computer. The Windows 95 **winipcfg** utility displays similar data in a GUI format. Run `winipcfg` from the **Run** command in the **Start** menu.

On a Windows NT computer, another method is to open a command prompt and enter the command `net config wksta`. Look for the address following the heading "Workstation active on." You can use this command without having to install TCP/IP protocols. (Unfortunately, **net config** does not provide this information on Windows 3.1x or Windows 95 computers.)

To create a reservation:

1. Start DHCP Manager.

2. In the **DHCP Servers** box, select the scope in which to define the reservation.

3. Choose **Add Reservations** in the **Scope** menu to open the **Add Reserved Clients** dialog box (see fig. 10.11).

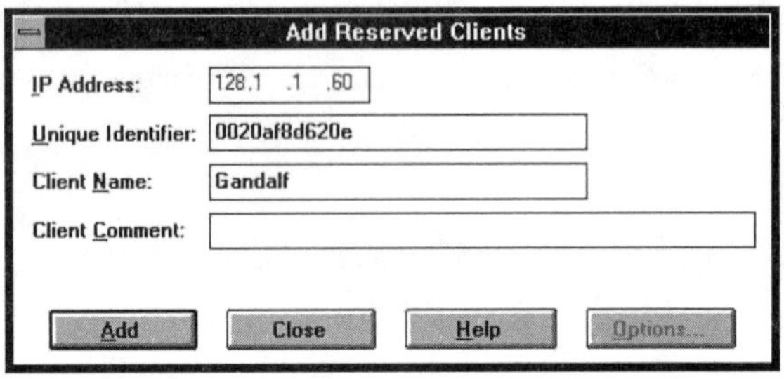

Figure 10.11

Adding a DHCP reservation.

Add Reserved Clients	
IP Address:	128.1 .1 .60
Unique Identifier:	0020af8d620e
Client Name:	Gandalf
Client Comment:	

Add   Close   Help   Options...

4. In the **IP Address** box, enter the IP address to be reserved. This address must fall within the range of available and nonexcluded addresses of the scope chosen in Step 2.

5. In the **Unique Number** box, enter the physical address of the client for which the address is being reserved. This address is often reported with punctuation such as, 00-00-6e-44-9f-4f. Do not include any punctuation in the **Unique Number** box. If you copied the address of the computer to the Clipboard, you can paste it by selecting the **Unique Number** box and pressing Ctrl+V.

6. Enter the client's name in the **Client Name** box.

7. If you want, enter a description in the **Client Comment** box.

8. Choose **Add** to store the reservation.

Reservations are listed in the **Active Leases** dialog box. As figure 10.12 shows, reserved leases are identified with the label "Reservation" and state the IP address that has been reserved.

Note Assigning a reservation to a client currently connected using an address leased from a scope does not force the client to release its current lease and obtain the reserved IP address. The client's current lease is deleted (expired), forcing the client to obtain a new address lease the next time it connects with the network. At that time, the client obtains the IP address that is reserved for it.

As with deleting active leases, therefore, a reservation should be added only when the client has released its current lease. Otherwise duplicate IP addresses may be assigned to the original client and to a new client that leases the address.

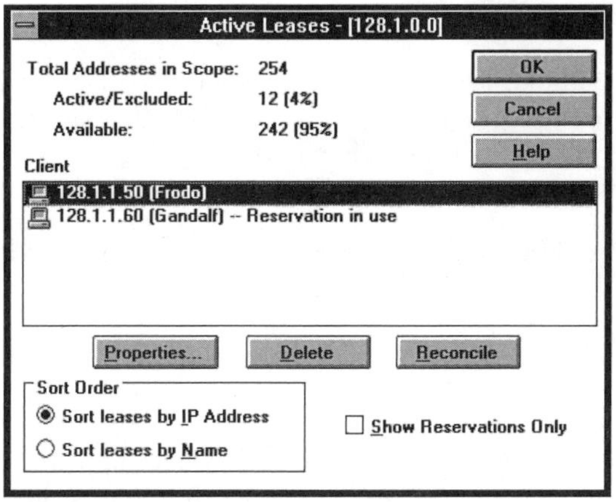

Figure 10.12

Active leases showing an IP address reservation.

Activating, Deactivating, and Deleting Scopes

Scopes may be active or inactive. An active scope services DHCP requests and is indicated in DHCP Manager by an illuminated (yellow) lightbulb icon to the left of the scope name. An inactive scope does not service DHCP requests and is indicated by a darkened (gray) lightbulb icon to the left of the scope name.

To deactivate an active scope, select the scope in DHCP Manager and choose **Deactivate** in the **Scope** menu.

To activate an inactive scope, select the scope in DHCP Manager and choose **Activate** in the **Scope** menu.

To delete a scope, first deactivate the scope. Then choose **Delete** in the **Scope** menu.

After a scope is deactivated or deleted, currently logged-in clients can continue to utilize the address leases assigned to them. When a client restarts or must renew an expired lease, it must obtain a lease from a different scope.

After deactivating or deleting a scope, you can force a DHCP client to obtain a lease from another scope by entering the command `ipconfig /renew` in a command prompt on the client. It might be necessary to restart the client. The Windows 95 **winipcfg** program provides a **Renew** button that accomplishes the same task.

Managing Leases

The duration of leases must be determined by the needs of the network.

◆ If the available address pool is larger than the number of hosts needing addresses, the lease duration can be fairly long. Indefinite leases are not recommended; all networks experience change to some degree and assigning a lease duration ensures that old leases are eventually purged.

◆ If the network configuration changes frequently, choose fairly short lease times so that addresses that become available can be reassigned quickly.

◆ If the number of TCP/IP users approaches the size of the address pool, a short lease duration may be in order.

When a client lease expires, it remains in the DHCP database for approximately one day. The DHCP client can attempt to renew its old lease within that period. The delay accommodates DHCP clients and servers that are in different time zones or that have unsynchronized clocks.

The **Active Leases** dialog box reports the sum of active and excluded addresses for the scope selected.

Managing Multiple DHCP Servers

A network can support any desired number of DHCP servers. Multiple DHCP servers reduce the workload on any one server, and enables DHCP address assignment to continue if one of the DHCP servers fails.

Unfortunately, having redundant DHCP servers for the same scope is impossible. DHCP does not provide a mechanism that enables DHCP servers to exchange lease information. If any IP addresses appear in the scope definitions for two DHCP servers, therefore, duplicate IP addresses might be assigned.

All DHCP servers can be managed centrally by a manager who has Administrator permissions for the servers. To add a DHCP server to the DHCP Manager, perform the following steps:

1. Start DHCP Manager.

2. Choose **Add** in the **Server** menu.

3. In the **Add DHCP Server to Server List** dialog box, enter the IP address of the DHCP server to add.

4. Choose **OK**.

Managing the DHCP Database

The key DHCP database files are stored by default in C:\winnt35\system32\dhcp. (If your system files are stored in a directory other than C:\winnt35, substitute the appropriate directory path.) The files are as follows:

◆ **DHCP.MDB.** The DHCP database file.

◆ **DHCP.TMP.** A file used by DHCP to store temporary working data.

◆ **JET.LOG and JET*.LOG.** These files record transactions performed on the database. This data can be used to recover the DHCP database in the event of damage.

◆ **SYSTEM.MDB.** Holds information about the structure of the DHCP database.

Windows NT Server periodically backs up the DHCP database and Registry entries. The default backup interval is 15 minutes, configurable using a Registry key.

Compacting the DHCP Database

The DHCP files should not be modified or removed. However, you might need to compact the database from time to time. Microsoft recommends compacting DHCP.MDB when it reaches 10 MB in size. To compact the database, follow this procedure:

1. Open a command prompt.

2. Enter the command **net stop dhcpserver** to stop the DHCP Server service on the computer. Users cannot obtain or renew DHCP leases while the DHCP Server service is stopped.

3. Change to the DHCP directory. If the directory is in the default location, enter the command **cd \winnt35\system32\dhcp**.

4. Enter the command **jetpack dhcp.mdb temp.mdb** to compact the database. **dhcp.mdb** is the file to be compacted, while **temp.mdb** is a name for a temporary file that **jetpack** uses during the compacting process.

5. After receiving the message jetpack completed successfully, restart DHCP with the command **net start dhcpserver**.

6. To close the command prompt, enter the command **exit**.

 Stop   jetpack should be used to compact only the DHCP.MDB file. Do not compact the SYSTEM.MDB file, period, per Microsoft.

Starting and Stopping the DHCP Server

You might need to periodically stop and restart the DHCP Server. You also might need to determine whether DHCP Server services are started. If users experience difficulty obtaining addresses from DHCP, the first troubleshooting step is to make sure that the DHCP Server service is started.

As explained in the previous section, you can start and stop the DHCP Server service from the command prompt. You also can use the Services tool in the Control Panel to start and stop it. To start, stop, or ascertain the status of the DHCP Server service, follow these steps:

1. Open the Services tool in the Control Panel. Figure 10.13 shows the **Services** dialog box.

2. Scroll through the list of services to locate the entry **Microsoft DHCP Server**. The status of the server is described by entries in two columns:

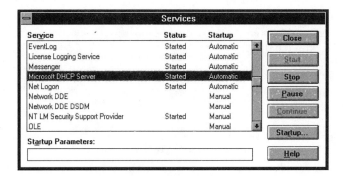

Figure 10.13

The Services tool displaying the status of the DHCP Server service.

◆ The **Status** column states whether the service is **Started**. If no entry is found, the service is not started.

◆ The **Startup** column indicates whether the service starts automatically when the system restarts. **Automatic** and **Manual** indicate whether manual intervention is required to start the service. A **Disabled** service cannot be started from the **Services** dialog box.

3. To change the startup mode for a service, choose **Startup** and change the Startup Type in the **Services** dialog box.

4. To stop a started service, select the service and choose **Stop.**

   To start a stopped service, select the service and choose **Start.**

   A disabled service cannot be started.

5. Choose **Close** to exit the Services tool.

Note   The information in this section is sufficient for the purpose of managing the DHCP Server service, but much more can be said about the Services tool. Consult NRP's *Inside Windows NT Server* for a complete discussion of the Services tool.

Repairing a Corrupted DHCP Database

The DHCP database files are backed up at periodic intervals. The default location for the backup copies of the database files is the directory C:\winnt35\system32\dhcp\backup\jet.

If the DHCP Server service is started but users still cannot obtain leases from DHCP, the DHCP database might have become corrupted, which would make DHCP unavailable. Restoring the DHCP database from the backup copy might be possible. To force DHCP to restore its database from the backup, stop and restart the DHCP Server service, using the techniques described in the previous two sections. If the DHCP Server service identifies a corrupted database during startup, it automatically attempts to restore from the backup database.

The section "Configuring DHCP in the Registry," later in this chapter, discusses the **RestoreFlag** key in the registry, which can be set to force DHCP to restore its database when the computer is restarted.

If neither procedure restores the database satisfactorily, stop the DHCP Server service. Then copy all files in C:\winnt35\system32\dhcp\backup to C:\winnt35\system32\dhcp. Finally, restart the DHCP Server service.

After you restore the database, you need to bring the database up to date on active leases not recorded in the backup copy of the database. This procedure is called *reconciling* the DHCP database. To reconcile the DHCP database:

1. Start DHCP Manager.

2. Select a scope in the **DHCP Scopes** box.

3. Choose **Active Leases** in the **Scope** menu.

4. Choose the **Reconcile button** in the **Active Leases** dialog box.

Note
The DHCP database is not fault tolerant, even though it is periodically backed up. A system crash during the backup process could corrupt both the database and the backup database.

To provide a greater degree of fault tolerance, you can use the Windows NT Replicator service to automatically copy the backup database to another Windows NT computer. After the server is restored to operation, the replicated copy of the backup database could be retrieved and used to restart DHCP.

NRP's *Inside Windows NT Server* offers a thorough discussion of the Replicator service.

Creating a New DHCP Database

If the database is corrupted and a valid backup is unavailable, you can force DHCP to create a new database with the following procedure:

1. Stop the DHCP Server service.

2. Copy the file C:\winnt35\system32\dhcp\dhcp.mdb to another directory.

3. Delete all files in the directory C:\WINNT35\SYSTEM32\DHCP (the default primary directory).

4. Delete all files in the directory C:\WINNT35\SYSTEM32\DHCP\BACKUP\JET (the default backup directory).

5. Copy the file SYSTEM.MDB from the installation CD-ROM or diskettes to the directory C:\WINNT35\SYSTEM32\DHCP.

6. Restart the DHCP Server service. The following four steps reconcile the new DHCP database with active leases.

7. Start DHCP Manager.

8. Select a scope in the **DHCP Scopes** box.

9. Choose **Active Leases** in the **Scope** menu.

10. Choose the **Reconcile** button in the **Active Leases** dialog box. When they renew their leases, clients are matched with active leases to complete rebuilding the database.

> **Note** You can force a client to renew its DHCP lease by entering the command `ipconfig / renew` at a command prompt on the client computer. With Windows 95, choose the **Renew** button in the `winipcfg` utility, which you can start by entering the command `winipcfg` in a **Run** dialog box.

DHCP Configuration Options

Your organization might choose to implement DHCP even though IP addresses are not assigned dynamically. DHCP *options* enable network administrators to configure many settings that affect the TCP/IP protocols. These DHCP options can be applied to any computer that obtains its address from DHCP, whether the address is dynamically allocated or reserved.

As shown in figure 10.14, DHCP options are applied in layers:

◆ Global options apply to all scopes on a given DHCP server unless overwritten by scope or client options.

◆ Scope options apply to all clients within the scope unless overridden by client options. Scope properties might be used to set options for a department or for hosts on a specific network.

◆ Client options supersede scope and global options for a specific client. Client-specific options may be configured for clients having DHCP reservations.

Figure 10.14

Priority of DHCP options.

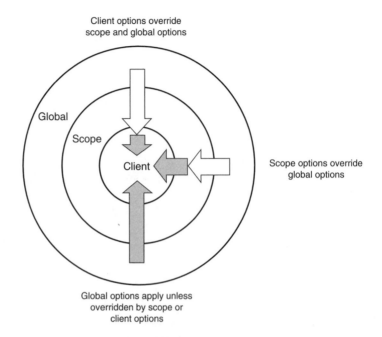

Specifying default options is another possibility. Specifying a default option establishes default values for any parameters associated with the option but does not put the option into effect. Options go into effect only when specified as global, scope, or client options.

A Microsoft DHCP packet can support a DHCP data payload of 312 bytes, which is generally sufficient. If too many DHCP options are configured, some can exceed the 312-byte capacity, making it necessary to trim options of lower priority.

Managing Default, Global, and Scope DHCP Options

Options are added, configured, and removed within DHCP Manager. Default, global, and scope options are managed from the **DHCP Manager** dialog box. To change options, follow these steps:

1. Start DHCP Manager.

2. Select an existing scope.

3. To set default parameter values for an option, choose the **Default** command in the **DHCP Options** menu.

   To set options for all scopes on the DHCP server, choose the **Global** command in the **DHCP Options** menu.

To set options for the selected scope, choose the **Scope** command in the **DHCP Options** menu.

4. The **DHCP Options** dialog box (see fig. 10.15) is used to add and delete options. The legend for the dialog box specifies whether default, global, or scope options are being configured. In this example, two options have been added.

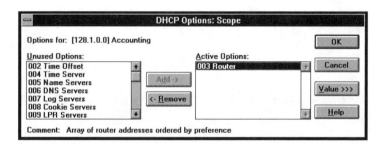

Figure 10.15

Adding options.

5. To add an option, select an option in the **Unused Options** box and choose **Add**.

6. To remove an option, select an option in the **Active Options** box and choose **Remove**.

7. Many options accept or require configuration values. To change the values of an option, select the option in the **Active Options** box and choose **Value**. The **DHCP Options** dialog box expands to display the currently assigned value or values (see fig. 10.16).

8. To edit values assigned to the option, choose **Edit Array**. An appropriate editor opens. Figure 10.17 shows the **IP Address Array Editor** dialog box. In this box, values may be added or removed from the array of addresses. (The order of the options determines their priority, and values should be added in order of priority. Unfortunately, no direct way exists for modifying the order of the values.)

Managing Client-Specific Options for Reservations

Client-specific options may be assigned to reservations only. Options may be assigned to leases only by assigning default, global, and scope options.

To assign options to a reservation:

1. Select the scope supporting the reservation in the **DHCP Manager** dialog box.

2. Choose the **Active Leases** command in the **Scope** menu.

3. Select the reservation in the **Active Leases** dialog box and choose the **Properties** button to open the **Client Properties** dialog box.

Figure 10.16

Expanding the DHCP Options dialog box to show option values.

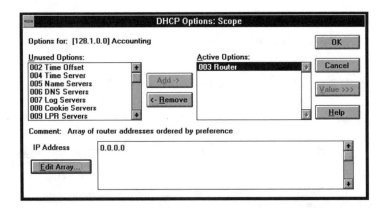

Figure 10.17

Registry subtrees shown in Registry Editor.

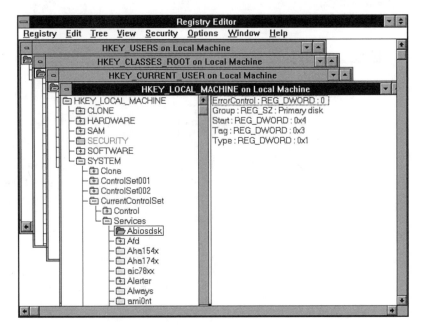

4. For reservations, the **Options** button in the **Client Properties** dialog box will be active. Choose **Options** to open the **DHCP Options: Reservation** dialog box, which is similar to the dialog box shown in figure 10.15. Use this box to add and configure options for the reservation.

5. Choose **OK** to exit the **DHCP Options** dialog box.

DHCP Options for Microsoft TCP/IP

Table 10.1 summarizes the predefined DHCP options that apply to Microsoft TCP/IP clients. The table includes only options that may be configured using the **DHCP Options** dialog box.

Several RFC1533 DHCP options are configured in the **Create Scope** or **Scope Proper-ties** dialog box. These options are as follows:

◆ 1. Subnet mask

◆ 51. DHCP Lease time

◆ 58. DHCP Renewal (T1) time

◆ 59. DHCP Rebinding (T2) time

Options 51, 58, and 59 are all functions of the lease duration specified in the **Create Scope** or **Scope Properties** dialog box.

Note RFC1533 specifies many other options not applicable to Microsoft TCP/IP clients. If non-Microsoft clients will be obtaining addresses from the Microsoft DHCP Server, you can include non-Microsoft options in the properties of the appropriate scopes and reservations.

TABLE 10.1   DHCP OPTIONS FOR MICROSOFT CLIENTS

Code	Name	Description
1	Subnet Mask	Specifies the client subnet mask. This option is configured in the Create Scope or Scope Properties dialog box, and cannot be directly configured as a scope option.
3	Router	Specifies a list of IP addresses for routers on the client's network.
6	DNS servers	Specifies a list of IP addresses for available DNS servers.
15	Domain name	Specifies the domain name to be used when resolving DNS host names.
44	WINS/NBNS servers	Specifies a list of IP addresses for NetBIOS name servers (NBNS). (See Chapter 11.)
46	WINS/NBT node type	Specifies the NetBIOS over TCP/IP node type. Values: 1=b-node, 2=p-node, 4-m-node, 8=h-node. (See RFC 1001/1002 and Chapter 11.)
47	NetBIOS ID scope	Specifies a string to be used as the NetBIOS over TCP/IP scope ID. (See RFC 1001/1002.)

Configuring DHCP in the Registry

The Registry is the fault-tolerant database in which configuration data are stored for Windows NT computers. Several Registry parameters are related to DHCP and can, like other Registry parameters, be modified using the Registry Editor. The Registry and Registry Editor are discussed more thoroughly in NRP's books *Inside Windows NT Server* and *Windows NT Server: The Professional Reference*.

> **Stop** The Registry includes configuration data for virtually every Windows NT system. Obviously, a great deal of damage can be done if errors are introduced into the Registry. Therefore, when browsing the Registry with the Registry Editor, you should choose **Read Only Mode** in the **Options** menu to prevent accidental changes.

The Registry is organized into four subtrees. Each of the subtrees has a window within Registry Editor (see fig. 10.17). The subtrees are delineated in the following list:

◆ `HKEY_LOCAL_MACHINE.` Current configuration parameters for the computer.

◆ `HKEY_CURRENT_USER.` The profile for the current user.

◆ `HKEY_USERS.` Stores user profiles.

◆ `HKEY_CLASSES_ROOT.` Object linking and embedding (OLE) and file-class associations.

Data associated with DHCP are stored in the HKEY_LOCAL_MACHINE subtree. The window for this subtree has been expanded in figure 10.17 to show the database structure. Note the similarity between the structure of the Registry and of the DOS/NT hierarchical file system. The equivalents of the directory in the Registry database are called *keys*. Data stored in Registry keys are called *values*.

Keys can contain other keys. In the figure, for example, **SYSTEM** is a key that contains several subkeys such as **ControlSet001** and **CurrentControlSet**.

In figure 10.18, the **CurrentControlSet** branch has been opened for several levels, revealing the **ComputerName** key. This key contains one value describing the NetBIOS name assigned to this computer. Keys can contain an indefinite number of values. All values have three components:

◆ A name, in this example, **ComputerName**

◆ A data type, such as **REG_SZ**

◆ A value, here, **RIVENDELL**

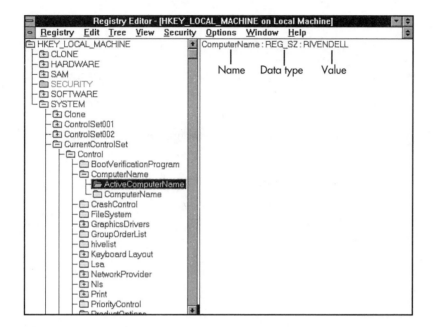

Figure 10.18

A value in the Registry.

Registry data have one of five data types:

◆ **REG_BINARY.** Raw binary data, the form used to store most hardware data.

◆ **REG_DWORD.** Numeric data up to 4 bytes in length, in decimal, hexadecimal, or binary form.

◆ **REG_EXPAND_SZ.** Expandable data strings that contain system variables. An example of this variable type would be **%SystemRoot\system32**.

◆ **REG_MULTI_SZ.** Data consisting of multiple strings in lists. Often used to store lists of human-readable values.

◆ **REG_SZ.** Character data, usually human-readable text.

The data types that apply to DHCP Registry entries are discussed along with the associated values. See the section "DHCP-Related Registry Values" later in this chapter.

Viewing and Editing DHCP-Related Values in the Registry

DHCP-related Registry values are stored in the HKEY_LOCAL_MACHINE subtree in the following subkey:

```
SYSTEM\CurrentControlSet\Services\DHCPServer\Parameters
```

To observe or modify the DHCP Registry values:

1. To start the Registry Editor, choose the **Run** command in the Program Manager **File** menu. In the **Command Line** box for the **Run** command, enter the command **regedt32** and choose **OK**.

2. If no subtrees are shown, choose the **Open Local** command in the **Registry** menu.

3. Expand the window for the HKEY_LOCAL_MACHINE subtree.

4. Click on the following keys to expand the appropriate branch of the tree:

   ◆ **SYSTEM**

   ◆ **CurrentControlSet**

   ◆ **Services**

   ◆ **DHCPServer**

   ◆ **Parameters**

   Completed, the window resembles figure 10.19.

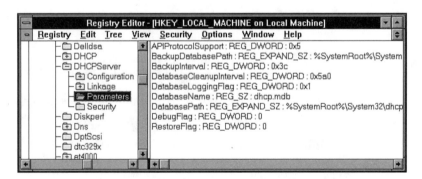

Figure 10.19

Registry values associated with DHCP.

5. To change a value, double-click on the value entry to open the appropriate editor. The editor that appears supports entry only of data that conform to the data type associated with this value. The example shown in figure 10.20 shows the DWORD editor, which accepts only a binary, decimal, or hexadecimal value. A String Editor is used to enter string-type values.

   Edit the value and, if necessary, click on the button associated with the data format. Then choose **OK** to save the value to the Registry.

6. To save changes, choose **Close** in the **Registry** menu.

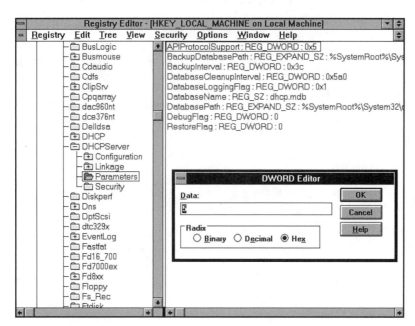

Figure 10.20

Editing a DWORD-type value in the Registry.

DHCP-Related Registry Values

The following Registry values can be viewed and edited using the procedure described in the previous section:

APIProtocolSupport

Data Type:	REG_DWORD
Range:	0x1, 0x2, 0x4, 0x5, 0x7
Default:	0x7

Specifies the protocols supported by the DHCP server. Edit this parameter to enable different computers to access the DHCP server. Available values are as follows:

0x1	RPC over TCP/IP
0x2	RPC over named pipes
0x4	RPC over local procedure call (LPC)
0x5	RPC over TCP/IP and RPC over LPC
0x7	RPC over TCP/IP, named pipes, and LPC

BackupDatabasePath

Data Type:	REG_EXPAND_SZ
Range:	*pathname*
Default:	%SystemRoot%\system32\dhcp\backup

Specifies the directory in which DHCP backup files are stored. The default value places the backup files on the same hard drive as the primary files, making both vulnerable to a single hardware failure. If the system has more than one hard drive, locating the backup directory on an alternative hard drive is preferable. This directory must be on a local hard drive because DHCP Manager cannot access a network drive.

BackupInterval

Data Type:	REG_DWORD
Range:	no limit
Default:	15 minutes

Specifies the interval in minutes between DHCP database backups.

DatabaseCleanupInterval

Data Type:	REG_DWORD
Range:	no limit
Default:	0x15180

DHCP periodically cleans up the database, removing expired records. This parameter specifies the interval in minutes between DHCP cleanup operations. The default value sets an interval of one day (0x15180 is 864,000 minutes, equivalent to 24 hours).

DatabaseLoggingFlag

Data Type:	REG_DWORD
Range:	0 or 1
Default:	1

If the value of this parameter is 1, database changes are recorded in the JET.LOG file. If the value is 0, changes are not recorded. The JET.LOG file is used to recover changes that have not been made to the database file. It might be desirable to turn off logging to improve system performance.

DatabaseName

Data Type:	REG_SZ
Range:	*filename*
Default:	dhcp.mdb

The name of the DHCP database file.

DatabasePath

Data Type:	REG_EXPAND_SZ
Range:	*pathname*
Default:	%SystemRoot%\System32\dhcp

The directory in which DHCP database files are created and opened.

RestoreFlag

Data Type:	REG_DWORD
Range:	0 or 1
Default:	0

If this value is 0, the database is not restored from the backup database when the DHCP Server service is started. Set this value to 1 to force DHCP to retrieve the backup database. This parameter is automatically set to 0 after a successful database restoration.

Summary

This chapter examined the DHCP (Dynamic Host Configuration Protocol). DHCP increases TCP/IP network administration efficiency by dynamically assigning IP addresses to hosts, practically eliminating the need to configure host addresses manually. Additionally, DHCP enables you to locally manage the majority of TCP/IP clients on an internetwork.

The chapter began with an overview of DHCP concepts and operation. You then learned how to install DHCP server services and how to set up DHCP scopes. Before DHCP clients can obtain IP addresses from a DHCP server, at least one scope must be created. A *scope* is a range of IP addresses along with a set of configuration options that apply to clients that receive IP addresses assigned from the scope.

After configuring DHCP, you can activate DHCP clients. The following section discussed how to enable a Windows NT computer as a DHCP client. (The configuration of Windows 95 and Windows 3.11 is covered in Chapter 13.)

The DHCP server maintains pools of IP addresses, called *scopes*. When a DHCP client enters a network, it requests and is granted a *lease* to use an address from an appropriate scope. There are prerequisites for DHCP clients to obtain addresses. After the prerequisites are satisfied, restarting a DHCP client causes it to obtain a lease for an IP address from a DHCP server. You can then view and manage active leases.

In some cases, it is important that a client always obtain the same IP address. It remains advantageous, however, to manage the IP address and its properties through DHCP. To support clients that require fixed addresses, *reservations* can be specified in DHCP Manager.

Scopes may be active or inactive. An active scope services DHCP requests. An inactive scope does not service DHCP requests. In the following section, you learned how to activate, deactivate, and delete scopes.

In subsequent sections, you learned how to manage multiple DHCP servers, and how to manage the DHCP database files. Multiple DHCP servers reduce the workload on any one server, and enable DHCP address assignment to continue if one of the DHCP servers fails.

The chapter concluded with a discussion of DHCP configuration options and configuring DHCP in the Registry. DHCP options enable network administrators to configure many settings that affect the TCP/IP protocols. The Registry is the fault-tolerant database in which configuration data are stored for Windows NT computers. Several Registry parameters are related to DHCP and can, like other Registry parameters, be modified using the Registry Editor.

Chapter 11 Snapshot

This chapter examines WINS in considerable depth, showing how to plan WINS services and how to implement and maintain WINS servers. It covers the following topics:

◆ Resolving names on Microsoft networks

◆ Architecture of the Windows Internet Name Service

◆ Naming on a non-WINS internetwork

◆ Installing the WINS server service

◆ Naming on a WINS network

◆ Naming versus browsing

◆ Managing WINS servers

◆ WINS registry parameters

◆ Managing LMHOSTS files

Managing WINS

The primary naming system for Microsoft networks is based on NetBIOS names. Each computer on the network is configured with a name that it broadcasts to the network to make its presence known to all other computers on the local network. This system is easy to maintain because whenever a computer inserts itself into the network, the global name database is updated. This system works well on local networks on which all protocols are supported by Microsoft network products. Microsoft operating systems configured using only TCP/IP protocols can use NetBIOS names within the context of a local, nonrouted network.

A significant limitation of NetBIOS naming in a TCP/IP environment is that the names do not propagate across routers. NetBIOS names are disseminated using broadcast datagrams, which IP routers do not forward. The NetBIOS names on one network, therefore, are invisible to computers on networks connected via routers.

Prior to the introduction of Windows NT Server, the Microsoft LAN Manager product supported internetwork name resolution using static naming tables stored in files named LMHOSTS. An *LMHOSTS* file is a text file that contains mappings between NetBIOS names and IP addresses. To enable computers on the internetwork to resolve names, a network administrator had to manually update the LMHOSTS file and distribute it to all computers on the internet. This was a distinctly labor-intensive method of maintaining NetBIOS naming.

With Windows NT Server, Microsoft introduced the Windows Internet Name Service (WINS). Like LMHOSTS, WINS maintains a NetBIOS global naming service for TCP/IP internets. Unlike LMHOSTS, WINS is dynamic, extending the automatic configuration of the NETBIOS name directory from local networks to internets. The WINS database is updated automatically as NetBIOS computers insert and remove themselves from the network.

If your Windows NT network will be connected to the Internet, using WINS in conjunction with DNS is possible, which would enable WINS to provide DNS with host names for Microsoft-based hosts within your network.

This chapter examines WINS in considerable depth, showing how to plan WINS services and how to implement and maintain WINS servers. Because LMHOSTS files might still be encountered and continue to be of value under some circumstances, LMHOSTS naming also is discussed.

Resolving Names on Microsoft Networks

Resolution is the process of associating host names with addresses. Resolution of NetBIOS names on TCP/IP environments is the responsibility of the NetBIOS over TCP/IP (NBT) service. NBT name resolution has evolved from a basic, broadcast-based approach to the current name-service approach. Before discussing WINS, it is necessary to examine the name resolution modes supported by NBT. The b-node, p-node, and m-node name resolution modes are defined in RFCs 1001 and 1002. H-node is currently an Internet-draft.

B-Node

Name resolution using broadcast messages (b-node) is the oldest method employed on Microsoft networks. Figure 11.1 illustrates b-node name resolution. When HOSTA needs to communicate with HOSTB, it sends a broadcast message that interrogates the network for the presence of HOSTB. If HOSTB receives the broadcast, it sends a response to HOSTA that includes its address. If HOSTA does not receive a response within a preset period of time, it "times out" and the attempt fails.

B-node name resolution works well in small, local networks, but poses two disadvantages that become critical as networks grow:

◆ As the number of hosts on the network increases, the amount of broadcast traffic can consume significant network bandwidth.

◆ IP routers do not forward broadcasts, and the b-node technique cannot propagate names through an internetwork.

B-node is the default name resolution mode for Microsoft hosts not configured to use WINS for name resolution. In pure b-node environments, hosts can be configured to use LMHOSTS files to resolve names on remote networks.

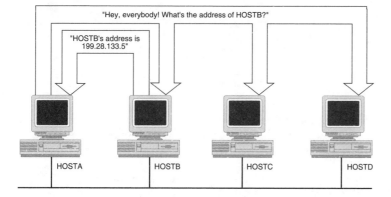

Figure 11.1

B-node name resolution.

P-Node

Hosts configured for p-node use WINS for name resolution. P-node computers register themselves with a WINS server, which functions as a NetBIOS name server. The WINS server maintains a database of NetBIOS names, ensures that duplicate names do not exist, and makes the database available to WINS clients. Figure 11.2 illustrates how WINS clients resolve names.

Each WINS client is configured with the address of a WINS server, which may reside on the local network or on a remote network. WINS clients and servers communicate via directed messages that can be routed. No broadcast messages are required for p-node name resolution.

Two liabilities of p-node name resolution are that:

◆ All computers must be configured using the address of a WINS server, even when communicating hosts reside on the same network.

◆ If a WINS server is unavailable, name resolution fails for p-node clients.

Because both b-node and p-node address resolution present disadvantages, two address modes have been developed that form hybrids of b-node and p-node. These hybrid modes are called m-node and h-node.

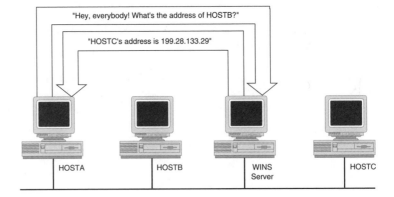

Figure 11.2

P-node name resolution.

M-Node

M-node computers first attempt to use b-node (broadcast) name resolution, which succeeds if the desired host resides on the local network. If b-node resolution fails, m-node hosts then attempt to use p-node to resolve the name.

M-node enables name resolution to continue on the local network when WINS services are down. B-node resolution is attempted first on the assumption that in most environments, hosts communicate most often with hosts on their local networks. When this assumption holds, performance of b-node resolution is superior to p-node. Recall, however, that b-node can result in high levels of broadcast traffic.

Microsoft warns that m-node can cause problems when network logons are attempted in a routed environment.

H-Node

Like m-node, h-node is a hybrid of broadcast (b-node) and directed (p-node) name resolution modes. Nodes configured with m-node, however, first attempt to resolve addresses using WINS. Only after an attempt to resolve the name using a name server fails does an h-node computer attempt to use b-node. M-node computers, therefore, can continue to resolve local addresses when WINS is unavailable. When operating in b-node mode, m-node computers continue to poll the WINS server and revert to h-node when WINS services are restored.

H-node is the default mode for Microsoft TCP/IP clients configured using the addresses of WINS servers. As a fallback, Windows TCP/IP clients can be configured to use LMHOSTS files for name resolution.

> **Note** Although networks can be configured using mixtures of b-node and p-node computers, Microsoft recommends this only as an interim measure. P-node hosts ignore b-node broadcast messages, and b-node hosts ignore p-node directed messages. Two hosts, therefore, conceivably could be established using the same NetBIOS name.

Architecture of the Windows Internet Name Service

WINS uses one or more WINS servers to maintain a database that provides name-to-address mappings in response to queries from WINS clients. The WINS database can be distributed across multiple servers to provide fault-tolerance and better service on local networks. A replication mechanism enables WINS servers to share their data on a periodic basis.

WINS is a particularly good fit when IP addresses are assigned by DHCP. Although the DHCP lease renewal process results in a certain stability of IP address assignments, IP addresses can change if hosts are moved to different networks or if a host is inactive for a time sufficient to cause its address to be reassigned. WINS automatically updates its database to respond to such changes.

Because WINS clients communicate with WINS servers via directed messages, no problems are encountered when operating in a routed environment. Figure 11.3 shows an internet with three networks. WINS servers are configured on two of the networks. The WINS servers can both resolve name queries, and are configured to periodically replicate their databases. WINS clients on all three networks can communicate with a WINS server to resolve names to addresses.

WINS proxies enable non-WINS clients to resolve names on the internetwork. When a WINS proxy receives a b-node broadcast attempting to resolve a name on a remote network, the WINS proxy directs a name query to a WINS server and returns the response to the non-WINS client.

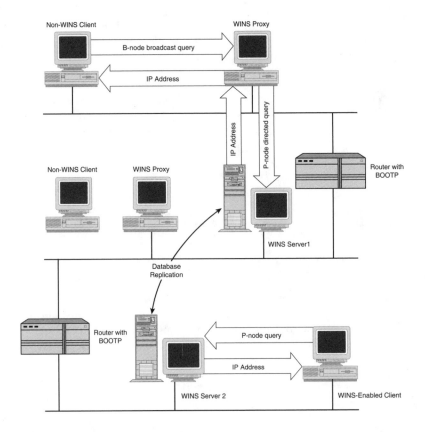

Figure 11.3

Architecture of a WINS name service.

WINS makes maintaining unique NetBIOS names throughout the internet possible. When a computer attempts to register a NetBIOS name with WINS, it is permitted to do so only if the name is not currently reserved in the WINS database. Without WINS, unique names are enforced only through the broadcast b-node mechanism on local networks.

When a WINS client is shut down in an orderly manner, it releases its name reservation in the WINS database and the name is marked as *released*. After a certain time, a released name is marked as *extinct*. Extinct names are maintained for a period of time sufficient to propagate the information to all WINS servers, after which the extinct name is removed from the WINS database.

If a computer has released its name through an orderly shutdown, WINS knows that the name is available and the client can immediately re-obtain the name when it reenters the network. If the client has changed network addresses (by moving to a different network segment, for example), a released name can also be reassigned.

If a computer is not shut down in an orderly fashion, its name reservation remains active in the WINS database. When the computer attempts to reregister the name, the WINS server challenges the registration attempt. If the computer has changed IP addresses, the challenge fails and the client is permitted to reregister the name with its new address. If no other computer is actively using the name, the client is also permitted to reregister with the name.

All names in the WINS database bear a timestamp that indicates when the reservation will expire. If a client fails to reregister the name when the reservation expires, the name is released. WINS supports definition of static name assignments that do not expire.

Naming on a Non-WINS Internetwork

Figure 11.4 illustrates the internet that will be used to demonstrate WINS operation. The internet consists of two networks, 128.1.0.0 and 128.2.0.0, connected by a multihomed Windows NT Server computer on which routing is enabled.

Four computers are attached to the internetwork:

◆ **VENICE.** A Windows 95 computer attached to network 128.1.0.0. VENICE has been assigned IP address 128.1.0.10.

◆ **URBINO.** A Windows 3.11 computer attached to network 128.2.0.0. URBINO's IP address 128.2.0.10.

◆ **ROME.** A Windows NT Server computer that is backup domain controller for the domain. ROME is statically configured with IP addresses 128.1.0.1 and 128.2.0.1.

◆ **FLORENCE.** A Windows NT Server computer configured as the primary domain controller. FLORENCE has been statically configured with IP address 128.2.0.2.

To access a shared resource, a computer must obtain the IP address of the server that shares the resource. VENICE could obtain the IP address of ROME without difficulty by sending a broadcast on the local network. But what happens when VENICE attempts to access a share on URBINO?

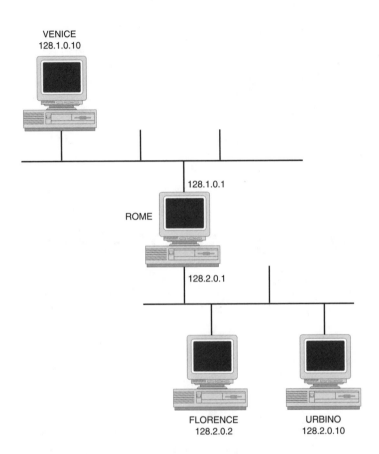

Figure 11.4

*An internetwork without
a WINS server.*

VENICE might be able to see an entry for URBINO in a browse window, or VENICE
could attempt to access a resource on URBINO by entering the UNC name of the
resource. When Venice attempts to connect with URBINO, the attempt fails with a
message similar to \\Urbino is not accessible. The computer or sharename could
not be found. VENICE attempted to identify URBINO using b-node broadcasts,
which cannot succeed because URBINO is on a separate network from VENICE.

The following sections examine the procedures for configuring WINS servers and
clients. Then discussion returns to this example network to see how WINS solves the
problem experienced by VENICE.

Installing the WINS Server Service

Any Windows NT Server computer can be configured as a WINS server, except WINS servers cannot receive their IP address assignments from DHCP. WINS clients communicate with WINS servers via directed datagrams, and you do not have to locate a WINS server on each network segment. However, non-WINS clients are supported only if at least one WINS proxy is installed on each network or subnetwork.

Note Multihomed computers should not be configured as WINS servers. A WINS server may register its name with only one network. The name of a multihomed WINS server, therefore, cannot be registered with all attached networks. Also, some client connection attempts fail with multihomed WINS servers.

Multihomed computers may be configured as WINS clients.

To install the WINS Server service, follow these steps:

1. Open the Network utility in the Control Panel.

2. Choose **Add Software** in the **Network Settings** dialog box.

3. Select **TCP/IP Protocol and related components** in the **Network Settings** box of the **Add Network Software** dialog box. Then choose **Continue**.

4. Check **WINS Server Services** in the **Windows NT TCP/IP Installation Options** dialog box. Then choose **Continue**.

5. Supply diskettes and path information as required to install the software.

6. Choose **OK** to close the **Network Settings** dialog box and restart the computer.

Configuring a Statically Addressed WINS Client

Clients configured using static IP addresses are enabled as WINS clients by supplying one or more WINS server addresses for the client's TCP/IP configuration. Figure 11.5 shows the TCP/IP configuration of a computer that includes an address for a primary WINS Server.

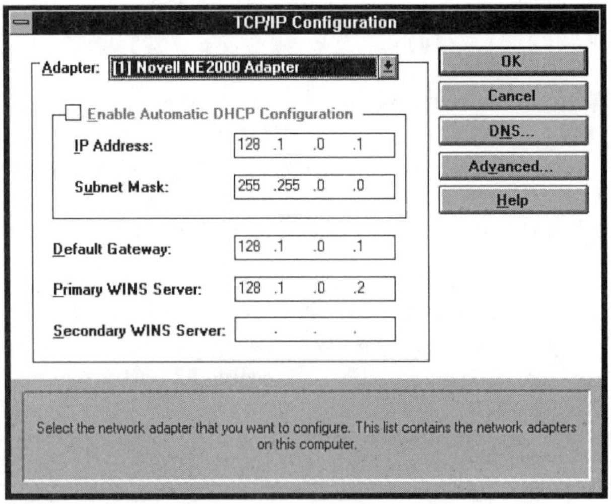

Figure 11.5

Configuring a TCP/IP host as a WINS client.

Configuring WINS Proxies

Windows NT, Windows 95, and Windows for Workgroups computers can be configured as WINS proxies, enabling them to receive broadcast b-node name requests from non-WINS clients and resolve them using directed h-node queries to WINS servers. WINS proxies enable b-node computers to obtain name resolutions from WINS.

For Windows NT and WfW computers, the WINS proxy feature is enabled in the **Advanced Microsoft TCP/IP Configuration** dialog box by checking the box labeled **Enable WINS Proxy Agent.**

Configuring DHCP Clients as WINS Clients

To enable DHCP clients to make use of WINS, the clients must be assigned the following two DHCP options:

◆ **44 WINS/NBNS Servers.** This option specifies the WINS servers that the computers will attempt to use. Because hosts in different scopes will probably access different scopes, this option should probably be assigned at the scope level.

◆ **46 WINS/NBT Node Type.** This option specifies the address resolution mode the WINS client will employ. In the vast majority of cases, all hosts should be configured in h-node mode, and it may be appropriate to assign this as a global option that applies to all scopes on a DHCP server.

To add option 44 to a scope, follow these steps:

1. Start DHCP Manager.

2. Select a scope in the **DHCP Servers** box.

3. Choose **Scope** in the **DHCP Options** menu.

4. In the **DHCP Options** dialog box (see fig. 11.6), select **044 WINS/NBNS Servers** in the **Unused Options** box and choose **Add**. Before the option is added to the **Active Options** box, you receive a warning, "Warning: In order for WINS to function properly, you must now set option 46(WINS/NBT Node Type)." Choose **OK** to continue.

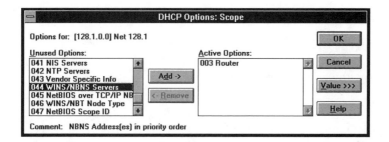

Figure 11.6

DHCP Options dialog box.

5. Choose **Value** to expand the dialog box and display the current values of the option. Option 44 accepts one or more addresses of WINS servers. To change the values, choose the **Edit Array** button (shown in fig. 11.7) to open the IP address array editor.

6. To add the address of a WINS server to the array, enter the address in the **New IP Address** box and choose **Add** to copy the address to the **IP Address** box. In the figure address 128.2.0.2 has been added to the array.

   To remove an address, select the address in the **IP Address** box and choose **Remove**. In the figure address 0.0.0.0 has been removed.

7. After addresses have been configured, choose **OK** and return to the DHCP Manager main window.

Figure 11.7

Adding addresses to the address array of WINS option 44.

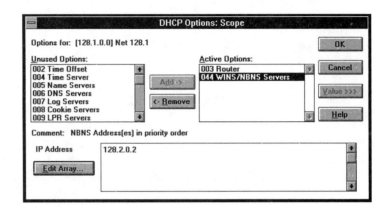

To add option 46 as a global option:

1. Start DHCP Manager.

2. Select a scope in the **DHCP Servers** box.

3. Choose **Global** in the **DHCP Options** menu.

4. In the **DHCP Options: Global** dialog box, select **046 WINS/NBT Node Type** in the **Unused Options** box and choose **Add**.

5. Choose **Value** to expand the dialog box and display the current values of the option (see fig. 11.8). Option 46 requires one of four values that specifies an NBT node type. In general option 0x8, h-node is the preferred choice. Enter the desired value and choose **OK**.

After the required options have been entered, they appear in the DHCP Server Manager main window (see fig. 11.9). Notice that option 046, which was entered as a global option, is identified by a global icon. This option applies to all scopes defined on this DHCP server unless overridden by a scope-level option.

After the WINS options have been added to the appropriate DHCP scopes, it is necessary to force the DHCP clients to release their leases so they can acquire new leases with the WINS options. You can delete the leases in the **Active Leases** dialog box, but clients cannot acquire new leases until their current leases expire.

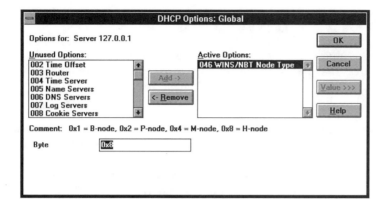

Figure 11.8

Editing the value of WINS option 46.

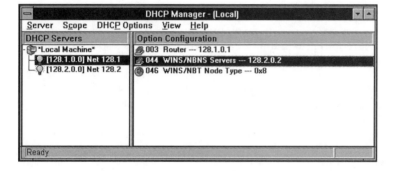

Figure 11.9

DHCP options configured for WINS.

> **Note** To force Windows NT and Windows 3.1x DHCP clients to release their current leases, enter the command `ipconfig /release` at a command prompt on the client computer. When the computer is restarted, the DHCP client acquires a new DHCP lease with the WINS options in effect.
>
> To force Windows 95 to release its DHCP lease, enter the command `winipcfg` at a command prompt and choose the **Rele_a_se** button.

Naming on a WINS Network

After WINS has been configured and all hosts have been registered with the WINS database, attempts to connect with remote hosts will succeed. Consider again now the example of VENICE attempting to connect to URBINO on a separate network. Under WINS, VENICE generates a p-node request for address information that is directed to VENICE's primary WINS server. The WINS server responds with the required address information that VENICE uses to establish a connection.

Naming versus Browsing

Users of Windows products in network environments become so familiar with browsing network resources that mistaking the Windows Browser for a name service becomes rather easy. Browsers, however, maintain databases only of host names. Addresses must still be derived from a name resolution process.

Browsing works somewhat differently on TCP/IP networks than on networks running NetBIOS and NWLink, although the difference becomes apparent only when routing is involved. Windows browsing is based on *browse lists*, which catalog all available domains and servers. When a user opens a **Connect Network Drive** dialog box (in File Manager of Windows NT or WfW) or a **Network Neighborhood** dialog box (Windows 95), the information that appears has been retrieved from a browse list.

Browse lists are maintained by *browsers*. By default, all Windows NT Server computers are browsers. Windows NT Workstation computers are potential browsers, and can become browsers if required. Windows 95 and WfW computers also are potential browsers.

Each domain has one *master browser* that serves as the primary point for collecting the browse database for the domain. Servers (any computer that offers shared resources) that enter the network transmit *server announcements* to the master browser to announce their presence. The master browser uses these server announcements to maintain its browse list.

Backup browsers receive copies of the browse list from the master browser at periodic intervals. Backup browsers introduce redundancy to the browsing mechanism and distribute browsing queries across several computers. An election process among the various browsers determines the master browser. In domains, the election is biased in favor of making the primary domain controller (PDC) the master browser, which always is the master browser if it is operational.

All Windows NT Server computers function as master or backup browsers. Windows NT Workstation computers can function as browsers. In the presence of sufficient Windows NT Server computers, no Windows NT Workstation computers will be configured as browsers. When no Windows NT Server computers are available, at least two Windows NT Workstation computers will be activated as browsers. An additional browser will be activated for every 32 Windows NT Workstation computers in the domain.

Servers must announce their presence to the master browser at periodic intervals, starting at one minute intervals and increasing to 12 minutes. If a server fails to announce itself for three announcement periods, it is removed from the browse list. Therefore, up to 36 minutes may be required before a failed server is removed from the browse list.

Domains are also maintained in the browse list. Every fifteen minutes, a master browser broadcasts a message announcing its presence to master browsers in other domains. If a master browser is not heard from for three 15-minute periods, other master browsers remove the domain from their browse lists. Thus, 45 minutes may be required to remove information about another domain from a browse list.

Internetworks based on NetBIOS and NWLink protocols can route broadcast name queries across routers. Maintaining a single master browser for each domain, therefore, is necessary.

Internetworks based on TCP/IP cannot forward broadcast name queries between networks. Therefore, Microsoft TCP/IP networks maintain a master browser for each network or subnetwork. If a domain spans more than one network or subnetwork, the domain master browser running on the PDC has a special responsibility of collecting browse lists from the master browser on each network and subnetwork. The domain master browser periodically rebroadcasts the complete domain browse list to the master browsers, which in turn update backup browsers on their networks.

> **Note** To enable browsing on a TCP/IP internetwork, at least one Windows NT Server computer must be present on each network (or subnetwork if subnetting is used). If WINS is not enabled for the network, each browser must be configured with an LMHOSTS file that contains entries for domain controllers on the internetwork.

Therefore, significant time might be required to disseminate browsing data through a domain on a large TCP/IP internetwork.

The browsing service is a convenience but is not required to enable clients to access servers on the internetwork. Client processes still can use shared resources by connecting directly with the UNC (Universal Naming Convention) name of the resource. If host URBINO shares its CD-ROM drive with the share name cd-rom, you can specify the resource as \\`urbino`\`cd-rom` in the **Path** box of a **Connect Network Drive** dialog box (see fig. 11.10). Alternatively, you can connect the resource using a **net use** command at a command prompt, for example:

```
net use f: \\urbino\cd-rom
```

It is unnecessary to be able to browse URBINO to connect using the UNC name. It is, however, necessary to be able to obtain the IP address for URBINO. On a TCP/IP internetwork, that makes WINS a near necessity. Browsing, on the other hand, is very convenient but is not essential.

> **Note**
>
> Multihomed hosts often present an ambiguous face to the network community. Different hosts can use different IP addresses to access services running on the host, with unpredictable results. One case in which this unpredictability seems to appear is browsing when the PDC for a domain is multihomed. Clients are not hard-wired with the addresses of browsers, and a multihomed master browser appears to confuse things, causing various clients to see different browse lists. More consistent results seem to be obtained when the PDC has a single IP address. In any case, the PDC cannot serve as a master browser for more than one network or subnetwork.

Figure 11.10

Entering a UNC path to connect to a resource.

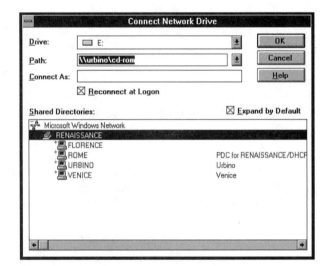

Managing WINS Servers

WINS functions are managed using WINS Server Manager. The icon for WINS Server Manager is installed in the Network Administration program group. WINS Server Manager is used to monitor WINS servers, establish static address mappings, and manage database replication. A few WINS database management tasks, such as compacting the database, are initiated from the command line.

Adding WINS Servers to WINS Server Manager

Figure 11.11 shows the main window for WINS Server Manager: WINS Manager has been configured to manage two WINS servers. A single WINS Service Manager can be used to monitor all WINS Servers on the internet.

If WINS Server Manager is run on a computer running the WINS Server service, the computer is listed in the WINS Servers list. To add a WINS server to the list of managed servers:

1. Choose the **Add WINS Server** command in the **Servers** menu to open an **Add WINS Server** dialog box.

2. Enter the IP address of the new WINS server in the **WINS Server** entry box and choose **OK.** The server is added to those in the **WINS Servers** box.

To remove a WINS server from the list, select the server and choose the **Delete WINS Server** command in the **Server** menu.

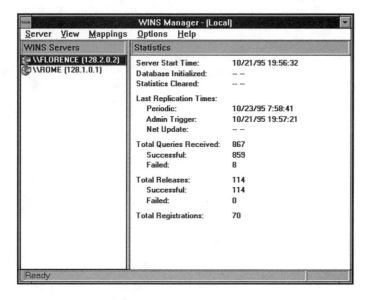

Figure 11.11

The WINS Server Manager main window.

Monitoring WINS

The main window of WINS Server Manager displays several statistics about the WINS server selected in the WINS Servers box. The statistics are as follows:

◆ **Server Start Time.** The date and time when the WINS Server was started. This is the time the computer was started. Stopping and starting the WINS Server service does not reset this value.

◆ **Database Initialized.** Static mappings can be imported from LMHOSTS files. This value indicates when static mappings were last imported.

◆ **Statistics Cleared.** The date and time when the server's statistics were cleared with the **Clear Statistics** command in the **View** menu.

◆ **Last Replication Time: Periodic.** The last time the WINS database was updated by a scheduled replication.

◆ **Last Replication Time: Admin Trigger.** The last time a WINS database replication was forced by an administrator.

◆ **Last Replication Time: Net Update.** The last time the WINS database was updated in response to a push request from another WINS server.

◆ **Total Queries Received.** The number of name queries this WINS server has received from WINS clients. Statistics indicate the number of queries that succeeded and failed.

◆ **Total Releases.** The number of messages indicating an orderly shutdown of a NetBIOS application. Statistics indicate the number of names the WINS server released successfully and the number that it failed to release.

◆ **Total Registrations.** The number of registration messages received from clients.

To refresh the statistics, choose the **Refresh Statistics** command in the **View** menu or press F5.

To clear the statistics, choose the **Clear Statistics** command in the **View** menu.

Setting WINS Manager Preferences

The **Preferences** command in the **Options** menu can be used to set a variety of optional features for WINS Manager. Figure 11.12 shows the **Preferences** dialog box. (In the figure, the **Partners** button has been clicked on to open the push and pull partner configuration options.) Options in this dialog box are as follows:

◆ **Address Display.** Contains four options that determine how WINS servers are listed in the WINS Servers list. The options are **Computer Name Only**, **IP Address Only**, **Computer Name (IP Address)**, and **IP Address (Computer Name)**.

◆ **Server Statistics: Auto Refresh.** Check this box to specify that statistics in the WINS Manager be automatically updated. Enter an update interval in the **Interval (Seconds)** box.

◆ **Computer Names: LAN Manager-Compatible.** Generally, this box should be checked to force computer names to conform to LAN Manager rules, which limit names to 15 characters. (Some NetBIOS environments use 16 character names.) LAN Manager uses the 16th byte to indicate the computer role (server, workstation, messenger, and so on). All Windows network products follow LAN Manager naming conventions.

◆ **Validate Cache of "Known" WINS Servers at Startup Time.** Check this option if the system should query all known servers when starting up to determine if the servers are available.

◆ **Confirm Deletion of Static Mappings & Cached WINS servers.** Check this option if a warning message should be displayed when static mappings or cached names are deleted.

◆ **New Pull Partner Default Configuration: Start Time.** This value specifies a default start time that will be applied to newly created pull partners. Specify a default replication interval in the **Replication Interval** fields. This value should be equal to or less than the lowest replication interval that is set for any active WINS replication partners.

◆ **New Push Partner Default Configuration: Update Count.** This value specifies the default for the number of registrations and changes that will cause a push partner to send a replication trigger. The minimum value is 20.

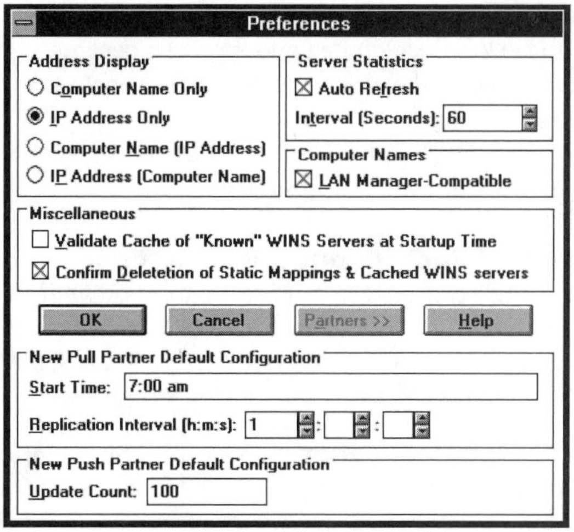

Figure 11.12

WINS Manager preferences.

Configuring WINS Server Properties

A number of properties can be adjusted for each WINS server. These properties are configured by selecting a WINS Server in the WINS Server Manager and choosing the **Configuration** command in the **Servers** menu. Figure 11.13 shows the **WINS Server**

Configuration dialog box. (In figure 11.13, the **Advanced** button was clicked on to open the **Advanced WINS Server Configuration** box.) The options in this dialog box are as follows:

◆ **Renewal Interval.** This option determines how frequently a client must reregister its name. A name not reregistered within the renewal interval is marked as *released*. Forcing clients to reregister frequently increases network traffic. A value of 32 hours enables a client to retain a registration from day to day, while ensuring that the registration is released in a reasonable period of time if it is not used. The maximum value for this field is 96 hours (4 days).

◆ **Extinction Interval.** This option determines how long for a *released* name to remain in the database before it is marked extinct and is eligible to be purged. Try setting this value to three or four times the renewal interval.

◆ **Extinction Timeout.** Specifies the interval between the time a record is marked *extinct* and the time when the record is actually purged from the database. The minimum value is one day.

◆ **Verify Interval.** Specifies how frequently the WINS server must verify the correctness of names it does not own. The maximum value is 24 days.

> **Note**   Setting renewal and extinction intervals is a balancing act between the needs of your users, keeping the WINS database up-to-date, and generation of network traffic. If you force renewal and extinction to occur at frequent intervals, network traffic increases and users can lose their name reservations if they are away from the office for a few days. On the other hand, if these intervals are too long, the database becomes cluttered with obsolete entries.

◆ **Pull Parameters: Initial Replication.** Check this box to have this server pull new data from its pull partners when it is initialized or when replication parameters change. Then specify a value in the **Retry Count** field to specify the number of times the server should attempt replication. If the server is unsuccessful, replication is retried according to the server's replication configuration.

◆ **Push Parameters: Initial Replication.** Check this box if the server should inform its push partners when it is initialized. If push partners should be notified when an address changes in a mapping record, check the **Replicate on Address Change** box.

◆ **Logging Enabled.** Check this box if database changes should be logged to the JET.LOG file.

◆ **Log Detailed Events.** Checking this box enables verbose logging. Due to the demand on system resources, this option should be used only when tuning WINS performance.

◆ **Replicate Only With Partners.** If this option is checked, an administrator cannot force a WINS server to push or pull from a WINS server that is not listed as a replication partner.

◆ **Backup On Termination.** If this option is checked, the database is backed up upon shutdown of WINS Manager, unless the system is being stopped.

◆ **Migrate On/Off.** Check this option if you are upgrading to Windows NT from a non-NT system. When checked, this option enables static records to be treated as dynamic so that they can be overwritten.

◆ **Starting Version Count (hex).** This value must be adjusted only if the WINS database is corrupted and must be restarted. In that case, set the value higher than the version number for this WINS server as it appears on all of the server's replication partners, to force replication of records for this server. The maximum value of this parameter is $2^{31} - 1$. Version counts are visible in the **View Database** dialog box.

◆ **Database Backup Path.** Specifies the directory in which the database backup files are to be stored. If a path is specified, a backup is performed automatically at 24 hour intervals. This backup can be used to restore the main database if it becomes corrupted. Do not specify a network directory.

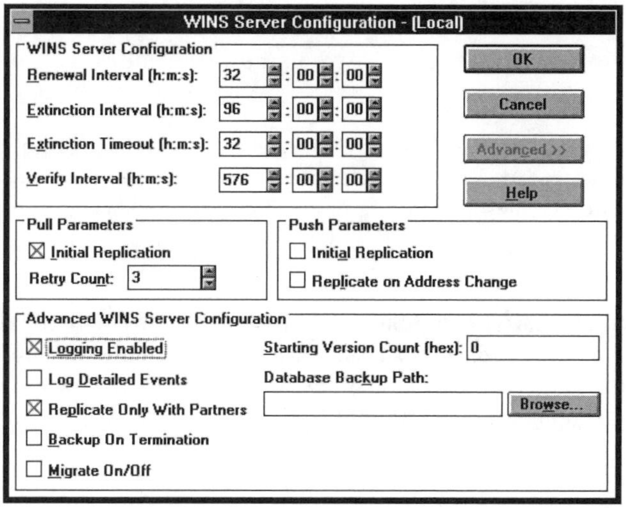

Figure 11.13

The WINS Server Configuration dialog box.

Viewing WINS Server Details

Detailed information for each WINS server may be displayed by selecting the server and choosing the **Detailed Information** command in the **Servers** menu. Figure 11.14 shows an example **Detailed Information** box. The fields in this box are as follows:

◆ **Computer Name.** The NetBIOS name of the computer supporting the WINS server.

◆ **IP Address.** The IP address of the WINS server.

◆ **Connected Via.** The connection protocol.

◆ **Connected Since.** The time when the WINS Server service was last activated. Unlike the **Server Start Time** statistic in the main window, **Connected Since** is reset when the WINS Server service is stopped and started.

◆ **Last Address Change.** The time when the last database change was replicated.

◆ **Last Scavenging Times.** The last time the database was scavenged to remove old data. Times are reported for the following scavenging events:

   ◆ **Periodic.** Timed scavenging.

   ◆ **Admin Trigger.** Manually initiated scavenging.

   ◆ **Extinction.** Scavenging of released records were scavenged because they had aged past the extinction time.

   ◆ **Verification.** Last scavenging based on the Verify interval in the WINS server configuration.

◆ **Unique Registrations.** The number of name registrations for groups that the WINS server has accepted. The **Conflicts** statistic indicates the number of conflicts encountered when registering names that are already registered. The **Renewals** statistic indicates the number of renewals that have been received for unique names.

◆ **Group Registrations.** The number of requests for groups that the WINS server has accepted. The **Conflicts** statistic indicates the number of conflicts encountered when registering group names. The **Renewals** statistic indicates the number of group name renewals that have been received.

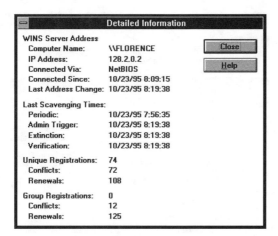

Figure 11.14

Detailed information about a WINS server.

Configuring Static Mappings

Sometimes dynamic name-address mappings are not desirable. At such times, creating static mappings in the WINS database proves useful. A *static mapping* is a permanent mapping of a computer name to an IP address. Static mappings cannot be challenged and are removed only when they are explicitly deleted.

Note   Reserved IP addresses assigned to DHCP clients override any static mappings assigned by WINS.

To add static mappings in WINS Manager, use the following procedure:

1. Choose **Static Mappings** in the **Mappings** menu to open the **Static Mappings** dialog box (see fig. 11.15), which lists all active static mappings. The mappings for ROME are tagged by a group icon because ROME was entered as a multihomed mapping. Figure 11.16 shows how the static mapping for ROME was entered.

2. To add a static mapping, choose **Add Mappings** to open the **Add Static Mappings** dialog box (see fig. 11.16).

3. Type the computer name in the **Name** box. WINS Manager supplies the \\ characters to complete the UNC name.

Figure 11.15

Static mappings.

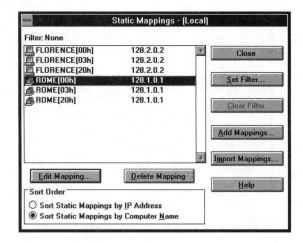

4. Enter the address in the **IP Address** box.

5. Choose one of the buttons in the **Type** box. (Group, internet group, and multihomed names are discussed further in the next section, "Special Names.") The following choices are available:

◆ **Unique.** The name will be unique in the WINS database and will have a single IP address.

◆ **Group.** Groups are targets of broadcast messages and are not associated with IP addresses. If the WINS server receives a query for the group, it returns FFFFFFFF, the IP broadcast address. The client then broadcasts on the local network.

◆ **Internet Group.** A group associated with the IP addresses of up to 24 Windows NT Servers plus the address of the primary domain controller, for a total of 25.

◆ **Multihomed.** A name that can be associated with up to 25 addresses, corresponding to the IP addresses of a multihomed computer.

6. Choose **Add.**

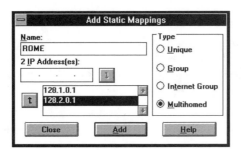

Figure 11.16

Adding static mappings.

To edit a static mapping, perform the following steps:

1. Choose **Static Mappings** in the **Mappings** menu.

2. Select the mapping to be modified in the **Static Mappings** dialog box and choose **Edit Mapping**.

3. In the **Edit Static Mapping** dialog box, make any required changes.

4. Choose **OK** to save the changes.

Static mappings for unique and special group names can be imported from files that conform to the format of LMHOSTS files, described later in this chapter in the section "Managing LMHOSTS Files." Choose **Import Mappings** in the **Static Mappings** dialog box to import mappings.

Special Names

WINS recognizes a variety of special names, identified by the value of the 16th byte of LAN Manager-compatible names. Special names are encountered when setting up static mappings and when examining entries in the WINS database. The special names recognized by WINS are discussed below.

Normal Group Names

Normal group names are tagged with the value 0x1E in the 16th byte. Browsers broadcast to this name and respond to it when electing a master browser. In response to queries to this name, WINS always returns the broadcast address FFFFFFFF.

Multihomed Names

A multihomed name is a single computer name that stores multiple IP addresses, which are associated with multiple network adapters on a multihomed computer. Each multihomed name can be associated with up to 25 IP addresses. This information is established when TCP/IP configuration is used to specify IP addresses for the computer.

When the WINS Server service is running on a multihomed computer, the WINS service is always associated with the first network adapter in the computer configuration. All WINS messages on the computer, therefore, originate from the same adapter.

Multihomed computers with connections to two or more networks should not be configured as WINS servers. If a client attempts a connection with a multihomed WINS server, the server might supply an IP address on the wrong network, causing the connection attempt to fail.

Internet Group Names

An internet group is used to register Windows NT Server computers in internet groups, principally Windows NT Server domains. If the internet group is not configured statically, member computers are registered dynamically as they enter and leave the group. Internet group names are identified by the value 0x1C in the 16th byte of the NetBIOS name. An internet group can contain up to 25 members, preference being given to the nearest Windows NT Server computers. On a large internetwork, the internet group registers the 24 nearest Windows NT Server computers plus the primary domain controller. Windows NT Server v3.1 computers are not registered to this group dynamically, and must be added manually in WINS Manager. Manually adding computers to the group makes the group static—it no longer accepts dynamic updates.

Other Special Names

Several other special names are identified by byte 16:

◆ 0x0 identifies the redirector name of a computer.

◆ 0x3 identifies the Messenger service name, used to send messages.

◆ 0x1B identifies the domain master browser, which WINS assumes is the primary domain controller. If it is not, the domain master browser should be statically configured in WINS.

◆ 0x1 identifies _MSBROWSE_, the name to which master browsers broadcast to announce their domains to other master browsers on the local subnet. WINS responds to queries to _MSBROWSE_ with the broadcast address FFFFFFFF.

Replicating the WINS Database

Having two or more WINS servers on any network is desirable. A second server can be used to maintain a replica of the WINS database that can be used if the primary server fails. On large internetworks, multiple WINS servers result in less routed traffic and spread the name resolution workload across several computers.

Pairs of WINS servers can be configured as replication partners. WINS servers can perform two types of replication actions: *pushing* and *pulling*. And a member of a replication pair functions as either a *push partner* or a *pull partner*.

All database replication takes place by transferring data from a push partner to a pull partner. But a push partner cannot unilaterally push data. Data transfers may be initiated in two ways.

A pull partner can initiate replication by requesting replication from a push partner. All records in a WINS database are stamped with a version number. When a pull partner sends a pull request, it specifies the highest version number that is associated with data received from the push partner. The push partner then sends any new data in its database that has a higher version number than was specified in the pull request.

A push partner can initiate replication by notifying a pull partner that the push partner has data to send. The pull partner indicates its readiness to receive the data by sending a pull replication request that enables the push partner to push the data.

In summary

◆ Replication cannot take place until a pull partner indicates it is ready to receive data. A pull request indicates a readiness to receive data as well as the data the pull partner is prepared to receive. Therefore, the pull partners really control the replication process.

◆ All data are transferred from a push partner to a pull partner. Data are pushed only in response to pull requests.

Pulls generally are scheduled events that occur at regular intervals. *Pushes* generally are triggered when the number of changes to be replicated exceeds a specified threshold. An administrator, however, can manually trigger both pushes and pulls.

Figure 11.17 illustrates a network that incorporates five WINS servers. In general, replication partners are configured for two-way record transfer. Each member of the partnership is configured as a push partner and a pull partner, enabling both servers to pull updated data from each other.

Figure 11.17

A network with several WINS replication partnerships.

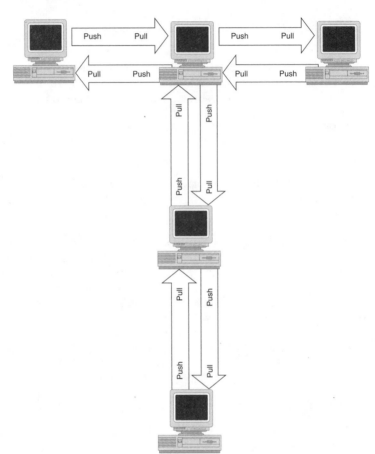

Adding Replication Partners

To configure replication on a WINS server

1. Select a WINS server in the WINS Manager main window.

2. Choose the **Replication Partners** command in the **Server** menu to open the **Replication Partners** dialog box (see fig. 11.18).

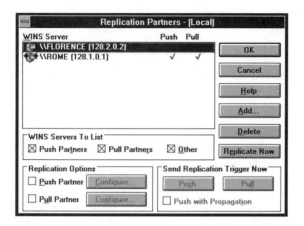

Figure 11.18

Configuring replication partners.

3. The **Replication Partners** dialog box lists all WINS Servers that have been added to the configuration of this WINS Manager.

4. To add a replication partner, choose **Add** and enter the name or the address of a WINS server in the **Add WINS Server** dialog box.

5. To specify a replication partner, choose a WINS server in the **WINS Server** box of the **Replication Partners** dialog box.

6a. To configure the selected server as a push partner

    a. Check the **Push Partner** box under **Replication Options**.

    b. Choose **Configure** to open the **Push Partner Properties** dialog box (see fig. 11.19).

    c. Enter a value in the **Update Count** field that indicates the number of updates that should trigger a push. The minimum value is 20. Choose **Set Default Value** to enter the value you selected as a default in the **Preferences** dialog box.

    d. Choose **OK** to return to the **Replication Partners** dialog box.

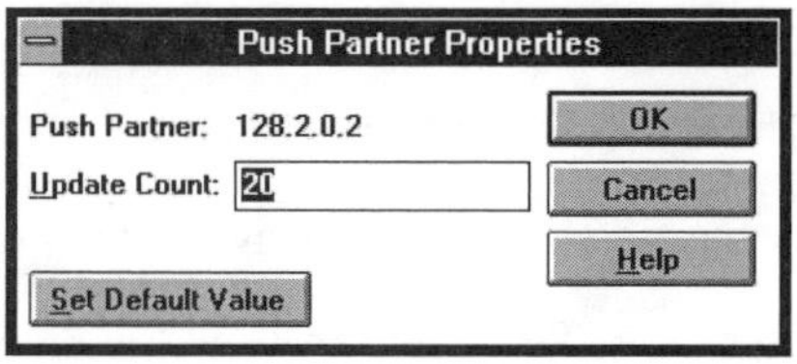

Figure 11.19

Configuring a push partner.

6b. To configure the selected server as a pull partner:

    a. Check the **Pull Partner** box under **Replication Options**.

    b. Choose **Configure** to open the **Pull Partner Properties** dialog box (see fig. 11.20).

    c. Enter a value in the **Start Time** that specifies when in the day replication should begin. The time format must conform to the setting in the International option in the Control Panel. Also, specify a time in the **Replication Interval** fields to determine the frequency of replication. Choose **Set Default Values** to enter the value you selected as a default in the **Preferences** dialog box.

    d. Choose **OK** to return to the **Replication Partners** dialog box.

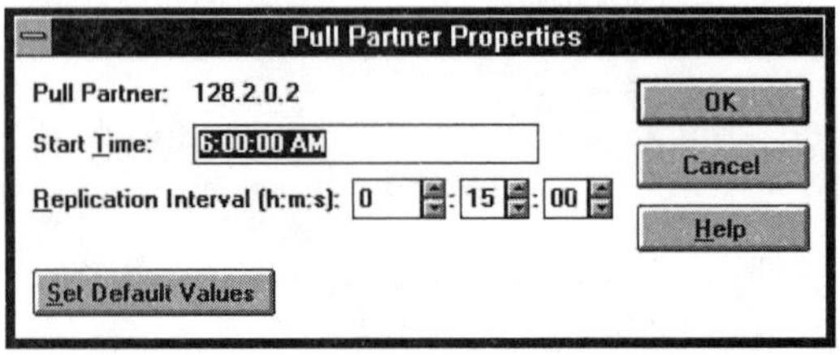

Figure 11.20

Configuring a pull partner.

7. Configure other replication partners as required. A WINS server can be configured simultaneously as a push and a pull partner, which is required if two-way replication is to take place.

8. Choose **OK** after replication partners are configured for this WINS server.

Manually Triggering Replication

After adding a WINS server, updating static mappings, or bringing a WINS server back online after shutting it down for a period of time, forcing the server to replicate its data with its replication partners might be advisable. WINS Manager enables administrators to manually trigger both push and pull replications.

To trigger a replication, follow these steps:

1. Choose a WINS server in the WINS Manager main window.

2. Choose the **Replication Partners** command in the **Server** menu.

3. Choose a replication partner in the **WINS Server** list of the **Replication Partners** dialog box.

4. Check the **Push with Propagation** box if you want to trigger a push replication to be propagated to all WINS servers on the internetwork. If you do not check this box, only the immediate push partner receives the replicated data.

5a. To send a replication trigger, in the **Send Replication Trigger Now** box, choose **Push** or **Pull**.

A push trigger notifies the pull partner that the push partner has data to transmit. It does not force the pull partner to accept a push. Data is not transferred until the pull partner sends a pull request to the push partner that originated the trigger.

A pull trigger requests updated data from a push partner.

5b. To start immediate replication, select a replication partner and choose the **Replicate Now** button.

Maintaining the WINS Database

Once configured, WINS generally requires little maintenance. Some tasks should be performed periodically, however, to improve the efficiency of WINS and to reduce the size of WINS database files. Additionally, when clients experience name resolution problems, you might need to view the contents of the WINS database to diagnose problems.

Viewing the Database

To view the database for a WINS server, select the server in the WINS Manager main window and choose the **Show Database** command in the **Mappings** menu, to open the **Show Database** dialog box (see fig. 11.21).

To display all database records for all managed WINS servers, select **Show All Mappings.**

To restrict the display to database records owned by a specific WINS server, select **Show Only Mappings from Select Owner** and select a WINS server in the **Select Owner** box. The owner of a WINS mapping record is the WINS server that first recorded the mapping.

Each record in the **Mappings** box includes the following data fields:

◆ **Icon.** A single terminal icon ⊟ indicates a *unique* name. A multiterminal icon

⊞ indicates a group, internet group, or multihomed name. (See the section "Special Names," earlier in this chapter.)

Figure 11.21

Showing the database of a WINS server.

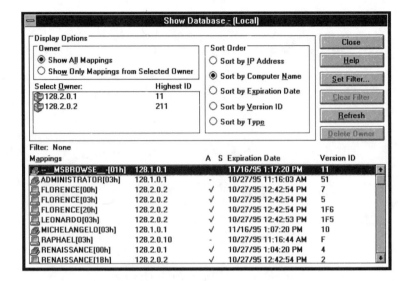

◆ **Computer Name.** Some computer names, such as _MSBROWSE_, are special names. User names also are shown in this listing. All are tagged with the hex number stored in byte 16 to identify the NetBIOS name type. See the previous discussion in the section "Special Names."

◆ **IP address.** The IP address associated with the computer name. Notice that several names may be associated with a single IP address.

◆ **A and/or S.** Indicates whether the name is established dynamically or statically. A name that was established dynamically and then entered as static can show checks in both columns.

◆ **Timestamp.** The day and time when the record will expire.

◆ **Version ID.** A stamp indicating the sequence in which the entries were established. When a pull replication partner requests new data, it requests entries with a revision number higher than the last record revision received from the push partner.

The database display does not update dynamically. Choose **Refresh** to update the display.

The **Sort Order** offers several options for sorting database records. You can also restrict displayed records by establishing a filter. Choose **Set Filter** and enter a computer name or IP address in the **Set Filter** dialog box to restrict the display to a specific computer.

To clear the database of entries for a specific WINS server, select the server in the **Select Owner** box. Then choose **Delete Owner**.

As discussed in the section "Special Names," NetBIOS names fall into several categories, identified by byte 16 of a LAN Manager-compliant NetBIOS name. Each name in the **Mappings** box of the **Show Database** dialog box is tagged with the value assigned to byte 16 of its name. (The WINS Show Database window uses the letter *h* to identify hex values. The value 01h is equivalent to 0x1.) Figure 11.21 illustrates several categories of NetBIOS names:

◆ **_MSBROWSE_ (tagged 01h).** The name browsers broadcast to on the local network.

◆ **RENAISSANCE (tagged 1Bh).** The master browser for the domain RENAISSANCE.

◆ **FLORENCE.** Identified by three special name tags: 00h identifies the FLORENCE redirector, 03h identifies the FLORENCE messenger service, and 20h identifies FLORENCE as a server. Multiple names are associated with the same network adapter to respond to different network dialogs.

In figure 11.22, the display has been scrolled to show entries for the domain name RENAISSANCE. Notice that the three entries for this name are identified by a group icon rather than an icon for an individual name. One of these entries, RENAISSANCE[1Ch], is an internet group name. Double-clicking on that entry opens the **View Mapping** dialog box (see fig. 11.23). Figure 11.23 shows how the name RENAISSANCE[1Ch] is associated with three IP addresses of Windows NT Servers running in the domain: 128.2.0.2 is singly homed and 128.1.0.1/128.2.0.1 is multihomed.

Adding static mappings to the internet group in the **View Mapping** dialog box is possible. Doing so alters the internet group so that it no longer can be updated dynamically, but might be necessary if Windows NT Server v3.1 computers are included in the domain as domain controllers.

Figure 11.22

An internet group in the Mappings list.

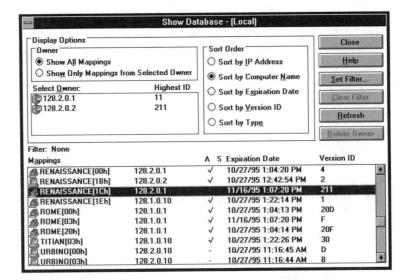

Backing Up the Database

WINS performs a complete backup of its database every 24 hours. The file name and path are specified by registry parameters, as discussed in the section "WINS Registry Parameters." On occasion, you might want to execute an unscheduled backup. The procedure, which must be performed on the computer running the WINS Server service, is as follows:

1. Choose the **Backup Database** command in the **Mappings** menu to open a Select Backup Directory dialog box (see fig. 11.24).

2. If desired, select a disk drive in the **Drives** box. The best location is another hard disk so that the database files remain available if the primary hard disk fails.

3. Specify the directory in which backup files should be stored. WINS Manager proposes a default directory.

4. If desired, specify a new directory name to be created in the directory chosen in Step 3. By default, a subdirectory named **wins_bak** is created to store the backup files.

5. To back up only records that have changed since the last backup, check the **Perform Incremental Backup** box. This option is meaningful only if a full backup has been previously performed.

6. Choose **OK** to make the backup.

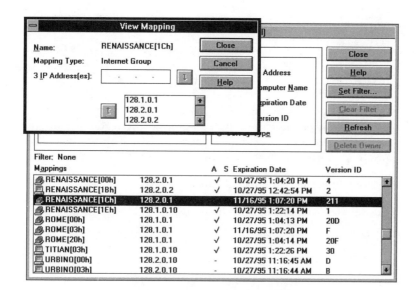

Figure 11.23

Mappings for the internet group RENAISSANCE.

Figure 11.24

Selecting a backup directory for WINS.

You also should back up the Registry entries related to WINS. To back up the WINS Registry entries, perform the following steps:

1. Run the REGEDT32.EXE program from a **Run** prompt in the **File** menu of Program Manager or File Manager. REGEDT32 can also be run from a command prompt.

2. Select the HKEY_LOCAL_MACHINE window.

3. Select the key **SYSTEM\CurrentControlSet\Services\WINS**.

4. Choose the **Save Key** command in the **Registry** menu.

5. Specify a directory and file name in which to store the backup files.

6. Choose **OK.**

Restoring the WINS Database

If users cannot connect to a server running the WINS Server service, the WINS database probably has become corrupted. In that case, you might need to restore the database from a backup copy. This may be done using menu commands or manually. The procedure must be performed on the computer running the WINS service.

To restore the WINS database using menu commands:

1. Stop the WINS Service using one of these methods:

   ◆ Stop the Windows Internet Server Service using the Services tool in the Control Panel.

   ◆ Open a command prompt and enter the command `net stop wins`.

2. Start the WINS Manager. Ignore any warning message that `The Windows Internet Naming Service is not running on the target machine, or the target machine is not accessible.`

3. Choose the **Restore Local Database** command in the **Mappings** menu.

4. In the **Select Directory To Restore From** dialog box specify the directory from which to restore.

5. Choose **OK** to restore the database.

6. Start the WINS service using one of the following methods:

   ◆ Start the Windows Internet Server Service using the Services tool in the Control Panel.

   ◆ Open a command prompt and enter the command `net start wins`.

To restore the database manually:

1. Stop the WINS Server service.

2. Delete all files in the directory C:\WINNT35\SYSTEM32\WINS.

3. Copy the file SYSTEM.MDB from the installation disks to the C:\WINNT35\SYSTEM32\WINS directory.

4. Make a backup copy of the file WINS.MDB to the C:\WINNT35\SYSTEM32\WINS directory.

5. Restart the WINS Server service.

Scavenging and Compacting the Database

The key WINS database files are stored by default in the directory C:\winnt35\system32\wins. (If your system files are stored in a directory other than C:\winnt35, substitute the appropriate directory path.) The files are as follows:

◆   **WINS.MDB.** The WINS database file.

◆   **WINSTMP.MDB.** Used by WINS to store temporary working data.

◆   **JET.LOG.** Records transactions performed on the database.

◆   **SYSTEM.MDB.** Holds information about the structure of the WINS database.

Stop   Never remove or modify the WINS files.

Windows NT Server periodically backs up the DHCP database and Registry entries. The default backup interval is 15 minutes, configurable through a Registry key.

Over time, the WINS database becomes cluttered with released and old entries from other WINS servers. *Scavenging* the WINS database clears these old records. After scavenging, compacting the database to reduce the size of the data file is a good idea.

Scavenging is performed periodically, as determined by parameters in the Registry, but you can choose to initiate scavenging manually—before compacting the database, for example.

To scavenge the database, choose the **I̲nitiate Scavenging** command in the **M̲appings** menu.

The WINS database is stored in the file named WINS.MDB, which is stored by default in the directory \WINNT35\SYSTEM32\WINS. To compact the WINS database, do the following:

1. Open a command prompt.

2. Enter the command `net stop wins` to stop the WINS Server service on the computer. Users cannot resolve names on this server while the WINS Server service is stopped.

3. Change to the WINS directory. If the directory is in the default location, enter the command **cd \winnt35\system32\wins**.

4. Enter the command **jetpack wins.mdb temp.mdb** to compact the database. **wins.mdb** is the file to be compacted, while **temp.mdb** is a name for a temporary file that **jetpack** uses during the compacting process.

5. After receiving the message jetpack completed successfully, restart WINS using the command **net start wins**.

6. To close the command prompt, enter the command **exit**.

> **Stop**   **jetpack** should be used to compact the WINS.MDB file only. Do not compact the SYSTEM.MDB file.

WINS Registry Parameters

The Registry was discussed briefly in Chapter 10, "Managing DHCP." Please review that discussion if necessary, or refer to NRP's *Inside Windows NT Server* for greater detail.

Unless otherwise specified, the Registry parameters related to WINS are stored in the HKEY_LOCAL_MACHINE subtree in the key **\SYSTEM\CurrentControlSet\Services \Wins\Parameters**. Not all parameters are inserted in the Registry during WINS installation. If you require the features associated with a parameter, use the Registry Editor to add the value to the Registry.

The **Parameters** key includes the subkey **Datafiles**, which specifies the files for WINS to use when it initializes the WINS database. The Registry values in the WINS Parameters key are as follows:

DbFileNm

Data Type:	REG_SZ or REG_EXPAND_SZ
Range:	*pathname*
Default:	%SystemRoot\system32\wins\wins.mdb

Specifies the complete path name for the WINS database file.

DoStaticDataInit

Data Type:	REG_DWORD
Range:	0 or 1
Default:	0

If this parameter is 1, the WINS database is initialized from files specified in the **Datafiles** subkey. Initialization takes place whenever WINS is started or when changes are made to parameters in the **Parameters** or **Datafiles** subkeys. If this parameter is 0 WINS does not initialize its database.

InitTimePause

Data Type:	REG_DWORD
Range:	0 or 1
Default:	0

If this parameter is 1, the WINS Server service starts in a paused state until it has been replicated from one of its replication partners or until replication has failed at least once. If this parameter is 1, the \WINS\Partners\Pull\InitTimeReplication parameter should be set to 1 or removed from the Registry.

LogDetailedEvents

Data Type:	REG_DWORD
Range:	0 or 1
Default:	0

This value ordinarily is set using the **Log Detailed Events** check box in the **WINS Server Configuration** dialog box. If 1, verbose logging is enabled. If 0, standard logging is enabled.

LogFilePath

Data Type:	REG_SZ or REG_EXPAND_SZ
Range:	*pathname*
Default:	%SystemRoot%\system32\wins

Specifies the directory in which to store WINS log files.

LoggingOn

Data Type:	REG_DWORD
Range:	0 or 1
Default:	0

If the value of this parameter is 1, logging takes place using the logging file specified by the LogFilePath parameter. This value ordinarily is set by checking the **Logging Enabled** check box in the **WINS Server Configuration** dialog box.

McastIntvl

Data Type:	REG_DWORD
Range:	2400 minimum
Default:	2400

Specifies the interval in seconds at which the WINS server sends a multicast message to announce its presence to other WINS servers. The minimum value of 2400 sets an interval of 40 minutes.

McastTtl

Data Type:	REG_DWORD
Range:	1 - 32
Default:	6

Specifies the number of times a multicast announcement can cross a router.

NoOfWrkThds

Data Type:	REG_DWORD
Range:	1 - 40
Defaults:	Number of processors on the computer.

Specifies the number of worker threads available to WINS. Can be changed without restarting the WINS server computer.

PriorityClassHigh

Data Type:	REG_DWORD
Range:	0 or 1
Defaults:	0

If this parameter is 1, WINS runs at a high priority, ensuring that it is not preempted by other processes on the computer. Use this parameter to emphasize WINS performance on a computer that functions primarily as a WINS name server. A value of 0 sets the WINS priority as normal.

RefreshInterval

Data Type:	REG_DWORD
Range:	Hex value for time in seconds, up to 96 hours, 59 minutes, 59 seconds.
Default:	96 hours

This parameter is a hex value that specifies the interval in seconds at which WINS names must be renewed on the server. The value ordinarily is set by specifying the **Renewal Interval** in the **WINS Server Configuration** dialog box.

TombstoneInterval

Data Type:	REG_DWORD
Range:	Hex value for time in seconds, up to 96 hours, 59 minutes, 59 seconds.
Default:	variable

This parameter is a hex value that specifies the interval after which nonrenewed names are marked as extinct. The value ordinarily is set by specifying the **Extinction Interval** in the **WINS Server Configuration** dialog box.

TombstoneTimeout

Data Type:	REG_DWORD
Range:	Hex value for time in seconds, up to 96 hours, 59 minutes, 59 seconds.
Default:	variable

This parameter is a hex value that specifies the interval after which extinct names are removed from the WINS database. The value ordinarily is set by specifying the **Extinction Timeout** in the **WINS Server Configuration** dialog box.

UseSelfFndPntrs

Data Type:	REG_DWORD
Range:	0 or 1
Defaults:	0

If this parameter is 1 and the network routers support multicasting, a WINS server can automatically identify other WINS servers and identify push and pull replication partners. If routers do not support multicasting, WINS servers can automatically identify only those WINS servers that are on the same network or subnet. WINS server automatic identification adjusts automatically as WINS servers are started or gracefully shut down.

WINS server automatic identification is overridden if WINS Manager is used to establish replication.

VerifyInterval

Data Type:	REG_DWORD
Range:	Hex value for time in seconds, up to 96 hours, 59 minutes, 59 seconds.
Default:	variable

This parameter is a hex value that specifies the interval after which the WINS server must verify entries in its database that it does not own. The value ordinarily is set by specifying the <u>V</u>erify Interval in the **WINS Server Configuration** dialog box.

Managing LMHOSTS Files

Although a complete name resolution system can be based on LMHOSTS files, static naming files can be a nightmare to administer, particularly when they must be distributed to several hosts on the network. Nevertheless, LMHOSTS files may be necessary if WINS will not be run on a network or if having a backup is desirable in case the WINS service fails.

Although LAN Manager host files supported little more than mappings of NetBIOS names to IP addresses, Windows NT offers several options that make LMHOSTS considerably more versatile.

Format of LMHOSTS Files

A sample LMHOSTS file is installed in the directory C:\WINNT35\SYSTEM32\DRIVERS\ETC. This file may be edited using any text editor to create LMHOSTS files for your network.

The basic format of an LMHOSTS entry is as follows:

```
ip address     name
```

The IP address must begin in column one of the line. Here is an example of a basic LMHOSTS file:

```
128.1.0.10    VENICE
128.2.0.2     FLORENCE
128.2.0.10    URBINO
```

Windows NT LMHOSTS files can be enhanced by a variety of keywords, discussed in the next section.

LMHOSTS Keywords

Here is an example of an LMHOSTS file augmented using keywords:

```
128.2.0.2    FLORENCE    #PRE
128.2.0.10   ROME        #PRE      #DOM:RENAISSANCE

#BEGIN_ALTERNATE
#INCLUDE \\FLORENCE\PUBLIC\LMHOSTS
#INCLUDE \\ROME\PUBLIC\LMHOSTS
#END_ALTERNATE
```

The #PRE keyword specifies that the entry should be preloaded into the name cache. Ordinarily, LMHOSTS is consulted for name resolution only after WINS and b-node broadcasts have failed. Preloading the entry ensures that the mapping will be available at the start of the name resolution process.

The #DOM keyword associates an entry with a domain, which might be useful for determining how browsers and logon services behave on a routed TCP/IP network. #DOM entries can be preloaded in cache by including the #PRE keyword.

The #INCLUDE keyword makes loading mappings from a remote file possible. One use for #INCLUDE is to support a master LMHOSTS file stored on logon servers and accessed by TCP/IP clients during startup. Entries in the remote LMHOSTS file are examined only when TCP/IP is started. Entries in the remote LMHOSTS file, therefore, must be tagged with the #PRE keyword to force them to be loaded into cache.

If several copies of the included LMHOSTS file are available on different servers, you can force the computer to search several locations until a file is successfully loaded. This is accomplished by bracketing #INCLUDE keywords between the keywords #BEGIN_ALTERNATE and #END_ALTERNATE, as was done in the example file just presented. Any successful #INCLUDE causes the group to succeed.

 Note   In the example listing, note that the hosts ROME and FLORENCE are explicitly defined so that the names can be used in the parameters of the #INCLUDE keywords.

Enabling Clients to Use LMHOSTS Files

Generally speaking, LMHOSTS files are unnecessary on networks that have a properly functioning WINS name service. If an internetwork does not use WINS, LMHOSTS lookups should be enabled and LMHOSTS files should be configured to enable computers to find critical hosts.

Any TCP/IP client can be enabled to use LMHOSTS files by checking the **Enable LMHOSTS Lookup** check box in the **Advanced Microsoft TCP/IP Configuration** dialog box.

Guidelines for Establishing LMHOSTS Name Resolution

B-node computers not configured to use WINS name resolution can use LMHOSTS to resolve names on remote networks. If the majority of name queries are on the local network, preloading mappings in the LMHOSTS file generally is not necessary. Frequently accessed hosts on remote networks can be preloaded using the #PRE keyword.

#DOM keywords should be used to enable non-WINS clients to locate domain controllers on remote networks. The LMHOSTS file for every computer in the domain should include #DOM entries for all domain controllers that do not reside on the local network. This ensures that domain activities, such as logon authentication, continue to function.

To browse a domain other than the logon domain, LMHOSTS must include the name and IP address of the primary domain controller of the domain to be browsed. Include backup domain controllers in case the primary fails or a backup domain controller is promoted to primary.

LMHOSTS files on backup domain controllers should include mappings to the primary domain controller name and IP address, as well as mappings to all other backup domain controllers.

All domain controllers in trusted domains should be included in the local LMHOSTS file.

Summary

Microsoft bases its primary naming system on NetBIOS names. Each computer on the network has its own specific name, and all other computers on the local network know what that name is. When the network acquires a new computer, the global name database is automatically updated. Consequently, system maintenance is relatively effortless when it comes to naming computers and keeping track of those names. This system works well on local networks. Microsoft operating systems can use NetBIOS names within the context of a local, nonrouted network.

One unfortunate drawback to the NetBIOS naming system is that the names do not propagate across routers. NetBIOS names are disseminated using broadcast datagrams, and IP routers do not forward them. Computers on one network, therefore, cannot read the NetBIOS names on another network when the two networks are connected via a router.

Microsoft did offer an alternative to the NetBIOS naming system that allowed for the recognition of names across networks (LMHOSTS), but the maintenance was considerable.

Enter WINS (Windows Internet Name Service). The introduction of this service by Windows NT Server combines easy maintenance (dynamic updating) with a global reading (one network recognizes the names of computers on another).

This chapter examined WINS in considerable depth, showing how to plan WINS services and how to implement and maintain WINS servers. Because LMHOSTS files might still be encountered and continue to be of value under some circumstances, LMHOSTS naming also was discussed.

Chapter 12 Snapshot

This chapter discusses the question of implementing a Domain Name Service on your server. It covers the following topics:

◆ Deciding whether to implement DNS

◆ Name resolution with HOSTS files

◆ Getting ready for DNS

◆ Obtaining and installing DNS for Windows NT

◆ Configuring DNS

◆ Starting the DNS Server Service

◆ Registering the DNS server

◆ Setting up a secondary name server

CHAPTER

12

Managing DNS

Domain Name Service (DNS) is the standard naming service used on the Internet and on most TCP/IP networks. Chapter 6, "The Process/Application Layer," describes DNS fairly thoroughly. This chapter focuses on two issues: whether you need to implement DNS on your network and, if so, how to implement a DNS server on Windows NT computers.

Deciding Whether to Implement DNS

If your Windows TCP/IP network is not connected to non-Microsoft TCP/IP networks, you do not need DNS. WINS can provide all the naming services required on a Microsoft Windows network. And because WINS configures name-address mappings dynamically, it requires little or no maintenance to cope with network equipment changes. A user can move a portable computer from one network on the private internet to another network and have no requirement for changes in WINS. WINS recognizes the new location of the host and adjusts its database accordingly.

You need DNS if you want to connect your TCP/IP hosts to the Internet or to a UNIX-based TCP/IP network, but only if you want to enable users outside the Windows network to access your TCP/IP hosts by name. If outside users do not use services hosted on your computers, or if identifying your computers by IP address is acceptable, identifying your network hosts in DNS is not necessary.

In other words, if your network is attached to the Internet, you do not need to include your hosts in the Internet DNS tree to enable your users to connect to outside resources. You need DNS name support only if outsiders connect to resources on your network.

If you decide that hosts on your network must be identified in DNS, ask the following questions:

◆ Must all hosts be added to DNS, or only a select few?

◆ How often will host name-address information change?

◆ Should the names of local hosts be provided by WINS?

◆ Will you be obtaining a domain name on the Internet?

◆ Will hosts under your domain name be dispersed geographically, or located in a single location?

The right answers to these questions might indicate that you can hire an internet service provider to manage your portion of the DNS tree. Recall from Chapter 6 that a single DNS server can manage multiple zones in the DNS tree. Many commercial Internet providers will manage your zone for a fee that often is considerably less than the cost of maintaining two private DNS servers. (Two are generally required to ensure fault tolerance.)

Consider contracting management of your portion of the DNS tree if any or all of the following circumstances apply:

◆ You obtain your Internet access through an Internet provider who offers DNS management as a service.

◆ You do not want to have local names of Windows TCP/IP hosts provided by WINS. The majority of Internet access providers run DNS on UNIX computers, which do not support links to WINS.

◆ Your network is too small to justify training two DNS administrators, allocating a portion of their work time, and maintaining two computers with the capacity to provide DNS services.

◆ Your network is fairly stable and you do not need immediate posting of changes.

Consider managing your own DNS server if any, some, or all of the following are true:

◆ You want to use WINS to provide host names of your Windows computers.

◆ You want local control of your organization's part of the DNS tree.

◆ Your network changes frequently.

◆ Your organization can justify the expense of administrative labor and DNS server hardware.

◆ Your network is local, and changes infrequently so that HOSTS files may be used.

Local networks that include UNIX hosts cannot use WINS for name resolution. Although DNS might seem to be the best solution for providing a local database, HOSTS files remain an option under some circumstances. Naming using HOSTS files generates no network traffic for name resolution, and HOSTS files can be maintained easily on a stable network. If the network changes frequently, maintaining DNS is easier than frequently distributing HOSTS files to all computers on the network.

Name Resolution with HOSTS Files

Before DNS, name resolution was accomplished using files named HOSTS that, on UNIX computers, were conventionally stored with the file name \etc\hosts. On Windows NT com-puters, HOSTS files are stored in the directory C:\WINNT35\SYSTEM32\DRIVERS\ETC.

Supporting a naming service is a simple matter of editing a master HOSTS file and distributing it to all computers, which could be accomplished by copying the file when a user logs on to a domain, or it could be done using a software distribution system such as Microsoft's System Management Server.

Basically, the same tasks are involved in maintaining a master HOSTS file and maintaining DNS database files. DNS saves labor because DNS database files need not be copied to all hosts, but rather, need only be installed on the primary and backup DNS servers. So, DNS begins to pay off when your network becomes so large that keeping everyone's HOSTS file up-to-date becomes too labor-intensive.

Getting Ready for DNS

If your network will never be on the Internet, you can use any naming conventions for DNS. If an Internet connection is a present or future requirement, however, you must do several things:

◆ Obtain one or more IP network address.

◆ Obtain an Internet connection.

◆ Obtain a domain name in the appropriate top-level Internet domain.

If an organization already connected to the Internet agrees to let you connect to the Internet by connecting to their network, you are responsible for obtaining IP addresses and domain names. Chapter 6 provides guidelines for identifying and contacting the authority for your parent domain. In these cases, IP addresses are assigned by the InterNIC Registration Service.

Increasingly, however, the principle way to connect to the Internet is to subscribe using an Internet access provider. IAPs are assigned blocks of IP addresses. You need to obtain an address from your IAP, who probably also would be willing to help you obtain a domain name. A good IAP can greatly simplify setting up an Internet connection.

Somewhere along the line, you need to coordinate with the contact for your domain's parent domain and for in-addr.arpa to obtain authority for your domain in the DNS tree. Before you attempt to hook into Internet DNS, however, you should have your DNS system in operation.

Obtaining and Installing DNS for Windows NT

The *Windows NT Resource Kit* includes an implementation of BIND, ported to Windows NT. Install the software by running the **install** program on the resource kit CD-ROM. The DNS software is installed in the \RESKIT35\dns directory.

Install DNS on a Windows NT computer by executing the INSTALL.BAT file in \RESKIT35\dns. This batch file installs the Domain Name Server service and copies the files to the working directory C:\WINNT35\SYSTEM32\DRIVERS\ETC. Before you start the DNS server, you need to edit the configuration files (as described in the next section).

Configuring DNS

Figure 12.1 illustrates an internetwork to be used as an example for configuring DNS. The University of Southern North Dakota at Hoople, a school of music (domain name hoople.edu), operates the network. Hosts have been named after the faculty's favorite composers.

The internetwork consists of two networks, connected by a multihomed host serving as an IP router. The internetwork connects to the Internet via a Cisco router. The primary DNS server will be mozart. The files configured for mozart will assume a secondary name server and will be set up on schubert. The details of configuring the secondary name server are discussed later in the chapter.

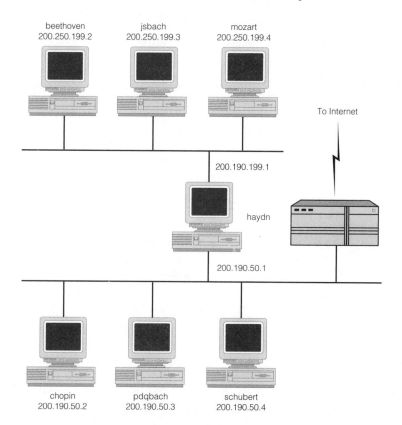

Figure 12.1

The example network.

The HOSTS file for this internetwork is as follows:

```
127.0.0.1          localhost

200.250.199.1      haydn.hoople.edu haydn papa1
200.190.50.1       haydn.hoople.edu haydn papa2

200.250.199.2      beethoven.hoople.edu beethoven
200.250.199.3      jsbach.hoople.edu jsbach jsb
200.250.199.4      mozart.hoople.edu mozart
200.190.50.2       chopin.hoople.edu chopin

200.190.50.3       pdqbach.hoople.edu pdqbach pdq
200.190.50.4       schubert.hoople.edu schubert
```

Much of the information in the HOSTS file shows up in the configuration files for DNS.

DNS is configured by editing several text files, which are located in the directory C:\WINNT35\SYSTEM32\DRIVERS\ETC. You need to maintain the following DNS files:

◆ **BOOT.** This file is the master configuration file. It declares all the various files used to initialize the DNS server.

◆ **CACHE.** This file contains host information that establishes basic DNS connectivity. Principally, this file defines the addresses of the root name servers for the DNS.

◆ **127.0.0.REV.** This file includes reverse lookup data for IP numbers on the 127 (loopback) network, such as **localhost.**

◆ *netid*.**REV.** For each network *netid* managed by the DNS server, a reverse lookup file is required to specify address-to-name mappings.

◆ *domain*.**DOM.** For each domain managed by the DNS server, a forward lookup file is required to specify name-to-address mappings.

The Windows NT DNS server software includes example files for each file type. Most files require considerable editing to customize the file for local use. The following sections examine each of these files in turn.

The BOOT File

The BOOT file is responsible for the following tasks:

◆ To specify the location of the directory that contains the DNS configuration files, if the location differs from the default directory.

◆ To declare the domains for which the server is authoritative, and the data file that describes each domain.

◆ To specify the name and location of the file that identifies the DNS root name servers.

Here is a possible BOOT file for the sample network:

```
;Directory entry not required. Files in default directory.
;directory        \winnt35\system32\drivers\etc

primary   hoople.edu                hoople.dom
primary   199.250.200.in-adr.arpa   200.250.199.rev
primary   50.190.200.in-adr.arpa    200.190.50.rev
primary   0.0.127.in-adr.arpa       127.0.0.rev

cache     .                         cache.dom
```

The BOOT file has three directives: `directory`, `primary`, and `cache`.

The `directory` directive specifies the location of the DNS database files. In the example, this line is prefixed with a semicolon (;), which designates it as a comment. The files are stored in the default directory and specifying the location is not necessary.

The `primary` directives declare the domains for which this server is authoritative, as well as the data file that contains data for each domain. This server is authoritative for four domains, and a `primary` directive is required for each. Each DNS server is authoritative for the loopback domain so that attempts to resolve loopback addresses are not propagated beyond the local DNS server.

The `cache` directive specifies the file that is authoritative for the root domain. Unlike files specified by `primary` directives, which are searched during the name resolution process, entries in the cache file are held in memory to make them immediately available.

Note	The example has stayed with the file name convention established by the Windows NT version of DNS: *domain*.dom files are for name domains and *address*.rev files are for reverse-matching domains (in-addr.arpa).

Domain Database Files

Each named domain for which the server is authoritative must be described in a database file. The database file for hoople.edu is as follows:

```
;The IN SOA record specifies the name server that is
;most authoritative for this domain.
@  IN SOA  mozart.hoople.edu.  peters.hoople.edu. (
                  1       ;serial
                  10800   ;refresh after 3 hours
                  3600    ;retry after 1 hour
                  691200 ;expire in 8 days
                  86400) ;minimum TTL 1 day


;The $WINS directive instructs DNS to use WINS to resolve names
;that cannot be found in DNS database files.
$WINS

;The IN NS directives name each name server for this domain.
@  IN NS  mozart.hoople.edu.
@  IN NS  schubert.hoople.edu.

;Each database file must have a name entry for "localhost"
localhost     IN  A  127.0.0.1

;Here are the name entries for the other hosts:

beethoven     IN  A  200.250.199.2
jsbach        IN  A  200.250.199.3
mozart        IN  A  200.250.199.4
chopin        IN  A  200.190.50.2
pdqbach       IN  A  200.190.50.3
schubert      IN  A  200.190.50.4
```

```
;This entry is for a multihomed host
haydn          IN  A  200.250.199.1
haydn          IN  A  200.190.50.1

;Aliases
jsb            IN  CNAME  jsbach
pdq            IN  CNAME  pdqbach
papa           IN  CNAME  haydn
papa250        IN  A      200.250.199.1
papa190        IN  A      200.190.50.1
```

The following sections examine each of the sections in the domain database.

The Start of Authority Record

A Start of Authority record is found at the beginning of each mapping database file. This block of information declares the host that is most authoritative for the domain, contact information, and some DNS server parameters.

An @ symbol at the beginning of the SOA header declares that this file defines members of the domain that was associated with the file in the BOOT file. Recall this entry in BOOT:

```
primary  hoople.edu                hoople.dom                      .
```

@ refers to the domain hoople.edu. Consequently, when the HOOPLE.DOM file declares an entry for the host mozart, the directive is defining information for mozart in the hoople.edu domain. That is, the directive is defining mozart.hoople.edu. In fact, the IN A entry for mozart could have been entered as follows with exactly the same effect:

```
mozart.hoople.edu.        IN  A  200.250.199.4
```

Notice that `mozart.hoople.edu.` is terminated with a period, indicating that its origin is the root domain. Without the period indicating the origin in the root domain, DNS would understand the name as `mozart.hoople.edu.hoople.edu`, because it would be understood in the context of the hoople.edu domain.

> **Stop** Improper use of trailing periods is a common cause of error in DNS database files.

The IN directive not surprisingly stands for Internet, one class of data that can appear in the database files. Following IN, the SOA directive declares this as a Start of Authority header.

Following the SOA directive are two internet names:

◆ The first, mozart.hoople.edu., is the domain name of the name server host that is most authoritative for this domain.

◆ The second, peters.hoople.edu., is the e-mail address of the primary contact for this name server. The actual e-mail address is "peters@hoople.edu." The @ has been replaced with a period. This e-mail name enables people to send messages when they have trouble with the name server.

Following the e-mail name are five parameters that set the operational characteristics of the DNS server, enclosed in parentheses to enable the parameters to span several lines, permitting a comment to label each parameter. A comment begins with a semicolon (;) and extends to the end of the line. All comment text is for human consumption and ignored by the computer.

Note that the closing parenthesis immediately follows the final parameter, not the comment for the parameter. A parenthesis in the body of the comment would be ignored.

Without comments, the SOA record could have been entered like this:

```
@  IN SOA  mozart.hoople.edu.  peters.hoople.edu. (1 10800 3600 691200 86400)
```

You probably agree that the comments make interpreting the record much easier. The five numeric parameters are as follows:

◆ **Serial.** A serial number that indicates the revision level of the file. The DNS administrator increments this value each time the file is modified.

◆ **Refresh.** The interval in seconds at which a secondary name server checks in to download a copy of the zone data in the primary name server.

◆ **Retry.** The time in seconds a secondary name server waits after a failed download before it tries to download the zone database again.

◆ **Expire.** The period of time in seconds that a secondary name server continues to try to download a zone database. After this time expires, the secondary name server discards data for the zone.

◆ **Minimum.** The minimum time to live in seconds for a resource record. This parameter determines how long a DNS server retains an address mapping in cache. After the TTL expires for a record, the record is discarded. Short TTL values enable DNS to adjust to network changes more adroitly, but increase network traffic and loading on the DNS server. A short TTL might be appropriate in the early days, while a network evolves, but you might want to extend the TTL as the network stabilizes.

The $WINS Directive

The $WINS directive is specific to the version of DNS that ships with the *Windows NT Resource Kit*. If an outside host queries a name from your DNS server, the server first attempts to resolve the name from DNS database files. If that is unsuccessful, the DNS server then attempts to resolve the name through WINS.

The $WINS directive enables DNS, WINS, and DHCP to cooperate. DNS name resolution is ordinarily static, based on manually maintained database files. Using the $WINS directive makes possible assigning IP addresses dynamically with DHCP, resolving NetBIOS names to dynamic addresses with WINS, and makes the name-to-address mappings available to DNS. In other words, you need not give up the advantages of DHCP dynamic address assignment to enable your network to support DNS name resolution.

Name Server Records

A name server record must declare each primary and secondary name server that is authoritative for the zone. Name servers are declared by IN NS records. Notice that the domain servers terminate with periods, indicating that the name originates with the root.

NS records might begin with the @ specifying "the domain for this database" or the @ might be omitted, in which case the domain is implied. If the @ is omitted, the IN should not occupy the first column of the line. In other words, the following declarations are equivalent in this context:

```
hoople.edu. IN NS  mozart.hoople.edu.
@           IN NS  mozart.hoople.edu.
            IN NS  mozart.hoople.edu.
```

Address Records

Each host name that DNS resolves must be specified using an A (address) declaration. One example from the hoople.edu database file is the following:

```
beethoven      IN  A  200.250.199.2
```

Multihomed hosts require an address declaration for each network adapter, as with the host haydn in the example database file.

Aliases

Many networks employ aliases. In most cases, aliases are declared using the CNAME ("canonical name") directive, as in this example:

```
jsb            IN  CNAME  jsbach
```

A more complex case is presented for multihomed computers. The aliases section of the sample database file includes three declarations related to the host haydn.edu:

```
papa           IN  CNAME  haydn
papa250        IN  A      200.250.199.1
papa190        IN  A      200.190.50.1
```

The CNAME declaration defines papa as an alias for the multihomed host haydn. DNS queries for papa or haydn are resolved to the first IP address in the configuration of haydn. A CNAME declaration maps to a canonical name, however, not to a specific network interface of the multihomed host.

Usually, applications don't care which address of a host they resolve to. When troubleshooting a network, however, you might prefer to be able to diagnose a specific interface, which is why two IN A declarations are included. papa250 and papa190 enable an administrator to, for example, ping by name a specific network attachment of haydn.

Backward Matching Database Files

A backward-matching (address-to-name matching) database file is required for each network ID for which the DNS server is authoritative. Recall that the file named 200.250.199.REV is the database for network 200.250.199, which appears in the reverse database tree as 199.250.200.in-adr.arpa.

The 200.250.199.rev file is constructed as follows:

```
@ IN SOA mozart.hoople.edu.  peters.hoople.edu. (
                1       ;serial
                10800   ;refresh after 3 hours
                3600    ;retry after 1 hour
                691200 ;expire in 8 days
                86400) ;minimum TTL 1 day


;name servers
@  IN  NS  mozart.hoople.edu.
@  IN  NS  schubert.hoople.edu.


;addresses mapped to canonical names
1  IN  PTR  haydn.hoople.edu.
2  IN  PTR  beethoven.hoople.edu.
3  IN  PTR  jsbach.hoople.edu
4  IN  PTR  mozart.hoople.edu
```

Similarly, the 200.190.50.rev file is constructed as follows:

```
@ IN SOA mozart.hoople.edu.  peters.hoople.edu. (
                1       ;serial
                10800   ;refresh after 3 hours
                3600    ;retry after 1 hour
                691200 ;expire in 8 days
                86400) ;minimum TTL 1 day


;name servers
@  IN  NS  mozart.hoople.edu.
@  IN  NS  schubert.hoople.edu.


;addresses mapped to canonical names
1  IN  PTR  haydn.hoople.edu.
2  IN  PTR  chopin.hoople.edu.
3  IN  PTR  pdqbach.hoople.edu
4  IN  PTR  schubert.hoople.edu
```

The reverse-naming files use the same Start of Authority header as the domain database file. As before, @ means "the domain specified in the BOOT file." Also, all host names are to be understood in the context of the domain name. Therefore, "2" in the IN PTR record refers to host 200.250.199.2 (which is 2.199.250.200.in-addr.arpa. in the reverse-naming database tree).

IN NS records declare the name servers that are authoritative for this domain.

IN PTR (pointer) records provide reverse mappings between IP addresses and host names. Notice that host names must be fully specified from the root domain.

The Localhost Database File

The 127.0.0.rev file includes reverse mappings for the localhost host name, which resembles the formats of the other reverse mapping files:

```
@ IN SOA mozart.hoople.edu.  peters.hoople.edu. (
                1       ;serial
                10800   ;refresh after 3 hours
                3600    ;retry after 1 hour
                691200  ;expire in 8 days
                86400)  ;minimum TTL 1 day


;name servers
@   IN   NS   mozart.hoople.edu.
@   IN   NS   schubert.hoople.edu.

;addresses mapped to canonical names
1   IN   PTR   localhost.
```

The Cache File

The CACHE.DOM file declares name-to-address mappings to be cached in the DNS server. Essentially, cached entries define the DNS servers that are authoritative for the root domain.

Root name servers change from time-to-time, and a DNS administrator should check the related information files at weekly intervals to ensure keeping the local cache database up-to-date. The official root name server list can be obtained in the following three ways:

- ◆ **FTP.** FTP the file /domain/named.root from FTP.RS.INTERNIC.NET.

- ◆ **Gopher.** Obtain the file named.root from RS.INTERNIC.NET under menu InterNIC Registration Services (NSI), submenu InterNIC Registration Archives.

- ◆ **E-mail.** Send e-mail to service@nic.ddn.mil, using the subject "netinfo root-servers.txt".

Note The naming scheme for the root name servers has recently changed considerably. Root name servers now have names such as A.ROOT-SERVERS.NET, where formerly they had names like NS.INTERNIC.NET or NS1.ISI.EDU. You still find references to the old names in much DNS literature.

The NAMED.ROOT file can be used unmodified as the cache database file, although you might want to rename the file based on local database file-naming conventions. At the time this book was being written, the NAMED.ROOT file had the following contents:

```
;       This file holds the information on root name servers needed to
;       initialize cache of Internet domain name servers
;       (e.g. reference this file in the "cache  .  <file>"
;       configuration file of BIND domain name servers).
;
;       This file is made available by InterNIC registration services
;       under anonymous FTP as
;           file                /domain/named.root
;           on server           FTP.RS.INTERNIC.NET
;       -OR- under Gopher at    RS.INTERNIC.NET
;           under menu          InterNIC Registration Services (NSI)
;               submenu         InterNIC Registration Archives
;           file                named.root
;
;       last update:    Sep 1, 1995
;       related version of root zone:   1995090100
;
;
; formerly NS.INTERNIC.NET
;
.                       3600000  IN  NS   A.ROOT-SERVERS.NET.
A.ROOT-SERVERS.NET.     3600000      A    198.41.0.4
;
; formerly NS1.ISI.EDU
;
.                       3600000      NS   B.ROOT-SERVERS.NET.
B.ROOT-SERVERS.NET.     3600000      A    128.9.0.107
;
; formerly C.PSI.NET
;
```

```
.                          3600000      NS    C.ROOT-SERVERS.NET.
C.ROOT-SERVERS.NET.        3600000      A     192.33.4.12
;
; formerly TERP.UMD.EDU
;
.                          3600000      NS    D.ROOT-SERVERS.NET.
D.ROOT-SERVERS.NET.        3600000      A     128.8.10.90
;
; formerly NS.NASA.GOV
;
.                          3600000      NS    E.ROOT-SERVERS.NET.
E.ROOT-SERVERS.NET.        3600000      A     192.203.230.10
;
; formerly NS.ISC.ORG
;
.                          3600000      NS    F.ROOT-SERVERS.NET.
F.ROOT-SERVERS.NET.        3600000      A     39.13.229.241
;
; formerly NS.NIC.DDN.MIL
;
.                          3600000      NS    G.ROOT-SERVERS.NET.
G.ROOT-SERVERS.NET.        3600000      A     192.112.36.4
;
; formerly AOS.ARL.ARMY.MIL
;
.                          3600000      NS    H.ROOT-SERVERS.NET.
H.ROOT-SERVERS.NET.        3600000      A     128.63.2.53
;
; formerly NIC.NORDU.NET
;
.                          3600000      NS    I.ROOT-SERVERS.NET.
I.ROOT-SERVERS.NET.        3600000      A     192.36.148.17
; End of File
```

The structure of the file is more clearly apparent if the comments are removed as follows:

```
.                          3600000  IN  NS    A.ROOT-SERVERS.NET.
A.ROOT-SERVERS.NET.        3600000      A     198.41.0.4
.                          3600000      NS    B.ROOT-SERVERS.NET.
B.ROOT-SERVERS.NET.        3600000      A     128.9.0.107
.                          3600000      NS    C.ROOT-SERVERS.NET.
```

```
C.ROOT-SERVERS.NET.      3600000    A     192.33.4.12
.                        3600000    NS    D.ROOT-SERVERS.NET.
D.ROOT-SERVERS.NET.      3600000    A     128.8.10.90
.                        3600000    NS    E.ROOT-SERVERS.NET.
E.ROOT-SERVERS.NET.      3600000    A     192.203.230.10
.                        3600000    NS    F.ROOT-SERVERS.NET.
F.ROOT-SERVERS.NET.      3600000    A     39.13.229.241
.                        3600000    NS    G.ROOT-SERVERS.NET.
G.ROOT-SERVERS.NET.      3600000    A     192.112.36.4
.                        3600000    NS    H.ROOT-SERVERS.NET.
H.ROOT-SERVERS.NET.      3600000    A     128.63.2.53
.                        3600000    NS    I.ROOT-SERVERS.NET.
I.ROOT-SERVERS.NET.      3600000    A     192.36.148.17
```

Each host is declared in two directives:

- **NS directive.** Declares the server by name as a name server for the root domain

- **A directive.** Declares the server name-to-address mapping

The NS and A directives include an additional parameter in the CACHE.DOM file. In early versions of DNS, a numeric parameter (here 3600000) indicated how long the data should remain in cache. In current versions of DNS, the root name server entries are retained indefinitely. The numeric parameter remains a part of the file syntax, but no longer serves a function.

Creating the cache file completes configuration of the DNS database files.

Starting the DNS Server Service

Starting the name server using the Services tool in the Control Panel is a simple matter. The service name is Domain Name Server Service, which is configured to start automatically when the server reboots. You can start the service manually by selecting in it the Services utility and choosing **Start**.

Thereafter, you should be able to use TCP/IP utilities, such as **ping**, to contact local computers by name.

Registering the DNS Server

After you connect your network to the Internet and configure the DNS server, you need to obtain administrative authority for your domains in the DNS and the IN-ADDR.ARPA trees.

You need to register with your parent domain in the DNS naming hierarchy. Your parent domain needs to know the names and addresses of your DNS servers. The exact registration procedure varies from domain to domain.

The InterNIC Registration Service is responsible for all registration in IN-ADDR.ARPA. Obtain the registration form in-addr-template.txt from RS.INTERNIC.NET.

Setting Up a Secondary Name Server

You probably want to set up one or more backup name servers to prevent failure of a single name server from disrupting name resolution for your domain. The difference between primary and secondary name servers is that secondary name servers obtain their data from other name servers, a process called *zone transfer*. Secondary name servers may obtain their data from primary or secondary name servers. This capability makes it possible to maintain the data on several name servers with only one set of master database files.

The example files in this chapter have configured the primary name server mozart. They have also anticipated establishment of a secondary name server on schubert, which this section addresses.

Install the DNS software on the secondary name server using the same procedures used to install the primary name server. The distinction between the primary and secondary name servers is found in the structure of the BOOT file.

The DNS directory of the secondary name server needs copies of the following files:

◆ BOOT

◆ CACHE.DOM

◆ 127.0.0.REV

The CACHE.DOM and 127.0.0.REV files are identical on all name servers and are physically copied to the secondary server. The BOOT file must be modified for the secondary server on schubert as follows:

```
;Directory entry not required. Files in default directory.
;directory        \winnt35\system32\drivers\etc

secondary  hoople.edu               200.250.199.4  hoople.dom
secondary  199.250.200.in-adr.arpa  200.250.199.4  200.250.199.rev
secondary  50.190.200.in-adr.arpa   200.250.199.4  200.190.50.rev
primary    0.0.127.in-adr.arpa      127.0.0.rev


cache      .                        cache.dom
```

In the three secondary directives, an IP address is added to the syntax. This IP address specifies the computer that serves as the repository for the database file. schubert loads hoople.dom from mozart (IP address 200.250.199.4). During operation, schubert makes backup copies of the database files in its local DNS directory, which enables schubert to start up if mozart goes down.

A name server can be a primary for some zones and a secondary for others. The role of a name server is specified by the use of the primary and secondary directives in the BOOT file.

Note The information in this chapter should be sufficient to enable you to configure a DNS name server in most situations. One configuration not considered here is the configuration of DNS to support e-mail routing. If your network incorporates e-mail, or if you want to know DNS in more intimate detail, consult the book, *DNS and Bind*, by Paul Albitz and Cricket Liu, from O'Reilly & Associates, Inc.

Summary

Chapter 6 described what DNS is, and this chapter discussed whether or not you should implement it on your network. Included in this discussion were questions that could help you decide if you should hire an Internet service provider to manage your portion of the DNS tree.

If you decided to manage you own DNS server, this chapter provided the information necessary to obtain, install, and configure a DNS server on Windows NT computers.

Chapter 13 Snapshot

This chapter examines installation and configuration of client software. It covers the following topics:

◆ Windows 95

◆ Installing TCP/IP for Windows for Workgroups, MS-DOS, and Windows 3.1

Installing TCP/IP on Microsoft Clients

C hapter 8, "Installing TCP/IP on Windows NT Computers," examines the procedures for setting up Windows NT computers as Microsoft TCP/IP clients. Besides Windows NT, Microsoft provides TCP/IP client software for the following environments:

◆ Windows 95

◆ Windows 3.11

◆ Windows 3.1 and MS-DOS

This chapter examines installation and configuration of client software in those three environments.

Windows 95

Windows 95 includes TCP/IP protocol support. The easiest way to install network support on Windows 95 is to use the Setup Wizard, which identifies most network adapters and simplifies adding network protocols. Therefore, discussion considers only the case of adding TCP/IP support to a Windows 95 configuration that already is network enabled.

To add TCP/IP protocols to a Windows 95 computer configured with basic network support, follow these steps:

1. Open the Control Panel in the My Computer window.

2. Start the Network tool in the Control Panel. Figure 13.1 shows the Network tool dialog box. The computer depicted in the example has been configured with a network adapter (3COM 3C589) and with the NetBEUI and NWLink protocols. Basic Microsoft network support has also been configured.

Figure 13.1

The Windows 95 Network tool before TCP/IP installation.

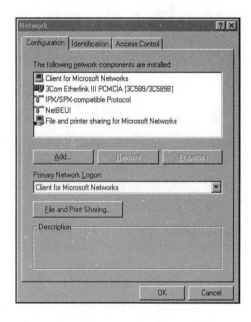

3. To add TCP/IP, choose **Add** in the Network tool dialog box. This will open the **Select Network Component Type** dialog box (see fig. 13.2). Select **Protocol** and choose **Add** to open the **Select Network Protocol** dialog box (see fig. 13.3).

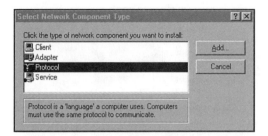

Figure 13.2

Selecting a network component.

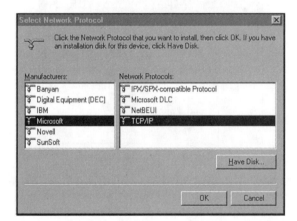

Figure 13.3

Selecting a network protocol.

4. In the **Manufacturers** box, select **Microsoft** to open a list of Microsoft protocols. Then, in the **Network Protocols** box, select **TCP/IP**. Choose **OK** to continue. The focus returns to the Network tool dialog box. Now TCP/IP is listed as a protocol (see fig. 13.4).

Figure 13.4

TCP/IP protocols installed in the network configuration.

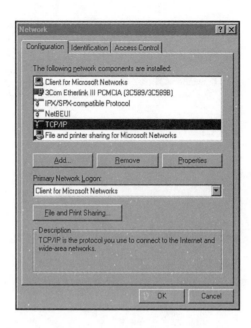

5. The TCP/IP protocols have been installed, but currently are configured with default properties. To review the protocol properties, select **TCP/IP** in the box labeled **The following network components are installed:**. Then choose **Properties** to open the **TCP/IP Properties** dialog box (see fig. 13.5).

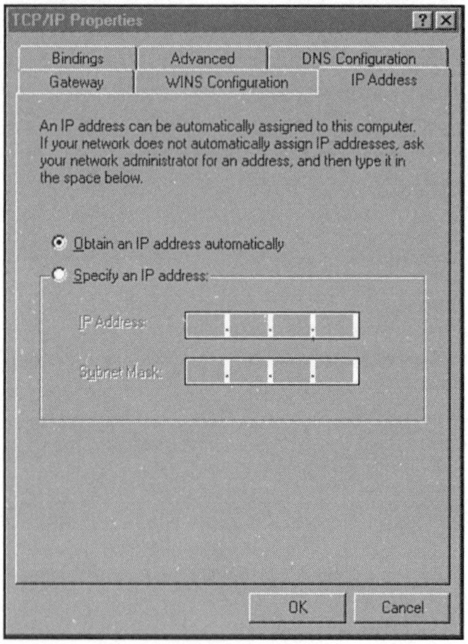

Figure 13.5

The TCP/IP Properties dialog box.

6. The **TCP/IP Properties** dialog box has several tabs that enable you to configure various aspects of the TCP/IP configuration. The information on these tabs is similar to the information that appears in the Windows NT protocol dialog boxes. After configuring the protocols, choose **OK** to return to the Network tool main dialog box.

7. After you exit the Network tool, you might need to supply diskettes and file paths required to copy files to the computer. After copying the files, restart the computer to activate the new protocols.

Installing TCP/IP for Windows for Workgroups, MS-DOS, and Windows 3.1

Windows NT Server includes TCP/IP client software for Windows for Workgroups 3.11. Also included is client software that supports Microsoft network access for MS-DOS computers, including computers running Windows 3.1. This section describes the procedures for creating client installation diskettes, and then discusses the procedures for installing TCP/IP support on Windows 3.1x and MS-DOS clients.

Creating Client Diskettes

Client installation diskettes must be created to install TCP/IP protocols on Windows for Workgroups 3.11, MS-DOS, or Windows 3.1. The diskettes are created using the Network Client Administrator utility, included with Windows NT Server. The icon for Network Client Administrator is installed in the Network Administration program group.

Network Client Administrator can be used to initiate a variety of client installation procedures. A complete discussion of the possibilities can be found in *Inside Windows NT Server*. The procedures covered in this section describe the procedures for creating two types of installation diskette sets and assume that Windows NT Server was installed from a CD-ROM:

◆ TCP/IP 32 for Windows for Workgroups 3.11

◆ Network Client v3.0 for MS-DOS and Windows

To create a set of client installation diskettes:

1. Start Network Client Administrator.

2. In the **Network Client Administrator** dialog box (see fig. 13.6) select the option **Make Installation Disk Set** and choose **Continue**.

Figure 13.6

Selecting a Network Client Administrator option.

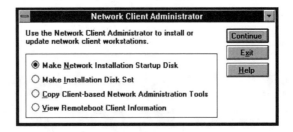

3. In the **Share Network Client Installation Files** dialog box (see fig. 13.7), select **Use Existing Path**. Then, in the **Path** box, enter the path to the \CLIENTS directory on your Windows NT Server CD-ROM. You can browse for the appropriate path by clicking on the **browse** button (the button with three dots on it) to the right of the **Path** box.

Figure 13.7

Setting the network client installation path.

4. The **Make Installation Disk Set** dialog box that appears next enables you to create five types of client disk sets (see fig. 13.8). To create a disk set, follow steps a through d:

   a. In the **Network Client or Service** box, select the disk set to create.

   b. Select the **Destination Drive** (A: or B:).

   c. Obtain the number of diskettes specified in the dialog box. The diskettes must be blank and formatted. To have the diskettes formatted before files are copied, check **Format Disks**.

   d. Choose **OK** and supply diskettes when they are requested.

Figure 13.8

Selecting a network client.

5. Quit Network Client Administrator.

6. Label the diskettes you prepared.

The following sections assume that appropriate client installation diskettes have been created using Network Client Administrator.

Windows for Workgroups 3.11

Windows for Workgroups 3.11 (WfW) is a network-ready implementation of Windows 3.x. Although WfW is network-ready, the standard package does not include TCP/IP protocols. You need to build a **TCP/IP 32 for Windows for Workgroups 3.11** client installation diskette using the Windows NT Server Client Administrator.

The following procedures assume that WfW has been installed and that a network adapter card has been configured. Only procedures for adding TCP/IP client support are covered.

To add TCP/IP to a WfW network configuration, perform the following steps:

1. Start the Windows Setup utility.

2. In the **Windows Setup** dialog box, choose the **Change Network Settings** command in the **Options** menu.

3. The **Network Settings** dialog box should resemble figure 13.9. The dialog box should specify support for **Microsoft Windows Network (version 3.11)**. Also, the **Network Drivers** dialog box should specify the network adapter that is installed in this computer.

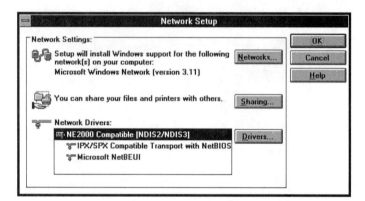

Figure 13.9

WfW network settings prior to installing TCP/IP.

4. To install TCP/IP client support, choose the **Drivers** button to open the **Network Drivers** dialog box (see fig. 13.10).

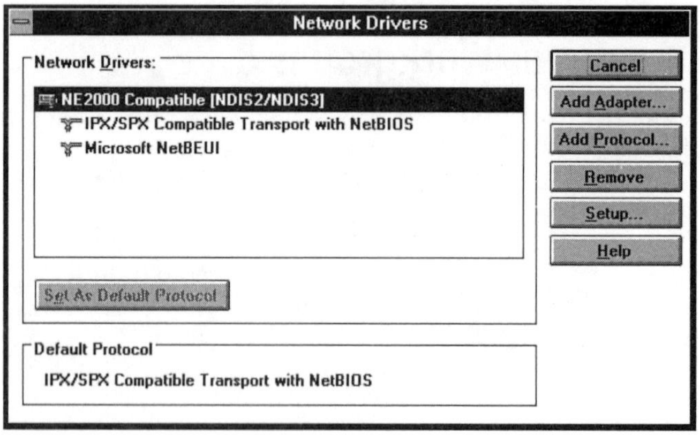

Figure 13.10

The Network Drivers dialog box.

5. In the **Network Drivers** dialog box, choose the **Add Protocol** button.

6. In the **Add Network Protocol** dialog box (see fig. 13.11), choose **Unlisted or Updated Protocol** in the protocol box and choose **OK**.

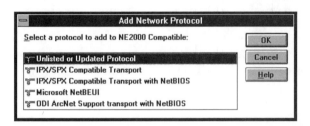

Figure 13.11

Selecting the protocol to install.

7. When prompted for the location of the protocol files, insert the **TCP/IP 32 Client for Windows for Workgroups** diskette in a diskette drive. Specify the drive path, and choose **OK**.

8. After the **Unlisted or Updated Protocol** dialog box appears, choose **Microsoft TCP/IP-32 3.11** and choose **OK**. Files are copied from the client diskette and Setup returns to the **Network Drivers** dialog box, which now shows **Microsoft TCP/IP-32 3.11** as an installed network driver.

9. To configure the TCP/IP protocols, in the Network Drivers dialog box, select **Microsoft TCP/IP-32 3.11** and choose **Setup** to open the **Microsoft TCP/IP Configuration** dialog box (see fig. 13.12).

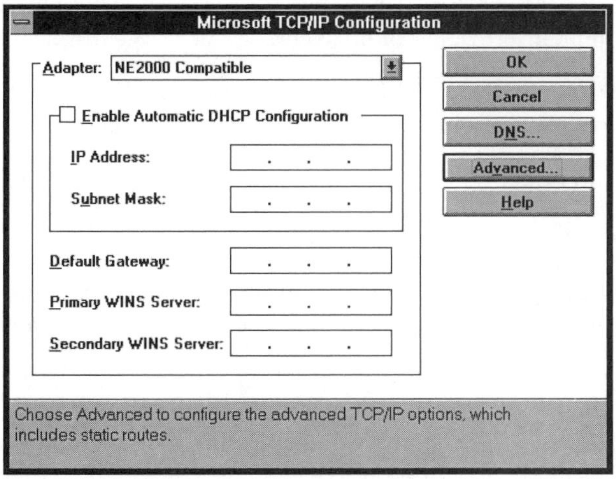

Figure 13.12

The W/W TCP/IP configuration dialog box.

The WfW TCP/IP protocol configuration dialog boxes are nearly identical to the dialog boxes used for Windows NT. Consult Chapter 8, "Implementing TCP/IP on Windows NT Computers," if you require additional information about these dialog boxes.

10. After entering the TCP/IP configuration, choose **OK**, exit the Windows Setup utility, and restart the computer.

Icons for the TCP/IP utilities **ftp** and **telnet** are installed in the newly created Microsoft TCP/IP-32 program group. Also installed in this program group are icons for Microsoft TCP/IP help and for a Release Notes file.

MS-DOS and Windows 3.1

Unlike Windows for Workgroups 3.11, Windows 3.1 does not include network client software. Windows 3.1 relies on DOS clients to provide the network redirector capability that enables Windows 3.1 to communicate with shared network resources. Therefore, the same client software is used to enable networking for MS-DOS and for Windows 3.1.

 Note   Windows 3.1 network support is extremely limited. If networking is important to your organization, it is strongly recommended that you upgrade to Windows for Workgroups 3.11 or Windows 95.

Follow the instructions in the previous section "Creating Client Diskettes" to build client diskettes for Network Client v3.0 for MS-DOS. To install the MS-DOS client, exit to an MS-DOS prompt, insert Disk 1 of the Network Client v3.0 disk set in a diskette drive, and do the following:

1. Change to the drive (A: or B:) in which the diskette was inserted.

2. Enter the command **setup**.

3. When the Welcome to Setup screen appears, press Enter.

4. Next, you are asked to specify the destination directory for the client files. The default directory shown is C:\NET. You can edit the directory. Press Enter to continue.

5. The next screen (see fig. 13.13) asks whether you want to optimize the client software for performance at the expense of memory. Buffers are used to store data waiting to be sent to the network or retrieved by MS-DOS. Increasing the number of buffers improves performance, at the cost of memory. Press Enter to

optimize the client for performance at the cost of reducing available MS-DOS memory. Press C to optimize memory usage at the cost of reduced performance.

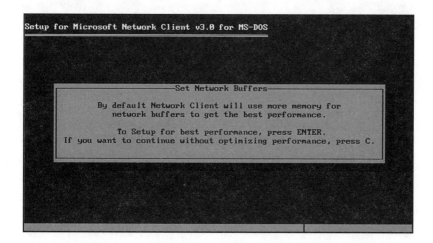

Figure 13.13

Setting client network buffers.

6. Next, Setup requests a username, to use as the default username when attempting to log on to the network. The screen (see fig. 13.14) lists the characters that may not appear in a logon name. After entering a name, press Enter.

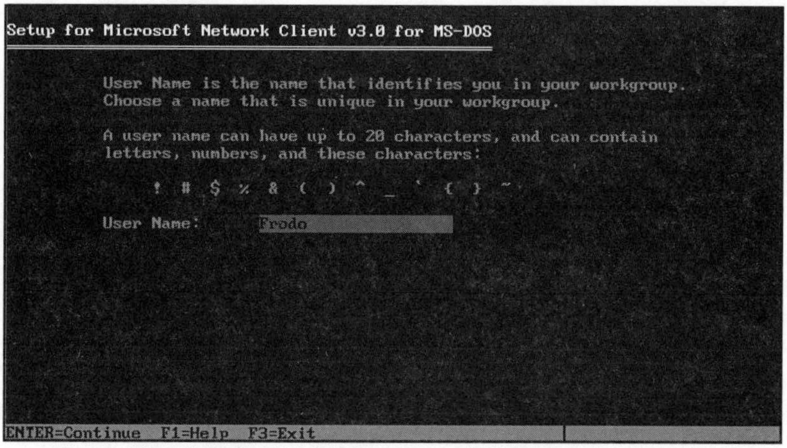

Figure 13.14

Entering a logon username.

7. The next screen (see fig. 13.15) displays several characteristics of the client configuration and is used to branch to several screens used to specify client options. Highlight **Change Setup Options** and press Enter.

Figure 13.15

Primary client configuration menu screen.

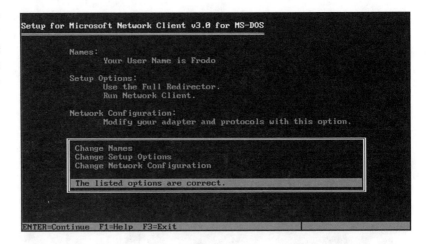

```
Setup for Microsoft Network Client v3.0 for MS-DOS

     Names:
              Your User Name is Frodo

     Setup Options:
              Use the Full Redirector.
              Run Network Client.

     Network Configuration:
              Modify your adapter and protocols with this option.

       ┌────────────────────────────────────────────────────┐
       │ Change Names                                         │
       │ Change Setup Options                                 │
       │ Change Network Configuration                         │
       ├────────────────────────────────────────────────────┤
       │ The listed options are correct.                      │
       └────────────────────────────────────────────────────┘



ENTER=Continue   F1=Help   F3=Exit
```

8. As shown in figure 13.16, the client software has four setup options. Highlight any option and press Enter to change the setting.

   ◆ **Use the Full Redirector** is the default redirector option that supports all redirector functions, including named pipes. You should probably retain the default setting, because the full redirector is required for Windows and remote access services. You can change this option to **Use the Basic Redirector** if only MS-DOS will be used.

   ◆ **Run Network Client** is the startup option that configures MS-DOS to start the network software when the system boots. In most cases, the default value should be retained. If you will be using the network pop-up utility, change the setting to **Run Network Client and Load Pop-up.** Disable both features by changing the setting to **Do Not Run Network Client**.

   ◆ The default logon validation option is **Do Not Logon to Domain.** If this computer will be logging on to a Windows NT Server domain, change the setting to **Logon to Domain.**

   ◆ The Net Pop-up is a DOS-based pop-up utility that can be used to connect to shared network resources. It loads automatically if **Run Network Client and Load Pop-up** are chosen, or can be started by typing the command **NET** at the command line. The hot key that pops the utility up can be changed from Ctrl+N.

   Choose **The listed options are correct** after options are configured as desired. You return to the primary client configuration menu.

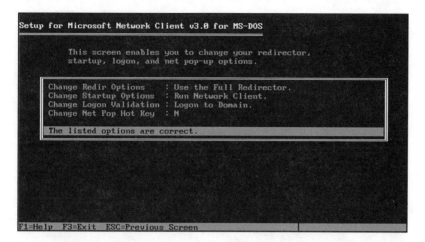

Figure 13.16

Configuring the client redirector.

9. To add a network adapter and the TCP/IP protocol, choose **Change Network Configuration**. The network adapter and protocol configuration screen is shown in figure 13.17.

   To change a setting on this screen, perform steps a and b:

   a. Choose an object in the **Installed Network Adapter(s) and Protocol(s)** box.

   b. Choose an option in the **Options** box.

   If a mouse is active, you can use it to select items in either box. Otherwise, use the Tab key to change boxes and then select an item with the arrow keys.

   Press Enter to execute an option for the selected adapter or protocol.

```
Setup for Microsoft Network Client v3.0 for MS-DOS

    Use TAB to toggle between boxes.

    Installed Network Adapter(s) and Protocol(s):

    ┌────────────────────────────────────────────────────┐
    │ NE2000 Compatible                                    │
    │        NWLink IPX Compatible Transport               │
    └────────────────────────────────────────────────────┘
    Options:

    ┌────────────────────────────────────────────────────┐
    │  Change Settings                                     │
    │  Remove                                              │
    │  Add Adapter                                         │
    │  Add Protocol                                        │
    ├────────────────────────────────────────────────────┤
    │  Network configuration is correct.                   │
    └────────────────────────────────────────────────────┘


ENTER=Continue  F1=Help  F3=Exit
```

Figure 13.17

Configuring client adapters and protocols.

10. If the appropriate adapter is not listed in the **Installed Network Adapter(s)** box, choose **Add Adapter** in the **Options** box. A series of dialog boxes enables you to select an adapter from those included on the client software disks or from a third-party disk (see fig. 13.18). Supply the third-party disk when it is requested. You are then returned to the adapter and protocol configuration screen.

Figure 13.18

Selecting a network adapter.

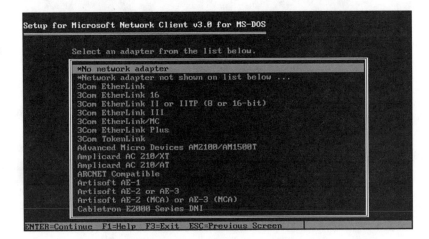

11. Select the adapter that has been installed and choose **Change Settings** to examine and change the adapter's hardware settings. Figure 13.19 shows example settings. The example shows an entry for **Adapter Slot Number**, an option that appears only on computers that have an EISA bus. Choose **The listed options are correct** when the adapter has been configured.

Figure 13.19

Setting the adapter hardware configuration.

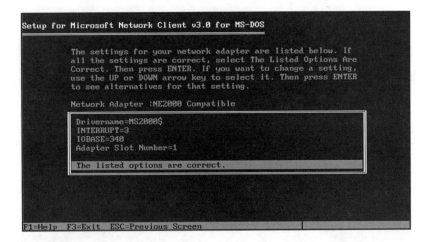

12. By default, adapters are configured with the NWLink protocols. These are not required on a purely TCP/IP network and can be removed. To remove the protocols, select **NWLink IPX Compatible Transport** and then choose **Remove** in the **Options** box.

13. To add the TCP/IP protocols, select the adapter in the **Installed Network Adapter(s)** box. Then choose **Add Protocol** in the **Options** box. Select the **Microsoft TCP/IP** protocol in the list shown in figure 13.20. You are returned to the main menu. The TCP/IP protocol is shown in the **Installed Network Adapter(s) and Protocol(s)** box.

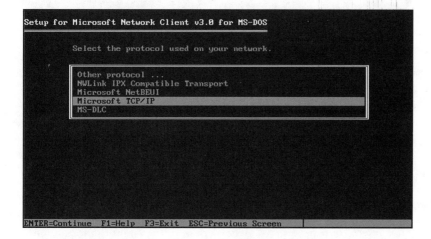

Figure 13.20

Selecting a protocol.

14. TCP/IP must be configured. Select the TCP/IP protocol in the **Installed Protocol(s)** list and choose **Change Settings** in the **Options** box. Figure 13.21 shows the TCP/IP settings.

    To configure the client to obtain an IP address from DHCP, retain the default setting of 0 for **Disable Automatic Configuration**. Set this parameter to 1 to manually configure addresses.

    If addresses are manually configured, enter appropriate information in the **IP Address**, **IP Subnet Mask**, and **Default Gateway** sessions.

    Choose **The listed options are correct** after completing the settings.

15. When adapters and protocols have been configured, select **Network configuration is correct** and press Enter to return to the Setup main menu.

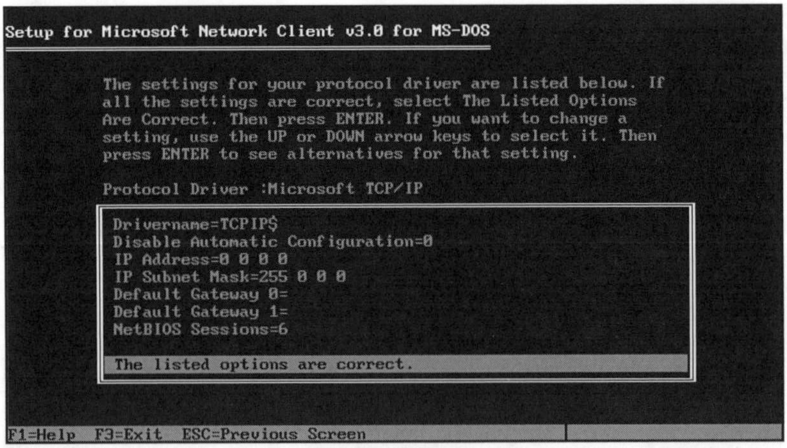

Figure 13.21

TCP/IP settings for the MS-DOS requestor.

16. When all configuration options are as desired, return to the Setup main menu, select **The listed options are correct** and press Enter.

   Even if you selected one of the prepackaged network adapter drivers, you are asked to insert an OEM drivers diskette. Insert Disk 2 of the client installation set to supply the driver files. For drivers not included with the client disk set, insert the OEM diskette.

17. After copying files, restart the computer to activate the client software.

When the MS-DOS client starts up, a logon dialog opens. If the client can locate the required workgroup or domain, the TCP/IP software has been properly configured. If not, check the settings in the file C:\NET\PROTOCOL.INI and edit them as required. Logon share settings are stored in the file C:\NET\SYSTEM.INI.

The NET utility is installed with the MS-DOS client. You can use the NET command or the pop-up shown in figure 13.22 to connect to resources. Type **NET HELP** for a list of the available NET commands. Type **NET** *command* **/?** for more detail about a particular command. See the Appendix of NRP's *Inside Windows NT Server* for more information about the NET commands.

If the computer uses Windows 3.1, use the Windows 3.1 System Setup utility to enable Windows 3.1 to operate as a Microsoft Network client. The steps are as follows:

1. Start the Windows Setup utility.

2. In the **Windows Setup** dialog box, **choose Change System Settings** in the **Options** menu.

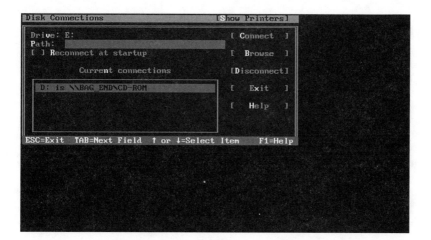

Figure 13.22

The MS-DOS client NET utility.

3. In the **Change System Settings** box (see fig. 13.23), pull down the list for the **Network** box and choose **Microsoft Network (or 100% compatible)**.

4. Exit the Windows Setup utility. You are prompted to supply diskettes from which Windows copies the required network support files. Restart Windows to activate networking.

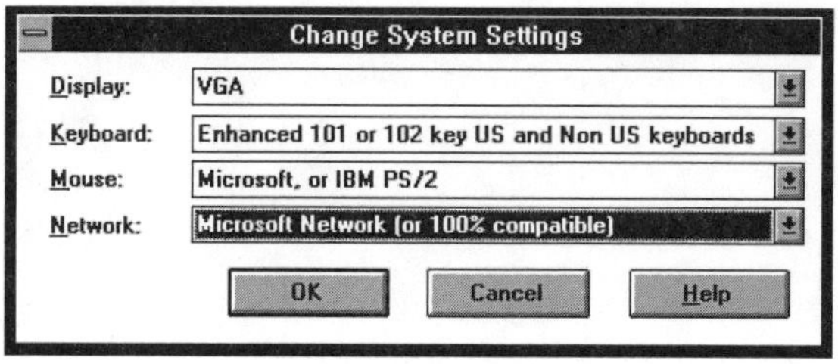

Figure 13.23

Activating Microsoft Network support for Windows 3.1.

Summary

Not only does Microsoft provide TCP/IP client software for Windows NT, it provides the software for the following environments as well:

◆ Windows 95

◆ Windows 3.11

◆ Windows 3.1 and MS-DOS

This chapter examined installation and configuration of client software in these three environments.

Chapter 14 Snapshot

This chapter discusses a variety of topics related to the management of Microsoft TCP/IP networks. It covers the following topics:

◆ Removing TCP/IP components

◆ Troubleshooting utilities

◆ Activating SNMP on Microsoft TCP/IP hosts

◆ Monitoring TCP/IP with Performance Monitor

Managing Microsoft TCP/IP

This chapter embraces a variety of topics related to the ongoing management of Microsoft TCP/IP networks, starting with instructions on how to remove TCP/IP software components from a Windows NT computer. The chapter then reviews some tools that can be used in addition to **ipconfig** to troubleshoot TCP/IP networks. Finally, the chapter examines installation of SNMP on network computers and how to use the Windows NT Performance Monitor to monitor TCP/IP computers.

The network management tools included with Windows NT are fairly limited, not surprising considering the high cost of the best network management tools. This chapter covers configuring SNMP on Microsoft systems, as well as monitoring Microsoft TCP/IP with the Windows NT Performance Monitor.

If your network depends on TCP/IP, you should seriously consider obtaining an SNMP management console. Among the best are:

◆ Microsoft's System Management Server, for Windows NT.

◆ Hewlett Packard's Open View, available for DOS, DOS/Windows, or UNIX.

◆ Sun Microsystem's NetManager, for UNIX.

◆ Novell's NetWare Management System (NMS), for DOS/Windows.

◆ SynOptics' (Bay Networks) Optivity, for DOS/Windows, UNIX, or for use in conjunction with Novell's NMS.

◆ Cabletron's Spectrum, for DOS/Windows, UNIX, or for use in conjunction with Novell's NMS.

This chapter also examines some tools that can be used to troubleshoot basic network problems.

Removing TCP/IP Components

Do not attempt to remove TCP/IP components manually. Most components require a number of files, which are not always installed in the same directories. And installation of all components involves adding keys and values to the Registry. Attempting to back out all of these changes is both trouble prone and unnecessary.

To remove a network software component:

1. Start the Network tool in the Control Panel.

2. In the **Network Settings** dialog box, select the component to be deinstalled in the **Installed Network Software** box.

3. Choose **Remove** to remove the component. All software is permanently removed. Reinstallation is required to restore the component.

Troubleshooting Utilities

Microsoft TCP/IP includes several utilities that can be used to troubleshoot the network. Chapter 8, "Implementing TCP/IP on Windows NT Computers," examines **ping** and **ipconfig**. The tools discussed in this chapter are **arp, tracert, netstat**, and **nbtstat.**

arp

All TCP/IP computers maintain an ARP cache in which are stored the results of recent ARP inquiries. The **arp** utility can be used to view and manage the ARP cache.

arp accepts three command options with the following syntaxes, where *ip_address* is an internet IP address, *mac_address* is the physical address of a network interface, and *ip_host_address* is the IP address of the host whose ARP cache is being examined or modified:

```
arp -a ip_address [-N ip_host_address]

arp -d ip_address [ip_host_address]

arp -s ip_address mac_address [ip_host_address]
```

If hosts cannot ping each other, their ARP cache entries could contain incorrect information. To view the ARP cache on a computer, enter the command **arp -a** at a command prompt. The following listing shows the results of an **arp** inquiry. If the MAC addresses in the ARP table are incorrect, delete the problematic entries.

```
C:\>arp -a

Interface: 128.1.0.1
  Internet Address      Physical Address      Type
  128.1.1.1             00-00-6e-44-9f-4f      dynamic
  128.1.1.60            00-20-af-8d-62-0e      dynamic

C:\>
```

To restrict **arp** to reporting cache entries for a specific IP address, include the address in the command. The following command lists cache entries on the local computer that relate to IP address 128.1.0.60:

```
arp -a 128.1.0.60
```

By default, **arp** reports on the cache table for the first network adapter in the computer's configuration. To access other adapters on multihomed hosts you must specify an interface using the **-N** option. This command reports cache entries on the second adapter of the host:

```
arp -a -N 128.2.0.1
```

To delete the cache record associated with an IP address, use the **-d** option. This command removes the entry for host 128.1.0.60 from the cache table for the first network adapter:

```
arp -d 128.1.0.60
```

The cache table for other network adapters can be specified using the **-N** option.

You can also manually add an entry to the ARP cache. The following example adds a cache entry mapping an IP address to a MAC address:

```
arp -s 128.1.0.60 00-20-af-8d-62-0e
```

As the following listing illustrates, entries added using the **-s** option are regarded as static, in that they are not determined by dynamic ARP inquiries.

```
C:\>arp -a

Interface: 128.1.0.1
  Internet Address       Physical Address       Type
  128.1.1.1              00-00-6e-44-9f-4f       dynamic
  128.1.1.60             00-20-af-8d-62-0e       dynamic

C:\>arp -s 128.1.1.60 00-20-af-8d-62-0e

C:\>arp -a

Interface: 128.1.0.1
  Internet Address       Physical Address       Type
  128.1.1.1              00-00-6e-44-9f-4f       dynamic
  128.1.1.60             00-20-af-8d-62-0e       static

C:\>
```

tracert

tracert is a route reporting utility that sends ICMP echo requests to an IP address and reports ICMP errors that are returned. Successive attempts are made starting with the Time To Live (TTL) field set to one and incrementing TTL by one with each attempt. Thus, each attempt gets one hop closer to the destination. The result is that **tracert** produces a report that lists all of the routers crossed. Here is an example of a tracert report:

```
C:>tracert ftp.microsoft.com

Tracing route to ftp.microsoft.com [198.105.232.1]
over a maximum of 30 hops:

  1     *        *        *       Request timed out.
  2    132 ms   138 ms   144 ms  iq-ind-gw1-en2.iquest.net [198.70.144.10]
```

```
 3    176 ms    166 ms    168 ms    border2-hssi1-0.KansasCity.mci.net [204.70.41.5]
 4    316 ms    237 ms    201 ms    core-fddi-1.KansasCity.mci.net [204.70.3.65]
 5    172 ms    176 ms    164 ms    core2-hssi-2.WillowSprings.mci.net [204.70.1.82]
 6    175 ms    167 ms    167 ms    core1-aip-4.WillowSprings.mci.net [204.70.1.61]
 7    189 ms    188 ms    185 ms    core2-hssi-2.Denver.mci.net [204.70.1.77]
 8    225 ms      *         *       core-hssi-4.Seattle.mci.net [204.70.1.90]
 9      *       224 ms    229 ms    border1-fddi-0.Seattle.mci.net [204.70.2.146]
10    227 ms    220 ms    223 ms    nwnet.Seattle.mci.net [204.70.52.6]
11    239 ms    232 ms    231 ms    seabr1-gw.nwnet.net [192.147.179.5]
12    227 ms    228 ms    229 ms    microsoft-t3-gw.nwnet.net [198.104.192.9]
13    238 ms    236 ms    232 ms    131.107.249.3
14    233 ms    240 ms    237 ms    ftp.microsoft.com [198.105.232.1]

Trace complete.

C:\WINDOWS>
```

netstat

The **netstat** utility reports current TCP/IP connections and protocol statistics. A basic **netstat** report appears in the following listing:

```
C:\>netstat

Active Connections

   Proto  Local Address        Foreign Address        State
   TCP    bag-end:1028         128.1.0.1:nbsession    ESTABLISHED
   TCP    bag-end:1069         128.1.1.60:nbsession   TIME_WAIT

C:\>
```

netstat reports the following information for each connection:

◆ **Proto.** The transport prototype with which the connection is established.

◆ **Local Address.** The name or IP address of the local computer, along with the port number the connection is using.

◆ **Foreign Address.** The foreign address and the port name or number associated with the connection. Both of the connections shown are NetBIOS resource sharing connections.

◆ **State.** For TCP connections only, the state of the connection. Possible values are:

CLOSED	FIN_WAIT_1	LISTEN	TIMED_WAIT
CLOSE_WAIT	FIN_WAIT_2	SYN_RECEIVED	
ESTABLISHED	LAST_ACK	SYN_SEND	

The syntax of **netstat** is as follows:

```
netstat [-a] [-e] [-n] [-s] [-p protocol] [-r] [interval]
```

netstat accepts several arguments that produce enhanced reports:

◆ **-a.** Displays all connections and listening ports, information not normally reported.

◆ **-e.** Displays Ethernet statistics. May be combined with the **-s** option.

◆ **-n.** Displays addresses and ports in numerical rather than name form.

◆ **-p protocol.** Shows connections for the specified protocol, which may be **tcp** or **udp.** If used with the **-s** option, *protocol* may be **tcp, udp,** or **ip.**

◆ **-r.** Displays routing table data.

◆ **-s.** Displays statistics separately for each protocol. By default, **netstat** reports statistics for TCP, UDP, and IP. The **-p** option can be used to display a subset of the three protocols.

◆ *interval.* Include an *interval* parameter to have **netstat** report repeatedly, with *interval* specifying the number of seconds between reports. Press Ctrl+C to stop **netstat.**

The following listing illustrates use of the -e option:

```
C:\>netstat -e
Interface Statistics

                        Received          Sent

Bytes                   124083            76784
Unicast packets         484               577
Non-unicast packets     195               96
Discards                0                 0
Errors                  0                 0
Unknown protocols       62
```

```
C:\>
```

The **-s** option reports statistics for the IP, ICMP, TCP, and UDP protocols, as in this example:

```
C:> netstat -s
```

IP Statistics

```
    Packets Received                     = 634
    Received Header Errors               = 0
    Received Address Errors              = 0
    Datagrams Forwarded                  = 0
    Unknown Protocols Received           = 0
    Received Packets Discarded           = 0
    Received Packets Delivered           = 634
    Output Requests                      = 658
    Routing Discards                     = 128
    Discarded Output Packets             = 0
    Output Packet No Route               = 0
    Reassembly Required                  = 0
    Reassembly Successful                = 0
    Reassembly Failures                  = 0
    Datagrams Successfully Fragmented    = 0
    Datagrams Failing Fragmentation     = 0
    Fragments Created                    = 0
```

ICMP Statistics

	Received	Sent
Messages	115	152
Errors	0	0
Destination Unreachable	0	0
Time Exceeded	109	0
Parameter Problems	0	0
Source Quenchs	0	0
Redirects	0	0
Echos	0	152
Echo Replies	6	0
Timestamps	0	0
Timestamp Replies	0	0
Address Masks	0	0
Address Mask Replies	0	0

```
TCP Statistics

    Active Opens                    = 6
    Passive Opens                   = 0
    Failed Connection Attempts      = 0
    Reset Connections               = 0
    Current Connections             = 1
    Segments Received               = 307
    Segments Sent                   = 374
    Segments Retransmitted          = 0


UDP Statistics

    Datagrams Received    = 211
    No Ports              = 1
    Receive Errors        = 0
    Datagrams Sent        = 132
```

nbtstat

nbtstat reports statistics and connections for NetBIOS over TCP/IP. The most basic option for **nbtstat** is **-r**, which reports complete name resolution statistics for Windows networking. Here is an example, which was generated on a network that did not incorporate a WINS server:

```
C:\>nbtstat -r

NetBIOS Names Resolution and Registration Statistics
-----------------------------------------------------


Resolved By Broadcast      = 6
Resolved By Name Server    = 0

Registered By Broadcast    = 11
Registered By Name Server  = 0

        NetBIOS Names Resolved By Broadcast
    -------------------------------------------
```

```
        GANDALF
        GANDALF
        RIVENDELL
        GANDALF
        MIDDLE_EARTH    <1B>
        RIVENDELL


C:\>
```

The syntax of **nbtstat** is as follows:

```
nbtstat [-a remotename][-A ipaddress][-c][-n][-r][-R][-s][-S][interval]
```

The following options are available for **nbtstat**:

◆ **-a *remotename*.** Lists the name table of a remote computer, specified by *remotename*.

◆ **-A *ipaddress*.** Lists the name table of a remote computer, specified by the computer's IP address.

◆ **-c.** Lists the contents of the local computer's NetBIOS name cache.

◆ **-n.** Lists local NetBIOS names.

◆ **-r.** Lists local Windows name resolution statistics, including broadcast and WINS-based name resolution.

◆ **-R.** Purges the name table and reloads it from entries in the computer's LMHOSTS file. (Clearly, the case of options makes a difference when using **nbtstat**!)

◆ **-s.** Displays workstation and server sessions, attempting to resolve remote IP addresses based on the HOSTS file.

◆ **-S.** Displays workstation and servers sessions, listed by IP address only.

◆ ***interval*.** Include an *interval* parameter to specify that **nbtstat** should report repeatedly with *interval* seconds between displays. Press Ctrl+C to terminate **nbtstat**.

The display produced by **nbtstat -s** illustrates the data that are available from the utility:

```
C:\>nbtstat -s
```

```
                     NetBIOS Connection Table

   Local Name              State    In/Out  Remote Host          Input    Output
   - - - - - - - - - - - - - - - - - - - - - - - - - - - - - - - - - - - - - - -
   RIVENDELL       <00>  Connected   Out   GANDALF    <20>       21KB       3KB
   RIVENDELL       <00>  Connected   Out   GONDOR     <20>        5KB       1KB
   RIVENDELL       <00>  Connected   Out   BAG_END    <20>       15KB       1KB
   RIVENDELL             Connected   In    BAG_END    <00>       25KB      82KB
   RIVENDELL       <03>  Listening
   RIVENDELL       <03>  Listening
   ADMINISTRATOR   <03>  Listening
   ADMINISTRATOR   <03>  Listening
   RIVENDELL       <1F>  Listening
   RIVENDELL       <1F>  Listening

   C:\>
```

Activating SNMP on Microsoft TCP/IP Hosts

SNMP agent support is an option on Windows NT and Windows 95. This section covers installation of SNMP in those environments.

Any SNMP configuration includes a *community* parameter, which is simply the name of a group of systems that exchange SNMP messages. The community name may be used to limit the extent to which some SNMP messages are propagated through the network. The default community name is *public*.

An SNMP agent also must specify at least one trap destination, the address of an SNMP computer to receive SNMP trap messages. Microsoft TCP/IP SNMP can send traps to IP and IPX addresses.

Configuring SNMP on Windows NT

The SNMP service is installed using the same procedures as for any TCP/IP software module:

1. Open the Network utility in the Control Panel.

2. Choose **Add Software** in the **Network Settings** dialog box.

3. Select **TCP/IP Protocol and related components** in the **Network Settings** box of the **Add Network Software** dialog box, then choose **Continue**.

4. Check **SNMP Service** in the **Windows NT TCP/IP Installation Options** dialog box. Then choose **Continue**.

5. Supply disks and path information as required to install the software.

6. Choose **OK** to close the **Network Settings** dialog box.

7. Next, you see the **SNMP Service Configuration** dialog box (see fig. 14.1).

    a. First, specify at least SNMP community to which this computer will belong. The default community is **public.** Enter SNMP community names in the **Community Names** box and choose **Add** to move them to the **Send Traps with Community Names** box.

    b. Also specify trap destinations for this computer. Enter IP addresses in the **IP Host/Address or IPX Addresses** box and choose **Add** to move them to the **Trap Destination** box.

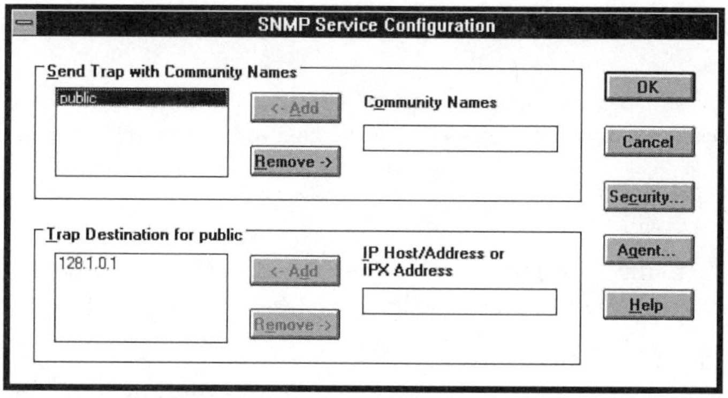

Figure 14.1

Specifying the SNMP configuration.

8. To specify security settings, choose the **Security** button to open the **SNMP Security Configuration** dialog box (see fig. 14.2).

    a. Check the box **Send Authentication Trap** if you want the computer to send a trap for a failed authentication.

    b. In the **Accepted Community Names** box, specify community names from which this computer will accept requests. Typically, all hosts belong to **public.**

    c. By default, the **Accept SNMP Packets from Any Host** option is checked. If this computer should accept packets only from hosts that have specific IP or IPX addresses, check **Only Accept SNMP Packets from These Hosts** and add the hosts in the associated box.

    d. Choose **OK** after entering security information.

Figure 14.2

Configuring SNMP security.

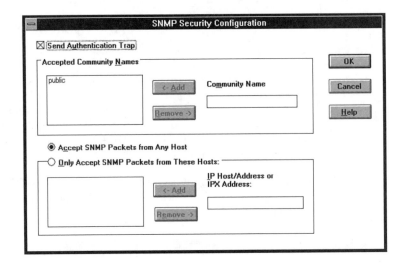

> **Note**
>
> Don't be lulled into a false sense of security. All of the SNMP security options can easily be circumvented. If your SNMP-managed network is connected to the Internet or any public internetwork, a firewall should be in place to prevent intrusion from outside SNMP management consoles.

  9. After returning to the **SNMP Service Configuration** dialog box, choose the **Agent** button to open the **SNMP Agent** dialog box (see fig. 14.3).

    a. In the **Contact** and **Location** boxes, enter the name of the computer user and the computer's location or other identification information.

    b. If additional TCP/IP services have been installed on the computer, check an SNMP service option in the **Service** box. The options are as follows:

        ◆ **Physical.** This computer manages a physical layer TCP/IP device such as a repeater.

        ◆ **Datalink/Subnetwork.** This computer manages a datalink layer such as a bridge or a subnetwork.

        ◆ **Internet.** This computer manages an internet layer device, that is, it functions as an IP gateway (router).

◆ **End-to-End.** This computer acts as an IP host. This option should be selected for all Windows NT computers.

◆ **Applications.** This computer supports applications that use TCP/IP. This option should be selected for all Windows NT computers.

10. Choose **OK,** exit the **SNMP Service Configuration** dialog box, and exit the **Network Settings** dialog box. The computer does not need to be restarted.

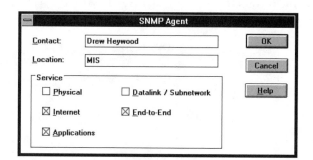

Figure 14.3

Configuring SNMP agent information.

Configuring SNMP on Windows 95 Computers

Setting up an SNMP agent on a Windows 95 computer involves two procedures, and possibly a third:

1. Installing the SNMP software.

2. Configuring the SNMP agent using the System Policy Editor.

3. If more than one community name is required, adding the community name to the Registry.

Installing the SNMP Software

To install the SNMP software:

1. Start the Network tool in the Control Panel.

2. In the **Network** dialog box, choose the **Add** button.

3. In the **Select Network Component Type** dialog box, select **Service** and choose **Add**. A box opens temporarily with the title **Building Driver Database**. When the box completes its work, the **Select Network Service** dialog box appears.

4. Choose **Have Disk** to open the **Install From Disk** dialog box. In the **Copy manufacturers files from** box, specify the path to the \ADMIN\NETTOOLS\SNMP directory on the Windows 95 CD-ROM.

   If necessary, choose the **Browse** button to open an **Open** dialog box and browse the local computer for its CD-ROM drive, or browse the Network Neighborhood for a shared CD-ROM drive that contains the Windows 95 CD-ROM. After specifying the drive letter of the CD-ROM, return to the **Install From Disk** dialog box and complete the path to the \ADMIN\NETTOOLS\SNMP directory. After you finish, the **Open** dialog box should resemble the one shown in figure 14.4.

Figure 14.4

Browsing for the SNMP files on the Windows 95 CD.

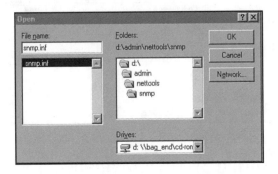

5. Choose **OK** to return to the **Install from Disk** dialog box. The **Copy manufacturers files from** box should now specify the path to the SNMP files. Choose **OK** to continue.

6. Next, the **Select Network Service** dialog box appears. Only the Microsoft TCP/IP agent is shown as an installable service, so nothing must be selected. Simply choose **OK** to continue.

7. Files now are copied from the CD-ROM to the hard drive. You might see messages concerning missing files. The reported files are part of a standard Windows 95 network installation and are already in place. You can choose **Skip** to ignore the missing files.

8. After returning to the Network utility, restart the computer to activate the SNMP agent.

Configuring the SNMP Agent

The SNMP agent is configured by editing the Registry using the System Policy Editor, which is not installed in a standard Windows 95 configuration. To install the System Policy Editor:

1. Open the Add/Remove Programs tool in the Control Panel. Click on the **Windows Setup** tab. Then click on **Have Disk**.

2. In the **Install From Disk** dialog box, specify the path to the \ADMIN\APPTOOLS\POLEDIT directory on the Windows 95 CD-ROM. You may browse for a CD-ROM drive as described in the previous section.

3. After specifying the path, choose **OK** to go to the **Have Disk** dialog box. Two entries appear in the **Components** box. Select **System Policy Editor** and choose **Install**.

4. After files are copied, quit the Add/Remove Programs tool.

To configure the SNMP agent using the System Policy Editor:

1. Choose the **Run** command in the Start menu. Enter the command `poledit` in the **Open** data entry field of the **Run** dialog box and choose **OK.**

2. In the **System Policy Editor** window choose the **Open Registry** command in the **File** menu. Two options are presented as icons in the System Policy Editor: **Local User** and **Local Computer** (see fig. 14.5).

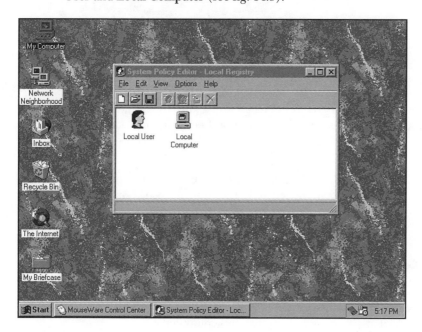

Figure 14.5

Options in the System Policy Editor.

3. Double-click on **Local Computer** to establish default SNMP policies for the computer. The next window you see is the **Local Computer Properties** window. In figure 14.6, the **Network** icon was double-clicked on to list the option's subcategories.

Figure 14.6

The Local Computer Properties window.

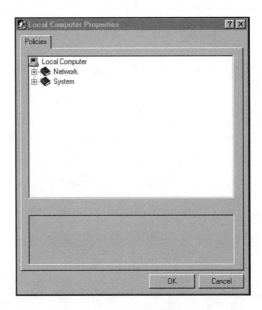

4. Double-click on Network, then double-click on **SNMP** to reveal the property entries for the SNMP agent, as shown in figure 14.7.

   Each entry in the policy editor is tagged with a box icon to the left of the option description. The box can be marked with a check mark, or it can be cleared.

   ◆ When the box is cleared, the Registry entry is not implemented.

   ◆ When the box is checked, the Registry entry is implemented and is configured using the values specified in the **Settings** dialog box.

   The four SNMP policy options are similar to options that have been discussed for Windows NT SNMP clients:

   ◆ **Communities.** Settings include one or more names of which the computer is a member.

   ◆ **Permitted managers.** Settings include IP or IPX addresses of computers that are permitted to manage this computer.

◆ **Traps for 'Public' community.** By default, only the public community is supported. Additional communities must be added to the Registry. Specify addresses of stations in the public community that are to receive traps from this station.

◆ **Internet MIB (RFC1156).** Settings are the contact name and location associated with this computer.

5. To set an SNMP policy:

    a. Click on the policy's box until it shows a check mark.

    b. Choose the **Show** button to open a **Show Contents** dialog box in which you can add and remove values.

    c. Choose **OK** after configuring all policies.

6. To remove a Registry entry along with previous configuration settings, click on the policy's box until it is cleared.

7. When the required settings have been entered, choose **OK** to return to the main window of the System Policy Editor.

8. Close the editor, and respond **Yes** when you are prompted, Do you want to save changes to the Registry?

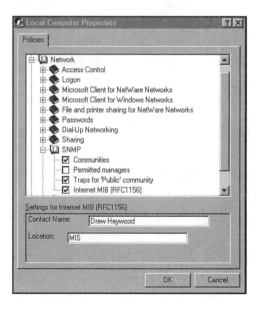

Figure 14.7

Policy properties for the SNMP agent.

Adding SNMP Communities

If more than one SNMP community will be active on the network, the community name and traps must be added to the Registry. This is most easily done with the Registry Editor. To add a community to the Registry:

1. Choose the **Run** command in the Start menu. Enter the command `regedit` in the **Open** field of the **Run** dialog box and choose **OK.**

2. Unlike the Windows NT Registry editor, here you will find all of the Windows 95 Registry subtrees merged into a single tree. Simply double-click on keys to open deeper levels of the Registry tree. In the Registry Editor, open the following key:

   `Hkey_Local_Machine\System\CurrentControlSet\Services\SNMP\Parameters\TrapConfiguration`

   At first, **Public** will be the only subkey of **TrapConfiguration**. Additional community names are created as additional subkeys of **TrapConfiguration**.

3. To create the subkey, be sure that **TrapConfiguration** is selected in the Registry tree.

   Click on the **Edit** menu. Then click on **New** to open the **New** submenu. Choose **Key** in the **New** submenu (see fig. 14.8).

4. A key will be added to the Registry tree with the name **New Key #1**. The key name is selected for editing. Type a community name for the key to overwrite the default name. Press Enter after typing the name.

5. Next, a value must be created for each console that will receive SNMP traps from this computer. These values are named with integers, starting with 1. The data portion of the value is an IP or IPX address.

   To assign a value to the key:

   a. Select the new key.

   b. Click on **Edit**, click on **New**, and click on **String Value** in the **New** submenu. A new value will be added to the values pane of the Registry Editor.

   c. The initial name of the new value is **New Value #1**, which is selected for editing when the value is created. If this is the first value in the community key, its name should be 1. Additional values should be named 2, 3, and so forth.

d. After renaming the value, click on **Edit** and click on **Modify** to open the **Edit String** dialog box (see fig. 14.8). In the **Value data** field, enter an IP address or an IPX address. Choose **OK** after finishing.

Figure 14.9 shows the state of the Registry editor after the new key has been added and values in the key have been defined.

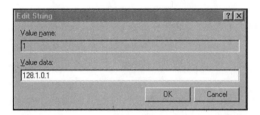

Figure 14.8

Editing the data for a Registry value.

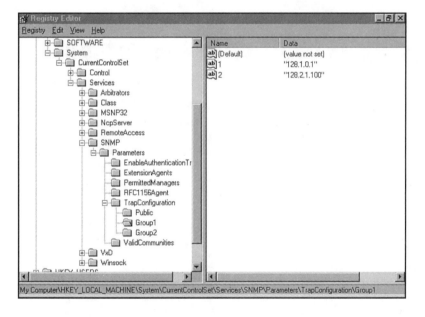

Figure 14.9

The Registry Editor after adding community keys.

6. Exit the Registry Editor to save the changes.

> **Stop**
>
> Remember, the Registry is critical to proper functioning of Windows 95. Make changes with care. You might want to save a copy of the Registry using the **Export Registry File** command in the **File** menu. Even if the Registry is damaged so that the system cannot be started, you can start the system using the emergency startup disk that is created during installation. A real-mode Registry editor on the startup disk can be used to import a working Registry from the export file.
>
> The Registry is stored in two files: SYSTEM.DAT, which contains general system information, and USER.DAT, which contains information related to user profiles.
>
> If you are certain that a backup file contains a complete Registry image, you can use the **regedit** utility on the startup disk to restore the complete registry by entering the command `regedit /c filename.reg` where *filename* is the name of the export file. Using the /c option with an export file that does not contain a complete Registry image will be disastrous!

Monitoring TCP/IP with Performance Monitor

Performance Monitor is a versatile tool, and it is beyond the scope of this book to exhaustively consider its features. Please consult *Inside Windows NT Server* for thorough coverage. This discussion examines the basics of charting statistics in Performance Monitor, along with some specifics that apply to monitoring TCP/IP objects.

Performance Monitor starts in chart mode. Before any data are displayed, you need to add a chart line using the following procedure:

1. Choose the **Add to Chart** command in the **Edit** menu. This opens the **Add to Chart** dialog box (see fig. 14.10).

2. In the **Computer** box, specify the UNC name of a computer to be monitored. If desired, you can browse for a computer by choosing the **Browse** button (the one with three dots on it).

3. In the **Object** box, select the object to be monitored. TCP/IP services adds the following objects to Performance Monitor:

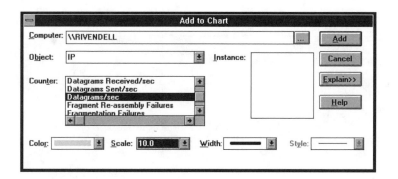

Figure 14.10

Specifying parameters for a chart line.

- ◆ ICMP
- ◆ IP
- ◆ Network Interface
- ◆ TCP
- ◆ UDP
- ◆ FTP (if the FTP Server service is installed)
- ◆ WINS (if the WINS Server service is installed

4. In the **Counter** box, select a counter to be charted.

5. If the counter you selected has more than one instance (such as two network interface adapters), select one in the **Instance** box.

6. If desired, customize the chart line by choosing options in the **Color**, **Scale**, **Width**, and **Style** boxes.

   Scale is an extremely useful option that enables you to adjust the magnitude of the line that will chart this counter. Choose a scale greater than 1 to increase the height of the chart and enhance display of counters reporting small values. Choose a scale less than 1 to reduce the height of the graph for counters reporting large values.

7. Choose **Add** to add the line to the chart.

8. Add other lines to the chart as desired.

9. Double-click on the legend for a chart line to edit the line's parameters.

Figure 14.11 shows a chart with several TCP/IP-related values.

Figure 14.11

*Example of a
Performance Monitor
chart.*

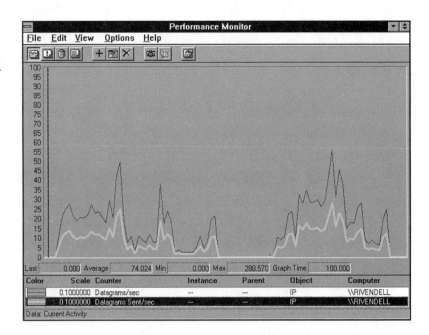

The majority of the available counters should require little explanation. Consult the Windows NT Server TCP/IP manual for descriptions.

Summary

This chapter first looked at how to remove TCP/IP software components from a Windows NT computer. Then it reviewed some of the tools that could be used to troubleshoot TCP/IP networks. These tools included arp, tracert, netstat, and nbdstat. Finally, this chapter examined the installation of SNMP on network computers, and how to use the Windows NT Performance Monitor to monitor TCP/IP computers.

Chapter 15 Snapshot

This chapter focuses on building an Internet server. It covers the following topics:

◆ Connecting to the Internet

◆ Using RAS to connect to the Internet

◆ Setting up an FTP server

◆ Setting up a World Wide Web server

Building an Internet Server

How you connect your computers to the Internet depends a great deal on what you want your Internet connection to accomplish. The following list presents just a few of the possibilities:

◆ A few of your users need light-duty access to services on the Internet.

◆ You want to enable all users on your LAN to connect to Internet services.

◆ You want to provide an FTP server to enable outside Internet users to send and receive files. Your users need access to files on the FTP server, but don't need Internet access.

◆ You want to set up a Web server.

◆ All of your users need to access the Internet. You also want to enable outside Internet users to access services offered on your network and to exchange data with your users via e-mail and file transfer.

After you define your organization's requirements, you can begin to answer several questions, such as the following:

◆ Do you need permanent access to the Internet, or is dial-up (switched) access sufficient?

◆ Do you need dedicated computers to provide services such as FTP or World Wide Web, or can you provide the required services on nondedicated systems?

◆ What are the security risks of the type of connection you intend to use and what precautions should you take?

This chapter begins by addressing these questions of connection methods and security risks.

Following that discussion, this chapter demonstrates how to enable your network to provide two popular Internet services: FTP and World Wide Web. FTP server software is included with Windows NT, and Windows NT Web server software is included with the *Windows NT Resource Kit*.

Connecting to the Internet

You can connect computers to the Internet in two ways: using a switched (dial-up) connection or using a dedicated communication channel. Switched and dedicated connections are suitable to different sets of Internet connection requirements.

Switched Internet Connections

The Windows Remote Access Server (RAS) can be configured to connect to the Internet in several ways:

◆ **Analog modems.** Dial connections using SLIP and PPP protocols at analog modem speeds.

◆ **ISDN.** High-performance dial-up connections using PPP.

◆ **X.25.** Packet switching, up to 56 Kbps.

Switched connections, as provided by analog modems and ISDN, are best suited to people who need occasional Internet connections. Although configuring a computer to route TCP/IP between a network and the Internet via an analog modem is possible, anyone who uses a modem to connect to the Internet knows that analog connections are quite slow, even when dedicated to servicing a single user. Several users successfully sharing even a 28.8 Kbps modem connection with any comfort is a highly unlikely proposition.

A common misconception about analog modems is that data compression is a reliable means of achieving high data rates. Although the majority of modems sold do support data compression, several factors limit the utility of data compression:

◆ Poor connection quality frequently prevents modems from using their highest data rates. Modems negotiate a data rate when they first connect, based on the fastest speed they can reliably use with the current connection quality. This data rate frequently is less than the theoretical potential of the modems.

◆ Poor connection quality can prevent attached modems from using data compression.

◆ Compressed data cannot be further compressed. Many data-intensive tasks involve downloading and uploading files, which are frequently already compressed. Modems cannot compress this data further, and the effective data rate is limited to the highest noncompressed rate the modems support.

Analog modems, therefore, should generally be regarded as individual connectivity tools.

Another switched communication method is ISDN. The most popular ISDN service provides two 64 Kbps "B" channels, which can be aggregated to support 128 Kbps data rates. ISDN data rates can support multiple users, but ISDN remains a switched connectivity option. A connection must be established each time access to the Internet is required. ISDN tariffs typically charge for connect time, and the cost of ISDN can escalate quickly if users connect for substantial periods of time.

The one nonswitched option RAS does support is X.25. Although obtaining a dedicated connection to an X.25 network is possible, data rates for X.25 are limited to 64 Kbps—sufficient for a few Internet users, but hardly adequate to accomodate dozens of users transferring files or accessing the Web.

Switched connections should be considered dial-out connections only. If you want a permanent presence on the Internet to offer a Web, FTP, or other server, you need a dedicated, permanent connection.

Permanent Internet Connections

A permanent connection to the Internet typically involves leasing a digital, dedicated line between your site and the site that provides your Internet connection. Dedicated lines are available in a wide variety of data rates, from 56 Kbps to several megabits per second. The cost of a dedicated line is high, but you cannot avoid the expense if you intend to maintain a permanent presence on the Internet.

Permanent connections to the Internet are inherently risky. The TCP/IP protocols were not designed with security in mind, and many Internet users have the expertise to crack into your network.

Isolating the Server

If your organization merely wants to offer a service to the Internet community without enabling your users to use the same connection to the Internet, limiting your security risk is easy. Figure 15.1 illustrates a configuration that completely isolates local users' computers from the Internet. If someone breaks into your Internet server, access is limited to the server itself.

Figure 15.1

An Internet server isolated from the local network.

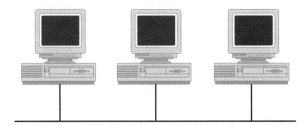

Consider this scenario, however. Your organization is a magazine publisher. You want to enable your authors to submit articles via **ftp**, and you want your editors to be able to retrieve articles from the FTP server through your LAN: this isn't possible if users are isolated from the Internet server, as in figure 15.1.

Windows supports protocols other than TCP/IP, however, and a possible solution to this problem is to use a different network protocol internally. Figure 15.2 shows an Internet server that connects to the Internet using TCP/IP. The server is connected to the organization's LAN using NWLink (IPX/SPX). Windows NT servers do not route between different protocol stacks, and this approach very effectively isolates outside TCP/IP users from inside users connected using NWLink.

Providing Full Internet Connectivity

Suppose, however, that you want your Internet connection to enable outside users to connect in and inside users to connect out. What is wrong with the network shown in figure 15.3? If an outsider attempts to violate security, you'll know it, won't you? After all, the intruder can be readily identified because he will be using a nonlocal netid.

Unfortunately, IP addresses aren't secure. Any reasonably knowledgeable Internet snoop can use a technique known as "IP spoofing" to make his packets appear to have originated on your local network. All the intruder needs to do is listen into your network for awhile, pick up a few usernames and passwords (which are transmitted in the clear), spoof an IP address, and break in. Once in, an intruder can gain entry to dozens of TCP/IP systems. If the intruder can "spoof in" using the address of a user logged on to a server, the intruder might be able to impersonate the logged-on user and access files using that user's security permissions.

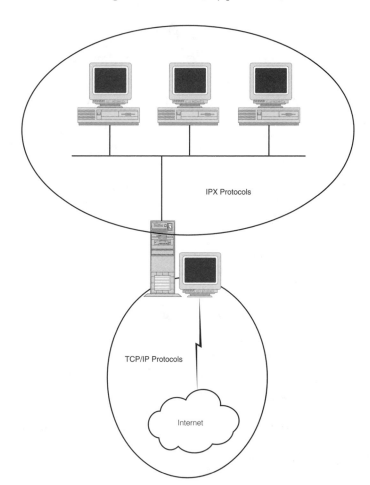

Figure 15.2

Isolating local computers using multiple protocols.

Figure 15.3

An insecure Internet connection.

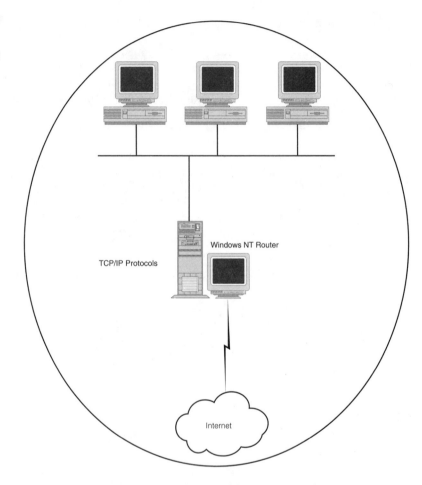

A basic rule of TCP/IP security is as follows: Never base security on IP addresses. Security must always be based on a secure login procedure that authenticates all users who are given access to critical systems.

Another basic rule is to isolate your Internet servers from your LAN clients. And isolation brings us to the subject of firewalls.

A *firewall* is a filter that can be configured to block certain types of network traffic. Traffic can be filtered in various ways:

◆ Restricting certain protocols

◆ Permitting inside traffic out, while preventing outside traffic from entering

◆ Restricting certain types of packets

A firewall is essentially an IP router that has had its routing function replaced by a more secure method of forwarding messages. Some firewalls are specialized pieces of hardware, while other firewalls might consist of software running on a multihomed TCP/IP host.

This is not the place to discuss the details of firewalls, which are quite technical. A look at some options for deploying firewalls, however, is worth taking. Figure 15.4 illustrates a firewall configuration in which one Internet host provides all Internet services *and* runs firewall software. The Internet server/firewall combination is configured to enable inside users to connect out to the Internet. Outside users, however, are not permitted to connect to the LAN.

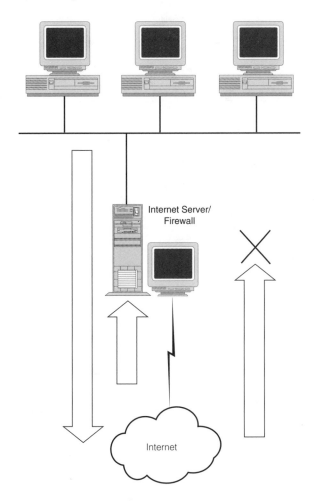

Figure 15.4

A basic firewall/Internet server combination.

If you must configure more than one Internet server, you should avoid the configuration shown in figure 15.5. No matter how tightly the firewall is configured to restrict outside users from accessing specific hosts, an intruder still could circumvent the firewall and gain access to other LAN-based hosts.

Instead, you should isolate the servers on a separate network segment and configure the firewall to route traffic appropriately. Figure 15.6 illustrates such an approach. The firewall permits outside users to access designated servers on one network segment, but prevents access to systems on the other segment.

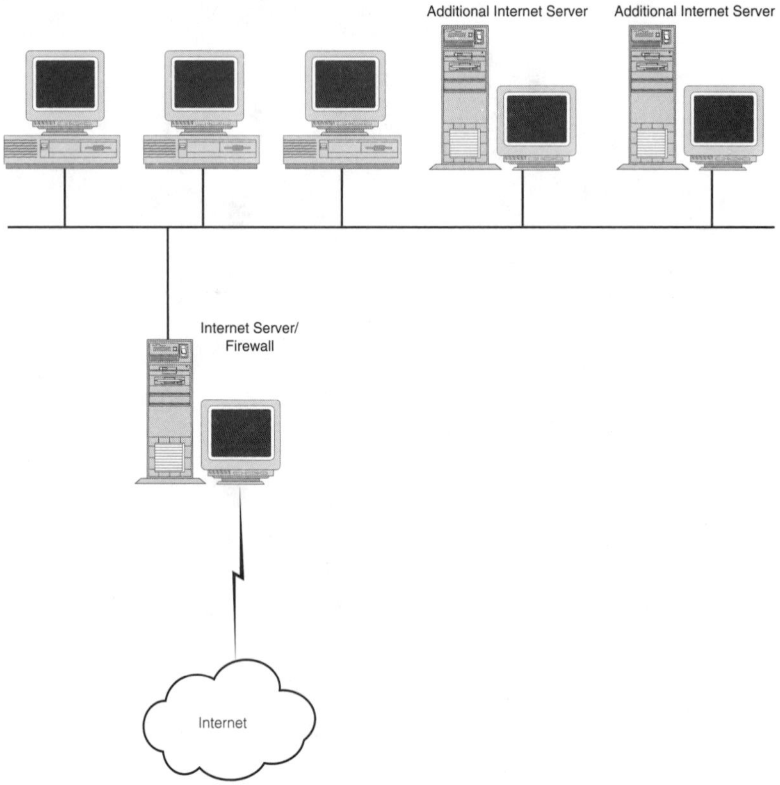

Figure 15.5

A firewall configuration that poses potential problems.

The techniques for cracking into TCP/IP networks are advancing at least as quickly as the techniques for building firewalls, and putting too much faith in the security you implement is unwise. For many, a secure network is merely an inspiration to try harder. For that reason, physical isolation of critical computers remains the one certain way to prevent intrusion.

Note Using the Windows NT router capability to make an Internet connection is possible, but the Windows NT router has limited performance and does not implement dynamic routing, such as RIP. Nor can the Windows NT router provide any firewall capabilities. In most cases, a commercial hardware router, preferably one that possesses firewall capabilities, is the most satisfactory way to connect to the Internet.

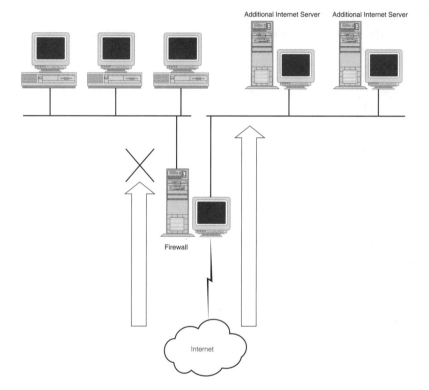

Figure 15.6

A more secure firewall configuration.

Using RAS to Connect to the Internet

For individuals and small LANs, connecting to a dial-up account using RAS may be an acceptable way to reach the Internet. This section covers installation, configuration, and use of RAS to access the Internet by dialing into an Internet access provider. This section shows how to install RAS, configure modem connections for the SLIP and PPP protocols, and access the Internet. It also shows you how to configure RAS to enable it to function as a router between LAN users and the Internet.

Two protocols are used with TCP/IP dial-in accounts. SLIP is an older protocol that offers high performance but provides nothing in the way of creature comforts or error checking. PPP is an improved protocol that is more reliable than SLIP and provides some management advantages, but operates somewhat more slowly than SLIP. The majority of Internet dial-in accounts are configured to use PPP.

To connect to the Internet, you need the following:

◆ A SLIP or PPP dial-in account with an Internet access provider. You need the following account information:

  ◆ Access telephone number
  ◆ Username
  ◆ Host name
  ◆ Password

◆ Unless these IP addresses are assigned dynamically when a connection is made, you need:

  ◆ IP address
  ◆ Subnet mask
  ◆ Default gateway address
  ◆ Primary and backup DNS server IP addresses

◆ You also need to know if Van Jacobsen (VJ) header compression should be on or off.

Installing RAS

RAS is installed using the Network tool in the Control Panel. The exact procedures vary depending on what software and hardware is already installed. The following procedure is fairly generic, and assumes that TCP/IP is already installed on the computer:

1. Start the Network tool.

2. If you use SLIP to connect, choose **Add Adapter** and select **MS Loopback Adapter** from the **Network Adapter Card** box in the **Add Network Adapter** dialog box. Specify **802.3** when you are prompted to select a frame type. Then choose **OK** to continue, complete the installation, and return to the **Network Settings** dialog box.

3. In the **Network Settings** dialog box, choose **Add Software**.

4. In the **Network Software** box of the **Add Network Software** dialog box, select **Remote Access Service**. Then choose **Continue**.

5. When prompted, supply the path to the installation files, after which files are copied to your system.

6. If a modem has not been configured on the computer, the **Add Port** dialog box opens (see fig. 15.7). Select a COM port to configure for RAS and choose **OK**.

7. If a modem has not been configured on the port, you receive the message, *Remote Access will attempt to detect the modem connected to the selected port*. Choose **OK** to initiate modem detection.

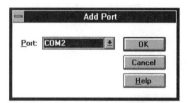

Figure 15.7

Adding a COM port to RAS.

8. If modem detection is successful, a **Detect Modem** dialog box appears, resembling the one shown in figure 15.8. The modems listed fit the profile of the equipment RAS detects. Select the candidate modem that most closely matches your hardware and choose **OK**.

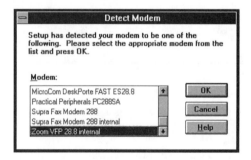

Figure 15.8

Selecting a modem for RAS.

9. Next, you see the **Configure Port** dialog box (see fig. 15.9). Select the option that specifies whether to use this port for dialing out, receiving calls, or both. Of course, the port must be configured for dialing out if it is to reach the Internet using a dial-in account. Selecting an option to receive calls enables this computer as a RAS dial-in server. Choose **OK** after making the selection.

If necessary, you can redetect the attached modem by choosing **Detect**.

Figure 15.9

Configuring the port connection mode.

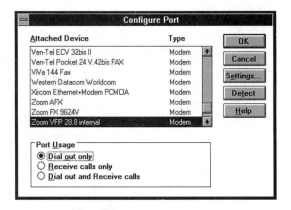

10. Next, the **Remote Access Setup** dialog box appears (see fig. 15.10). This dialog box enables you to add modems to the RAS modem pool, and to remove and reconfigure modems. Perform any required maintenance and choose **Continue.**

Figure 15.10

Managing modems in Remote Access.

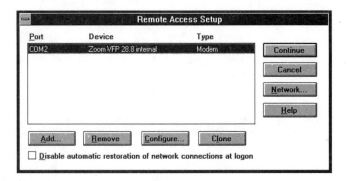

11. Next, the RAS files are installed and a Remote Access Service program group is created in Program Manager. The new program group contains icons for RAS-related programs. Supply the path to the installation directory when prompted and choose **Continue**. After files are copied, you are returned to the **Network Settings** dialog box. Choose **OK**. Restart the computer when prompted.

Configuring RAS for a PPP Connection

To configure RAS to dial an IAP account configured for PPP, do the following:

1. Start Remote Access (the icon is located in the Remote Access Server program group). The **Remote Access** dialog box appears (see fig. 15.11). The list of phone book entries initially is empty. The figure shows Remote Access after a phone book entry has been added.

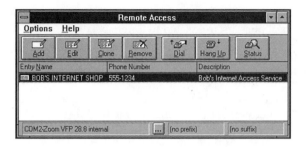

Figure 15.11

The Remote Access dialog box.

2. Choose **Add** to open the **Add Phone Book Entry** dialog box (see fig. 15.12). If the **Modem** and other buttons are not visible at the bottom of the dialog box, click on the **Advanced** button. Then complete the entries in this box as follows:

   ◆ Identify the entry in the **Entry Name** (required) and **Description** (optional) fields.

   ◆ Complete the **Phone Number** field. Click on the **Browse** button (a button with three periods on it) to browse telephone numbers that have already been entered into RAS.

   ◆ Select a port in the **Port** box.

   ◆ Remove the check mark from the **Authenticate using current user name and password** check box.

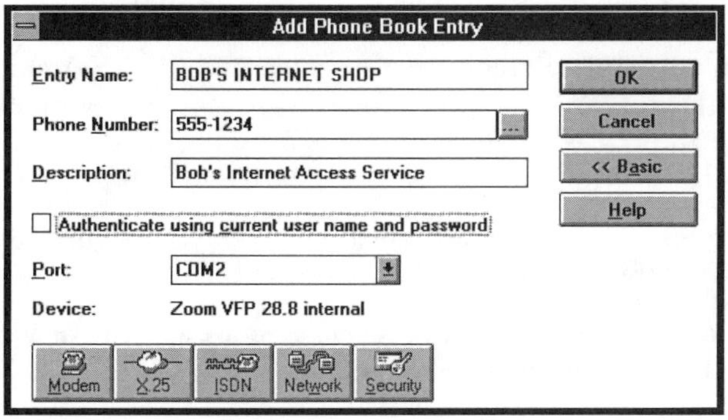

Figure 15.12

Adding a phone book entry.

3. Choose the **Modem** button to open the **Modem Settings** dialog box (see fig. 15.13). Complete this dialog box as follows:

   ◆ Set the **Initial speed** field to the highest connection speed for the modem. Generally speaking, a 14.4 Kbps modem can be configured for a speed of 38400. A 28.8 Kbps modem can be configured for a speed of 57600. These speeds are possible only if the computer is equipped with a 16550 UART. Older-style serial ports are restricted to lower speeds.

◆ Check **Enable hardware flow control**, **Enable modem error control**, and **Enable modem compression**.

◆ Unless you have trouble and need to manually debug modem commands, do not check **Enter modem commands manually.**

Choose **OK** to return to the **Add Phone Book Entry** dialog box.

Figure 15.13

Configuring a RAS modem.

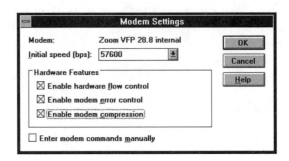

4. Choose **Network** to open the **Network Protocol Settings** dialog box (see fig. 15.14). The dialog box in the figure is filled out appropriately for PPP.

   Consult your IAP to determine whether their PPP software supports RFC 1570. If so, check **Request LCP Extensions**.

5. Only the TCP/IP protocols are required. Check the **TCP/IP** box. You may deselect **NetBEUI** and **IPX** unless those protocols are required for other RAS activities. Choose the **TCP/IP Settings** button to open the **PPP TCP/IP Settings** dialog box (see fig. 15.15). Complete this dialog box as follows:

   ◆ If an IP address is assigned automatically on connection, check **Server assigned IP address**. This generally will be the correct option.

   ◆ If a specific IP address will be used, check **Require specific IP address** and enter the IP address in the **IP address** entry box.

   ◆ If a DNS server will be configured at connection time, check **Server assigned name server addresses**.

   ◆ If a DNS server must be specified in the RAS configuration, check **Use specific name server addresses.** Then enter the IP addresses of the primary and backup DNS server (if any) in the **DNS** and **DNS backup** entry boxes.

◆ Check **Use VJ header compression** if your IAP supports Van Jacobson IP header compression while establishing a PPP connection.

◆ Check **Use default gateway on remote network**.

Choose **OK** after you complete the dialog box. Choose **OK** again to return to the **Add Phone Book Entry** dialog box.

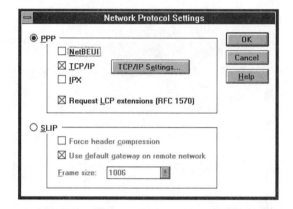

Figure 15.14

Selecting a TCP/IP dial-in protocol.

6. Choose the **Security** button to open the **Security Settings** dialog box (see fig. 15.16). Check **Accept any authentication including clear text**.

You can use the **Before Dialing** and **After Dialing** dialog boxes to specify login scripts that are executed before and after RAS connects to the IAP. Many IAPs use a standard logon dialog that matches the default RAS configuration. In that case, both login script settings might be set to **(none)**. Try those settings first. If **(none)** does not provide proper logon, change **After Dialing** to **Generic login** and try again.

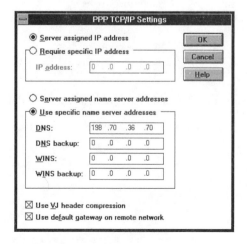

Figure 15.15

Configuring PPP.

If the default logon procedure does not work, change **After Dialing** to **Terminal**. After RAS achieves a connection, a terminal is enabled that permits you to conduct a login dialog by entering your username and password in terminal mode.

When entries are complete, choose **OK** twice to return to the **Remote Access** dialog box.

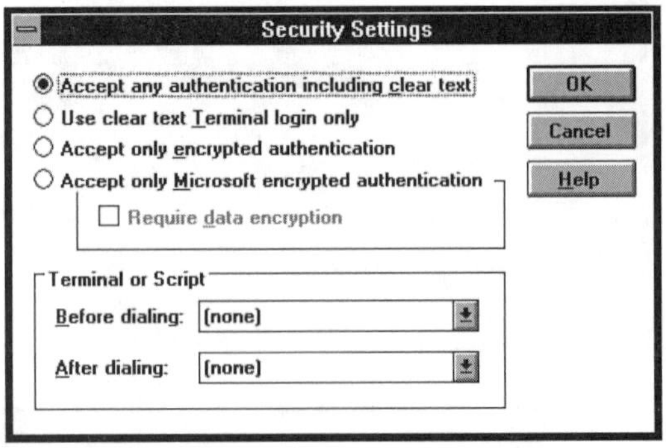

Figure 15.16

Configuring dial-in security settings.

7. To test the new entry, double-click on it in the **Remote Access** dialog box. The **Authentication** dialog box opens (see fig. 15.17). The username initially matches your account name on the Windows network. Change the entry in **User Name** to the logon name of your Internet account. Also, enter your password in the **Password** box. Then choose **OK** to connect.

If the connection is successful, you see the message *Registering your computer on the network.*

If the connection is unsuccessful, check your entries in the RAS configuration dialog boxes. If everything appears correct, try the following changes:

◆ Change the setting for **Use VJ header compression**.

◆ Change the setting for **Request LCP Extensions**.

◆ Change **After Dialing** to **Terminal** and attempt a terminal-mode logon.

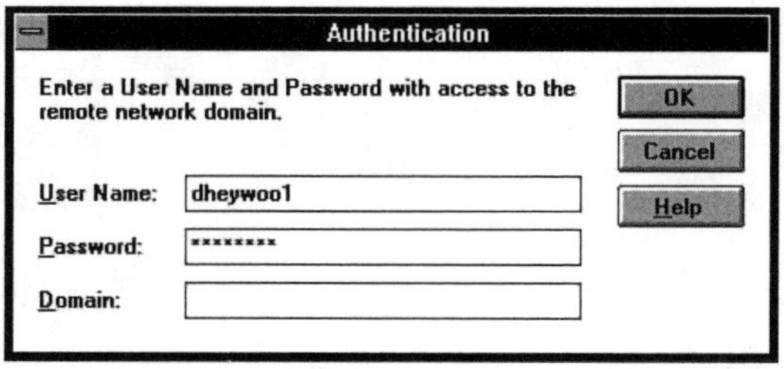

Figure 15.17

Entering a username and password.

Configuring RAS for a SLIP Connection

To configure RAS to dial an IAP account configured for SLIP, you must first install the MS Loopback Adapter in the Network utility and configure TCP/IP. Then you can configure a Phone Book entry in RAS. Before setting up a Phone Book entry, do the following:

1. Start the Network utility in the Control Panel. In the **Network Settings** dialog box, choose **Add Adapter** to open the **Add Network Adapter** dialog box.

2. In the **Add Network Adapter** dialog box, search the list of adapters in the **Network Adapter Card** box and select **MS Loopback Adapter**. Then choose **Continue.**

3. In the **MS Loopback Adapter Card Setup** dialog box, select a frame type of **802.3**.

4. Choose **OK**. When prompted, supply the path to the installation files and choose **Continue**.

5. After you are returned to the **Network Settings** dialog box, choose **OK**.

6. Network setup configures the network and then opens the **TCP/IP Configuration** dialog box, shown in figure 15.18. In the **Adapter** dialog box, choose **MS Loopback Adapter** and configure the adapter, as follows:

   a. In the **IP Address** box, enter the IP address your IAP assigned you.

   b. Enter a subnet mask in the **Subnet Mask** box. The subnet mask is almost always 255.255.255.0.

   c. In the **Default Gateway** box, enter the IP address your IAP supplied.

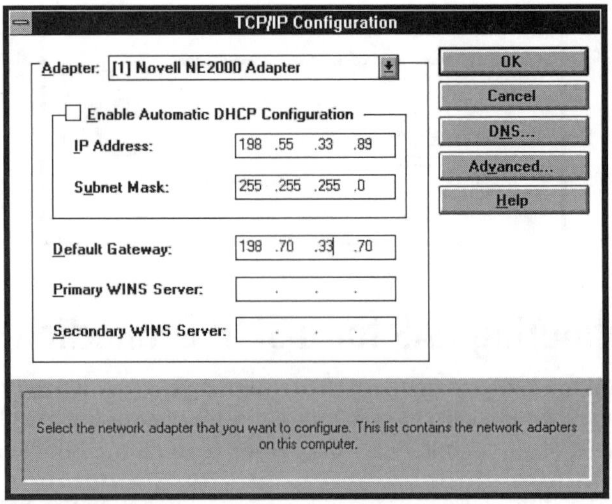

Figure 15.18

Configuring the MS Loopback Adapter.

7. After configuring the adapter in the **TCP/IP Configuration** dialog box, choose the **DNS** button to open the open the **DNS Configuration** dialog box (see fig. 15.19). Configure the entries in this box as follows:

   a. In the **Host Name** field, enter the host name your IAP assigned you.

   b. In the **Domain Name** field, enter the domain assigned to your IAP.

   c. In the **Domain Name Service (DNS) Search Order** box, add the IP address of the DNS server, as specified by your IAP. If backup name servers are available, add their addresses as well.

   Choose **OK** to return to the **TCP/IP Configuration** dialog box.

8. Choose **Advanced** to open the **Advanced Microsoft TCP/IP Configuration** dialog box (see fig. 15.20). Ensure that the **Enable DNS for Windows Name Resolution** box is not checked.

9. Choose **OK** and exit the Network utility. Restart the computer to establish the new settings.

After you configure the MS Loopback Adapter, you can set up a Phone Book entry to access a SLIP account.

1. Start Remote Access, using the icon located in the Remote Access Server program group. The **Remote Access** dialog box appears (refer to fig. 15.11). At first, the list of phone book entries is empty. The figure shows Remote Access after a phone book entry has been added.

2. Choose **Add** to open the **Add Phone Book Entry** dialog box (refer to fig. 15.12). If the **Modem** and other buttons are not visible at the bottom of the dialog box, click on the **Advanced** button. Then complete the entries in this box as follows:

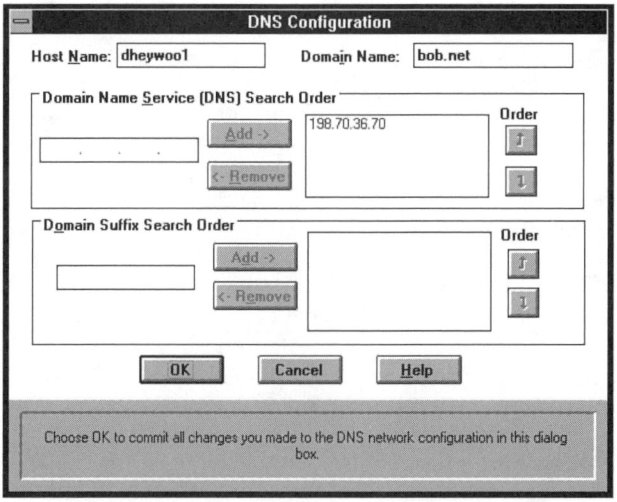

Figure 15.19

Configuring account and DNS server information.

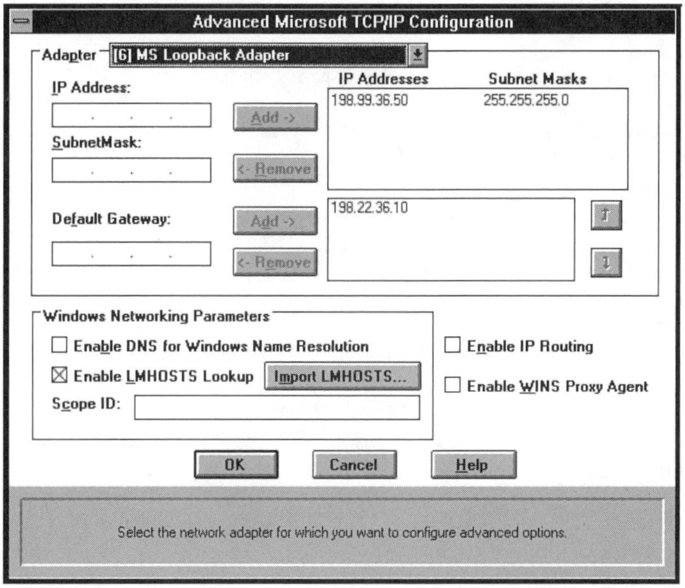

Figure 15.20

Advanced configuration for the MS Loopback Adapter.

◆ Identify the entry in the **Entry Name** (required) and **Description** (optional) fields.

◆ Complete the **Phone Number** field. Click on the **Browse** button (the button with three dots) to browse telephone numbers that have already been entered into RAS.

◆ Select a port in the **Port** box.

◆ Remove the check mark from the **Authenticate using current user name and password** check box.

3. Choose the **Modem** button to open the Modem Settings dialog box (refer to fig. 15.13). Complete this dialog box as follows:

◆ Set the **Initial** speed to the highest connection speed for the modem. Generally speaking, a 14.4 Kbps modem can be configured for a speed of 38400. A 28.8 Kbps modem can be configured for a speed of 57600. These speeds are possible only if the computer is equipped with a 16550 UART. Older-style serial ports are restricted to lower speeds.

◆ Check **Enable hardware flow control**, **Enable modem error control**, and **Enable modem compression**.

◆ Unless you have trouble and need to manually debug modem commands, do not check **Enter modem commands manually.**

Choose **OK** to return to the **Add Phone Book Entry** dialog box.

4. Choose **Network** to open the **Network Protocol Settings** dialog box (see fig. 15.21). The dialog box in the figure has been filled out appropriately for SLIP.

Check **SLIP** and configure the options as follows:

◆ Check **Force header compression** and **Use default gateway on remote network**.

◆ Leave **Frame Size** at the default value of 1006 unless your IAP specifies a different value.

Choose **OK** after you configure the dialog box. You are returned to the **Add Phone Book Entry** dialog box.

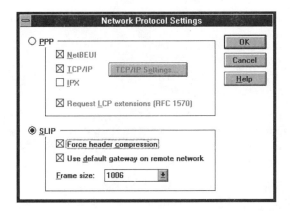

Figure 15.21

*Configuring RAS for a
SLIP connection.*

5. Choose the **Security** button to open the **Security Settings** dialog box (refer to fig.
   15.16). Check **Accept any authentication including clear text**.

   The **Before Dialing** and **After Dialing** list boxes can be used to specify login
   scripts to execute before and after RAS connects to the IAP. Many IAPs use a
   standard logon dialog that matches the default RAS configuration. If so, both
   login script settings can be set to **(none)**. Try those settings first. If **(none)** does
   not provide proper logon, change **After Dialing** to **Generic login** and try again.

   If the default logon procedure does not work, change **After Dialing** to **Terminal**.
   After RAS achieves a connection, a terminal is enabled that permits you to
   conduct a login dialog by entering your username and password in terminal
   mode.

   When entries are complete, choose **OK** twice to return to the **Remote Access**
   dialog box.

6. To test the new entry, double-click on it in the **Remote Access** dialog box, which
   opens an **Authentication** dialog box (refer to fig. 15.17). The username initially
   matches your account name on the Windows network. Change the entry in **User
   Name** to the logon name of your Internet account. Also, enter your password in
   the **Password** box. Then choose **OK** to connect.

   If the connection is successful, you receive the message *Registering your
   computer on the network*.

   If the connection is unsuccessful, check your entries in the RAS configuration
   dialog boxes. If everything appears correct, try the following changes:

♦ Check all TCP/IP configuration settings.

♦ Change the setting for **Force header compression.**

Using RAS as an Internet Router

After RAS has been configured and tested, you can configure RAS as a router that enables other users on your network to access the Internet. Performance is limited by the slow bit rates supported by analog modems, but routing through RAS is one possible way to connect multiple users to the Internet.

To configure RAS as an Internet router, you need the following:

♦ A PPP connection to the Internet

♦ An Internet class C network ID or a valid IP subnet and subnet mask, assigned by your Internet Access Provider.

♦ A domain name and name server if you want to have your local computers identified through DNS.

♦ A Windows NT computer configured with a high-speed modem and serial card.

> **Stop**   You cannot perform this procedure if your IAP uses Windows NT computers to provide dial-in connections.

Figure 15.22 illustrates a Windows network that uses RAS to route traffic to the Internet. To configure a network with a RAS Internet router:

1. Configure your local TCP/IP hosts with IP addresses that have been assigned to your site.

2. Configure the default gateway for all TCP/IP computers to the IP address that matches the LAN adapter card in the RAS server.

3. On the RAS server, use `regedt32` to add a value to the Registry in the following key:

   `\HKEY_LOCAL_MACHINE\System\CurrentControlSet\Services\RasArp\Parameters`

   The value to add is

   ♦ Name: `DisableOtherSrcPackets`

   ♦ Data Type: `REG_DWORD`

   ♦ Value: `1`

This value ensures that packets routed through the RAS server retain the IP addresses of the clients that originated the packets.

4. If the network number on your network is the same class as the network number used by the network provider (a netid is shared by subnetting) add a value to the following key:

`\HKEY_LOCAL_MACHINE\System\CurrentControlSet\Services\RasMan\PPP\IPCP`

The value to add is

◆ Name: `PriorityBasedOnSubNetwork`

◆ Data Type: `REG_DWORD`

◆ Value: `1`

Setting this value to 1 enables RAS to route traffic to the LAN adapter. Otherwise, all traffic for the network ID is routed to the RAS adapter. This value is needed only if the same netid is found on both networks to which the RAS server is attached.

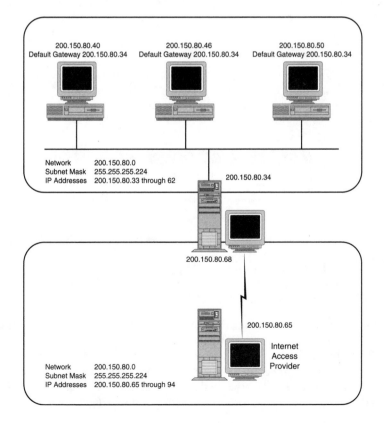

Figure 15.22

A network using RAS as a router to the Internet.

Setting Up an FTP Server

An FTP server is an excellent tool for distributing files to customers and contacts, as well as a good way to receive files from Internet users. Windows NT Server includes FTP Server software, which makes establishing an FTP Server presence on the Internet very easy.

Installing the FTP Server Service

To install the FTP server software:

1. Open the Network utility in the Control Panel.

2. Choose **Add Software** in the **Network Settings** dialog box.

3. Select **TCP/IP Protocol and related components** in the **Network Settings** box of the **Add Network Software** box. Then choose **Continue**.

4. Check **FTP Server Service** in the **Windows NT TCP/IP Installation Options** dialog box. Then choose **Continue**.

5. Supply disks and path information as required to install the software.

6. You receive the warning shown in figure 15.23, which serves notice that an FTP server can be a security risk because FTP passwords are not encrypted as they are routed through the network. Properly configuring the FTP server can minimize this risk. Choose **Yes** to continue.

Figure 15.23

The FTP server installation warning.

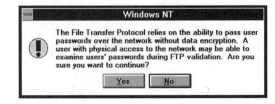

7. Next, the **FTP Service** dialog box appears (see fig. 15.24). This dialog box is used to configure the basic parameters that control operation of the FTP Server service. Configure this dialog box as follows:

   a. The **Maximum Connections** value determines the number of users who can be connected to the FTP server at a given time, ranging from 0 to 50. A value of 0 means that no maximum is set. Users who attempt to connect when connections are at maximum receive a message defined by the administrator. See the section "Registry Keys Associated with FTP Server" later in this chapter for instructions on specifying the message.

b. The **Idle Timeout** determines how many minutes an inactive user can remain connected. This value ranges from 0 to 60 minutes. A value of 0 disables the idle timeout and users can remain connected indefinitely.

c. The **Home Directory** field specifies the directory in which users are initially placed. This directory should be located on a disk that FTP users are permitted to access. See the section "Configuring FTP Server Security" later in this chapter for more information.

d. Checking **Allow Anonymous Connections** permits users to log on using the username **anonymous**. If this box is checked, specify valid account information in the **Username** and **Password** boxes. Anonymous users have the same permissions as the account you specify. The **Guest** account frequently is used for this reason.

The username and password must be correct and the account must be enabled because anonymous users effectively log on to the server using the username and password. Attempts by anonymous users are denied if they cannot successfully log on to the account you specify.

e. To prevent users from connecting using their Windows usernames and passwords, check **Allow Only Anonymous Connections**. This option prevents exposure of Windows network usernames and passwords to prying eyes on the Internet.

8. Choose **OK** to close the **FTP Service** dialog box and restart the computer. Then choose **OK** to quit the Network tool. Restart the computer to complete the installation.

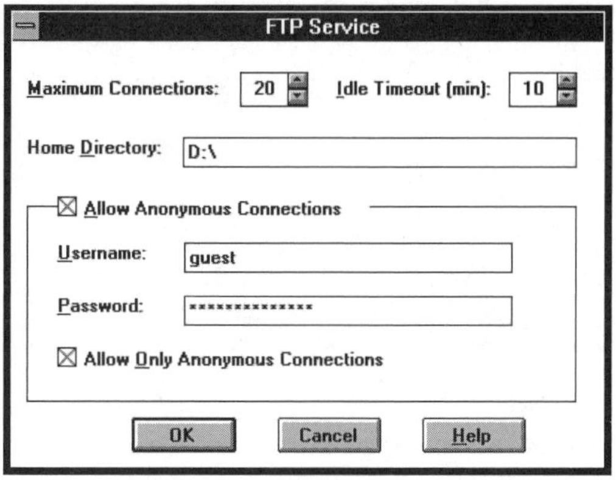

Figure 15.24

Configuring the FTP Server.

| Note | FTP security isn't very secure because passwords aren't encrypted when they are passed from the FTP client to the FTP server. As a result, you should not place great reliance on FTP password security. |

When accessing an FTP server, users should be discouraged from using their standard network username and password, because they can be observed on the network. In fact, standardizing on anonymous connections to protect user's account information is probably the best choice. Consequently, you might want to check **Allow Only Anonymous Connections**.

The files an anonymous user can access are limited in two ways: by the permissions assigned to the account specified in the **FTP Service** dialog box, and by the drives that FTP users are permitted to access. See the next section, "Configuring FTP Server Security," for the procedures used to restrict drive access.

Configuring FTP Server Security

Installing the FTP Server software adds an FTP Server option to the Control Panel. This option is used to configure FTP server security, which must be done during installation of the FTP server. You can change security settings at any time.

To configure FTP Server security, perform the following steps:

1. Choose the FTP Server tool in the Control Panel to open the **FTP User Sessions** box (see fig. 15.25). The figure shows two users logged in to the FTP server. The next section, "Managing the FTP Server Service," discusses information and techniques for managing the server.

Figure 15.25

Monitoring FTP user sessions.

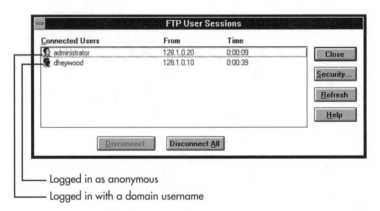

2. To configure FTP security, choose the **Security** button to open the **FTP Server Security** dialog box (see fig. 15.26). This dialog box serves to specify which volumes FTP users are given read and write access.

3. By default, read and write access is disabled for all partitions. To enable access to a partition, follow these steps:

    a.   Select a partition in the **Partition** box.

    b.   Check **Allow Read** to enable read access for the partition.

    c.   Check **Allow Write** to enable write access for the partition.

4. Choose **OK** after security has been configured. You do not need to restart the server—the changes take effect immediately.

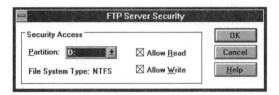

Figure 15.26

Setting FTP Server partition security.

Note

The following two factors limit the capabilities an FTP user can exercise:

◆ Whether FTP Server security grants read or write access for the partition with which the user works. These permissions affect all files on the partition.

◆ The permissions assigned to the domain user account under which the user is logged on to FTP. These partitions can be assigned to specific directories or files as required.

The restrictions placed on a user are the sum of these two sets of permissions. If FTP Server security does not permit FTP users to write to a volume, users are restricted from writing, even if their domain user accounts grant write permissions.

Similarly, if FTP Server security permits writing to a volume but the user's account has not been given write permissions for any or all of the volume, the account permissions restrict the user's write access.

Managing the FTP Server Service

To administer the FTP Server service, you must be logged on as a member of the Administrators group.

Any time changes are made to the FTP server (except FTP Server security settings), the FTP Server service must be stopped and started. Restarting the service disconnects any users currently connected. Two methods are available for starting and stopping the service:

◆ Open the Services tool in the Control Panel. In the **Services** dialog box, select **FTP Server.** Then choose the **St̲op** button followed by the **S̲tart** button.

◆ Open a command prompt and enter the command `net stop ftpsvc`. Then enter the command `net start ftpsvc`.

The FTP Server can be monitored using the FTP Server tool in the Control Panel, which opens the **FTP User Sessions** dialog box (refer to fig. 15.25). This dialog box lists each active FTP session. Two types of sessions are identified by icons:

◆ Users who log on using a domain username are identified by their username and by a user icon. In figure 15.25, one user is logged in as **administrator.**

◆ Users who log on using anonymous FTP are identified by an icon that is tagged with a question mark. If the user entered an e-mail address as a password, the name displayed is the username portion of the e-mail address. In figure 15.25, user **dheywood** has logged in as anonymous with a password of **dheywood@email.net**.

An administrator can disconnect specific users by selecting the user and choosing **D̲isconnect**, or he can disconnect all users by choosing **Disconnect A̲ll**.

Registry Keys Associated with FTP Server

Several FTP Server features are configured by editing the Registry. See Chapter 10, "Managing DHCP," for brief instructions on using the Registry Editor. The following Registry values are associated with the FTP Server service:

AnnotateDirectories

Data Type:	REG_DWORD
Range:	0 or 1
Default:	0

If this directory is 1, directory annotation is on. Directory annotation enables administrators to post directory descriptions in directories in a file named ~FTPSVC~.CKM, which usually is assigned the hidden attribute. FTP users can view these files by using the command `quote site ckm`.

ExitMessage

Data Type:	REG_SZ
Range:	String
Default:	"Goodbye"

This string appears as a signoff message after users enter the ftp **quit** command. Customize this message as required for your site.

GreetingMessage

Data Type:	REG_MULTI_SZ
Range:	String
Default:	None

Edit this value to present a message to users who have been logged on to the FTP server. If the user logs on as **anonymous** and prefaces the password using a minus sign (-) the greeting message is not sent.

LogAnonymous

Data Type:	REG_DWORD
Range:	0 or 1
Default:	0

If this value is 0, anonymous logons are not logged in the System event log. If the value is 1, anonymous logons are logged.

LogNonAnonymous

Data Type:	REG_DWORD
Range:	0 or 1
Default:	0

0 disables logging of non-anonymous logons. 1 enables logging.

LogFileAccess

Data Type:	REG_DWORD
Range:	0, 1, or 2
Default:	0

This value determines how the FTP Server logs file access:

0   File accesses are not logged

1   File accesses are logged to FTPSVC.LOG in the FTP server's current directory.

2   File accesses are logged to FT*yymmdd*.LOG where *yy*, *mm*, and *dd* define the year and month and day on which the file was generated.

Stop   FTP file access logs are verbose and can quickly become quite large.

LogFileDirectory

Data Type:	REG_SZ
Range:	Pathname
Default:	*systemroot*\\SYSTEM32

Specifies the directory in which log files will be created.

LowercaseFiles

Data Type:	REG_DWORD
Range:	0 or 1
Default:	0

If this value is 1, when a noncase-preserving file system generates a **list** or **nlist** command, the file names that are returned are mapped to lowercase. If the value is 0, the case of characters in file names is not altered. FAT is the only noncase-preserving file system this value affects.

MaxClientsMessage

Data Type:	REG_SZ
Range:	String
Default:	"Maximum clients reached, service unavailable."

This value specifies the message to be sent to users who attempt to connect to the FTP server after the maximum number of connections has been reached.

MsdosDirOutput

Data Type:	REG_DWORD
Range:	0 or 1
Default:	1

If this value is 1 (the default), the FTP server returns directories in MS-DOS directory format using backward slashes (\\). Change this value to 0 to generate UNIX-style listings with forward slashes (/). The majority of FTP servers on the Internet are UNIX machines and generate UNIX-style listings.

Setting Up a World Wide Web Server

A *World Wide Web server* is a server that communicates using the *HyperText Transfer Protocol (HTTP)*. Web servers present pages of information that are created using *HyperText Markup Language (HTML)*, which permits the pages to contain formatted text as well as links to, among other things, graphics and other Web pages. The flexibility of the tools available for displaying information on Web pages is expanding almost daily.

The Web is the fastest growing part of the Internet, and many companies are rushing to get their Web servers up and running. But that is not the only reason for setting up a Web server. Many organizations are setting up Web servers on their private networks, and are using them to disseminate information. Many of the information distribution capabilities commonly associated with groupware software packages can be easily and inexpensively implemented using a Web server and free software.

The *Windows NT Resource Kit* includes HTTPS, a freeware Web server produced by the European Microsoft Windows NT Academic Centre (EMWAC), a consortium that supports use of Windows NT within academia. This section shows you how to install the HTTP server and how to configure a very basic Web page. After that, you should be ready to obtain a book on HTML and expand the capabilities of your Web pages.

Installing and Configuring the EMWAC HTTPS Server

During installation of the *Windows NT Resource Kit* software, the EMWAC software is installed in the directory \RESKIT35\emwac. Besides the HTTPS server, you can find software and documents that enable you to set up Gopher and WAIS servers.

To install the HTTPS server, perform the following steps:

1. Decide the directory in which to install the HTTPS software. (C:\WINNT35\SYSTEM32 is the recommended directory.) Copy the files HTTPS.EXE, HTTPS.CPL, and HTTPS.HLP to the directory you select.

   Documentation is supplied in several formats. Look for the files HTTPS.DOC (Word), HTTPS.WRI (Write), and HTTPS.PS (PostScript) in the EMWACS directory.

2. Open a command prompt. Change to the directory to which you copied the program and execute the command **https -install**.

3. Open the Services tool in the Control Panel. HTTP Server will now be one of the listed services. It has not been started and is configured to be started manually. If the HTTP Server should start automatically:

    a. Select **HTTP Server**.

    b. Choose **Startup**.

    c. In the **Service** dialog box, check **Automatic.**

4. To configure the HTTP server, open the HTTP Server tool that was installed in the Control Panel. This opens the **HTTP Server** dialog box (see fig. 15.27).

5. In the **Data directory** field, specify the root of the directory tree that will be available to users of the Web server. If the data directory is a network directory on another computer, you must specify the directory using UNC notation, for example, *SERVER**DIRECTORY*. You cannot specify the directory using connected drive letters.

6. In the TCP/IP port, specify the port to use to listen for incoming HTTP connections. This value must be an integer value that corresponds to an unused port (the default is 80). Ports occasionally are used to restrict access to a Web server to users who know the correct port number. Unless that is your goal, stay with the default port.

7. You should not need to change any of the MIME file time mappings. Consult the HTTPS documentation for more information about MIME type matching.

8. If you want to log HTTP transactions, check **Log HTTP transactions** and specify a logging directory in the **Log file directory** field. HTTPS logs the time and date of each request, the IP address of the server and the client, the HTTP command, the URL requested, and the version of HTTP that was used.

9. If users should be permitted to browse directories, check **Permit directory browsing.** To prevent browsing of a specific directory, create a file named NOBROWSE in the directory. The contents of the file do not matter.

10. Start the HTTP Server service using the Services tool in the Control Panel. Or enter the command **net start "http server"** at a command prompt. The quotation marks are required.

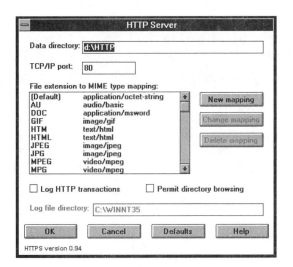

Figure 15.27

Setting up the HTTPS server.

Creating Web Pages

The complexity of a Web page is unlimited. HTML is a versatile graphic markup language that goes far beyond the scope of this chapter. The purpose here, therefore, is merely to set up a basic Web page or two to show you the mechanics of putting pages on the HTTPS server.

Dozens of books have been written about HTML, and many are available from sister imprints of New Riders Publishing. Be sure to check the catalogs of Que and Sams.

Another source of information is, of course, the Web itself. You can, for example, get plenty of information from the Web site at the University of Illinois at Urbana-Champaign (UIUC). The UIUC has been at the forefront of Web research, originating the popular Mosaic Web browser, available as freeware for noncommercial use. The URL for the UIUC Web server is as follows:

```
http://www.ncsa.uiuc.edu/
```

A brief but informative document about HTML can be obtained from the following URL or ordered in printed form for a small fee from the UIUC:

```
http://www.ncsa.uiuc.edu/General/Internet/WWW/HTMLPrimer.html
```

Creating a Home Page

Every directory of an HTTPS server can contain a file named DEFAULT.HTM, displayed automatically anytime the directory is opened in a Web viewer. Consequently, creating a home page for your Web server is no more complicated than creating an HTML document named DEFAULT.HTM and placing the file in the data directory specified during configuration of the HTTPS server (refer to fig. 15.27). The home page is the first document users see when they connect to your Web server.

The following is an exceedingly basic home page that illustrates the basic principle. Figure 15.28 shows how this page appears in a Web viewer.

```
<HTML>
<TITLE>This is home page #1</TITLE>
<H1>Welcome to our home page!</H1>
<H2>This is a second level heading</H2>
<HR>
<P>
This is the first paragraph of the Web page.<P>
And this is the second paragraph.
</HTML>
```

Note   This server was being operated on a local network without a naming service. In figure 15.28, notice that the URL for the Web server uses an IP address—a useful way to conceal a Web server while debugging it. Don't add it to DNS until the server passes muster. Then, only users who know the IP address can connect and try out your pages.

Figure 15.28

Appearance of the first home page.

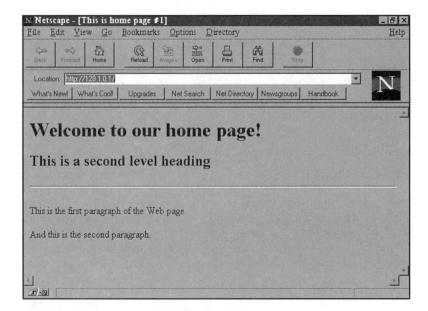

You can see how each element in the DEFAULT.HTM file is reflected in the page that appears in the Web viewer, but some general characteristics of HTML files should be noted before looking at the specifics.

The entries in angle braces (such as *<TITLE>* and *</H2>*) are called HTML *tags*. Tags specify HTML options, such as formatting or links to other documents. These tags are the commands that form the HTML language. Essentially, building documents using HTML is a form of programming. Observing the rules of applying HTML tags to the document is important, because violating the rules can result in bugs that are just as troublesome as the bugs that afflict application programmers. The first rule of programming is to know the language, which is your tool set for building your product.

Some HTML tags are used individually. The *<HR>* tag, for example, draws a *hard rule*, a line across the display. Another individual tag is *<P>*, which marks a paragraph break, much like pressing Enter while using a word processor. A *<P>* tag typically causes the Web browser to end the current paragraph and insert a blank line.

Other tags are used in pairs that essentially say "begin this feature here" and "end this feature there." The *<TITLE>* tag begins a title, for example, which defines the text used to title the window in which the Web page appears. The *</TITLE>* marks the end of the title. The simple rule is that / marks the *end* tag for the feature it specifies. Whenever tags are used in pairs, you must be certain to match beginning and ending tags. Using a *<TITLE>* tag without a *</TITLE>* tag can confuse the user's Web browser into interpreting the entire document as a title. Mismatched tags are common causes of HTML bugs.

Be careful about improperly nesting pairs of tags. The following sequence certainly confuses things:

```
<H1>This is heading 1
<H2>This is heading 2</H2>
</H1>
```

One set of tags you should include are *<HTML>* at the beginning of the document and *</HTML>* at the end. These tags aren't required for HTTPS, but they make your Web page more portable by identifying the document protocol. Other HTML viewers, which might not automatically identify HTML, will recognize the *<HTML>* tags and interpret the document properly.

Clearly, HTML does a lot for you. All you need to do to specify nested headers is specify different header levels using the *<H1>* through *<H6>* tags. The example includes instances of the *<H1>* and *<H2>* tags. As figure 15.28 illustrates, each header level has its own conventions for displaying the header text.

Now that you know how to build a basic home page, examining two more advanced HTML techniques should prove useful: linking to other documents and displaying graphic images.

Linking to Another Document

Before you can link to another document, you need another document. The second document is named DOC2.HTM and stored in a subdirectory of the HTTPS data directory, named Documents.

Here the DEFAULTS.HTM file has been modified to include a link to the new file:

```
<HTML>
<TITLE>This is home page #1</TITLE>
<H1>Welcome to our home page!</H1>
<H2>This is a second level heading</H2>
<HR>
<P>
This is the first paragraph of the Web page.<P>
And this is the second paragraph.<P>
<A HREF="Documents\doc2.htm">Here is another document!</A>
</HTML>
```

When this new home page is viewed on a browser (see fig. 15.29), the text *Here is another document!* appears in a distinctive typeface that identifies it as a hot link. To display the linked document, you need only double-click on the hot link.

The new element is the *<A> anchor* tag, which has the following structure:

```
<A HREF="The path to the document">Displayed message</A>
```

In the example, the document path is simply a relative directory path, because the file is located in a subdirectory of the HTTPS data directory. However, this path can also be a URL to any server on the Internet. You could, for example, add a link to the Microsoft Web server home page using this line:

```
<A HREF="http://www.microsoft.com/">Microsoft's home page</A>
```

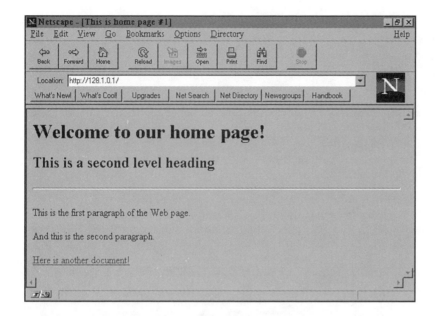

Figure 15.29

A Web page with a document link.

Links can extend to services other than HTTP. The available link types are as follows:

◆ **http.** A file on a World Wide Web server.

◆ **file.** A file on a local server or an anonymous FTP server.

◆ **gopher.** A file on a Gopher server.

◆ **wais.** A file on a WAIS server.

◆ **news.** A Usenet newsgroup.

◆ **telnet.** A service offered by a Telnet server.

In other words, Web pages can provide entrées to the vast majority of resources available on the Internet.

Providing In-Line Images

Graphic Web browsers can display images on the same pages as text. This capability makes embedding graphics into Web pages easy. Two file formats are supported: GIF (graphic interchange format) and XBM (X Bitmap). A GIF file is used as an example here. Here is a home page that includes an embedded graphic. Figure 15.30 shows how the page appears on a Web browser.

```
<HTML>
<TITLE>This is home page #1</TITLE>
<H1>Welcome to our home page!</H1>
```

```
<H2>This is a second level heading</H2>
<HR>
<IMG ALIGN=MIDDLE SRC=software.gif>
<A HREF="Documents\doc2.htm">Here is another document!</A>
</HTML>
```

The new element is the `<IMG>` tag, which identifies an image file to be embedded. The file is identified by the SRC= parameter. In this case, the file SOFTWARE.GIF is located in the HTTPS data directory, and a path is not required. But you can include a directory pathname to access files elsewhere on the server. You can also include a URL to access files on other Web servers.

By default, the text that appears with an image is aligned with the bottom border of the image. In the example, the ALIGN=MIDDLE option is included to align the text with the center of the graphic. To match the text with the top of the graphic use the ALIGN=TOP option.

Figure 15.30

A Web page with an embedded graphic.

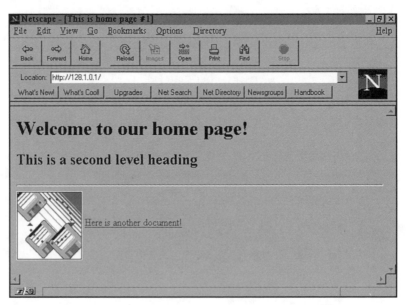

This discussion of HTML was intended to demonstrate the basics of the HTML language and to convince you that Web pages aren't necessarily difficult to build. If you want to investigate the subject further, first investigate the UIUC's "Beginner's Guide to HTML," mentioned at the beginning of this section. If you want more, any bookstore is likely to offer a selection of a dozen or more titles.

If you want to set up a Web site without getting too wrapped up in HTML, consider obtaining an HTML editor accessory. Most vendors of word processors now offer tools for converting documents to HTML format. You can also find several shareware and freeware tools on the Internet that can simplify preparation of HTML files.

Summary

This chapter began by addressing the questions of Internet connection methods and security risks. Several connection methods were discussed, along with their relative security risks. Also, alternative security methods were mentioned.

Then the chapter demonstrated how to enable your network to provide FTP and World Wide Web. It also covered configuring FTP server security and creating Web pages.

When working with TCP/IP, encountering binary, decimal, and hexadecimal number representations is unavoidable. Subnet masks, for example, are written in dotted decimal form, but the workings of subnet masks must be understood in binary. And some computer numbers, such as the contents of large blocks of memory, can comfortably be expressed only in hexadecimal form. It is the purpose of this appendix to simplify these number systems.

All data in computers are represented internally by switches, which are either on or off (or high/low, or some other either/or situation). A single switch that represents a two-state value is called a *bit*, a name which derives from the expression *binary digit*. *Binary* refers to a numbering system in which digits have only two states, making binary a natural match for computer memory.

A single bit is pretty limited in the range of data it can represent. Most data are more complex than the either/or data that can be represented by a single bit, and it usually takes many bits to represent any substantial real-world value. When working with large sequences of bits, engineers need a shorthand method for representing the positions of all those switches. Writing down "on-off-off-on-off-off-off-on" whenever representing the positions of a series of computer switches isn't very convenient.

That is why binary representation was adopted for computers. If 1 represents one state of the switch and 0 the other state, representing a group of switches as something like 10001001 is easy. Binary numbers aren't that hard to understand. Before attempting an explanation, however, reviewing the way everyday decimal numbering works should prove useful. Decimal notation is based on powers of 10, and you probably have no trouble understanding that the decimal number 5,821 is evaluated as follows:

5 represents 5×10^3 ($5 \times 10 \times 10 \times 10 = 5 \times 1,000$)

8 represents 8×10^2 ($8 \times 10 \times 10 = 8 \times 100$)

2 represents 2×10^1 (2×10)

1 represents 1×10^0 (1×1)

This same procedure applies with binary and hexadecimal numbers. Binary numbers are based on powers of 2, and the binary number 1011 evaluates like this:

1 represents 1×2^3 ($1 \times 2 \times 2 \times 2 = 1 \times 8$)

0 represents 0×2^2 ($0 \times 2 \times 2 = 0 \times 4$)

1 represents 1×2^1 (1×2)

1 represents 1×2^0 (1×1)

From the preceding breakdown, you can see that the binary number 1011 is equivalent to the decimal value 11.

Because you encounter binary numbers quite frequently, you should find remembering the powers of 2 through 28 useful:

$2^0 = 1$ $2^1 = 2$ $2^2 = 4$ $2^3 = 8$ $2^4 = 16$ $2^5 = 32$ $2^6 = 64$ $2^7 = 128$ $2^8 = 256$

If you were to apply these values to a byte that consists entirely of 1s, you would see that the highest value that eight bits can represent is 11111111, which is 255 decimal.

Long series of binary digits are very difficult for humans to scan, and the networking profession frequently uses two different representations to make long binary numbers more human-friendly.

One form is the dotted-decimal form used to represent IP addresses. In dotted-decimal notation, a 32-bit IP address is broken into four 8-bit groups like this:

   01101101 11101101 00010001 11110010

Each 8-bit group is then represented by a decimal number in the range of 0 through 255 like this:

   109   237   17   242

The preceding is then represented in dotted-decimal form as 109.237.17.242. Granted, not many of us can convert 8-bits to a decimal value without considerable help, but the end result is much easier to handle.

Apart from IP address, however, the most common way to represent large binary numbers is hexadecimal notation, usually called *hex*. Hex notation begins by breaking binary numbers into groups of four bits, like this:

0110 1101 1110 1101 0001 0001 1111 0010

Each four-bit group represents a decimal value in the range of 0 through 15. Hex notation uses the digits 0 through 9 for values up to 10. For 10 through 15, hex uses the letters A through F. Table A.1 summarizes the binary, decimal, and hex values through fifteen.

TABLE A.1   BINARY, DECIMAL, AND HEXADECIMAL EQUIVALENTS

Binary	Decimal	Hexadecimal
0000	0	0
0001	1	1
0010	2	2
0011	3	3
0100	4	4
0101	5	5
0110	6	6
0111	7	7
1000	8	8
1001	9	9
1010	10	A
1011	11	B
1100	12	C
1101	13	D
1110	14	E
1111	15	F

Because each hex digit corresponds to four bits, representing any binary number in hex form is easy. Consider the following example:

0110 1101 1110 1101 0001 0001 1111 0010

   6   D   E   D   1   1   F   2

Two common notations are used to identify hexadecimal numbers. One is a trailing h; for example, 29h. Another is the representation used in C programming, which prefixes the hex number with 0x; for example, 0x29. You encounter both notations when working with Microsoft TCP/IP.

Note   The Windows Calculator applet is a handy tool for converting numbers among various base representations. Choose **Scientific** in the **View** menu to display the scientific calculator options.

Index

E